I0889332

Figures of the World

FLASHPOINTS

The FlashPoints series is devoted to books that consider literature beyond strictly national and disciplinary frameworks, and that are distinguished both by their historical grounding and by their theoretical and conceptual strength. Our books engage theory without losing touch with history and work historically without falling into uncritical positivism. FlashPoints aims for a broad audience within the humanities and the social sciences concerned with moments of cultural emergence and transformation. In a Benjaminian mode, FlashPoints is interested in how literature contributes to forming new constellations of culture and history and in how such formations function critically and politically in the present. Series titles are available online at http://escholarship.org/uc/flashpoints.

SERIES EDITORS: Ali Behdad (Comparative Literature and English, UCLA), Editor Emeritus; Judith Butler (Rhetoric and Comparative Literature, UC Berkeley), Editor Emerita; Michelle Clayton (Hispanic Studies and Comparative Literature, Brown University); Edward Dimendberg (Film and Media Studies, Visual Studies, and European Languages and Studies, UC Irvine), Founding Editor; Catherine Gallagher (English, UC Berkeley), Editor Emerita; Nouri Gana (Comparative Literature and Near Eastern Languages and Cultures, UCLA); Susan Gillman (Literature, UC Santa Cruz), Coordinator; Jody Greene (Literature, UC Santa Cruz); Richard Terdiman (Literature, UC Santa Cruz), Founding Editor.

A complete list of titles begins on p. 259.

Figures of the World

The Naturalist Novel and Transnational Form

Christopher Laing Hill

NORTHWESTERN UNIVERSITY PRESS | EVANSTON, ILLINOIS

Northwestern University Press
www.nupress.northwestern.edu

This title is licensed under the Creative Commons Attribution-NonCommercial-NoDerivatives 4.0 International License (CC BY-NC-ND). Read the license at https://creativecommons.org/licenses/by-nc-nd/4.0/legalcode.

A Study of the Weatherhead East Asian Institute, Columbia University
The Studies of the Weatherhead East Asian Institute of Columbia University were inaugurated in 1962 to bring to a wider public the results of significant new research on modern and contemporary East Asia.

This book is freely available in an open access edition thanks to TOME (Toward an Open Monograph Ecosystem)—a collaboration of the Association of American Universities, the Association of University Presses, and the Association of Research Libraries—and the generous support of the University of Michigan. Learn more at the TOME website: openmonographs.org.

Copyright © 2020 by Northwestern University Press. Published 2020.
All rights reserved.

Printed in the United States of America

10 9 8 7 6 5 4 3 2 1

Library of Congress Cataloging-in-Publication Data

Names: Hill, Christopher L., 1964– author.
Title: Figures of the world : the naturalist novel and transnational form / Christopher Laing Hill.
Other titles: FlashPoints (Evanston, Ill.)
Description: Evanston, Illinois : Northwestern University Press, 2020. | Series: Flashpoints | Includes bibliographical references and index.
Identifiers: LCCN 2020003924 | ISBN 9780810142145 (paperback) | ISBN 9780810142152 (cloth) | ISBN 9780810142169 (ebook)
Subjects: LCSH: Naturalism in literature. | Literature, Modern—19th century—History and criticism. | Literature, Modern—20th century—History and criticism. | Comparative literature.
Classification: LCC PN601 .H49 2020 | DDC 809.3912—dc23
LC record available at https://lccn.loc.gov/2020003924

For my family

Contents

Acknowledgments

This book would not have been possible without the work of many scholars of naturalist fiction, especially the contributors to two journals dedicated to the field, *Cahiers Naturalistes* and *Excavatio*. To them I owe great thanks.

Over the years I received inspiration and support for this project from Paul Anderer, Chris Bush, Sebastian Conrad, Vilashini Cooppan, Seth Fein, Shel Garon, Carol Gluck, Eric Hayot, June Howard, Sabu Kohso, Neil Levi, Janet Walker, and colleagues at the universities where I have taught. The editors of Northwestern University Press's FlashPoints series, especially Susan Gillman and Richard Terdiman, and my editors at the Press, Trevor Perri and Gianna Mosser, saw the value of the project and ushered it into print.

I received advice on the manuscript from David Bell, Héctor Hoyos, Youngju Ryu, Jiwon Shin, and Xiaobing Tang, and an anonymous reader for the Weatherhead East Asian Institute at Columbia. Jonathan Arac, Marshall Brown, Nina Cornyetz, Reginia Gagnier, and Keith Vincent gave guidance on early versions of several chapters. Members of panels and seminars at the American Comparative Literature Association, Asian Studies Conference Japan, Association for Asian Studies, Association for Japanese Literary Studies, Modern Language Association, and Society for Novel Studies provided feedback. Mélissa Gélinas, Paul Martin, and Mariane Stanev assisted with the research.

Many people gave me opportunities to speak on the project. I thank Jonathan Abel, Susan Andrade, Geoffrey Baker, Caroline Eckhardt, Narve Fulsås, Manu Goswami and Kristin Ross, Indra Levy, Ted Mack, Numano Mitsuyoshi, Stefan Nygård and Johan Strang, Nancy Ruttenburg, Alan Tansman, Umemori Naoyuki, Stefan Vandamme and Blaise Wilfert, Tobias Werron, and Jonathan Zwicker.

I would not have been able to complete this book without those who provided indispensable support to keep working, including Victoria de Grazia and Jacques Revel. I received institutional and financial support from Columbia University, the École des Hautes Études en Sciences Sociales, the Freie Universität Berlin, the University of California at Berkeley, the University of Michigan, Waseda University, and Yale University.

Finally, this book owes everything to Miki Higasa and members of my family.

Portions of "The Travels of Naturalism and the Challenges of a World Literary History," in *Literature Compass* 6, no. 6 (2009), are reproduced with the permission of Wiley. Article copyright © 2009, Christopher L. Hill, journal compilation copyright © 2009, Blackwell Publishing Ltd.

Portions of "Exhausted by Their Battles with the World: Neurasthenia and Civilization Critique in Early Twentieth-Century Japan" in *Perversion and Modern Japan: Experiments in Psychoanalysis* (London: Routledge, 2009) are reproduced with permission of the Licensor through PLSclear. Chapter copyright © 2009, Christopher L. Hill, editorial selection copyright © 2009, Nina Cornyetz and Keith Vincent.

Portions of "Haven't We Met? On the Scales of Connection," in *Verge: Studies in Global Asias* 3, no. 2 (2017), are reproduced with permission of the publisher. Copyright © 2017, University of Minnesota Press.

An earlier version of chapter 3 was published as "Nana in the World: Novel, Gender, and Transnational Form," in *Modern Language Quarterly* 72, no. 1 (2011): 75–105. Copyright © 2011, University of Washington. All rights reserved. Republished by permission of the copyright holder, and the present publisher, Duke University Press. www.dukeupress.edu.

Conventions

Japanese names are given in the order of family name followed by personal name. Following custom, however, I refer to Japanese authors who used a pseudonym in place of their personal name by the pseudonym on second reference. This may cause some confusion, so for clarity's sake the most important cases are: Hasegawa Tenkei (referred to as "Tenkei"), Ihara Saikaku ("Saikaku"), Kosugi Tengai ("Tengai"), Mori Ōgai ("Ōgai"), Nagai Kafū ("Kafū"), Ozaki Kōyō ("Kōyō"), Shimamura Hōgetsu ("Hōgetsu"), Shimazaki Tōson ("Tōson"), Tayama Katai ("Katai"), and Tsubouchi Shōyō ("Shōyō").

To aid readers, each chapter except the conclusion provides the original title and date of publication of works the first time they are mentioned, regardless of whether they have been mentioned in preceding chapters.

With the exception of customary titles, all translations are my own.

Preface

This book is about a kind of fiction known as "naturalism," a genre of social documentation and critique that first appeared in France in the 1860s and was adopted in many parts of the world over the next sixty years, from the Americas to East Asia. The book is also about how one might study the history of literary form on a large geographic scale. As naturalist fiction traveled the world, adopted in some places and rejected in others, it encountered new social conditions and other ways of writing about society. In the process its topics, themes, and literary form—methods of narration, techniques of description, figurative language, and so on—changed significantly and sometimes unexpectedly. It became not one but many naturalisms. *Figures of the World* is about that history, that process, and how one can learn from it to understand other "big" cultural phenomena.

Two things led me to write this book. First, in my earlier work on the transnational history of literature and thought I often encountered a certain kind of comment: that naturalism's impact in a country had been lamentably great, that a promising writer's career had been warped by interest in it, or—the same thing the opposite way—that naturalism's impact was fortunately slight, and the interest in it was merely a passing phase. If these kinds of comments were so frequent, about place after place, what was more significant, the great impact of naturalism, or the view that its impact was a shame? Critics seemed to be saying, effectively, the opposite of what they meant. Even in the national or regional frames of most literary history, naturalism in fiction seemed more important than many people wanted it to be.

Second, as someone who has tried to push comparative literature and intellectual history outside their European boundaries—often through comparative work encompassing nineteenth and twentieth-century Japan—I was impatient with the debates on "world literature" that erupted in Anglophone criticism around 2000. The arguments over world literature seemed to devolve into competition to define the phrase: world literature is *this*, no, world literature is *that*. Whatever world literature was to be, moreover, Europe seemed to lurk in what Dipesh Chakarabarty would call the "theoretical subject" of the definition.[1] Explorations of literary form on a "world" scale based on substantial research were scarce.[2] Meanwhile, critique of the world-lit debate often rejected any literary history on a scale bigger than nation or region altogether, on the grounds that it reproduced neoliberal fantasies about globalization. On the one hand, I thought, regarding "world literature": theory is best when it follows practice. Let's do some research, then start talking. On the other hand, regarding world literature's critics: do we really want to ignore the circulation of texts and genres that we know has been occurring for centuries, and is only increasing in importance, or do we want to find better ways to approach it?[3] I knew that naturalism had affected fiction in many countries of the world, and I knew that progress on how to study a transnational phenomenon like this was slow. Hence this book about the history of naturalist fiction, which is meant to trace out this interesting and occasionally strange episode in the history of the novel, but also to explore, concretely, ways to study the history of expressive forms, from surrealism in painting and haiku in poetry to video games and martial arts films, on what I think we should call "geographically extensive"—though not global or world—scales.

Figures of the World approaches the transnational history of naturalist fiction from two perspectives. The first chapter presents the history of naturalism on a large scale and explores problems in conceptualizing a history in which geographical circulation is an inextricable part of changes in literary form. To better understand how the themes and techniques of naturalism moved around the world, I examine three circuits through which naturalism reached, and circulated within, South America, North America, and East Asia. I then examine essential contexts for naturalism's dissemination: the manifestos and other writings *about* naturalism that writers and critics used to promote and defend it; the "fellow travelers," from Positivism to neurology, that supported, and gained support from, their adoption by naturalist writers; and the concurrent travels of other varieties of realism. At the end of the chapter I turn to ways to theorize a geographically extensive literary field like that of naturalist fiction and how to periodize its emergence, growth, and dissolution. In this chapter I rely greatly and gratefully on many other scholars' work on the history of naturalism and realism in different parts of the world. On the one hand, the goal is to bring together research that generally has stayed in narrower boundaries, and on the other to develop methods for working on a scale that is "big" but not—for reasons I will explain—"world" or "global."

Chapters 2, 3, and 4 trace the history of three topoi of representation common in naturalist fiction that experienced successive appropriations and revisions as naturalism turned into naturalisms. These three "figures," as I call them, played rhetorical, structural, and analytical roles in the naturalist text. They are the "body figure," which emerged through attempts to show the relationship between physical, psychological, and social life; the "Nana figure," which staged social contradictions through self-liberated female characters; and the "social figure," through which naturalist fiction created models of social structure and development. I use each of these figures as what Erich Auerbach called a "point of departure" (*Ansatzpunkt*) to understand how the techniques and form of naturalist fiction changed as they traveled. Auerbach defined a point of departure as "a firmly circumscribed, easily seen, set of phenomena whose interpretation is a radiation out from them and which orders and interprets a greater region than they themselves occupy."[4] This is precisely my strategy: there are any number of ways to enter this complicated transnational history, but these three figures illuminate many aspects of the naturalist text. Through the body figure I explore how naturalist writers' figurative language coalesced into a characteristic diagnostic-explanatory technique; through the Nana figure, I explore the role that the circulation of figures played in the history of form; and through the social figure, I explore the limits to the adaptation of naturalist technique as writers faced conditions different from those in which naturalism first emerged.

In contrast to the first chapter, chapters 2, 3, and 4 shift between literary history (including the history of translation, pirating, and emulation of novels by Émile Zola) and the formal analysis of texts from France, the United States, and Japan. The goal is to use close analysis in the original languages as a bulwark against any assumptions of the easy translatability of naturalist techniques, and in so doing get meaningful answers—different in different places—to Roberto Schwarz's question of what happens to literary forms when they are put to use in conditions different than those in which they first took shape.[5] Chapter 2 examines the role of the degenerate body in naturalist mimesis in Zola's *L'Assommoir* (1877), Frank Norris's *McTeague* (1899), and Shimazaki Tōson's *Spring* (*Haru*, 1908). It traces the role that *L'Assommoir*, the novel that was Zola's springboard to international fame, played in the diffusion of the body as organizing motif, and shows how Norris and Tōson broke apart the connection Zola drew between body and fate to address the contingent relationship between labor, money, and value in American capitalism (*McTeague*) and the "civilizing" projects forced on Japanese society by a reformist state (*Spring*).

Chapter 3 turns to the character of the self-liberated woman in naturalist fiction, drawing on Zola's *Nana* (1880), Kosugi Tengai's *New Year's Finery* (*Hatsu sugata*, 1900), and Theodore Dreiser's *Sister Carrie* (1900) as principal examples. The international response to Zola's novel, the chapter shows, created a character type that evolved through successive iterations into a mobile social diagnostic. Where Zola created the actress-prostitute Nana as the perfect enabler of a corrupt world, however, Tengai and Dreiser placed their heroines Oshun and Carrie in antagonistic positions toward their societies, with Oshun's capture and containment and Carrie's ambiguous self-liberation showing the authors' views of the relationship of gender, ideology, and sexualized labor in their countries.

Chapter 4 explores naturalism's creation of fictional spaces to model social relations and focuses on Zola's *Germinal* (1885), Jack London's *The Sea-Wolf* (1904), and Tayama Katai's *The Country Teacher* (*Inaka kyōshi*, 1909). The complex reception of *Germinal* reveals the limits of naturalist techniques when confronted with different social conditions and shows that the metamorphoses of naturalist form reflected the uneven political and economic geography of the planet. London unpacked naturalist techniques of social modeling to denaturalize the transition from liberal to monopoly capitalism underway in the United States, while Katai used them to depict the unevenness of economic and social development in Meiji Japan and in the process developed methods of describing the relationship of individual, social, and nonhuman worlds that were formally and analytically far from anything Zola might have undertaken.

These three paths through the history of naturalist fiction reveal both the possibilities and limits of naturalism as a way of describing and analyzing societies. Some writers seized on unexplored aspects of earlier texts to take naturalist fiction in new directions, while others, facing qualities in their societies beyond the ken of conventional naturalist techniques, revised so radically that the eventual dissolution of naturalism as a transnational phenomenon came into sight. The conclusion of *Figures of the World* briefly traces a few of the afterlives of naturalist fiction—of which there were as many as versions of naturalism itself—and returns to the problem of how to approach a history like that of the naturalist novel, which stretches across both decades and oceans and is characterized by formal changes in different parts of the field that were coeval but perhaps irreconcilable. It argues that transformation in movement must be at the heart of transnational studies of expressive forms.

A project like this involves choices beyond my points of departure. Probably foremost in some readers' minds is how I define naturalism in literature, a notorious and unsettled issue. Begging patience, I defer the problem until chapter 1, where I advocate an inductive approach that foregrounds what writers thought naturalism to be. Before explaining other choices, I want to second Aamir Mufti's rejection of the claim that the literary archive becomes unmanageably large once one steps outside the European canon, which was the rationale for the program of "distant reading" that Franco Moretti proposed in one of the first interventions in the world literature debates. In Mufti's view, the argument for distant reading—relying on others' work instead of reading novels oneself—is a transformation of the qualitative histories of practices of writing in different parts of the world into a spurious quantitative problem. Resolution of this non-problem by distant reading amounts to an erasure of history.[6] The assertion that close reading is impossible on a "world" scale moreover puts tools for understanding such a qualitative history out of reach. Close reading is necessary: as a way to understand the particularities of the text in itself, in relation to the literary history of the place where it was written, and in relation to other naturalist texts; as a means to investigate both the obvious and subtle ways writers responded to their local situations; and in the broadest sense, as I have said above, to block simplistic assumptions about the equivalence and translatability of texts and contexts in a "global" perspective. Pursuing a project of large-scale history *and* close reading requires rejecting some dubious aspirations of "world literature" (particularly an aspiration to totality), while finding practical ways to make a project like this possible, and, crucially, trying to ensure that practical choices do not lead to blinkered conclusions. As I have put it elsewhere, the goal has to be an openness in argumentation that invites further work leading to, ideally, *additional* rather than *contrary* conclusions. Such an openness requires being forthright about the points of departure one has adopted while acknowledging that others were possible, and explaining one's choices in terms of the history surrounding them to show that they are meaningful rather than arbitrary.[7]

A critical set of choices in this book concerns my selection of works from France, the United States, and Japan for the close reading in chapters 2, 3, and 4 that is the counterpart of the "macro" perspective of chapter 1. One reason for choosing works from these three countries is linguistic: they are written in languages in which I am accustomed to doing close analysis. Scholars with different linguistic abilities would reach other—and one hopes, additional—conclusions about what happened to the naturalist text as it moved through the world. Because of the inevitability of paying close attention to the French school, which emerged as part of the history of realism in Europe but also through domestic literary and ideological battles, there were also good reasons to choose two non-European examples where distinct forms of naturalism emerged in different circumstances, with different literary antagonists, and with long-term, but quite different impacts. For reasons both global and local, for example, race and immigration had a central place in the social analytics of naturalist fiction in the United States, though they were largely absent in French naturalism.[8] Naturalist writers' throaty contributions to the discourse on race were part and parcel of their assault on the genteel realism of writers like William Dean Howells. In Japan, naturalism emerged in the wake of a decades-long political, economic, and cultural project meant to avert colonization that included establishment of the "novel" (*shōsetsu*) as a form of fiction, the central event in a dramatic reorganization of the local literary field. Naturalist writers' battles within the field were inseparable from a critique of the Japanese state's reformist project and the ideology of civilization that supported it. Notably different varieties of naturalism thus appeared in the United States and Japan in response to their different circumstances. These two countries also played roles in naturalism's transnational history. American translations of French works (which appeared earlier than translations in Britain) were critical in the dissemination of naturalism outside of areas where Romance languages were dominant, while Japanese translations (often via English) were a further vector for the transmission of naturalism elsewhere in East Asia. The histories of naturalism in France, Japan, and the United States thus illustrate some of the many ways that naturalist fiction developed, several of the mechanisms through which it traveled, and some of the reasons why its afterlives differed so greatly.

If novels and stories from France, the United States, and Japan show how some writers responded to conditions around them, reshaping the naturalist text in the process, other examples would open other questions and reveal other responses. One of the more obvious paths not taken in this book would lead to Germany, the second concentration of naturalist fiction in Europe after France. In particular, Germany would be critical for a history of the transnational impact of naturalism in theater, which is not a topic here.[9] A list of other possible examples would be long, but I should especially note the importance of naturalist fiction in the literary histories of the Spanish- and Portuguese-speaking Americas, particularly Argentina and Brazil. The history of naturalist fiction in these countries upsets Europe-centered chronologies and reveals the importance of intermediaries—former metropoles—in the dissemination of techniques that emerged in France. Socially, politically, and economically speaking they also present a range of circumstances to which naturalist writers responded that is significantly different from North America and East Asia. While I discuss the circuits through which naturalism reached Argentina and Brazil in chapter 1 and refer to writers from the region throughout the book, I regret not being able to engage more closely with their works.

Because textual genealogies are at the center of this book's literary history, the novels of Zola get a lot of attention, at the risk of making the transnational history of naturalist fiction look like the history of Zola's influence. The history of naturalism is complex and multi-stranded, but there is no way to get around the singular importance of Zola as promoter and his works as models. It is no coincidence that naturalism's watershed year of 1880 saw the publication of both *Nana* and *The Experimental Novel* (*Le Roman expérimental*), Zola's most important programmatic tract. I will argue that Zola's work played a legitimating rather than simply prescriptive role in the transnational naturalist field. The attention to Zola nonetheless may give the false impression that this history and my attempt to trace it are Eurocentric. Yes, Zola was a European novelist, but some of the most interesting moments in this history come when novelists departed from his model, not for lack of talent but because when unrevised, the model could not address the circumstances at hand. The alternative to Zola would not be a different novelist (or several different ones), but a more structural approach that would necessarily shrink the room for the kind of close reading that shows the importance of such "deviations." The shortcomings of the work of Pascale Casanova—like Moretti, another driver of debates on world literature—show, moreover, that such a structural approach can easily privilege so-called literary centers more, not less.[10] Instead of trying to maneuver around Zola in this history, I take the position that genealogy does not equal servility. Zola's works themselves were not sui generis: the dossiers he compiled for his novels are full of notes on books about everything from working-class slang to neurology. Research on the reception of Zola's works reveals abundantly, moreover, that once they were out in the world they were no longer his own but material for others' interpretive translations, imitations, parodies, and inspiration. This book is more concerned with the process of such transformation than with Zola as an originator.

Finally, before turning to that process, I want to say plainly that I do not consider this a book about "world literature." The history of naturalist fiction unfolded in the space of the planet but did not reach all its corners. Its history was not "global." For other reasons, this examination of the naturalist novel's many, sometimes contradictory careers is not meant to be "globalizing." Much of the recent work in literary history and the circulation of expressive forms on a large scale is at its weakest when its ambitions are greatest. The problem, again, is not the quantitative challenge of the sheer mass of works one might examine. Rather, the ambition to work on a "global" scale seems operatively paired with a blindness not only to the great variety of ways of telling stories in the history of human expression, but also to the great unevenness and inequality in political, economic, and cultural relations between different parts of the world. As in economic discourse, talk of cultural "globalization" often assumes a barrier-free space of "flow" in which globality overcomes obstacles to its realization. Arjun Appadurai argued almost three decades ago, however, that the global cultural economy is a contest of homogenization and heterogenization: globalization produces difference.[11] Given this reality, approaches to geographically extensive literary history that aspire to "go global" are likely to produce poorer arguments than approaches which assume from the start that global explanations are impossible. Put another way: many naturalist novels are "totalizing" in their intention to offer a synthetic portrait and analysis of society. This book, however, has no intention of presenting a totalizing history of the form. The goal instead is porousness, partiality, and recognition that the order of the globe is a myth, the pandemonium of the planet a reality to be welcomed.

Figures of the World

CHAPTER I

Literary Travels and Literary Transformation

Naturalism is a problem. This shifting amalgam of documentary description, ideas from the nascent social sciences, and entropic plots had a tremendous impact on prose fiction in many parts of the world from the middle of the nineteenth century into the early twentieth century. Critically, however, naturalism is more or less reviled. Its reputation never really recovered from the attacks leveled against it in the 1930s by the great Marxist critic Georg Lukács.[1] It is the elephant in the room of the history of the novel. Naturalism should be a problem these days for another reason. Its history was essentially transnational. The techniques that writers and critics described at the time as "naturalistic" developed through the circulation of texts and the multiplication of naturalism into many different naturalisms. Yet the methods that we have in the early twenty-first century for understanding the histories of genres and schools on a large scale fall short in explaining something like the history of naturalism. Naturalist fiction itself can be a matter of taste. Some is great, but some is more of a curiosity, euphemistically speaking. Yet inasmuch as naturalism is a problem, it is also an opportunity to develop new methods for understanding expressive culture in transnational times.

What literary historians call "naturalism" in fiction began to emerge in the 1860s in France, in a convergence of currents in European realism. While acknowledging the hazards of "firsts," we may say that among its first examples were two novels named for their female protagonists, Edmond and Jules de Goncourt's *Germinie Lacerteux* (1864), about a maid who lives a secret amorous life, and Émile Zola's *Thérèse Raquin* (1867), about a woman who conspires with her lover to kill her husband. Around this time Zola, who also wrote about art, began to use the word "naturalist" (*naturaliste*) to describe painters and then his own fiction. (Zola's source for the term probably was an 1858 essay on Honoré de Balzac by the critic and historian Hippolyte Taine, which used "naturalist" in an analogy to the natural sciences to connote precision, objectivity, and disinterest.) In the 1870s Zola complemented the term "naturalist" with "naturalism" (*naturalisme*), turning the quality into a tendency. By relentlessly peppering articles with the two terms, Zola managed to lodge them in the critical vocabulary and get them applied to young protégés.[2]

Led with brio by Zola, French naturalism gained attention during the 1870s and reached an apogee in the early 1880s. It was supported by a stream of manifestos and critical essays, most importantly Zola's *The Experimental Novel* (*Le Roman expérimental*, 1880). Two events are symbolic: the "Trapp Dinner" held by Zola's protégés to celebrate the release of his novel *L'Assommoir* in 1877, and the publication three years later of *Evenings in Médan* (*Les Soirées de Médan*), a collection of stories by Zola and the same group named for the town where he had a country house.[3] The self-congratulation was undue. By the mid-1880s denouncing naturalism was a way for young writers to attract attention. Onetime associates of Zola such as Joris-Karl Huysmans went their own aesthetic ways. In 1891 a survey of French writers concluded that naturalism was finished.[4] In response Paul Alexis, Zola's most stalwart follower, quickly telegrammed him: "Naturalism not dead. Letter follows."[5] Even Zola, however, confided to the critic Jules Lemaître that he was tired of the Rougon-Macquart series, his massive "natural and social history" of Second Empire France.[6] When he finished the twentieth novel in 1893 his work moved in new directions, arguably still "naturalistic," but far from the physio-psychological anatomy of *Thérèse Raquin*.

Yet Alexis was right in his contention that naturalism was not dead, if not in the way he meant. From the 1870s into the twentieth century self-declared naturalist writers appeared across Europe, in the Americas, and Asia, adopting both the label and what they considered to be the method. The circulation of the work of Zola and other French writers, in French and in English, German, Russian, and Japanese translations, assisted the emergence of naturalism in these far-flung places. In some parts of the world naturalism was still shaping fiction directly in the 1920s, and its long-term impact in places where vigorous schools appeared is clear—even if sometimes lamented. A surge of critical debate and original works in Europe in the 1880s and 1890s became the foundation for approaching naturalism as an "international" movement.[7] And indeed it was, although one should pause to consider what "international" may seem to imply: a basic similarity in "national" writers' intents; comparability in the social contexts in which they worked; an analogous relationship of naturalism to local literary pasts; and a resemblance in naturalism's afterlives and legacies. Most work on naturalism as an international phenomenon, including studies of individual writers that assimilate them to the movement, takes a European scale, implying a shared chronology if not a geographical evenness. Lurking in the background is not just an empirical limitation of examples, but a presumption of cultural unity that legitimates comparison. Histories of naturalism in other parts of the world, whether national or regional in scale, are not often different in this respect: they typically begin with the matter of literary "imports."

Even on a European scale, the complexity of this history and its relation to other tendencies in fiction quickly appears. Writers and critics used the terms "naturalism" and "realism" (*naturalismo*, *realismo*) interchangeably in Portugal, where literary historians consider naturalism to have appeared in the 1870s with the work of José Maria Eça de Queirós; and in Spain, where it appeared in the 1880s with that of Benito Pérez Galdós, Emilia Pardo Bazán, and Clarín (Leopoldo Alas).[8] On the one hand we have the real difficulty of differentiating naturalism from the broader phenomenon of realism, but on the other hand there is the fact that fiction engaged with Zola achieved a dominance in these countries that naturalism never had in France, effectively becoming synonymous with realism because it was the only variety of the latter in practice. In Italy, where "naturalism" too was a common synonym for "realism," the reception of French naturalism in the 1870s was so entwined with the history of the "veritism" (*verismo*) espoused by writers like Luigi Capuana and Giovanni Verga that it is impossible to tell them apart, but also impossible to say they are the same.[9] Yet certainly the impact of naturalism was great. Not always so elsewhere: in Francophone Belgium a naturalism appeared around 1880 with the work of Paul Heussy and Camille Lemonnier, but the response to French naturalism in Flanders and the Netherlands was hostile, its impact minimal.[10] In southeastern Europe, Eugen Kumičić proclaimed his affiliation in Croatia in the 1880s, followed by Fran Govekar in Slovenia in the 1890s, but their reputations were minor and their followers were few.[11] A group of naturalist writers appeared in Serbia in the 1880s, but they were criticized for following Zola too closely. The most Zolean of the prominent Serbian realists, Simo Matavulj, was careful to keep his distance.[12] A school appeared in Greece in the 1890s—Andréas Karkavitsas and Alexandre Papadiamantis, among others—but only more than a decade after the debates incited by the serialization of Zola's *Nana* there in 1879.[13]

In the Nordic countries, naturalist fiction was part, but not all, of the "modern breakthrough" promoted by the Danish critic Georg Brandes. Naturalism emerged in Denmark in the 1870s with the early work of Jens Peter Jacobsen; in Norway at the end of the decade with Arne Garborg, followed by Amalie Skram, Hans Jaeger, and others; in Sweden in 1879 with August Strindberg's first novel, joined by the fiction of "Young Sweden" writers such as Victoria Benedictsson and Gustaf af Geijerstam in the 1880s; and in the same decade in Finland with writers such as Minna Canth, in Finnish, and Ina Lange, in Swedish.[14] But here realist writers who kept a critical distance from naturalism (Jonas Lie, in Norway) were as important as Zola to younger writers who espoused it (Herman Bang, in Denmark).[15] Other important writers, such as Alexander Kielland in Norway, drew from naturalism and other realisms alike. By the end of the 1880s naturalism was being denounced as "shoemaker realism" and a shift toward more psychological fiction began.[16]

Looming over this European history are two great outliers, Britain and Russia. A naturalist school appeared in Britain beginning in the 1880s (George Moore, George Gissing, Thomas Hardy), but the reception of naturalism was so hostile there that Zola's publisher was tried for obscenity.[17] Zola's work gained early notice in Russia through his contributions to the liberal periodical *Messenger of Europe* (*Vestnik Evropy*) and the efforts of Ivan Turgenev, but the work of the major writers usually conscripted into "international" naturalism—Turgenev and Fyodor Dostoevsky—is quite different from that of Zola or the Goncourt brothers. A group of writers embracing Zola's methods appeared in the 1870s, among them Pyotr Boborykin and L. L. Stečkina, but their place in the Russian literary scene was relatively minor, and the criticism of Zola's theories was harsh.[18] This is an intentionally partial history, but some lessons should be clear: naturalism's impact was great in some places, scant in others; there might be a school here, only a few writers there; some naturalist upsurges were contemporaneous with what was happening in France, while others "lagged"; noisy adherents often faced vociferous abstainers.

The same was generally true outside Europe. To take up the examples of the Americas and East Asia: fiction that writers and critics called naturalism appeared in Brazil and Argentina in the 1880s, with writers like Aluísio Azevedo and Júlio Ribeiro in the one, and Eugenio Cambaceres and Juan Antonio Argerich in the other. Their fiction was informed by both the work of Zola and Portuguese and Spanish intermediaries. (As in Portugal and Spain, "naturalism" and "realism" were interchangeable terms.) In other Spanish-speaking countries in the Americas, however, it was common to find naturalism mixed with well-entrenched romanticism, for example in the work of Mercedes Cabello de Carbonera in Peru and Carlos Reyles in Uruguay in the 1880s and 1890s.[19] To the north, arguments over "naturalism" began in the United States in the late 1870s, while the first works seen as examples appeared in the 1890s with the novellas of Stephen Crane. Some naturalist fiction, such as Jack London's, was widely read, but much of it was viewed with opprobrium. (The disapproving publisher of Theodore Dreiser's *Sister Carrie* tried to escape from his contract.)[20] In Japan, adherents of Zola such as Kosugi Tengai and Nagai Kafū began publishing around the turn of the century, but the naturalist school that developed there emphasized individuality in a way that reflected as many contributions from German as French naturalism. In the 1920s this form of naturalist fiction passed from Japan to China and Korea, where it had an anticolonial thrust. I will say more about these examples later, but again some preliminary lessons: adherents of Zola could be found in many places, but not everywhere, and naturalism was more often a hybrid than not. There were not one but many naturalisms, which differed according to the circumstances in which they formed. Some were in practice not only after Alexis's telegram but after Zola and most who attended the Trapp Dinner had passed on.

This plethora of naturalisms, however, reveals many elements in common, beginning with commitments to documentary description and the exposure of unwelcome truths, often legitimated by reference to the social and medical sciences. Among frequent topics one finds sexuality (for example, works by Ribeiro in Brazil and Kafū in Japan), hypocrisy and corruption (Guy de Maupassant in France and Cambaceres in Argentina), and the fate of individuals facing gigantic forces (Bang in Denmark and Verga in Italy).[21] The city is a favored setting (Strindberg in Sweden and Joanis Kondylakis in Greece), with the far-from-bucolic countryside as a counterpart (Manuel Zeno Gandía in Puerto Rico and Tayama Katai in Japan).[22] The same goes for the bourgeois household and the working-class quarter (Eça in Portugal and Skram in Norway on the one hand, Pardo Bazán in Spain and Azevedo in Brazil on the other).[23] Favored characters include the prostitute (Federico Gamboa in Mexico and Kim Tong-in in Korea), the atavistic criminal (Zola in France and Frank Norris in the United States), the oppressed worker (Baldomero Lillo in Chile and Fran Saleški Finžgar in Slovenia), and the opportunistic capitalist and the gluttonous corporation (Clorinda Matto de Turner in Peru and Dreiser in the United States).[24] These elements often developed into tropes that functioned as social analytics. Three such "figures" that this book examines closely are the degenerate body (the "body figure"), the self-liberated woman (the "Nana figure"), and the bounded milieu (the "social figure").

Another point in common is the controversy that naturalist fiction seems almost as a rule to have incited. To give only a few examples: in Spain, debates over the work of Zola in the 1880s split writers and critics into two camps, with conservatives opposing the foreign influence from France. Naturalism was called a threat to religion and country.[25] In Italy, where the major naturalist writers were from Sicily, writers and critics used the promotion of naturalism to insert the South into national literary debates. The Neapolitan critic Francesco De Sanctis advanced his reputation—and perhaps his political career—by supporting and then denouncing it.[26] The Greek translation of *Nana* in 1879 incited a controversy that lasted a decade, the foreword by Ayissalaos Yannopoulos Ipiriotis propounding naturalism as a way to rejuvenate the country's literature.[27] Around the same time, a transatlantic debate involving Eça de Queirós and Joaquim Maria Machado de Assis shaped fiction in Portugal and Brazil alike, pushing Eça to reevaluate the methods of his early work and helping Machado to develop his own realist alternative to naturalism.[28] In Japan, the early reception of naturalism was embroiled in a debate on "submerged ideals" (*botsu risō*) between the critic Tsubouchi Shōyō and the writer Mori Ōgai in the 1890s, the arguments continuing after the first naturalist works appeared at the end of the decade.[29] In China and Korea in the 1920s, as in many countries, quarrels over naturalism were part of efforts to establish realism in fiction.[30] This kind of effect was not unusual: the debate *about* naturalism, even when it produced few or even no naturalist writers, could deeply affect local literary fields.[31]

Finally, one should note the importance of Zola's fiction and critical essays as shared points of reference for writers, so much that "Zolaism" was a pejorative synonym for naturalism. The convention of gesturing to Zola reinforced the sense that naturalism was a program one could sign on to. Yves Chevrel, who is careful not to reduce the entire history to Zola and his influence, describes Zola's role in the dissemination of naturalism as "inciter, unifier, catalyzer."[32] This may understate the importance of Zola's works in propagating naturalist tropes and methods. Chapters 2, 3, and 4 of this book examine specific examples of this process. The many shout-outs that can be found in naturalist fiction amply illustrate Zola's importance as a unifying figure. Capuana dedicated his 1879 novel *Giacinta* to Zola, as the German writer Karl Bleibtreu did his 1885 story collection *Wicked Society* (*Schlechte Gesellschaft*).[33] The dedication of Ribeiro's *The Flesh* (*A carne*, 1888) is two pages long, in French, addressed to Zola; and the title of *Potpourri*, Cambaceres's satire of the Argentine elite, alludes to Zola's caustic portrait of bourgeois sexual mores in France, *Pot-Bouille* (both 1882).[34] Norris's 1896 story "His Sister" has a character named Gervaise Coupeau, after the protagonist of *L'Assommoir*.[35] Characters in Govekar's *In the Blood* (*V krvi*, 1896) and the Chilean novelist Augusto D'Halmar's *Juana Lucero* (1902) read *Nana* (1880), while one of the final scenes in Katai's *Country Teacher* (*Inaka kyōshi*, 1909) alludes to its ending.[36] Zola was not the only French naturalist whose work got such attention: a character in Bang's *By the Wayside* (*Ved Vejen*, 1886), for one, has a dog named Bel-Ami, after the hero of a novel published a year earlier by Maupassant.[37] With so much of naturalism associated with Zola, however, some writers felt forced to declare their independence. The preface to Lemonnier's *The Flesh-Eater* (*Happe-Chair*, 1886), about a factory strike, is a letter to Zola which avows that Lemonnier was already writing the novel when *Germinal*, Zola's mine-strike saga, appeared in 1885.[38] A character in the German playwright Gerhart Hauptmann's *Before Dawn* (*Vor Sonnenaufgang*, 1889) says that Zola and Henrik Ibsen are not real writers but "necessary evils."[39] Doubtless Hauptmann understood that like it or not, references to Zola were required to join what I will call the naturalist literary field.

There are good reasons, then, to approach the history of naturalist fiction as a history of literary form that unfolded on a large—but not "global"—scale. It is a history that is fundamentally heterogeneous, with writers who identified themselves as naturalists in one part of the world writing in ways their counterparts in other areas might not have recognized. It is also chronologically ragged. Naturalist fiction waxed in some places when it was waning in others, but the creativity to be found in some writers who wrote after others should dissuade us from seeing them as laggards, much less imitators. As readily as one can discern large-scale commonalities, moreover, the scales of the battles around naturalism inevitably were "small": the near-at-hand social, political, and literary contexts in which writers worked. Naturalism's history is geographically extensive *and* local, neither a monolithic history of globalization and homogenization nor a collection of separate national or regional histories that one can approach with conventional methods of comparison.

Questions of definition run throughout this history. The French critic Lemaître said in 1891 that the only naturalist was Zola.[40] Some writers now commonly considered to be naturalists in France and other countries did not adopt the label. As we have seen, however, many other writers were in the habit of announcing their association with naturalism through prefaces, dedications, and allusions to Zola's work. Critics at the time, moreover, thought that something new had appeared in fiction, calling it naturalism, "Zolaism," or the "experimental novel." Historians of many literatures agree that a shift occurred, have settled on calling it "naturalism" as it was called at the time, and have applied the label both to writers who did and did not identify themselves with the new trend. In the terminology of conceptual history, naturalism is partly a native category (used by writers and critics at the time) and partly a category of analysis (used by literary historians now). In a pair of anthropological terms lately adopted in literary criticism, it is partly "emic" (originating in the culture in question) and partly "etic" (used to describe that culture).

Recognizing the double quality of "naturalism" as a term compounds rather than settles the problem of definitions, because we seem to be faced with a choice between what "naturalism" may have meant then and what it may mean now, each depending on who was or is talking. The problem gets worse the wider one casts the geographical net. Naturalist writers are said to be anticlerical in Spanish America, intentionally romantic in Brazil, symbolist in Japan, and anticolonial in Korea.[41] It may be impossible to come up with a definition that accommodates all the ways of writing that are considered "naturalistic." Some might follow Lemaître, give up the label entirely even though it was commonly used at the time, and in giving it up, effectively abandon the project of studying these texts collectively. Among scholars of naturalism it is common to take a different view, that this is not a phenomenon which can be studied through a priori definitions. One must instead study it historically, while taking care with the category confusion that can be caused by the label itself.[42] Setting aside a priori definitions lets one acknowledge that what writers and critics called naturalism was a changing combination of elements that could include on-site fieldwork, ideas from neurology and criminology, tropes from other genres, popular clichés, and of course depressing plots. That the constellation varied over time and space as writers adapted naturalist techniques to new locales attests to the fact that many writers seem to have considered naturalism to be a method rather than a prescribed form.

When it comes to definitions, then, I propose taking writers and critics at their word: if they called it naturalism, then naturalism it was. By the same token, I suggest accepting what scholars of different literatures consider to be "naturalism" in their contexts. As we have already seen, there was not one naturalism; rather there werc many naturalisms, in the plural, linked by connection to the school that emerged in France and the ubiquity of the term *naturalisme* and its many translations. Instead of asking "Naturalism: what?" we might ask "Naturalism: when and where?" Indeed, the question behind this book is how a tendency in French fiction in the 1860s could turn into so many different naturalisms in some sixty years. Such an approach to the problem of defining naturalism will make some readers want to pull out their hair. But then: who are we to say that Amalie Skram was not doing what she thought she was doing in Norway in the 1880s because we can't define it the same way as what Yŏm Sang-sŏp thought he was doing in Korea in the 1920s, their own descriptions of their work as "naturalism" notwithstanding? To those risking baldness: let's see what we can learn by trying to make sense of this messy history.

LITERATURES IN THE WORLD

Some of the questions that the history of naturalist fiction raises should be clear by now: How exactly did this form of realism move around the world, becoming in the process not one but many naturalisms? Why did writers embrace the method and the label? Is there a pattern to where it was rejected? Why were new versions of naturalism appearing in some places when writers and critics thought it was "over" in others? Did the prestige of French writers—which was a political and economic, not just a cultural matter—inevitably tilt the field in their favor? If this is not a history of influence or even imitation—as some critics insist—just what kind of history is it? Following the example of the great historian of Brazilian literature, Roberto Schwarz: how do literary forms fare in places with different social conditions—and, I would add, different literary pasts—than those where they originated?[43] And finally: what methods do we need to figure all this out? The last question is the critical one for this book.

Some recent work on "world literature" helps illuminate these questions, although I do not consider this book a contribution to the world literature debate, for reasons noted in the preface. To begin, we might ask if naturalist fiction was world literature in David Damrosch's sense of "works that circulate beyond their culture of origin," whether in translation or the original language.[44] Certainly this would describe many of the novels of Zola and other prominent naturalist writers, which would-be naturalists read avidly. At the other end of the spectrum, however, were writers known only in the countries where they worked, if that—Oguri Fūyō in Japan or Ina Lange in Finland, for example. These days they belong at best to what Damrosch calls the "shadow canon."[45] Damrosch's paradigm explains part of this history—the part without which the rest would not have happened—but not all of it. That Damrosch's definition of world literature does not wholly apply reveals the basic unevenness of the naturalist literary field, in contrast to the barrier-free space of circulation that much world literature scholarship assumes.[46]

Alexander Beecroft's argument that literature circulates in "ecologies" with differing characteristics and scales reveals another aspect of this history. Beecroft proposes six ecologies in which literary works circulate, of which the last two—national and global—would be most relevant to the history of naturalist fiction.[47] Beecroft distinguishes the literatures of national ecologies, in which a literature corresponds to a people, state, and national language, from those of "panchoric" ecologies, for example, which address speakers of a language who may be spread across several states whose sovereignty does not depend on claiming to represent a nation. In what Beecroft sees as the emerging global ecology, literary circulation "truly knows no borders," and fiction written in a globalized language such as English may not be identified with any particular location (Beecroft, *Ecology of World Literature*, 35–36, 199). Beecroft's typology, which hinges on the changing relations among languages, literatures, and states, dislodges the reflexive assumption in much work on world literature that literatures are nothing but national before they become global. Yet the history of naturalist fiction does not quite fit here either. Many of the battles that writers and critics waged around naturalism were national in scale, and the polemical social portraits that naturalist writers created were addressed to the societies at hand. Against this evidence that the history of naturalist fiction can be explained in a framework of national literary ecologies, however, we have the fact that these writers imagined themselves taking part in something on an other-than-national scale. At the same time, only some of this fiction can be seen to exist in an ecology of global circulation. The history of naturalism is neither simply national nor global in Beecroft's terms.

Emily Apter's argument against the study of "world literature" as commonly practiced, but *for* de-provincialized comparative studies, opens up other approaches to the history of naturalist fiction. Apter's recent work foregrounds problems of translation in many registers. Translation in the usual sense—language to language—played an important role in the spread of naturalist themes and techniques. Translations of Zola's novels, especially *L'Assommoir*, *Nana*, and *Germinal*, were crucial vectors. More metaphorically, the travels of naturalism involved translations of a method, in the sense of adaptation and revision. Apter draws attention to the importance of *failures* of translation, and failed translations of method are also an important part of naturalist itineraries.[48] The charge that some naturalists were imitators was essentially a charge that they were unable to translate the method—although in another way it could mean that they were all too successful, producing an exact but out-of-place equivalent. Other translation failures—when writers working in conditions different from those in which naturalism emerged found they could not adapt naturalist method in its entirety—led to productive departures from the metropolitan norm. Such productive failure is a running issue in this book and is especially important in chapter 4, on how naturalist fiction modeled social relations.

Apter also questions the assumption of the equivalence—translatability—of literatures and cultures in the work of Damrosch, Franco Moretti, and others involved in world-literature studies (Apter, *Against World Literature*, 2–4). Aamir Mufti's work on how Orientalist scholarship contributed to ideas of world literature traces the forgotten history behind such an assumption: the universalization, beginning in eighteenth-century Europe, of the category of "literature," which created a spurious "plane of equivalence and comparability" on which current world-literature studies are founded.[49] How the European category of literature was universalized outside Europe is a problem that Lydia Liu, and more recently Michael Allan, have examined.[50] Naturalist writers worked in the throes of this transformation: they assumed that their literary methods were universal, thus helping naturalize "literature" per se. Their attitude allowed naturalism to become an imitable program and lent coherence to the heterogeneous transnational field. Yet the history of naturalist fiction belies their faith in the universality of the method. It was only partly translatable. The result, as I have said, was the multiplication of naturalisms. The logic and significance of this process is only apparent if one sets aside simple assumptions of equivalence and indeed resists them through close textual analysis. That is the essential method of the second, third, and fourth chapters of this book.

Apter's and Mufti's interventions ultimately address a confusion between history and category that appeared in Moretti's influential kickoff to the world literature debates of the 2000s and remains in much work on what Mariano Siskind calls the "globalization of the novel." Rather than rehearse the numerous responses to Moretti's "conjectures" on the diffusion of literary forms, I will get straight to several points that should inform large-scale literary history.[51] Moretti argues that when writers outside western Europe tried to write the kind of long prose fiction that began to appear there in the eighteenth century, they confronted a mismatch between the western European novel as form and the social conditions at hand which forced them into a "compromise" between foreign form, local material, and local form, or as he rephrased it, between foreign plot, local characters, and local narrative voice. However successful they may have been in finding a compromise, the mismatch remained as a "fault line" between story and discourse (Moretti, "Conjectures on World Literature," 60, 65). The pattern of compromise and crack can be found in countless variations everywhere except Spain, France, and Britain, the places that usually are taken as paradigmatic for the "rise of the novel." In light of what is to be found in other parts of the world, Moretti says with brio that these countries are not the rule but the exception ("Conjectures on World Literature," 61).

How Moretti handles the exception is more instructive than his discovery of the supposed rule. The "law of literary evolution" that Moretti claims to have discovered is so indiscriminate as to simply say: "Their fiction is not like our fiction." Moretti's argument that such conclusions can be reached through "distant reading"—relying on the work of other scholars instead of reading novels oneself—remains controversial. The paradox of rule-as-exception does not follow from the way he gathers evidence, however, but simply from turning one history of prose fiction in a small part of Europe into a critical category. Moretti's diction reenacts the transposition, which is rooted deeply in comparative literature as a discipline: speaking initially of "the Western European Novel," he slides toward "the modern novel" and then settles on simply "the novel."[52] I do not mean to over-parse, but given such a confusion of history and category, Moretti's conclusion about compromise is nearly inevitable: only the historical examples from which the category of "the novel" was abstracted can ever meet its measure.[53] Recent interventions have not avoided this problem. Siskind's argument on the globalization of the novel produces a curious inversion of Moretti's law. Moretti says that novels everywhere show the same compromise, while Siskind says that they serve the same "institutional and political function"—the cultivation of bourgeois hegemony—regardless of place. For Moretti, novels never work the same way outside western Europe; for Siskind they work *exactly* the same way.[54] The real obstacle in these analyses is not how they treat the diffusion of historical literary forms, but how they collapse a disorderly transnational history into a genre category that supports reductive comparative conclusions.

Finally, I should address Pascale Casanova's theory of "world literary space," because my argument about the history of naturalist fiction is fundamentally at odds with her view of literary relations between spatially distant parts of the world. Casanova defines world literary space as a hierarchically organized cultural field, in the manner of Pierre Bourdieu, arranged around autonomous and heteronomous (independent and other-dependent) poles. Countries in the autonomous portion of the field are rich in "literary resources" and provide models for writers elsewhere aspiring to aesthetic independence. Heteronomous portions of the field are resource-deprived and dependent on political authorities.[55] The "oldest" parts of the field—European countries whose writers fought over vernacular languages in the fifteenth and sixteenth centuries—are the most autonomous, and France the most autonomous of all. As first among peers France determines "Literary Mean Time," the up-to-date "present" of literary aesthetics (Casanova, *World Republic of Letters*, 85, 87, 90). Writers and critics in heteronomous parts of the field tend to perpetuate styles that are already outmoded in autonomous parts, leaving them backward and anachronistic. Their acceptance of aesthetic standards set in France is an aspect of "literary belief" and an effect of domination (*World Republic of Letters*, 10, 93–94, 100–101). (Casanova is not beyond bending the evidence to suit the model: among other examples, she suggests that naturalist fiction—the blackest of bêtes noires—came into vogue in South America in the 1930s and 1940s, for example, while we have already seen that writers there embraced it around 1880, when naturalism was also rising in Europe.)[56] What results from a conflation of aesthetic history and geographical space—reinforced by phrases like "aesthetic distance"—is a spatialized teleology of literary development that is abstracted from the literary history of several countries in Europe, and ends with the modernism for which Casanova shows an obvious preference (*World Republic of Letters*, 88).

Still more problematic for large-scale histories of literary form is the circular and cynical logic that Casanova uses to describe "peripheral" writers' attempts to determine their own aesthetics, a variety of what Kristin Ross calls the "Bourdieu effect" in sociological argument.[57] In Casanova's view, invoking Literary Mean Time is the only way for writers in heteronomous parts of the world literary field to escape local restraint (*World Republic of Letters*, 109). In doing so, however, they only reproduce their subordinate position in the world. Essentially, peripheral writers are dominated because they can't understand why they are, and they cannot understand why they are because they are dominated. Casanova's circular logic depends, on the one hand, on the assumption that writers who engage metropolitan aesthetics are playing for the attention of metropolitan critics, and on the other that engagement can only mean imitation. As we will see, the history of naturalist fiction instead shows frequent revisions of metropolitan norms, precisely because the conditions where writers worked—including the degree of autonomy of local literary fields—were different from those in the place where the first iteration of this kind of realism appeared.

The history of naturalist fiction is a particularly good case for finding fresh answers to the questions about the travel of expressive forms raised by Damrosch, Beecroft, and others. That naturalist writers frequently announced themselves through manifestos and pointed allusions makes it relatively easy to see the outlines of naturalism's travels. Moreover, where naturalism appeared, it often was consequential for local literary fields—even when its opponents prevailed. Although some writers' ambitions outstripped their abilities, the impact of naturalism's rise, travels, and disappearance thus can be observed on several scales.

As I will discuss later in this chapter, naturalism also competed with other varieties of realism that were on the move in the nineteenth and twentieth centuries, and it mixed with romanticism and modernism in "non-sequential" combinations that unsettle linear teleologies of form. The history of naturalist fiction thus illuminates a complex episode in literary history that analogical reasoning (globalization, ecology, underdevelopment) struggles to explain. As a concrete case, naturalist fiction offers an opportunity to begin building properly *historical* explanations of the circulation of literary forms, concepts, and expressive culture in the broadest sense.

NATURALIST CIRCUITS

The history of the naturalist novel is usually told as an internal European story, sometimes with an extra-European coda or two. The narrative given by Yves Chevrel, whose important work set the agenda for much subsequent scholarship, is a representative example. Chevrel describes the history of naturalism as a process of diffusion that proceeded through successive "waves."[58] The emergence of the naturalist novel proper was preceded by a preliminary wave of realistic depictions of everyday life and social mores that appeared independently in several countries. Examples are Gustave Flaubert's *Madame Bovary* (1857); Gustav Freytag's *Debit and Credit* (*Soll und Haben*, 1855); and Leo Tolstoy's *Sevastopol Sketches* (*Sevastopol'skie rasskazy*, 1856). Out of such realist currents came the first wave of naturalist novels, among them the Goncourt brothers' *Germinie Lacerteux* (1864), Zola's *Thérèse Raquin* (1867), and Dostoevsky's *Crime and Punishment* (*Prestuplenie i nakazanie*, 1866). Although other developments in Europe could be considered to contribute to this first wave, the main force was French. It was supported by a series of reflections on technique such as the Goncourts' preface to *Germinie Lacerteux*. In Chevrel's second wave, the naturalist "groundswell" in the years around 1880, these separate national developments became an international phenomenon, with the French school of *naturalisme* gaining a dominant position through a flood of new novels, translations, and programmatic statements. (It was from this time that naturalism was increasingly identified with Zola.) Chevrel identifies naturalist novels (and several plays) in this period from Germany, Denmark, Spain, Italy, Norway, Sweden, Russia, and England. A third wave followed in the late 1880s, in which naturalism achieved near domination of the novel across Europe, with major writers who had previously kept their distance showing signs of accommodation. At the same time, the movement began to split from inside, as young writers in France penned the "Manifesto of Five" to denounce Zola while Ibsen—seen as a naturalist since *A Doll's House* (*Et dukkehjem*, 1879)—also declared his differences with him. In Chevrel's final wave, in the early 1890s, naturalism was moribund in France (with Zola alone carrying on) but was still a vital force elsewhere, particularly in Germany but also in the United States, where Crane made his debut with *Maggie, A Girl of the Streets* (1893). By the turn of the century, Chevrel says, naturalism had ceased to exert a direct influence on the development of literary form (Chevrel, *Naturalisme*, 37–48).

Chevrel's account annexes a great number of works to a movement that he defines mainly through the work of Zola and his followers. As we have seen, not all would agree that *verismo* in Italy was identical to *naturalisme* in France. Still others might object to the unqualified inclusion of Russian realists such as Dostoevsky in this story. Several of Chevrel's waves, moreover, are too close to each other to be meaningfully distinct, and by his own admission some key works such as Zola's *L'Assommoir* (1877) fall in troughs between the waves (Chevrel, *Naturalisme*, 48). Momentarily setting aside such objections to Chevrel's synthesis, we can draw out several basic assumptions. Chevrel relies on an organic scheme in which literary forms emerge through internal evolution. The realist novel is a determinate stage in such evolution, the naturalist novel is an extension of its inherent tendencies, and realism-naturalism is inevitably succeeded by further phases. The chronology of forms unfolds in an area bounded by Asian Russia and the Atlantic, the Arctic and the Mediterranean; the transactions that turn scattered national trends into an international movement likewise observe these boundaries in a closed circuit. Chevrel's argument that the tendencies of the realist novel achieved their naturalist germination in France, from which the new school radiated to distant areas, shows that the "waves" of his history of naturalism are not only temporally serial but also spatially concentric.[59] In Chevrel's scheme, writers outside Europe do not contribute to naturalism's development, although they can, like Crane, be enlisted to extend the life of the school when it is in decline. Chevrel's suggestion that the naturalist novel does not leave Europe until it has achieved maturity (or even old age) is something we find again in Moretti's assumption that "the modern novel" departs Europe in a relatively fixed form which extra-European writers struggle to accommodate to social conditions at the point of arrival. One may observe as well that Chevrel's view of French writers as the propagators of new literary forms, which pass to Europe and the rest of the world, persists in structural paradigms of world literature such as Casanova's, in which France sets aesthetic standards that peripheral writers yearn to imitate.

A look at the lives of naturalist fiction in other parts of the world yields a different story. It is not one in which the centrality of Europe, as assumed in so much work on the history of the novel, is simply challenged by agency on the cultural periphery. Rather, it suggests a different view of circulation and chronologies in "world literature." I will illustrate with examples from the history of naturalism in South and North America and East Asia. I do not intend these short histories of naturalism to stand in for the longer and more complex histories of fiction in these regions of the world. Given the goal of sketching out the history of naturalism on a large scale, there is no way around being reductive in the ways I situate naturalist fiction in "local" literary histories. As I have said earlier, however, I believe the compensation for focusing on a specific and identifiable thread such as the naturalist novel ultimately will be a more informed way of approaching the relationship between local literary practices, the circulation of genres and forms, and large-scale political and economic forces.

Naturalism's history in Latin America is chronologically ragged and geographically uneven. In some countries, such as Brazil and Argentina, naturalist writers were numerous enough that one can legitimately see a "school." In other countries one finds a writer or two or—more commonly—works in which elements of European naturalism are mixed with other tendencies in fiction. Fiction-writing in Portuguese and Spanish emerged in part through the appropriation of aspects of European romanticism in the middle of the nineteenth century. The European writers most often identified as models or influences are Sir Walter Scott and François-René de Chateaubriand. European historical romance also arrived via James Fenimore Cooper, Scott's North American disciple.[60] The appropriation of these writers coincided with the creation of national identities, resulting in what Doris Sommer calls "foundational fictions" that created national pasts and imagined futures. Two of the best-known examples are José de Alencar's *The Guarani* (*O Guarani*, 1857) in Brazil and José Marmol's *Amalia* (1855) in Argentina, each by writer-politicians who considered their work to have a public purpose.[61] The authors of these and other national romances took the utilitarian approach of borrowing what was useful from European romanticism and leaving the rest, sometimes producing a paradoxical mix of a romantic plot and realistic descriptions of daily life, particularly life in the hinterland. The resulting *costumbrismo*—"literature of customs"—was concerned with the social "real" but was not a study of mores. Its function rather was to make different social strata comprehensible to each other.[62] The dominance of romantic *costumbrismo* was the backdrop for the rise of literary trends usually kept apart—naturalism, other realisms, and stylistically innovative poetry—that Siskind advocates approaching collectively as *modernismo* in the broad sense of asserting one's modernity.[63]

In Brazil, social conditions that the romantic aesthetic could not accommodate—such as the freedom granted to the descendents of slaves by the Law of the Free Womb of 1871 and the fall of the Empire in 1889—led to crises of representation that provided the opening for naturalism's more challenging depiction of social reality.[64] While writers across the region followed developments in French literature closely—generally reading it in the original language—naturalism was introduced to Brazilian letters not through the work of Zola but by *Cousin Basilio* (*O Primo Basilio*), the 1878 novel by Eça de Queirós, Zola's most prominent advocate in Portugal.[65] Eça's account of the liaison of Basilio, who has returned to Portugal after making a fortune in Brazil, with Luisa, a bourgeois wife, set off the first great controversy over the novel in Brazil. The argument spread to Eça's *The Sin of Father Amaro* (*O Crime de Padre Amaro*, 1875) and to French naturalism through charges that *Father Amaro* plagiarized Zola's *The Sin of Father Mouret* (*La Faute de l'Abbé Mouret*, 1875).[66] Aluísio Azevedo's *The Mulatto* (*O Mulato*, 1881), which uses the life and death of its mixed-race protagonist to indict the slaveocracy of provincial Maranhão, is usually called the "first" work of naturalism in Brazil, although there are other candidates such as Herculano Marcos Inglês de Souza's novel *Colonel Sangrado* (*O Coronel Sangrado*, 1877). Certainly *The Mulatto* was the first novel to provoke the controversy that typically accompanied the emergence of naturalist schools. Azevedo was accused not just of imitating Zola but also of plagiarizing Eça, and in his birthplace of São Luís Azevedo was accused of obscenity, immorality, and threatening respect for social order.[67] Although he wrote many potboilers, Azevedo followed up with other "serious" novels such as *The Man* (*O Homem*, 1887) and *The Slum* (*O Cortiço*, 1890). Other examples of naturalism in Brazil include Ribeiro's quasi-clinical examination of sexuality, *The*

Flesh (1888); Inglês de Sousa's *The Missionary* (*O Missionàrio*, 1891); and Adolfo Caminha's *The Teacher* (*A Normalista*, 1892) and *Bom-Crioulo* (1895), about a black sailor who becomes sexually obsessed with a white cabin-boy.

Critics have noted scenes, motifs, and characters in these novels that echo the work of Eça and Zola. (In addition to the preface addressed to Zola, *The Flesh* reproduces a scene of oral sex from *Cousin Basilio*, while *The Slum* reprises a lesbian love scene from *Nana*.)[68] The critic José Guilherm Merquior calls Brazilian naturalism "transoceanic plagiarism."[69] Others see the naturalist novel in Brazil as an original synthesis because writers were intent on using what they found in Eça and Zola to address the physical and social conditions around them.[70] Most notably, they confronted the history and legacy of slavery and racism. Although Zola's Rougon-Macquart series was written when France was expanding its empire, racial difference had no role in the hereditary scheme that organized it. Although the series' novels frequently address the problem of labor, moreover, its enslaved form never appears. In Brazil, where slavery was not abolished completely until 1888, issues of race were necessarily part of naturalist writers' confrontation with national romance (in which the Indian was the favored other) and the Comtean political orthodoxy of the times (which could not account for slavery in its theory of progress).[71] Critics leaven their insistence on innovation with observations about the "native" contradictions of naturalism in Brazil. The plot of Azevedo's antiracist, antislavery novel *The Mulatto*, for example, dramatizes the "whitening solution" promoted by liberals, who thought that sexual relations between blacks and whites would improve the population by increasing the "white influence" in it.[72] Without excusing such pseudo-enlightened racism, one should note that its role in naturalism in Brazil is not a sign of imitation or "compromise": rather, Brazilian naturalists' imaginary resolutions of actual social problems reflected common political positions in the society of their time.

In the Spanish-speaking Americas, a Balzacian variety of realism had been available since the publication of *Martín Rivas* by the Chilean doctor Alberto Blest Gana in 1862, but *costumbrismo* romanticism remained entrenched into the 1870s.[73] As in Brazil, literary historians note romanticism's greater utility until its aesthetic could no longer accommodate changes wrought by industrialization, immigration, and the embrace of Positivism and liberal political economy. The turn to naturalism as a method of social investigation was most notable in areas where such changes had the greatest impact, particularly Argentina.[74] As in Brazil, too, writers encountered naturalism directly from France (Argentina's Cambaceres discovered Zola's work during a stay there, as Blest Gana had Balzac's) and through the former metropole, via the novels of Galdós, Pardo Bazán, and other Spanish writers.[75]

As happened so often, the first naturalist works by "early adopters" in Argentina were preceded by a polemic. In this case, the uproar followed the publication of a single installment of a Spanish translation of *L'Assommoir* in August 1879. The confrontation between supporters and detractors of Zola continued with *Nana*, whose French edition went on sale in Buenos Aires in March 1880 only one week after the volume was released in Paris. The anonymous publication of Cambaceres's *Potpourri* two years later reignited the debate. Although this "first" naturalist novel in Spanish America did not greatly resemble Zola's work in method, it was associated with naturalism because of its cynical assessment of the Argentine elite and its proximity to the Zolean uproar.[76] (In point of view and tone it more resembles Machado de Assis's Brazilian *anti*-naturalist novel *Memórias póstumas de Brás Cubas* or *The Posthumous Memoirs of Brás Cubas*, 1881.) Cambaceres's following novels—*Sentimental Music* (*Musica sentimental*, 1884), *Without Direction* (*Sin Rumbo*, 1885), and *In the Blood* (*En la sangre*, 1887)—did move increasingly toward the Zolean model, signaled by motifs in *Sentimental Music* recalling *Nana* and the analytical framework of heredity announced by the title of *In the Blood*.[77] Other writers added to the naturalist upsurge, notably Antonio Argerich with *Innocent or Guilty?* (*¿Inocentes o culpables?* 1884) and Manuel Podestá with *Irresponsible* (*Irresponsable*, 1889).

Many of these novels set out to demystify ideas of the nation that had been promoted by *costumbrismo* fiction such as Marmol's *Amalia* in light of sudden increases in wealth, inequality, and conflict between old elites and the new, immigrant masses. In these conditions, naturalist methods of describing social relations seem to have been particularly useful.[78] Much like naturalist writers in Europe, Cambaceres, Argerich, and their peers enlisted the hegemonic "scientific" languages of their era in their analyses of the situation, in this case Positivism, Social Darwinism, and European race theory. They took notable aim at immigrants (*In the Blood* and *Innocent or Guilty?*) and the idle landed class (*Without Direction*) as threats to the social order.[79] The naturalist assault was ambiguous: Cambaceres attacked the language of the status quo from within and ultimately delivered an even bleaker critique than did Zola, but the intensity of his and Argerich's depiction of the forces reshaping society comes in part from their uncritical acceptance of theories of racial hierarchy.[80] Cambaceres's *In the Blood* was well received when it was published in 1887, indicating that in the short span of six years naturalism had been more or less accepted in Argentina, leaving one to wonder if this fiction meant to disrupt the status quo in fact gave comfort to it.[81]

Elsewhere in Spanish America naturalism emerged later and more fitfully. Fiction posing a naturalist challenge to the romantic norm began to appear in Uruguay in the 1880s with Carlos Reyles's *For Life* (*Por la vida*, 1888), followed by *Drink* (*Beba*, 1894) and Javier de Viana's *Gaucha* (1899). Reyles soon embraced the new vogue for decadentism, however, while *Gaucha* was Viana's only piece of long fiction.[82] In Puerto Rico, Zeno Gandía published two "chronicles of a sick world" in the 1890s, *The Pond* (*La Charca*, 1894) and *Marten* (*Garduña*, 1896), with a clinical, "scientific" perspective.[83] Writers who adopted only a few elements of French naturalism were more common than this relative handful of naturalist true believers, however. One example is Matto de Turner, whose novels *Birds without a Nest* (*Aves sin nido*, 1889) and *Inheritance* (*Herencia*, 1895), about the treatment of Andean Indians in Peru, incorporated both naturalist and romantic techniques into what became known as "indigenist" fiction.[84] Another is the Mexican writers who published fiction with varying connections to European naturalism in the 1890s and 1900s. The most prominent of these, Federico Gamboa, is known for shifting the focus of fiction from countryside to city in novels such as *Santa* (1903), which has elements recalling *Nana*. (Gamboa too encountered the work of Zola while in France.)[85] Writing in defense of his novel *Appearances* (*Apariencias*, 1892), Gamboa granted a place to neoclassicism and romanticism in poetry, but maintained that naturalism had "triumphed" in prose, which henceforth could "only be naturalistic." Surveying the horizon, he found different naturalisms in different lands: "excessive" in France, "sweet" in England, "penetrating" in Norway, and "admirable" in Bret Harte's California sketches.[86] However unusual it might seem now to include Harte in the list, Gamboa's view of naturalism as a capacious transnational form was strikingly at odds with the common denunciation of it as a foreign import, while his recognition that naturalism manifested itself in the plural was an acknowledgment of writers' abilities to adapt it to their own circumstances.

Naturalism in Brazil and Argentina emerged through contact with multiple currents in European naturalism: French and Portuguese in the first case, French and Spanish in the second. Writers from Germany or other European countries where naturalism was flourishing were not involved. Azevedo, Cambaceres, and their peers embraced naturalism not only as a method of examining their societies in a critical light, but also as a way to overturn romantic representations of national life, which were themselves the result of an earlier appropriation of European fiction. Naturalism, other realisms, and the loose collection of poetic aesthetics that became known as *modernismo* emerged at essentially the same time in response. The victory was not complete: naturalistic and romantic techniques of representation coexisted, sometimes in the same work. The reason was more than just habit, since romantic *costumbrismo* and naturalism-realism shared a sense of social vocation, however different their approaches may have been to describing social relations.[87] The more time passed, moreover, the more likely were naturalist and modernist techniques to mingle, for example in the work of Gamboa and the poet Amado Nervo's short novel *Pascual Aguilera* (1896) in Mexico.[88]

Beginning around 1880, then, we can identify distinct circuits for the circulation of naturalist fiction to and around Latin America that overlapped with the more densely traveled circuits of naturalism in Europe. The chronology of naturalism in Latin America too shares certain events with the history of European naturalism while remaining distinct from it. Yet in this history, several "periods" of conventional literary historiography—romanticism, realism, modernism—collapse into relations of mutual influence. The seemingly strange hybrids of romantic naturalism and naturalistic modernism were not temporal aberrations, as Casanova's spatialized theory of literary history would need them to be, but a common consequence of the travel of forms, which facilitates such "non-sequential" juxtapositions. The idea that all of this is a compromise between foreign form and what Moretti calls "local voice" too seems increasingly unsustainable: the history of the novel in Latin America is largely a history of writing in the colonizers' languages, but even within that history, parsing the relationship between recent and less recent appropriations as "compromise" is not just artificial but perhaps meaningless. Instead, we need to reckon historically with the prospect of multiple chronologies (rather than a single linear evolution) and multiple circuits (rather than concentric circles) that contribute to the heterogeneous history of a transnational literary phenomenon.

The history of naturalist fiction to the north, in the United States, further complicates the picture. There, naturalism emerged in opposition to an already existing realism and continued to thrive well into the twentieth century. Translation, moreover, played an important role in the circulation of naturalist fiction to North America. Realistic fiction began to appear in the United States in the 1860s, showing on the one hand a commitment to documentary observation—Rebecca Harding Davis's *Life in the Iron Mills* (1861), for example—and on the other hand an overt antagonism toward sentimental and romantic fiction and the attitudes they were blamed for promoting—one way, perhaps, of reading *Miss Ravenel's Conversion from Secession to Loyalty* (1867) by John William De Forest. By the 1880s a variety of realism classically represented by the trio of William Dean Howells (*The Rise of Silas Lapham*, 1885), Henry James (*The Bostonians*, 1886), and Mark Twain (*The Adventures of Huckleberry Finn*, 1885) had established itself, although not without controversy.[89] Ongoing debate also created a critical discourse on realism that extended to naturalist fiction. While defending their work in the "realism war" of the 1880s, Howells and James moved critical opinion of Zola and other French naturalists from dismissive hostility (*L'Assommoir* being "loaded with moral contagion") to a grudging recognition that naturalist exposés could have humanitarian goals.[90]

Stephen Crane published *Maggie*, usually considered the first work of naturalism in American fiction, under a pseudonym in 1893, followed by *The Red Badge of Courage* (1895) and *George's Mother* (1896). (The latter was a companion piece to *Maggie*, which Crane revised and republished the same year under his own name.) In the classic canon, Crane's volley was followed by Frank Norris's *Vandover and the Brute* (1895, published posthumously in 1914), *McTeague* (1899), and *The Octopus* (1901), which was the first novel in a planned trilogy called *The Epic of the Wheat*. The new trend in fiction continued with Theodore Dreiser's *Sister Carrie* (1900), and after a lull, *Jennie Gerhardt* (1911); and stories and novels by Jack London such as *The Call of the Wild* (1903) and *The Sea-Wolf* (1904). Readers at the time perceived these works, which depicted violence and desire without moral restraint, as departures from the more decorous realism associated with Howells.[91] They were called both "realist" and "naturalist." The naturalist upsurge is often expanded to include work by other writers such as Harold Frederic (*The Damnation of Theron Ware*, 1896), Kate Chopin (*The Awakening*, 1899), and Edith Wharton (*The House of Mirth*, 1905). Critics also frequently extend this history until well after naturalism had fallen out of practice in other parts of the world, to include, for example, John Dos Passos's *Manhattan Transfer* (1925), William Faulkner's *The Sound and the Fury* (1929), and James T. Farrell's *Studs Lonigan* trilogy (1932–35).

The sources for this new kind of fiction were multiple. Although some historians have tried hard to separate naturalism in the United States from European sources—especially French ones—Zola's novels undeniably played an important role in naturalism's emergence there.[92] His books were largely known in English translation. U.S. publishers often released English-language versions of them years before authorized translations appeared in Britain because they were unhindered by international copyright law. Typically the translations were pumped up in title and watered down in content. *The Fortune of the Rougons* (*La Fortune des Rougon*, 1871), which has a subplot about ill-fated sweethearts, was released both as *The Girl in Scarlet; or, The Loves of Silvère and Miette* and, more to the point, as *Wedded in Death*. Zola's novel *The Belly of Paris* (*Le Ventre de Paris*, 1873), set in the bazaar of Les Halles, became *La Belle Lisa; or, The Paris Market Girls*.[93] Between their covers, translations of French naturalism, like those of Russian realism, were edited and expurgated, with scenes deemed too provocative modified or cut.[94] Even mediated by translation and self-protective scruple, however, they left an impression. Crane said of *Nana*: "this girl in Zola is a real streetwalker . . . Nana, in the story, is honest."[95] Norris, who read Zola's work in French, openly acknowledged its impact. (He repeated the shout-out to *L'Assommoir* in his story "His Sister" when he had a "decayed French laundress" cook for the central characters in *McTeague*.)[96] While Crane resisted the label of naturalist, when Norris reviewed *Maggie* he found traces of *L'Assommoir* in it, and as if to drive home the point that Crane was part of the family, another character in "His Sister" is referred to as "George's mother." Scholars also see elements of Zola's *The Debacle* (*La Débâcle*, 1892), a Rougon-Macquart novel about the Franco-Prussian War that Crane is known to have read, in *The Red Badge of Courage*.[97]

Just as the transnational movement cannot be reduced to the international impact of Zola, so too not all naturalist fiction in the United States has such direct connections to his work. It was the Zola fan Norris who recommended *Sister Carrie* to his employer, Doubleday, Page, for publication, but Dreiser vowed that he had not read any of Zola's work before writing the novel, leading many to speculate on indirect connections.[98] London's fiction too shows no direct connection to Zola, although by common consensus it was part of the turn-of-the-century naturalist upsurge. Here one strand of late nineteenth-century intellectual history, evolutionary ideas of the "survival of the fittest," illuminates the connections among naturalist authors in the United States: a battle of street urchins in the opening scene of *Maggie* found echoes in the life of a wolf pack in London's *Call of the Wild* and in a famous episode in Dreiser's *The Financier* (1912), in which an aquariumed lobster devours a squid. Another important source was the school of Midwestern realism, raw fiction about an embittered farming population that culminated in the work of Hamlin Garland, whose best-known story, "Under the Lion's Paw" (1890), depicts a world of impersonal, crushing force.[99] Garland gave critical encouragement to Crane in his early career. So too did Howells, whose realism—along with James's—was a source for naturalist fiction even though Norris dismissed it as literature of "small passions" about "things that are likely to happen between lunch and supper."[100] Crane referred to Howells and Garland as his "literary fathers."[101]

And then there is the question of the relationship of naturalism in the United States to the romance and to romanticism. While the genres of sentimental and historical romance were the ultimate enemy for naturalist writers in the United States, many saw and continue to see a connection between naturalism and the methods of mid-nineteenth-century "romantic" writers such as Herman Melville and Nathaniel Hawthorne. Howells was one; and Norris, who considered Zola an essentially romantic writer, was another.[102] Donald Pizer argues that to Norris "naturalism" meant a dialectical resolution of the faults of realism and romanticism, Howells and Victor Hugo, with the one "accurate" at the cost of being "true," and the other having the opposite problem. Norris responded with novels that found the sensational in the commonplace (a neighborhood dentist's murder of his wife in *McTeague*); Crane with novels finding the commonplace in the sensational (the deflation of heroism in *The Red Badge of Courage*); Dreiser by confounding the difference between them (an epic fall leading to a banal suicide in *Sister Carrie*).[103] Other literary historians see naturalist writers in the United States appropriating and inverting the conventions of the popular romances of the day.[104] To see naturalists reaching either back or to the side is not to collapse the differences among texts that are conventionally called romantic, realist, and naturalist—they reveal, for example, radically different conceptions of the self and ways of representing it—but rather to acknowledge that there is no one-way path from the first to the last.[105]

In the United States, then, we find a distinct history, different from the one found in Latin America, within the career of this transnational phenomenon. Although some writers and critics encountered French naturalism in the original language, it mainly was known through unauthorized, often expurgated translations. The French school was hotly debated in the United States in the 1880s, but original naturalist works did not appear there until the 1890s, a decade after Argentina and Brazil and at a time when naturalism was waning in Europe. Also unlike the Portuguese- and Spanish-speaking Americas, where naturalism and the novel were supplanted by *modernismo* and poetry, naturalist fiction remained part of the scene in the United States until the middle of the twentieth century. Most significantly, however, in the United States naturalism emerged in antagonism to other, already existing realisms. Their existence changed the relationship of naturalist fiction to romances and romanticism. As in Latin America and both the central and peripheral areas of Europe, "naturalism" meant both a method and a position taken against other players in the local literary field, yet the content of the method and the meaning of the position differed from these other places (as the confrontations in them differed from each other). Finally, the relatively long life of naturalism in the United States evinces a different relationship to what followed. If Dos Passos's *Manhattan Transfer* is a work of naturalism (not modernism), it is so because its disunified, multi-strand social narrative uses a naturalistic descriptive method; if Faulkner's more psychologically focused *The Sound and The Fury* too is naturalism, it is so because it maintains an anatomizing relationship between character and narrative observer.

Naturalist writers in the settler societies of South and North America did battle with forms of fiction linked directly and indirectly to forms also found in Europe—varieties of national romanticism on the one hand, of realism and popular romance on the other. In East Asia, not only was there was a long history of prose fiction in Chinese and Japanese—including fiction concerned with the representation of social relations and the everyday—but writers in the region became familiar with European romanticism and several kinds of European realism, including naturalism, at essentially the same time. As in the United States, English played an important role as a language of translation, but it was joined by Japanese as a medium through which writers in China and Korea encountered European fiction and criticism. By the 1920s, moreover, a naturalism that had emerged in Japan, along with critical essays promoting it, was shaping fiction and criticism in Japan's neighbors.

Japanese writers turned their attention to the European novel beginning in the 1870s during the era of "civilization and enlightenment" (*bunmei kaika*) that followed the Meiji Restoration of 1868. Progressive intellectuals saw the reform of culture—in the senses both of arts and letters and of everyday life—as a means of strengthening the country, with the ultimate goal of withstanding European imperialism. *The Essence of the Novel* (*Shōsetsu shinzui*, 1886), a programmatic tract by the critic and would-be novelist Tsubouchi Shōyō, formalized the program. Shōyō called for fiction that would depict "human emotions and manners" (*ninjō setai*) instead of resorting to the recycled plots and stock characters common in eighteenth- and nineteenth-century fiction.[106] A search for native precedents for realism led to a revival in the 1890s of the work of the eighteenth-century writer Ihara Saikaku—a parodic chronicler of urban life—in the fiction of Ozaki Kōyō and the young writers in his circle.[107] Their "serious" (*shinkoku*) fiction came to be known as "novels of misery" (*hisan shōsetsu*). Like Howells's work in the United States, their novels became the target of the early naturalist writers in Japan.

Zola's work was first introduced to Japan at second hand, through a translation of the French philosopher and critic Eugène Véron's *Aesthetics* (*L'Esthétique*, 1878) by Nakae Chōmin in 1883–84.[108] Zola's name surfaced again in 1888, when the politician Ozaki Yukio wrote about the obscenity trial of Zola's English publisher in a travelogue serialized in the *Chōya shinbun* newspaper.[109] In 1889 the writer Mori Ōgai, writing from Germany, first discussed Zola's work as a whole in an article based on the German poet and dramatist Rudolf von Gottschall's disapproving evaluation of the "naturalistic and photographic" French novel in his collection *Literary Death Rattles and Life Questions* (*Literarische Todtenklänge und Lebensfragen*, 1885).[110] Critical discussion of naturalism resurged in one of the first great controversies in modern Japanese literary circles, the "suppressed ideals debate" (*botsu risō ronsō*) between Ōgai and Shōyō in 1891 and 1892. Ōgai, responding to Shōyō's opinion that writers and critics sometimes suppress their own views in order to allow a work's "ideals" to emerge unimpeded, argued that in the end even Zola, seemingly the epitome of a writer who suppressed his presence, was a "great idealist" who relied on the imagination.[111] Kawauchi Kiyoshi has shown that the positions that Shōyō and

Ōgai took ultimately trace back to debates on objectivity in literature in France (for Shōyō, via Hippolyte Taine; for Ōgai, via Gottschall and Ferdinand Brunetière).[112] That is: the discourse on naturalism—which extended far beyond Europe, as we have already seen—preceded and conditioned the reception of naturalist works in Asia.

Zola and naturalism (*shizen shugi*) were one and the same in Japan until the early years of the twentieth century.[113] Literary critics viewed Zola primarily as a theorist of heredity and environment, but many writers in the 1890s—who read Zola in English translation—looked to him for new techniques for the representation of social relations and human behavior.[114] Original works of what critics called *Zoraizumu*—Zolaism—appeared at the turn of the century. These include Kosugi Tengai's novels about the world of entertainment and prostitution, *New Year's Finery* (*Hatsu sugata*, 1900) and *Popular Song* (*Hayari uta*, 1902); and Nagai Kafū's *Flowers of Hell* (*Jigoku no hana*, 1902) and *Woman of Dreams* (*Yume no onna*, 1903), which were similarly focused on female protagonists. Tayama Katai's story "The End of Jūemon" ("Jūemon no saigo," 1902), about a rural delinquent murdered by the villagers he torments, directed naturalist fiction not just to depicting social reality but also to puncturing social myths.[115] These writers' antagonists were the "novels of misery" by Kōyō protégés such as Hirotsu Ryūrō, which they considered sentimental and moralistic, but the unadorned style they aspired to was in itself an attack on the literary establishment. They propounded their goals in prefaces and manifestos, most importantly Tengai's preface to *Popular Song* and Katai's essay "Plain Description" ("Rokutsu naru byōsha," 1904), which attacked novelists who put artistry and technique ahead of description as "slaves to writing."[116] As this early period of naturalism in Japan unfolded, the work of Maupassant and of German naturalists such as Hermann Sudermann, with their greater interest in human liberation, joined Zola's fiction as influences.[117]

Naturalism in Japan is commonly thought to have taken a turn with Katai's *The Quilt* (*Futon*, 1907), which recounts his real-life obsession with a female protégé, lightly camouflaged by changes of name and a third-person point of view. In the mid-1920s *The Quilt* was retroactively dubbed the first "I-novel" (*shishōsetsu*), a confessional genre that openly relied on episodes of an author's life, and the history of naturalism in Japan began to be reduced to the emergence of this kind of autobiographical fiction. Tomi Suzuki points out that treating *The Quilt* as the beginning of the I-novel is both anachronistic (the term was coined in 1920 or 1921) and critically inept, because unlike many such works of the 1910s and early 1920s, Katai takes an undeniably ironic view of his stand-in.[118] The turn that began with *The Quilt* might rather be viewed in two ways. First, many more writers began writing fiction regarded as "naturalistic" following Katai's succès de scandale. Second, while not all of this fiction was connected to the authors' lives, much of it rejected the purely external description of writers like Tengai in favor of psychological autopsy that is closer in some ways to the free-indirect-discourse mental anatomies of Zola novels such as *L'Assommoir* than to *New Year's Finery* and other early naturalist works in Japan. The thread leading from the first to the second period of naturalism in Japan is thus a concern with mimesis.[119]

Writers of "egocentric" naturalism frequently used the double perspective of protagonist and narrator as a means to protest what they considered the oppressive weight of custom on individual freedom.[120] Naturalist fiction in this socio-psychologically indicting mode was theorized by critics such as Shimamura Hōgetsu and Hasegawa Tenkei, who coined the influential phrase "the sorrow of exposing reality" (*genjitsu bakurō no hiai*) in 1908 to explain its world-weary tone.[121] By the 1910s some writers and critics had had enough of naturalist pessimism. Shiga Naoya, Mushakōji Saneatsu, and others associated with the coterie magazine *White Birch* (*Shirakaba*) turned egocentric second-period naturalism into a fiction of the self premised on sincerity and authenticity.[122] (An influential example was Shiga's 1917 novella *Wakai* or *Reconciliation*.) In Japanese critical parlance their work also is called naturalism, although it scarcely resembles the fiction of Zola, the Goncourts, or Maupassant. Rather than considering this a misnomer, however, one should recognize that the practice of naturalist fiction had significantly changed over some dozen years in Japan.

Naturalisms—in the plural—played complex roles in the establishment of realism in China and Korea, where writers and critics also sought new forms of fiction. In China, arguments for realism in fiction appeared in the late Qing and early Republican periods. In 1902 the historian and social critic Liang Qichao was one of the first to advocate *xieshi*, an import of the Japanese coinage *shajitsu* ("realism") which he encountered while studying in Japan.[123] In the following decades critics such as Chen Duxiu and Hu Shi continued the argument, which became central to literary debates in the May Fourth movement, a wide-ranging push for social, political, and intellectual reform that began in 1919. Realism in literature, proponents argued, would encourage public engagement with social and political problems, an attitude best exemplified in the fiction of Lu Xun.[124] Their basic ideas about realism came from criticism in English and Japanese, including Hōgetsu's essay "Naturalism in Literature" ("Bungei jō no shizenshugi," 1908), which had an especially strong impact on May Fourth critics such as Mao Dun when it was translated into Chinese in 1921.[125] Students in or recently returned from Japan played a key role in these arguments because of their familiarity with Japanese literature and literary criticism and European literature and criticism translated into Japanese.[126]

Mao Dun began promoting realism and naturalism as the editor of *Short Story Monthly* (*Xiaoshuo yuebai*) and a leader of the Chinese Literary Association (Wenxue yanjiu hui), founded in 1921. He and others involved in the debates considered realism and naturalism to be related but they distinguished between them, in a sense as epistemology versus method, but perhaps too for the polemical value that "naturalism" (*ziran zhuyi*) commanded.[127] Mao Dun said that he personally favored symbolism and neoromanticism but the naturalism of Zola, whom writers generally read in English translation, was his model for fiction that would be able to address the problems of the present moment.[128] He made an extended case for it in "Naturalism and Contemporary Chinese Fiction" ("Ziran zhuyi yu Zhongguo xiandai xiaoshuo"), an influential essay from 1922 informed by Hōgetsu. Mao Dun called objective observation and scientific description "naturalist treasures" that would allow writers to overcome the defects in both old and new styles of writing fiction.[129]

Although Mao Dun became known as the Chinese spokesman for Zola, he kept a critical distance. Zolean determinism, he argued, reflected on the one hand a subjective bias that mistook the pathologies of bourgeois society for essential human depravity, and on the other an ideological presumption that society cannot be changed. Adopting Zola's methods, however, did not require accepting his view of social relations.[130] Mao Dun later recalled that when he began writing fiction with the linked novellas of *Eclipse* (*Shi*, 1927), he found himself drawn as much to Tolstoy as to Zola.[131] From the perspective of the continual adaptation of ideas and literary form, it is notable that in *Eclipse* and later works Zolean determinism becomes a matter of class and ingrained ideology, not biology or milieu. In David Wang's view, Mao Dun may have intentionally "misread" Zola so that he could accommodate a new social and historical environment.[132] As I have argued about other naturalist writers, we might also say that he adapted naturalism to address the world at hand, amalgamating it with aspects of other realisms such as Tolstoy's when they proved useful.

Around the same time that Mao Dun began promoting naturalism, a group of Chinese students in Japan formed the Creation Society (Chuangzaoshe) and introduced Japanese naturalism to Chinese fiction.[133] Familiar with the theory and practice of Japanese naturalism and the *White Birch* group, several members embraced "egocentric" Japanese fiction and poetry with zeal. They soon produced their own works, among them Yu Dafu's "Sinking" ("Chenlun," 1921), Guo Moruo's "Lingering Spring" ("Can chun," 1922), and Zhang Ziping's "Lives of a Group of Good-for-Nothings" ("Yiban yongyuan de shenghuo," 1922). Creation Society writers broke with the apolitical attitude of Japanese chroniclers of the self like Shiga and Mushakōji, turning the form to address not only their personal experience but the collective situation in China. The protagonists of these stories are not closed off from society but rather embedded in it.[134] Yu Dafu's "Sinking," the best known of the group's stories, examines the mind of a Chinese student in Japan who commits suicide after experiencing prejudice, romantic frustration, and growing anguish over China's shortcomings. Just before succumbing he calls for reform. Psychological anatomization of the author-protagonist becomes a means of social critique, while assertion of the self is both a motif and a means of national regeneration. The "translingual" introduction of Japanese naturalism (itself a transformation of French and German varieties) into Chinese fiction thus was part of the May Fourth-era proposition of individualism as the antagonist of tradition.[135] Cheng Fangwu, showing the taste for polemic characteristic of the entire group, said that such uninhibited self-expression was "true realism" (*xieshi zhuyi*) in contrast to the "trivialism" (*yongsu zhuyi*) promoted by Mao Dun and the Literary Association.[136] Christopher Keaveney argues that the form was both liberating and constricting: writers could use it to explore new ideas of the self and truths that would serve society, but the form itself constantly pulled them toward a more inward focus.[137]

These two naturalisms, the one inspired by the naturalism of Zola and the other by that of Japanese writers such as Katai and Shiga, came into conflict during the debates over realism and reform in the 1920s. Soon after the Creation Society was founded in 1921, Yu Dafu published an advance notice for its magazine that criticized the Literary Association for "monopolizing" the literary scene and depriving other writers of opportunities. Mao Dun for his part criticized Creation Society writers for subjectivism, despite his reservations about Zola's faith in objective description.[138] Comments like Cheng Fangwu's on Literary Association "trivialism" suggest that the Creation Society may have promoted its version of naturalism as a way of gaining position against the larger group. In 1924, as many writers in China returned to political engagement, members of the Creation Society embraced a Marxist program of literary struggle, denounced individualism in art, and in the process rejected their earlier egocentric fiction.[139] In the increasingly vituperative arguments, Cheng Fangwu and a new generation of Creation Society members denounced writers including Mao Dun, Lu Xun, and onetime members of their own group. (Yu Dafu had withdrawn bitterly in 1927.)[140] Although Chinese writers continued to engage with Japanese and European naturalism, one might say that during the debates on literature and politics, an issue that moved from theme to form during the transformation of naturalism in Japan—the relationship of the writer to society—moved fully outside the text as the debate on the revolutionary role of the writer.[141]

In Korea, a Japanese colony since 1910, naturalist fiction flourished in a moment of political despair between the suppression of the anti-Japanese protests in 1919 that came to be known as the March First Movement and the formation of the militant Korean Artist Proletarian Federation (KAPF) in 1925. Japanese naturalism, the criticism associated with it, and the fiction of the self descended from it, had a deeper impact here than in China because most knowledge of European realism and naturalism passed through Japan and Japanese.[142] Zola's work was introduced to criticism beginning in 1915, at a time when authors such as Yi Kwang-su who pushed for new forms of fiction in Korea were writing the didactic poetry and fiction known as enlightenment literature, whose main goal was nation-building. The critic Paek Tae-jin presented naturalism (*chayŏn chuŭi*) as a more materialist and "scientific" fiction that could address the dark sides of contemporary life.[143] The literary climate changed after the anticolonial demonstrations that erupted in Seoul in March 1919. Although the campaign for independence was suppressed brutally, the Japanese colonial government was forced to loosen restrictions on publishing as part of a new policy of "Cultural Rule." Naturalism emerged in the burst of literary activity that followed, which was permeated by a sense of hopelessness.[144] As in China, students in or recently returned from Japan played key roles.[145] Kim Tong-in, one of the writers most responsible for introducing naturalism to Korean fiction, formed the influential Creation (Ch'angjo) group there in 1919 and launched a coterie magazine to disseminate its work. The other, Yŏm Sang-sŏp, brought together a group of writers around the journal *Ruins* (*P'yehŏ*) in 1920 after returning to Seoul from Tokyo.

The first works of naturalism were part of the literary wave that followed the March First movement, beginning with Kim's "The Sorrow of the Weak" ("Yakhanja ŭi sŭlp'ŭm," 1919) and "A Man with a Weak Heart" ("Maŭm i yŏt'ŭn chayŏ," 1920) and Yŏm's "The Green Frog in the Specimen Room" ("P'yobonsil ŭi ch'ŏnggaeguri," 1921). These early stories by Kim and Yŏm were influenced by the fictions of the self that they encountered in Japan.[146] Their literary antagonists were the idealism and didacticism of enlightenment fiction.[147] Kim, inspired by the Japanese *White Birch* group, demanded literary autonomy. His essay "The World Created by Self" ("Chagi ŭi ch'angjohan segye," 1920) explained the approach: true art required "egoism." The writer should use it to create fictional worlds in which he is a "puppeteer" manipulating and scrutinizing his characters.[148] The art-for-art's sake attitude notwithstanding, stories by Kim such as "A Seaman's Chant" ("Paettaragi," 1921) and "Potatoes" ("Kamja," 1925) adopted a Zolean "experimental" method. He and others associated with naturalism in Korea such as Hyŏn Chin-gŏn pitilessly observed their characters' struggles against a fatal social environment. (The central figure in Hyŏn's 1924 story "Unsu choŭn nal" or "A Lucky Day" is a rickshaw puller who goes to work in order to care for his ailing wife, only to find her dead upon his return.)[149] Yŏm Sang-sŏp, in contrast, wrote in the mode of the I-novel. "The Green Frog in the Specimen Room," which recalls Japanese naturalism after *The Quilt*, is about a degenerate writer, recently returned from Japan, who is haunted by the image of a vivisected frog. Yŏm explained his position in his 1922 essay "Individuality and Art" ("Kaesŏng kwa yesul"): to depict life truly one must also depict "the sorrow of exposing reality." The phrase, which Yŏm borrowed from the title of Hasegawa Tenkei's 1908 essay, became a buzzword in the Korean literary scene. Naturalist fiction was Yŏm's chief example of "individualistic" art.[150] The double perspective of scrutinizing both social reality and the self observing it allowed Yŏm a position that was critical but nondidactic.[151] Whether in Yŏm's individualistic or Kim's puppeteer mode, naturalist fiction in Korea reversed the inward turn of naturalist writers in Japan to direct readers' attention to the brutality of colonial rule and craft metaphors of national awakening and resistance, a change similar to the one undergone by Japanese naturalism in China.[152]

While egocentric naturalism was nearly synonymous with the novel per se in Korea in the early 1920s, those who practiced it confronted restraints similar to those that Chinese authors such as Yu Dafu faced in their early work. The autonomous literature that was the aim of Japanese I-novelists such as Shiga was socially and politically impossible in colonial Korea. Not only did the colonial government restrict artistic freedom through censorship and other means, but there was also no practical way to make a living as a writer.[153] Yŏm dramatized the problem in his novella *On the Eve of the Uprising* (*Manse chŏn*, 1924), whose Japanophile narrator, traveling through colonial Korea before the March First protests, concludes that "the grumblings of a satiated belly" had little to do with "the facts," that is, Korea's colonization.[154] *On the Eve of the Uprising* signaled a turning point not just for Yŏm but also for the realism of the 1920s. Naturalism was displaced by more conventional third-person realism with an anticolonial and increasingly Marxist orientation, dominated by the "New Tendency Literature" (Sin kyŏnghyangp'a munhak) promoted by the KAPF, whose program was influenced by ideas about proletarian literature that were now in international circulation. Pak Yŏng-hŭi, the chairman of the KAPF and one of the theorists of New Tendency Literature, criticized naturalism for degrading its heroes and taxing the reader with tedious description. He called for "outcry over form, reality over description, power over beauty," phrases that recall Mao Dun's view in China that the naturalist description of social problems could leave readers with no sense of solutions.[155] In newspaper columns in the late 1920s and 1930s, Kim Tong-in bemoaned the encouragement that Zola's work gave Korean writers to indulge in "yawn-worthy descriptions."[156] Although as in China, writers in Korea continued to engage with individual works of Japanese naturalism, the turn away from naturalism as a style was decisive.[157] Yet however brief its career, writers and critics at the time acknowledged naturalism's impact on the formation of Korean literature. Im Hwa, the first critic to attempt a history of Korean literature, said in the 1920s that one could not understand literary history without it.[158]

The history of naturalist fiction in East Asia reveals additional patterns of circulation and contexts for the rise and disappearance of naturalist schools. Putting it together with the wax and wane of naturalisms in other parts of the world, we can see just how complex was the interaction of local, regional, and global contexts in this sprawling, variegated history. In East Asia, not only French but also German naturalist fiction, each usually read in English or Japanese translations, contributed essential elements to local naturalist schools. They were joined by Japanese works, which had their own impact in China and Korea. Naturalist writers in all three countries, as in Brazil, Argentina, and the United States, took positions against earlier forms of fiction in the context of a general push for the literary new. Their most cherished targets, however, were near-contemporaries who had led the break with the past such as Ozaki Kōyō in Japan and Yi Kwang-su in Korea. The travels of naturalism within Asia were facilitated by the prestige of a Japan that seemed to offer an alternative to European and North American modernities, political, economic, and literary. Yet the Chinese and Korean literary movements of the 1920s followed anticolonial demonstrations, and even the works most evidently descended from the variety of naturalism that appeared in Japan included Japan's formal and informal colonialism in their panoramas of social ills.

As naturalism's travels to and in East Asia differed from its travels elsewhere, so too did its aftermath. In Spanish America naturalism was supplanted around the turn of the century by *modernismo*, which occasionally adopted some of its techniques; in the United States it thrived for almost half a century longer. In Japan, the fiction of the self that began to appear during naturalism's heyday was practiced into the 1920s and remains influential today. In both China and Korea, naturalism was fairly soon succeeded by realisms that were more militant both in their politics and in their insistence on describing society, not the self. The realisms that formed in part through the denunciation of naturalism were anticolonial and often Marxist, and the decline of naturalism in East Asia thus coincided with the rise of what Michael Denning calls the "Novelists' International" of leftist fiction (a movement with its own conflicted relationship to naturalism, beginning with Zola's *Germinal*).[159] The history of naturalist fiction was one of multiple mediations—via a number of countries and languages—shaped by multiple poles of international power, with multiple, discrepant outcomes. While this investigation could continue in other parts of the world, the lesson should be clear: one must approach something like the transnational rise and fall of naturalist fiction as *history*—convoluted and unruly—not as a matter of "rules" and models.

Returning to Chevrel's literary historiography, it is obvious that naturalist fiction in various guises continued to thrive and change long after its fortunes fell in Europe. Lest one conclude that we can just add more waves to the map of diffusion, however, we should recall how dissimilar were the paths through which naturalism traveled the world, and how dissimilar its careers in distant parts. Naturalism's circuits were hardly synchronized: they had a common starting point in the 1860s, but their chronologies were vastly different, from the coevality of schools in Brazil and Argentina with Europe to the "late" and short-lived schools in China and Korea. The vitality of arguments about naturalism in fiction across some sixty years shows moreover that not only was there no Parisian "Mean Time" in literature, but also that naturalist writers were more concerned with how to describe and criticize the conditions around them than with what Parisian critics might have thought about what they were doing (if Parisian critics knew about them at all). And while undeniably there was a "naturalist moment" in the fiction of many parts of the planet, and thus in the literatures of the world—in the plural—this moment was coeval and even in rivalry with other literary moments, such as modernism and socialist realism, each with their own heterogeneous chronologies and geographies.

The chronological and geographical unevenness of naturalism's careers shows that its history was not global in the sense of reaching all parts of the planet. Nor was it a history of "globalization" in the sense that Mufti identifies in some arguments on world literature: barrier-free circulation in a space of absolute comparability. On the contrary, many naturalist writers responded to the domestic and international inequalities created by capitalism and the differing power of states, that is, to precisely the inequalities that the discourse of globalization erases. Tracing the history of a transnational phenomenon like naturalism does not mean falling for myths about globalization. It can instead be an opportunity to better understand the relationship between political economy and expressive forms. But if so, how do we contextualize and conceptualize a phenomenon that seems to upend so many explanations of things like it?

CONTEXTS

Naturalist fiction emerged around the world as a result of contexts both local and large in scale. What I am approaching as "local" contexts in this book were not necessarily limited in geographic reach, but rather were specific in their impact on naturalist fiction in different parts of the world. The history of slavery in the Americas and the transnational discourse on race that supported it are essential to understanding

Azevedo's *Mulatto*, for example, but they do not tell us much about the underdevelopment of the Japanese countryside that is the subtext of Katai's *Country Teacher*. I will address several such local contexts for the history of naturalist fiction in the following chapters of this book. (In this sense, I am practicing a kind of "serial contextualism" as proposed by David Armitage to extend intellectual history across longer expanses of time.)[160] A number of large-scale contexts, in contrast, shaped the history of naturalist fiction as a whole: the manifestos and sympathetic literary criticism whose history most closely parallels that of naturalism itself; fellow-traveling genres of thought with which naturalism had mutually supportive relationships; and the other varieties of realism that were naturalism's rivals in the transnational literary scene. Such contexts were *large* in scale in that they were manifest in many parts of the world, but they were not *global* in the sense either of spanning the planet or of providing a totalizing explanatory ground for the phenomenon of naturalism in literature. In the same spirit, "large" and "local" should not be understood as a subordinated pair, with the former more important than the latter. The point is that to understand a history like that of the naturalist novel one needs to be able to operate on several scales, fluidly: to move along a gamut of scales, as Jacques Revel puts it, acknowledging that different scales have their own cognitive value; or take the fractal approach that Wai-Chee Dimock advocates, in which every scale of analysis produces a different set of relevant detail.[161]

We have already seen that naturalist fiction was accompanied—and sometimes preceded—by critical discourse *about* naturalist methods, goals, and (im)moral worth. Any work of literature is surrounded by a context of discourse on literature. What distinguishes naturalism is the plethora of programmatic statements and the intensity of critical debate that turned it into an "ism" that writers could embrace or denounce, in either case using it as a means to position themselves in local literary fields. In this respect "naturalism" functioned less like "realism"—a looser and more inclusive term—than like the many -isms of the so-called modernist turn, futurism, vorticism, and so on, which writers invented or embraced as labels to consolidate relational positions toward other writers and tendencies.[162] The critical apparatus that supported the travels of naturalism and provided an arsenal in the local controversies it sparked surrounded the fiction in widening circles, from prefaces, through criticism and programmatic statements by naturalist writers, to pieces by like-minded critics. Perhaps the first example was the Goncourt brothers' preface for *Germinie Lacerteux*, which described it as a "clinical study of love," explaining that the novel must emulate "the studies and duties of science," thereby becoming a "history of contemporary mores."[163] Other examples of naturalist paratexts—material that frames and guides consumption of the work itself—are Cletto Arrighi's preface to *Nana in Milan* (*Nanà a Milano*, 1880), which was seen by many as an important step in the Italian reception of naturalism even if the novel to which it was attached was a knockoff of Zola's book; the Peruvian novelist Cabello's preface to *White Sun* (*Blanca Sol*, 1889); and the Japanese writer Tengai's preface to *Popular Song*, which declared that nature (*shizen*) is "not good, bad, beautiful, or ugly," but only said to be so by moralists.[164]

Efforts to create a legitimating discourse for naturalism continued in essays and manifestos written by writers who espoused it, such as the essays by Kim Tong-in and Yŏm Sang-sŏp in Korea discussed earlier. Pardo Bazán's collection of essays *The Vital Question* (*La Cuestión palpitante*, 1883) criticized the moralistic opposition to naturalism in Spain.[165] In Denmark, Bang staked out an independent position in Nordic literature's "modern breakthrough" by advocating naturalism in a dispute with the literary kingmaker Brandes in 1883.[166] Literary critics further elaborated the discourse on naturalism. The careers of a relative minority of critics, such as Hōgetsu and Tenkei in Japan, were closely tied to naturalism. At somewhat greater remove were critics such as Mao Dun in China and De Sanctis in Italy who evaluated naturalism critically if sympathetically. Finally, the essays and manifestos of Zola, particularly those published as *The Experimental Novel* in naturalism's blockbuster year of 1880, were widely cited and reprised in the discourse on naturalism. I will discuss their role in the naturalist field in the following section.[167]

Naturalism's self-generated critical apparatus alone cannot explain why an approach to the novel that incited so much opposition was nevertheless adopted in so many places. Naturalism had a number of "fellow travelers" on its circuits around the world, including slum reportage, sexology, and Social Darwinism. Like naturalist fiction, these genres of social knowledge combined empirical investigation with normative assertions concerning society and individual behavior. (In this sense they contributed to a naturalist "social imaginary" as defined by Charles Taylor.)[168] An example is a cluster of theories of morbid heredity that appeared in mid-nineteenth-century Europe, represented most famously by the Austrian physician Bénédict Auguste Morel's *Treatise on the Physical, Intellectual, and Moral Degeneracies of the Human*

Species (*Traité des dégénérescences physiques, intellectuelles et morales de l'espèce humaine*, 1857). Theories of degeneration such as Morel's, which typically assumed the inheritance of acquired characteristics, organized Zola's cycle on the Rougon-Macquart family, whose members are driven to the heights and depths of society by inherited pathologies.[169] Cesare Lombroso, an Italian founder of modern criminology, drew on them for the theory of atavistic criminality in his influential *Criminal Man* (*L'Uomo deliquente*, 1876).[170] Lombroso's ideas on criminal regression contributed to Zola's *The Human Beast* (*La Bête humaine*, 1890), about a train engineer who feels a chronic impulse to murder, and also were an inspiration for *Degeneration* (*Entartung*, 1892), a widely read book of social criticism by the Paris-based physician Max Nordau who argued that the work of "degenerate" artists such as Tolstoy, Richard Wagner, Walt Whitman, and Zola caused inheritable moral degeneracy in their fans.[171] In 1897 Frank Norris published "A Case for Lombroso," about an Anglo-Hispanic love affair turned wrong by racial degeneration, and on his clipping of the story added a subtitle: "A Subject for Max Nordau."[172] In the meantime, the theory of degeneration had inspired the new medical diagnosis of "neurasthenia"—nervous decay caused by the stress of modern life—which was popularized by the American neurologist George Beard in *A Practical Treatise on Nervous Exhaustion* (1880) and other books and articles. The transnational discourse on neurasthenia (which also contributed to Nordau's *Degeneration*) had a broad impact on naturalist fiction at the turn of the century, and as we will see in chapter 2, it played a central role in the Japanese novelist Shimazaki Tōson's criticism of the "civilizing" projects of the Meiji period in his novel *Spring* (*Haru*, 1908).[173]

The examples of naturalism's intersections with fellow travelers abound, and I will examine more of them in the following chapters. The travel of each of these genres supported the travel of others. (Zola cited Lombroso, but Lombroso also cited Zola.)[174] While the naturalist novel was consistently imbricated with related genres of social knowledge, however, the composition of these constellations varied. In South America, Positivism was an important ally; in Japan, discourses of public hygiene.[175] Although these forms of social investigation and regulation were moving around the world at the same time, moreover, the chronologies and paths of their travel were nonsynchronous and nonparallel with respect to each other and naturalist fiction. We can attribute naturalism's shifting affiliations to the varying histories of its fellow travelers, which rose and fell in credibility and arrived in different regions at different times, but also to differences in the dominant social imaginaries in specific parts of the world, which were the result of their respective intellectual and social histories.

Finally, during its peregrinations naturalist fiction frequently confronted other varieties of literary realism. We already have seen how naturalism built on, yet positioned itself against, existing realisms in the United States and Japan (James, Howells, and Twain in the one; Kōyō, his protégés, and other writers such as Natsume Sōseki in the other). Although Jacobsen's novella *Mogens* (1872) is usually seen as the first work of naturalism in the Nordic countries, the writers who identified most with Zola, such as Bang and Jaeger, were in the second generation of the problem-oriented literature that Brandes called the "modern breakthrough."[176] They were both indebted to and critical of Jonas Lie and others in the first generation of realists, and Brandes himself.[177] In Brazil, Machado's realism rivaled the work of naturalists such as Azevedo and Ribeiro; in Argentina, the realism of writers such as Lucio V. López (*La Gran Aldea* or *The Great Town*, 1884) was an alternative to the naturalism of Cambaceres and Argerich. In Japan, Kōyō read Zola but looked to Saikaku as his "native" source.[178]

Circulating around and through these confrontations was the work of several European realists with international impact: from France, Balzac, Stendhal, and Flaubert; from Russia, Dostoevsky, Tolstoy, and Turgenev.[179] If naturalism incited debate wherever it went, other realisms sometimes won the argument. In southeastern Europe naturalists such as Kumičić and Govekar made little headway against the examples of Russian writers such as Turgenev and Nikolai Gogol.[180] For writers in Finnish and Finland Swedish, the Norwegian realists Lie and Kielland were as important as the naturalist Arne Garborg. They also drew on examples from Russia—not only Tolstoy and Turgenev but also the critic Vissarion Belinsky's theory of realism.[181] In China, as we have seen, Mao Dun turned from Zola to Tolstoy when he began writing fiction, while the efflorescence of Japanese-influenced egocentric naturalism was foreclosed by socialist realism in both China and Korea. Christophe Charle argues that in Paris itself, a vogue for Russian fiction in the 1880s was motivated partly by French critics' desire to push Zola out of his dominant position.[182]

This is not to downplay the impact that naturalism had in many parts of the world, but rather to stress that naturalism's career unfolded within a broader "realist moment" of the late nineteenth and early twentieth centuries that encompassed these many varieties of literary realism and included areas where the impact of naturalism in its heyday was slight.[183] For many writers this moment began as a push against national romanticisms which had themselves been inspired, mutatis mutandis, by English, French, and German romantic and historical fiction. (Examples can be found in Finland, Serbia, and the United States, among many places, in addition to those from South America discussed earlier.)[184] Such was not always the case: as noted earlier, writers in East Asia became familiar with European romanticisms and realisms at essentially the same time, against the backdrop of long literary histories that included genres of socially descriptive fiction. Within this broad history of realism, naturalism differentiated itself from the realisms associated with individual authors—Jamesian, Tolstoyan—through the apparatus of manifestos and criticism that made it a program distinct from the work of Zola, if always shadowed by it. Naturalism's shifting relationships with fellow-traveling genres of social thought lent it further, quasi-scientific legitimacy against other realisms. Like its beginnings, the endings of this "moment" are imprecise: the antipathy of late nineteenth- and twentieth-century modernisms and the avant-gardes toward realism is famous, but they never fully dispensed with its techniques, while many realists, bourgeois or socialist, kept on writing regardless of the formal experimentation around them. While I think it is correct to speak of a realist moment, then, it would be difficult to write a history of it, at least right now. It is, however, precisely the programmatic quality of naturalism, including the tendency of naturalist writers to announce themselves, that makes tracing its geographically extensive history possible in a way that tracing the history of realism as a whole is not. Perhaps by tracing the history of naturalism we may find the methods and categories needed to construct other large-scale histories of expressive forms.

THE STRUCTURE OF THE TRANSNATIONAL FIELD

One can begin by theorizing the geography of the transnational naturalist field, and then turning to ways to periodize its history. The challenge is the heterogeneity of practices that writers considered to be naturalistic, even as many of the writers in question identified themselves as naturalists through prefaces, references to Zola, and so on. Although there have been many attempts to define naturalism, mostly concerned with the phenomenon in Europe, as I argued earlier the multiplicity of naturalisms requires one to set aside a priori definitions and instead proceed historically and inductively. By "induction" I simply mean reasoning from parts to wholes or from particulars to generals, that is, making general statements based on inferences from observed examples. Inductively, we can describe the size and shape of the naturalist field at a particular time in terms of the paths of circulation of texts and the constellation of points of local production. Given the tendency of naturalist writers to announce their affiliation, the most proximate sign of the latter is the citation of other naturalist writers—especially but not only Zola—through paratexts, character names, allusions to specific scenes, and the many other means already observed.[185] So defined, the transnational naturalist field would encompass both the qualities that all of the instances share and the range of topical, thematic, and formal possibilities that they collectively illustrate.

From this perspective, the scale of the naturalist field was large but never "global," if global implies planetary reach and a kind of uniformity. Its shape was irregular: in the 1880s it extended to Serbia but not Greece, and to several countries in South America, but none in North America. Some parts were "thick" and some "thin"—many writers in Germany, few in England. The character of the web of citations also varied: it was more multidirectional in the densely traveled circuits of Europe, increasingly unidirectional the farther one was from them.[186] Nonetheless, local manifestations of naturalism clearly emerged through a global dynamic. To be clear: the field was defined by the activities of all participating in it, but this does not mean it was level. Differing degrees of reciprocity in the work of citation, for example, show that relationships in the field could be profoundly asymmetrical. The prominence of writers such as Zola was only increased by the number of acts of homage to them.[187] Beyond their immediate regions, moreover, contact between naturalist writers was rare. (Azevedo gave up his career as a novelist, entered Brazil's diplomatic service, and spent some two years in Yokohama as a vice-consul at the time when Katai and other Japanese Zolaists were starting their careers in Tokyo. Even as close as he was, however, there is no evidence that he met them or any other Japanese writers.)[188] While we should recognize that naturalist writers who did not know others' work directly were connected through the mediation of the field as a whole, the general absence of "periphery-to-periphery" connections distinguished the transnational naturalist field from the modernist field, where such connections were more frequent if far from the rule, and from the intentional cultivation of writerly relations that were unmediated by Europe during the era of decolonization.[189]

Yet the geographical extension of the field largely was the work of the citers, not those who were cited. Certainly the citers produced many epigonistic imitations and knockoffs. The following chapters of this book, however, trace revisions of literary form that were inventive responses to new conditions. In writing on Azevedo and the Brazilian literary historian Antônio Cândido, Roberto Schwarz raises the possibility that in some cases the seeming "copy"—Azevedo's *The Slum*, in Schwarz's example—may have been superior to the original—Zola's *L'Assommoir*. In such works one finds both textual filiation and fidelity to a different social reality. The challenge of the latter forces revision—not rejection—of the former.[190] Put another way, the recognition (probably unwelcome) that a true copy is impossible could have unexpectedly positive results. Schwarz warns against concluding that peripheral writers who thus surpassed their models achieved reputations equal to those of their metropolitan counterparts.[191] On the contrary, one should see that such writers' interventions in topic, theme, and form by naturalist writers were propelled precisely by inequalities in economic, political, and cultural relations. The extension of the field could generate new possibilities, but the possibilities themselves reflected the unevenness of both the naturalist field and the world political economy.

The role of Zola in the structure of the naturalist field was great, but not in the most expectable ways. The circulation of Zola's works, especially *L'Assommoir*, *Nana*, *Germinal*, and *The Experimental Novel*, provided literary models and a method to espouse. The many departures from models and method show, however, that Zola's role in the field was not simply prescriptive. "Zola"—the author, works, and program rolled into one—also had a legitimating function. He might be called an "initiator of discourse" in Michel Foucault's sense, that is, a figure to whom reference was obligatory.[192] The concept is useful when talking about center-periphery cultural relations because it distinguishes the legitimating function of such figures from their chronologically prior position. There was much to be gained in local literary battles through cosmopolitan references to Zola and naturalism. Stefan Nygård and Johan Strang observe that playing the international against the local—often cast as the "up-to-date" against the "backward"—is a common way of taking a position in peripheral cultural fields.[193] The history of naturalism is rife with examples of this strategy: Bang in Denmark,

Katai in Japan, Norris in the United States, and Kumičič in Croatia all invoked Zola against the literary establishment. (The inverse, no less common, was to denounce naturalism as a foreign import.)

Zola's relentless promotion of naturalism aside, why would he have such a legitimating role in the naturalist field? As a writer working in a language with many readers outside his own country, Zola could achieve a prominence that naturalist writers in "small" languages could not.[194] Naturalism as a transnational phenomenon probably would not have been possible if it had not first emerged in a language with wide currency such as French. As we have seen, its travels were aided by translation into another such language, English. French and British imperialism ultimately were behind the two languages' reach, and thus were a condition for the recognition that naturalism gained outside France. But more specifically, about Zola: Bourdieu observes that in the circulation of ideas, sometimes it is not what an author *says* but what he or she can be *made to say* that counts. Writers who are particularly "elastic"—who can be made to say many different things—circulate well.[195] Elastic, stretchy: a paradoxical quality of Zola's work is that his fiction ranged far beyond—and often contradicted—his statements of method. Naturalism as a program indeed proved rather flexible (hence the variety of practices that writers considered to be naturalistic). This is not to say that Zola's position in the field was neutral. While invoking Zola did not amount to imitation—or as Casanova would put it, the reproduction of domination—the role of "Zola" in structuring the naturalist field reflected the cultural, political, and economic asymmetries of the world in which the field existed.

Finally, if the structure of the naturalist field followed from the circulation of key texts, the productive necessity of revision, and the legitimating function of Zola, it was also defined by opposition to other realisms. "Naturalism" was a position in a broader field composed of the variety of realisms in local practice and international circulation. Position-taking in Bourdieu's sense between naturalism and other realisms occurred mainly at the local level, in what conventionally are considered national literary fields. The consequences of such battles were both local and transnational, however, beginning with naturalism's achievement of a dominant position in France around 1880, which was requisite for the entire far-flung phenomenon. The evolution of naturalist fiction in Argentina from deplored to accepted practice lent legitimacy to naturalist writers elsewhere in Spanish America, while the ascension of an egocentric naturalism in Japan was a bridge for naturalism's travels in East Asia. Naturalist writers thus worked in a double frame. Their participation in the transnational field was premised on their activities in their local one, but the existence of the former also gave them leverage in the latter.[196] Understanding the history of naturalist fiction requires the kind of multi-scalar and cross-scalar analysis that Harsha Ram has advocated for the study of global modernisms.[197]

How should one periodize a literary history like this one, which spans more than half a century and several oceans? To recall the challenges: naturalist writers and schools appeared in some places far from France before they appeared in some places nearer. Naturalism was pronounced dead at its place of origin when writers elsewhere were still adapting and revising its techniques—and they continued to do so for decades. Some later developments were impossible to predict from earlier ones—and some would have been hard to reconcile with each other. (If they had met in Japan, would Azevedo have recognized Katai as a naturalist, and vice versa?) The boundaries between naturalism and other ways of writing fiction, moreover, were indistinct, not only because beginnings and endings are hard to identify, as with any literary trend, but also because some writers freely mixed techniques that literary historians usually see as incompatible.

The influential attempts by Casanova and Moretti to theorize literary production on a supranational ("world") scale cannot account for the peculiarities of this history because they rely on teleologies derived from European literature. Moretti's narrative of the formal evolution of the novel compares later, extra-European manifestations to earlier, European ones and concludes that all non-European novels are formally "cracked" compromises. While Moretti means to explain the incorporation of local techniques into a foreign form, the fact remains that his theory explains the dissemination of the European novel as deviations from a European norm. Nonetheless, Moretti regards the "rise of the novel" as a developmental necessity: it must happen everywhere, even though in most places it doesn't turn out right.[198] Casanova's proposition of "world literary space" relies, in a sense, on the opposite comparative conclusion. Manifestations far from Europe of literary trends that originated on the continent are over-eager, "anachronistic" imitations of fashions that the center of the world is done with. Here backwardness is a function of distance, as compromise is for Moretti. For all of Casanova's attempts to map so-called world literary space in terms of relationality and symbolic domination, as I have said earlier, the landscape she creates simply spatializes an allegedly inexorable movement from romanticism through realism to modernism. There are good ethical reasons to object to attachments like Moretti's and Casanova's to "Eurochronologies" (as Arjun Appadurai named them), on the grounds that they deny creative agency to writers outside a handful of European countries.[199] Just as important, however, is the simple fact that arguments which rely on them fail empirically.

Rather than relying on evolutionary teleologies, we should approach the history of a phenomenon like literary naturalism as the development as a whole of the kind of synchronically structured literary field that I described earlier. If we imagine such a field comprising all the instances of naturalism in practice at a given moment, in relational position toward each other, then varieties of naturalism that had appeared chronologically earlier and later would exist in the same synchronic "present" of the field as a whole as long as they were in use. The history of the field would be the entry, change in relative position, and disappearance of participants, or put another way, the history of the constellations of topic, theme, and form that appeared and disappeared as writers adopted, adapted, and abandoned naturalistic ways of writing fiction. Critically, the field's geographic extension, which was the major cause of successive revisions, would be part of the history of the structure of the field and thus of the history of form in naturalist fiction. The vital difference of the approach I am suggesting from arguments about "diffusion"—of the European novel, for example—is precisely the emphasis on the emergence and transformation of a relational field in which each new intervention changes the field as a whole. The history that would result would not be an enumeration of individual innovations (although these would be an important part of it), but rather a properly transnational and multi-scale account of the heterogeneous development of literary form.

We could call the periodization of such a history a "geochronology," which in naturalist fiction shows four phases. First, the appearance of initial examples such as *Germinie Lacerteux* and *Thérèse Raquin* in the 1860s, as one of several contemporaneous developments in European realism, and the subsequent appearance of a group of affiliated writers in France—the Médan group of Paul Alexis, Henry Céard, Léon Hennique, Joris-Karl Huysmans, and Guy de Maupassant. Second, the emergence of "Zola" as a legitimator starting in the late 1870s—through the dissemination of his work outside France and announcements of affiliation by writers elsewhere—and the beginning of the geographical expansion of the field. Third, the multiplication of practices that writers identified as "naturalist" from the 1880s onward. The geographic extension of the field resulted in heterogeneity, not uniformity. Some writers and schools began to exit. Most notably, by the mid-1880s Paris no longer was a source of new writers, and geographically speaking was a "hole" in the field. Fourth, a thinning out and the appearance of more and larger holes as fewer writers practiced the naturalisms that had emerged in their parts of the world. By the 1920s, naturalism no longer was a *transnational* field, even though some writers continued working in this mode until mid-century. In light of naturalism's lasting but varied impact on local fields, we could call this the start of a period of naturalist afterlives.

There are some aspects of a geochronology like this that literary historians will have to get used to. The history of the field was inseparable from changes in its size and shape. This history was not global, but neither was it the sum of national histories; rather, it was a shifting transnational topography. In addition, literary tendencies conventionally thought of as "eras" sometimes were coeval. Writers in some parts of the world were working with techniques considered "modernist" in current critical parlance while others, in other parts, were working with techniques considered naturalist. None of the techniques were more advanced or backward. Moreover, some writers mixed them and in the process generated new formal possibilities. What appear to be nonsequential juxtapositions are a frequent result of the circulation of literary forms, to the point that "hybridization" may be more common than not. (If so, instead of marveling over hybridity one should ask what conditions led to specific combinations, and what writers accomplished thereby.) Finally, an approach to large-scale literary history that gives up the teleologies submerged in the present categories of literary study would also give up paradigms of original or originator and copy or copier to imagine the history of literary form instead in terms of successive iterations of formal possibilities.

I will return to questions of method throughout this book. Before doing so, however, it is essential to dive into examples of the revision of naturalist form from some of its first iterations through later, "peripheral" interventions. My Auerbachian points of departure for this exploration are the degenerate body, the self-liberated woman, and the bounded milieu, three important "figures" in which naturalist topics, themes, and form intersected.

CHAPTER 2

The Degenerate Body

If naturalist fiction aspired to be the most mimetic of nineteenth-century realisms—as Émile Zola's claims to scientific objectivity attest—the body was among the most privileged sites in its system of mimesis. Examples of the topical and thematic importance of bodies in naturalist fiction abound: the body of an ill-fated youth in Alphonse Daudet's *Jack* (1876), of the sexually curious Lenita in Júlio Ribeiro's *The Flesh* (*A Carne*, 1888), of the celebrated prostitute Yukie in Kosugi Tengai's *Popular Song* (*Hayari uta*, 1902), of the superhuman captain Wolf Larsen in Jack London's *The Sea-Wolf* (1904), among many others. The body—usually ailing or otherwise pathological—also played a critical role in naturalism's techniques of description, from the representation of individual characters to neighborhoods and societies. One scholar of Zola argues that his essential impulse was to somaticize his fictional worlds.[1] How naturalism enlisted bodies in the representation of large and abstract social forces—the acts of a state, the production of value in a capitalist economy—are the points of departure in this chapter for considering how particular techniques in naturalist fiction aided the emergence of naturalist schools in distant parts of the world. Figurative treatment of the degenerate body made it into a motif that could be detached from early texts and circulate independently of them.

Naturalism's gravitation toward the body as a keystone of mimesis is evident from the earliest examples in France, such as Edmond and Jules de Goncourt's *Germinie Lacerteux* (1864) and Zola's *Thérèse Raquin*

(1867). Zola's ideas about the role of the body in society and his work came together in *The Fortune of the Rougons* (*La Fortune des Rougon*, 1871) after extensive reading in medicine and new studies of heredity. *The Fortune of the Rougons* was the foundation for a "natural and social history" of the Second Empire, to be organized by the physiologically propelled behavior of successive generations in an intertwined family, and it might be expected to have become the model for naturalism's body-based analysis of human social relations. In fact, a novel about one member of the family, *L'Assommoir* (1877), was most responsible for spreading this technique of mimesis around Europe and across oceans through skill and scandal. The novel combined medical discourse on physiology and behavior with figurative language concerning specific parts of the body in order to describe individual mentalities and the social environment. The "body figures" of *L'Assommoir* (as I will call them) amalgamated conceptual and stylistic elements to form metonymies and synecdoches referring to each other as much as to the fictional world, even while—according to Zola at least—naturalism meant to describe individuals and society with pure objectivity. As naturalism traveled, body figures were put to new uses. In two later examples I will examine, Frank Norris used the technique to explore primitivism in American capitalism in *McTeague* (1899), while Shimazaki Tōson used it to anatomize the social transformations of Japan's Meiji period in *Spring* (*Haru*, 1908).

The circulation of naturalist techniques for representing the body was an important aspect of the naturalist field. New formal and thematic possibilities appeared as writers adopted and adapted them. Zola's body figures often reveal heredity and milieu combining ineluctably to determine a character's behavior. In *McTeague* and *Spring*, however, such a determinist circle breaks up to allow a more pointed—because less fatalistic—critique of the here and now. The physiological determinism of body figures remains, ultimately becoming part of naturalist form. Perhaps through the act of bringing naturalist methods to bear on new social conditions, however, contingency—history—entered naturalist representation and with it the possibility, often remote in Zola's work, that societies may change. Concurrently with this shift one can begin to find a reflection on method and form in "peripheral" naturalist texts.

THE GENEALOGY OF THE NATURALIST BODY

A genealogy of the naturalist body might begin with Honoré de Balzac, whose *Human Comedy* (*La Comédie Humaine*) preoccupied Zola as he planned the Rougon-Macquart series. The character portraits for which Balzac became known establish a figurative relation between body, character, and milieu that later was one of the foundations of naturalist mimesis. An example is the portrait of Madame Vauquer, owner of the pension in *Old Goriot* (*Le Père Goriot*, 1835) where Goriot and a young student from the provinces, Eugène de Rastignac, reside. From the "wizened, pudgy face, from the middle of which protruded a parrot's beak of a nose" to the "skirt made of an old robe, whose wadding poked out through rents in the worn cloth," Balzac's description of Madame Vauquer's outward appearance presents a string of figures for her dolorous yet vainly hopeful personality. In the synecdoche of the first phrase, a part—the face—represents the whole; in the metonymy of the second, something contiguous—the skirt—represents the woman who wears it. By synecdoche again, Madame Vauquer explains the world of the pension: her appearance "harmonizes" with her building's fetid rooms, to the point that "her whole person explained the boarding house, as the boarding house supposed her presence." Finally, through a comment that she resembles "all *women who have had misfortunes*," she stands in for a social type. (Balzac's italics indicate the common wisdom that legitimates the typology.) The figurative qualities of the portrait thus confirm the typicality of the setting where Eugène encounters Goriot, and by extension of their seemingly coincidental meeting.[2]

In his semiotic analysis of description in the classic European novel, Philippe Hamon observes the privileged place of the character portrait in the readerly—realistic—text. The portrait provides a focus for description of a character, which may otherwise be diffuse to the point of incoherence, and a location for the character's meaning. Portraits are essentially digressions via metonymy and synecdoche in the place of direct explanation. The mass of details that such figures summon are connected anaphorically, that is, they refer not only to the character but also to each other. As a consequence, a realist like Balzac may describe character and milieu reciprocally, to the point that they are redundant.[3] The reciprocal relationship reflects assumptions about the connection of individual behavior with social circumstances that naturalist writers such as Zola expressed more overtly when they took an interest in the emerging social sciences. More critically for naturalist mimesis, the reciprocity established a continuum of description in which a physical detail and the rhetorical figure it supported could be vehicles for comment on both individual and society.

In Balzacian realism and naturalism alike the kind of body-centered figurative language found in the portrait of Madame Vauquer—its "body figures"—served both descriptive and narrative purposes. The longer and less conclusive portrait of Balzac's title character opens a question that the novel answers: "Who is Goriot?" With a well-kept figure and apparently well off when he moved into the boarding house, Goriot's "fleshy calf" and "long straight nose" conveyed moral qualities, confirmed by the gentleman's "round and naively simple face," of which Madame Vauquer approved. She entertained thoughts of a new marriage, excursions to the theater, "the whole Eldorado of little Parisian households" (*Père Goriot*, 43). Goriot's appearance began to decline, however, at the same time he moved to progressively smaller quarters in the house. By the time the story proper begins, his appearance, "which secret woes had rendered imperceptibly sadder day by day," was the most unhappy of all the diners at the communal table. To his fellow boarders his dirty, olive gray hair, sunken chest, and ravaged eyes all were proof of moral turpitude. "The problem that his physical and moral situation presented," however, was still unsolved (*Père Goriot*, 53, 54). Although the novel is more Eugène's story than Goriot's, the uncertainty provides the impetus for the narrative. Eugène's social education gives him the means to learn who Goriot is, individually and typically, thereby resolving the problems introduced by the portrait.

Physical details are the key to the portrait of Goriot, but unlike that of Madame Vauquer their figurative referents—the qualities of personality they are meant to reveal—are unstable. Hamon argues that the length of a portrait places a character in a hierarchy, with secondary characters getting the sparer treatment.[4] Note also a qualitative difference: the portrait of a secondary character may render it redundant with its milieu, but the portraits of primary characters are typically inconclusive. As we will see in the case of Gervaise, the protagonist of *L'Assommoir*, the more extensive chain of anaphoric connections that contribute to body figures for primary characters leaves each open to a multiplicity of meanings, and therefore able to explain social forces far greater than the characters themselves. Balzac's portraits offered a double lesson for the naturalist novel: description of the body not only could propel narrative, but also provide the foundation for synthetic *social* portraits.

In a memo entitled "Differences between Balzac and Me" ("Différences entre Balzac et moi," composed in late 1868 or early 1869), Zola tried to dispel an evident anxiety of influence by distinguishing the approach of *The Human Comedy*, which he viewed as analogical, from the one he would pursue in the Rougon-Macquart series, which was to be physiological. Balzac's history of mores was inspired by the observation that just as there are lions, dogs, and wolves in the animal kingdom, there are artists, administrators, lawyers, and so on in society. Balzac imagined his novels as a zoology of humanity, Zola observes. The "mirror of society" that Balzac created, however, was riddled with normative political and religious judgments. In contrast to the Catholic and royalist sympathies that underlay Balzac's analogical zoology, Zola imagined basing his novels on laws of heredity and behavior, using the method of a "pure physiologist" that would be "less social than scientific."[5] Two responses to Balzac can be found in the memo's musings on method. On the one hand, in order to avoid Balzac's distortion of the social mirror, Zola would try to remove the narrator from the description of individuals and society. On the other hand, he would ground the figurative language of Balzacian description in physiological science. Zola found the means he needed in a craze for "anatomical" fiction exemplified by the Goncourt brothers.

The rhetoric of the laboratory—anatomy, dissection, analysis—was ubiquitous in Parisian literary circles in the 1850s and 1860s. One reason was the growing prestige of medicine. Against the mystic capaciousness of romanticism and the self-congratulatory discretion of the polite realism of the day, medicine was an alibi for precision and audacity.[6] Another was the liberty that writers and critics felt, at a time when intellectual fields were divided differently than they are now, to exploit the metaphorical possibilities of medical language. Gustave Flaubert said that *Madame Bovary* (1857) was "above all a work of criticism, or rather of anatomy."[7] The critic Charles-Augustin Sainte-Beuve said upon reading that novel: "Anatomists and physiologists, I find you everywhere," noting the science and "spirit of observation" of the new generation of writers.[8] The critic Hippolyte Taine praised Balzac's "moral anatomy," while a protégé, Émile Deschanel, wrote an entire book on the *Physiology of Writers and Artists* (*Physiologie des écrivains et des artistes*, 1864).[9] In their preface to *Germinie Lacerteux*, one of naturalism's founding texts, the Goncourt brothers described their novel as "a clinical study of love" (*Germinie Lacerteux*, 23). Indeed, in its early stages the naturalist novel took shape through its creation of a point of view analogous to anatomical examination. The dissection of characters' behavior and mental states, often relying heavily on the vocabulary of neurology, went hand in glove with a narrative observer who was meant to be clinically impartial.

Germinie Lacerteux is the story of a Parisian maid who, propelled by a good-willed desire to help others and the need for sexual satisfaction, slides into debt, alcoholism, and debauchery. She dies of tuberculosis contracted after a night spent in the rain spying on a former lover. At the end of the novel the spinster who employed her, Mademoiselle de Varandeuil, is astonished to learn of her maid's double life as faithful servant and habituée of the city's outer boulevards. (Germinie was modeled on the Goncourts' own maid, whose death led to similar revelations; Mademoiselle de Varandeuil's surprise was the Goncourts' own.) Germinie is created almost exclusively through description of her bodily features, appearance, and actions. An early passage catalogs the "ugly" Germinie from hair to hips, noting a protruding forehead, deep eye sockets, a distance "too great" between upturned nose and large mouth, a back whose lymphatic whiteness seems both angelic and unhealthy, dangling arms, delicate wrists, hands unaffected by work, and an impossibly narrow waist that she lets move with lazy grace, "adorable like all that, in women, has the monstrosity of smallness." Despite her ugliness, Germinie's gestures, gait, and least movements radiate a "sensual temptation." A low-cut dress exposing her shoulders, upper chest, and the top of that pale back compounds the air of "acrid and mysterious seduction" conveyed by her body and movements. Although emotion, pleasure, and passion are said to pass across Germinie's gray eyes in flashes of light, such descriptions' stress on the body gives the impression that these too are physical phenomena (*Germinie Lacerteux*, 68–70).

While Mademoiselle de Varandeuil tries to fathom her maid without success, what other novels might describe as Germinie's "inner" life is visible in conditions of her body and outward behavior. When Germinie falls in love with a shopkeeper's son, the narrator notes the "singular physiological phenomenon" that results: a "marvelous animation" overtakes her, replacing the "miserable nervous energy" that sustained her before with a "healthy activity" and a "burning, restless, overflowing exuberance." With her new "bodily good humor," Germinie incessantly walks, runs, scrubs, cleans, and shakes; her fingers move on their own and her feet dance when she is seated. Later, Germinie reacts to news of the death of her daughter with the young man with a violent, minutely detailed convulsion (*Germinie Lacerteux*, 84–85, 123–24). Even what Germinie hides from Mademoiselle de Varandeuil—sexual adventures, growing debt—go unconnected to inward sentiments such as remorse or guilt. Hiding them too is an action: Germinie lets "nothing come to her lips . . . nothing be seen in her face, nothing appear in her manner";

on her deathbed she "gathers into herself all exterior signs of her ideas" (*Germinie Lacerteux*, 155, 234). In narrative discourse, then, there is no real difference between Germinie's appearance and behavior, what she keeps from Mademoiselle de Varandeuil and the keeping of it. Germinie is only what she does, and therefore only what can be seen.

Considering the role that the rhetoric of anatomy plays in *Germinie Lacerteux*, one might call its narrative standpoint an "anatomical point of view." Germinie is broken into parts of the body, details of clothing, and movements that amount to symptoms of her corporeal state, which are reassembled without comment into the novel's description of her behavior. Unlike Balzac's portraits, where physical features denote unseen qualities, the isolated parts of Germinie do not refer to anything that is not already visible to the people around her. The narrative's diagnostic expertise is legitimated by its ubiquitous medical language, in particular the language of neurology. Germinie is subject to "nervous disorders" that upset the equilibrium of human joy and sorrow, allowing each to reach extremes. Ominously, she casts "the shadow of a woman of the Salpêtrière"—a leading center of neurological research and a lockup for prostitutes (*Germinie Lacerteux*, 142, 146). The replacement of moral judgment by quasi-medical observation is signaled ironically near the end, when a doctor pronounces Germinie "a lost woman" (*une femme perdue*), meaning only, however, that she will soon die (*Germinie Lacerteux*, 223–24). The resolute restriction to the "observable" was a naturalist conceit that outlasted the anatomical point of view: literary invention presented as scientific observation.

Germinie's dismemberment is a technique that the Goncourts extended to the observation (i.e., creation) of her social world. Patrick O'Donovan shows that in this novel as in others by the Goncourts, interaction in public spaces is frequently described as an entanglement of body parts. Hands, waists, and so on serve as synecdoches for the people mingling them, but simultaneously as elements of a metonymy: their contact figures the sexualized social practices to which Germinie becomes habituated and then abandons herself. Observation of the body becomes a variety of ethnography.[10] Dissection of Germinie indeed becomes a rationale for narrative excursions to *café-concerts*, the outer gates of Paris, and other places where Germinie acts out her hidden life in plain sight. As in their description of Germinie's mental life, however, the Goncourts maintain a characteristic distance from her milieu, which likewise is described through visible behavior. Social description remains grounded in the body.

Zola shared the Goncourts' enthusiasm for narrative anatomy and the new nerve science in *Thérèse Raquin*, an early novel in which the ideas and narrative forms behind the Rougon-Macquart novels appeared. (Zola's laudatory review of *Germinie Lacerteux* recounted the "scientific curiosity" of examining an "unknown creature.")[11] In his preface to the novel's second edition, responding to those who denounced it as "putrid literature," he explained: "I simply carried out on two living bodies the analytical work that surgeons carry out on cadavers." Thérèse and her lover Laurent are "human beasts" (*brutes humaines*) dominated by their nerves and blood, who experience "cerebral derangements" after the "nervous crisis" that follows their murder of Thérèse's husband. "What I was obliged to call their remorse," Zola explained, "consists of a simple organic disorder, the rebellion of a nervous system stretched to the breaking point."[12] As these remarks suggest, the physical nerve became the privileged body part in *Thérèse Raquin*'s figurative system.

The novel's story is compelling and grisly: Thérèse, a strong-willed woman living a somnolent life with her cousin and husband Camille and his mother, comes alive when Camille brings home his friend Laurent. They become lovers. Constrained by Camille's presence, they drown him and bide their time until they can marry. Carnally reunited after some fifteen months, they discover that they cannot bear each other's company. After pursuing their separate pleasures, each resolves to murder the other. When the moment arrives they discover the mutual plots and commit double suicide. Sequences relating each stage of their relationship are punctuated with chapters that amount to medical exams of the lovers' physiological and mental states, with special attention to the nerves. Even before their reunion they begin to suffer simultaneous "nervous derangements," from an obsession with a scar on Laurent's shoulder from his struggle with Camille to hallucinations of the dead man himself. The lovers' decay is a "fact of psychology and physiology" often seen in people thrown together by "great nervous shocks" (*Thérèse Raquin*, 154). Although they are able to marry without suspicion, the physiological equilibrium of their relationship is gone. Thérèse's "overexcited nerves" push Laurent into a state of "nervous hypersensitivity." Any remorse that Laurent feels is "purely physical," however, and Thérèse's daily scenes of repentance before Camille's mother—now paralyzed and mute from a stroke, in another neurological touch—likewise are manifestations of her nervous decline (*Thérèse Raquin*, 182, 183).

Synecdoches of the nerve have a privileged explanatory role in *Thérèse Raquin*. The state of characters' nerves explains their mentalities, behavior, and relations with others. But the nerve is also the indispensable part of a single mind-body, and figuratively refers to the entire being. It moreover is the channel for intertextual references meant to strengthen the novel's claim to scientific precision. Each bit of neurological vocabulary—"cerebral derangement," "nervous hypersensitivity"—adds to the explanatory power of the nerve as figure.[13] Note a significant departure from the methods of *Germinie Lacerteux*: while the Goncourt brothers' novel evokes Germinie's mental state through the visible signs of a nervous disorder, *Thérèse Raquin* comments extensively on a part of the body that is not observable from the outside. The premise of medical examination remains, but an all-seeing diagnostic eye replaces the Goncourts' insistence on the outwardly visible. This is just one sign of an evident circularity of description and explanation (the novel creating the characters that it proposes to explain) which Zola perhaps acknowledged through a *mise en abyme*: Laurent makes daily trips to the morgue where he scrutinizes bodies until he finds Camille's, which he and Thérèse left in the Seine.[14] As a material cause for mentalities and behavior, however, the nerve provided a rationale for approaching psychological description as a kind of anatomy. In Laurent's case in particular, Zola began to move fluidly between descriptions of behavior, indirect reporting of thought, and representation of it via free indirect style.[15] The nerve lay between behavior and the activity of thinking in a single spectrum of mimesis.

NERVES AND CRACKS

Between *Thérèse Raquin* and *The Fortune of the Rougons* the nerve underwent a critical transformation: it gained a place in the life of society, no longer of individuals alone. Comments by Taine on *Thérèse Raquin* were a proximate cause. In a letter to Zola, Taine said the novel's central characters were so ghastly that they monopolized the reader's attention. Without a counterweight from other characters, or contradictory qualities in Thérèse and Laurent themselves, the novel became a phantasmagoria. Zola needed to enlarge his scope and balance his effects, because "a book must always be, more or less, a portrait of the whole, a mirror of the entire society."[16] The issue for Taine was typicality: a synthetic social portrait cannot be based on characters outside the norm. In Taine's famous formula, every person's actions come from the interaction of "lineage" (Fr. *race*), "milieu," and "moment": hereditary and innate dispositions, the natural and social environment, and the cumulative weight of history.[17] Applied in reverse, the formula says that only typical characters can convey how these forces combine in society, which is the novelist's proper object of study.

Taine's theory is usually seen as Zola's basic model for the reproduction and variation of characteristics across generations of the Rougon-Macquart family. Zola struggled with Taine's prescriptions, however. In his plans for the series Zola wrote of two character types, the Emma (after Flaubert's heroine) and the Germinie. The one acquires a generality while the other becomes exceptional. He conceded that Thérèse and the heroine of *Madeleine Férat* (1868) were the latter, with the self-rebuke: "I may no longer set forth [*sortir*] from the exception." The destination was another matter. Instead of creating generalizeable, Flaubertian characters as Taine urged, he would create exceptional characters in the manner of Stendhal, whose characters were typical yet not restricted to the banal everyday. (Julien Sorel of *Le Rouge et le noir* or *The Red and the Black*, 1830, was Zola's prime example.) Zola's method would be to start with the general, avoid "monstrosities too great," but use "particular cases of brain and flesh" to create exceptional beings that epitomize an era.[18] Stendhal provided a precedent for social analysis founded on social exception and, happily, for the dramatic plots that exceptional characters allow. The terms of anatomical narrative, however, required something more: a scientific basis for the exceptional character that would let him or her *embody*, not just epitomize, the state of society at a given moment.

Zola found his solution in a complex of works concerned with physiology, behavior, and society that were part of the intellectual context for the emergence and circulation of naturalism discussed in the previous chapter. He favored those works that gave special explanatory power to the nerve, such as Charles Letourneau's *Physiology of Emotion* (*Physiologie des passions*, 1868), which called the nervous system "the theater and organ of psychological life" and claimed that scientists would show it to be the source of all that metaphysicians had attributed to the soul.[19] Behind the scientific confidence were anxious arguments since mid-century about individual and social "degeneration," advanced by weighty tomes such as Bénédict Morel's *Treatise on the Physical, Intellectual, and Moral Degeneracies of the Human Species* (*Traité des dégénérescences physiques, intellectuelles et morales de l'espèce humaine*, 1857). The arguments on degeneration collapsed environmental and hereditary causes of undesirable behavior into synthetic explanations that were ostensibly medical, not moral.[20] By their Lamarckian logic, pathological behavior passed to future generations in the form of hereditary predispositions that would spread inexorably through society. Because theories of degeneration thus allowed an analyst to move back and forth between individual and social pathology, they evolved into all-encompassing explanations of social problems during the time that Zola planned and wrote the Rougon-Macquart novels.[21] Such attempts to bring the causes of social problems to light, however, tended to produce an ever greater sense of crisis. Analysts responded by returning to the degenerate body as the locus, if not the source, of the disorder.[22]

One contribution to the medical-moral alarmism, Prosper Lucas's *Philosophical and Physiological Treatise on Natural Heredity* (*Traité philosophique et physiologique de l'hérédité naturelle*, 1847–50), arguably had greater impact than Taine's work on Zola's views of the relationship between the individual and the social structure.[23] Critical opinion minimizes the importance of Lucas's ideas for Zola, perhaps because they differ so greatly from the post-Mendel science of heredity (according to Lucas, a woman's first lover left a hereditary imprint on all of her children). In Henri Mitterand's view, Lucas's *Treatise* was simply a treasury of character types and a rationale for placing them in a family tree. Jean-Louis Cabanès argues that Zola plumbed Lucas's system for myths, while Auguste Dezalay asserts that Lucas let Zola work out long-held ideas about return and repetition.[24] I would say that Lucas offered more: the elements of a body-based theory of social structure and a rationale for overcoming the dichotomous structure of anatomical narrative, with its strict separation between narrative observer and observed body. As Zola put Lucas's ideas to work, figurative language concerning the body became a way to describe entire societies and the movement of history itself.

Lucas meant to set out to solve the major problem facing existing theories of heredity, the proliferation of exceptions.[25] To account for the spontaneous appearance of new traits Lucas proposed a law of "inneity" to complement one of heredity, and illustrated their interaction through hundreds of examples culled from earlier studies. The theory encompassed a spectrum of traits from an organism's physical form—or "mechanism"—to its mental form (*forme morale*)—or "dynamism." Physical form included the tissues, fluids, and organs of the body; mental form, the organism's faculties, energies, and "modes of activity." Between them lay the nervous system, the body's "principle organ." In Lucas's view, the study of "dynamic heredity"—the transmission of aptitudes and forms of behavior—led immediately to the nervous system and thus to "the very heart of material life [*vie plastique*]."[26]

Lucas's law of inneity explained "originality, imagination, and liberty" in the making of the individual, that is, spontaneous variation, while the law of heredity explained "repetition and memory," the perpetuation of traits.[27] The *Treatise*'s numerous sub-laws and classifications defy summary, but several aspects are notable for asserting a reciprocal relationship between individual heredity and social structure. Lucas assumed not only that characteristics acquired during a parent's life were passed on in some form to the child, but also that circumstances at the moment of conception affected the child's traits—two ways that the "dynamic life" of one generation affected the physical life of the next. (The product of an adulterous liaison was likely to be a girl.)[28] Generations were shaped as well by the "heredity of institutions." A system of aristocracy, for example, encouraged endogamy and thereby the reproduction of behaviors supporting the system. Ultimately, however, "social facts" followed from "vital facts." Natural heredity was "the primordial reason and the real source" of the heredity of institutions, thus grounding social structures in biological traits.[29] His keen attention to "morbid heredity" and "pathological modification"—such as inherited or spontaneously occurring propensities for drunkenness, crime, and madness—similarly reflects Lucas's legitimation of social structures via heredity. He typically looked to the lower classes for examples.[30] His theory of individual heredity ultimately offered a synthetic—and complacent—explanation of social forms.

Zola's notes leave little doubt of Lucas's importance as he imagined characters and their relationship to each other in the Rougon-Macquart clan. The notes include detailed explanations of the permutations of characteristics across generations, with special attention to the transmission and spontaneous appearance of behavioral pathologies.[31] Zola made much of Lucas's views that nervous illnesses followed the maternal line and that parents' "moral state" at the time of conception affected the child (Zola, "Documents et plans," 1705, 1724–25, 1728). Lucas's work thus provided the basic scheme for the whole series: the madness of the matriarch Dide appears in varying form in all of her descendants, whether their genealogy begins in her marriage to the opportunistic farmhand Rougon or her affair with the alcoholic smuggler

Macquart. The impact on Zola's methods as a novelist seems even more profound. Character portraits could now be organized by theories of heredity and put into a matrix of synchronic and diachronic—intra- and inter-generational—relations.[32] The ramifications were triple. First, Lucas provided Zola with a scientific rationale for drawing characters in gigantic, even pathological terms. Because the three-decade drama of the Rougon-Macquart series would be driven by "the effect of heredity itself" shaped by "the great democratic upheaval of our times," such characters would not be exceptional, strictly speaking, even if they seemed larger than life ("Documents et plans," 1738, 1757). Second, because social forms derived from the aggregate of individual physiologies, a family history could be scientifically, not just metaphorically, a microsmic summation of social history.[33] Zola would demonstrate the connections among characters who at first glance seem strangers, study "the total of the wills of each" and "the general thrust of the ensemble," and thereby create "typical actors that sum up the epoch" ("Documents et plans," 1756–57). Finally, because physical and mental life were on a single spectrum linked by the nerve, any kind of behavior, whether outwardly visible or the behavior known as thinking, could be the object of naturalist description. That is, Lucas's *Treatise* was a physiological justification for the free indirect style that lies at the heart of *L'Assommoir* and other naturalist landmarks.

Zola laid the foundation for his "natural and social history" in *The Fortune of the Rougons* (1871), where pathological bodies begin to provide simultaneously scientific and figurative means of describing individual behavior, social structure, and their interrelation. The novel is at once the story of Dide's immediate descendants and the victory of Bonapartists in the Provence town of Plassans during the coup d'état that founded the Second Empire in 1851. Dide, who suffers from "a lack of equilibrium between the blood and the nerves, a kind of derangement of the brain and heart," has experienced convulsions and other "nervous crises" from a young age. According to the town's common wisdom she has a "cracked brain" (*cerveau fêlé*) (*Fortune*, 67, 70). After inheriting a farm on the outskirts of Plassans she impulsively married Rougon, a worker who knew a good chance when he saw it. Although he soon died, they had a son, Pierre. Dide's affair with Macquart—smuggler, poacher, drinker—began shortly after and produced a son, Antoine, and a daughter, Ursule. Left essentially to themselves, the three children grew up according to their respective instincts (*Fortune*, 72). Jealous that his illegitimate siblings led comfortable lives, Pierre tricked his mother out of her property, sold it, bought into a firm trading olive oil, and married the socially ambitious daughter of one of the firm's founders, with whom he plotted a way into bourgeois society. Antoine, meanwhile, has found a hard-working woman off whom he can live while nursing his rancor. Pierre's politics are strictly establishment, reflecting his ambitions; while Antoine's are pseudo-republican (as Zola presents them), based on resentment. Pierre rids himself of Ursule by arranging her marriage to a milliner with whom she has several children, among them a son, Silvère, who is drawn into Antoine's orbit but develops a sincere reverence for the Republic.

When the story proper begins in 1851, Pierre's opportunity seems to be at hand. He has maneuvered to lead Plassans' anti-republican opposition. His son Eugène, who moves in Bonapartist circles in Paris, has alerted him to the coming coup by Louis-Napoléon. When a republican army enters Plassans, Pierre hides in the hovel where Dide lives; after the republicans leave—Silvère and his sweetheart among them—he leads an attack to recapture the town hall, where Antoine is in charge. Although Pierre is acclaimed a hero, the conservative town remains uneasy. His wife Félicité cuts a deal with the jailed Antoine to lead Plassans' remaining republicans into a massacre, securing Pierre's reputation as a defender of order and clearing the path to a lucrative government post. Silvère, meanwhile, is captured and returned to Plassans, where he is summarily executed by a policeman he injured. Dide witnesses the execution and suffers a nervous crisis from which she does not emerge.

The Fortune of the Rougons establishes both a historical and figurative relationship between the family's rise and the coup d'état. The novel offers three linked origins for the family: Dide's nervous "crack" (*fêlure*), the coup, and the murder of Silvère. Dide's condition allows Pierre and Antoine to grow up according to their own hereditary dispositions, thus allowing the emergence of complementary opportunisms that are critical in the denouement of the coup in Plassans, when the corrupt reestablishment of order leads to Silvère's execution. The characters embody three political positions, as Zola explained when he pitched the novel to his publisher: Pierre the conservative opportunist, Antoine the "spurious and disgraceful" democrat, and Silvère, the "very soul" of Republic, love, and liberty ("Documents et plans," 1759). The Rougon-Macquart series tracks the hereditary permutations of the first two attitudes, while the third reemerges as a possibility in the next-to-last novel, *The Debacle* (*La Débâcle*, 1892), about the collapse of the Second Empire and the Paris Commune. The Empire's fall in 1870—unanticipated when Zola planned the series—added a layer of historical irony as the succeeding novels mapped the permutations of the "crack" against the background of the Empire's fetid opulence.[34]

The metonymic (if not chronological) connection of the three origins was one inspiration for the influential turn to poetics in Zola criticism in the 1970s, as scholars examined the role of myth and rhythm in the Rougon-Macquart novels' recurring themes and proliferating symbols.[35] Nonetheless, we must take the family tree and its origins in the work of Lucas seriously. As Nicholas White puts it, for Zola the family tree—which he introduced with Lucas's terminology—was both object and model of analysis.[36] It had the obvious functions of providing a "scientific" basis for the family members' attitudes and behavior and a scaffolding that linked the novels, but it also gave Zola the means to treat physiology as a systemic factor in history, making lineage a dynamic, not static, complement to the milieu and moment of Taine's three-part formula. Zola told himself that it did not matter if the "generating fact" of all this—Dide's "crack"—was credible. As a hypothesis it could serve as an axiom from which all else derived.[37]

Counterintuitively, however, the fictional genealogy may have been most important as a way for Zola to study the abstract, impersonally mediated social relations characteristic of capitalist modernity.[38] The differences between *The Fortune of the Rougons* and the following novels are instructive. Although Zola distinguished between inherited tendencies and the social environment that shapes their manifestation, in the first Rougon-Macquart novel the two intermingle. Members of the family are the most significant part of any character's milieu in Dide's "house of lucid madness" (*Fortune*, 72). Dide and her children make their own social environment, which is conjointly physiological and interpersonal. Colette Becker observes the contrast with the ossified social geography of Plassans, which is divided between a noble quarter, the "new town" of the bourgeoisie, and the "old town" of workers and merchants.[39] The town limits the family's ability to make its own world; fittingly they attack it. The victory that Pierre and Antoine engineer together is the decisive blow: now opportunists rule and social boundaries will dissolve.

Direct relations among members of the family diminish, however, as individuals depart Plassans in search of opportunity. In the subsequent novels it is mainly parents and children who are in contact, and the legitimate and illegitimate branches of the family rarely cross paths.

(The main exception is *La Conquête de Plassans* or *The Conquest of Plassans*, 1874, in which Pierre Rougon's daughter Marthe and Ursule Macquart's son François are married.)[40] As direct relations diminish, mediating social institutions become the focus of several novels: the capitalist economy in *The Kill* (*La Curée*, 1872), the state in *His Excellence Eugène Rougon* (*Son Excellence Eugène Rougon*, 1876), and the Catholic Church in *The Conquest of Plassans*, among other examples. The forces that these institutions unleash now shape the process through which the hereditary dispositions of physical life become the attitudes and behavior of dynamic life. Members of the family shape these institutions in turn. They continue to influence the manifestations of Dide's crack in each other, but the influence now is mediated, for example, by the system of equivalencies of capitalist value. The reciprocal relationship of individuals and institutions, and the mediating role of institutions in relations between individuals, thus emerge as perhaps the most fundamental topics of the Rougon-Macquart novels. Ultimately theories of heredity were a means for Zola to think through the production and reproduction of social relations in a complex society, a preoccupation shared with the sociology of the era, from Émile Durkheim's theory of the division of labor to Gabriel Tarde's theory of imitation.[41]

Zola's formula for understanding the process, as noted, was to study both "the total of the wills" of each member of the family and "the general thrust of the ensemble." In the belief that individual will was a manifestation of physiology, he began with the description of physical bodies, passed on to behavior, then to social relations, and finally to institutions and forces operating at the largest scale. Put differently, he moved from individual heredity to what Lucas called the heredity of institutions, from individual appetites (the topic of every Rougon-Macquart novel) to their aggregate in his era's "democratic upheaval." The description of individual bodies was thus the keystone of systematic social description. In contrast to *Thérèse Raquin*, in the Rougon-Macquart novels body parts figure not only mentalities but also the forces and institutions shaping the social environment. Critically, however, the physical and figurative body were strictly connected: Dide's descendants "embody" aspects of Second Empire society both figuratively and scientifically. (For this reason, I resist the view that Zola wrote a history of a purely figurative "social body.")[42] Because bodies are doubly implicated in the social transformations that are the topic of each novel and the whole series, descriptions of the body can propel narrative in ways different from *Thérèse Raquin*, where fixed dispositions simply become more manifest. While many aspects of anatomical narrative remain, starting with *The Fortune of the Rougons* we can see the binary structure of observer-observed giving way to a descriptive text that produces multiple coordinated meanings.

And so we find, in *The Fortune of the Rougons*: an intricate foundation for writing a history of the Second Empire through the history of pathological bodies; a framework for addressing the still unsettled sociological question of how individuals, separately and in aggregate, produce, maintain, and are shaped by mediating institutions; and a rigorous, because scientific, means of establishing the relationship between human physiology and the largest structures of human life. The axiom of Dide's "crack," traced through its permutations across five generations, would put the investigation in motion.

But that's not how it worked out, even in France, and it's not necessarily bad that it didn't.

The serialization of *The Fortune of the Rougons* began in *Le Siècle* on June 28, 1870, but was suspended after August 10 because of the outbreak of the Franco-Prussian War. The final four installments of the novel, telling the dénouement of Louis-Napoléon's coup, appeared beginning on March 18, 1871, the day the Commune was declared in Paris, and more than seven months after the end of the Second Empire. Political chaos further delayed the release of the novel as a volume until October. Critical and popular response was tepid: on top of the delays, Napoleon III's fall meant that the novel's indictment of his rise was not as provocative as planned. Meanwhile, Zola pushed ahead: by the time a third edition of *The Fortune of the Rougons* appeared in December 1872, with revisions to better set up subsequent novels, he had already published *The Kill.*[43] The Rougon-Macquart series did not truly gain critical attention and popular interest, moreover, until *L'Assommoir*—the seventh novel, about Antoine's daughter Gervaise—appeared in 1877. The scandal of *L'Assommoir* and novels about two of Gervaise's children, Anna (*Nana*, 1880) and Étienne (*Germinal*, 1885), cemented Zola's reputation, but it was certain that many readers did not know the genealogy, and pathology, that connected the series' characters and novels. (Although a family tree was published for the first time in the eighth novel, *Une page d'amour* or *A Page of Love*, 1878, it is doubtful that readers felt compelled to pick up *The Fortune of the Rougons.*)

Zola's design of the series also worked against his overall plan. Most of the novels after *The Fortune of the Rougons*, as noted earlier, center on members of only one or two generations. Several, such as *Nana* and

The Human Beast (*La Bête humaine*, 1890), are about a single member whose connections to the clan are explained only by the narrator. Taken alone, most of the novels can be read as biographically organized stories of a single character or as nuclear family dramas. While organizing the series around smaller groups of the family served the goal of studying social mediation, without the context of the pathological genealogy it was less than obvious how characters such as *The Human Beast*'s Jacques, a railroad engineer who is afflicted with an atavistic impulse to murder, could "sum up" the era. Instead, what stood out were the larger-than-life characters and their stories, "twisted from the ordinary," as Zola's American admirer Frank Norris put it.[44] As a matter of method for large-scale literary studies, then, one might note: history and form intervene in the best-laid plans.

Elements of Zola's plan nonetheless survived historical complications and formal contradictions because they were central to every novel in the series. Most important was the focus on pathological bodies. Pierluigi Pellini points out that the inheritance of benign qualities would hardly have made compelling history. Inherited madness was a more interesting choice.[45] Yet the connection between the description of pathological bodies and that of equally pathological Second Empire society was also the foundation of a critical stance. Ipso facto, social description that began with pathological bodies rejected any positive notion of an organic social order. The proposition that society would not only allow but welcome the spread of the family's pathologies, moreover, amounted to a prediction that any regime so corrupt must fall. This is not to say that Zola's social critique did not reproduce any number of stereotypes—the man-eating whore, the criminal proletarian, the sexually inert bourgeois—but rather that describing ailing, degenerating bodies was part of the bravado with which Zola and later naturalist writers set out to show truth to societies that did not want to look.

The disconnection of individual novels from the Rougon-Macquart series' intricate plan may paradoxically have aided such a project. Absent the genealogical explanations of *Fortune of the Rougons* and the final novel, *Doctor Pascal* (*Le Docteur Pascal*, 1893)—in which Pierre's middle son reconstructs the history of inherited madness—the pathological body could float free of the "crack." That is, unyoked from the theories that assigned it a spot in the family tree, it could be attached to many aspects of social life. For the same reason its figurative meanings could multiply. The most prominent novels of the Rougon-Macquart series allow just that, which is testament that the programmatic and sometimes plodding *Fortune of the Rougons* enabled, rather than restricted, a free-ranging project. The example of *L'Assommoir*, the novel that launched French naturalism into the world, shows Zola using a malformed leg to illuminate an entire sector of society.

THE STORY OF THE LEG

L'Assommoir (1877) is the story of Antoine Macquart's daughter Gervaise, who has migrated to the Paris neighborhood of La Goutte d'Or with her lover, Lantier, and their two sons. Formally innovative and critically scandalous, *L'Assommoir* launched Zola and naturalism internationally. It is also one of the clearest examples of how naturalist fiction used figurative language to connect individual and social pathologies, an adaptable technique that aided naturalism's travels. The novel's richness is manifest in its title: an *assommoir* is the part of a slaughterhouse where animals are bludgeoned, but when the novel was published the term was also Parisian working-class slang for any bar specializing in rotgut liquor. In the novel, "L'Assommoir" is the common name of the bar that Gervaise and her eventual husband Coupeau frequent. More broadly, the *assommoir* signifies the noxious neighborhood of the Goutte d'Or, a surrounding society indifferent to "the rank milieu of our suburbs" (as Zola wrote in his preface), the malefic work of fate, and Gervaise's entire crushing life.[46] (The title's complex resonances are the reason why it now typically goes untranslated.)

"Conceived in drunkenness," Gervaise inherited from Antoine and her mother Josephine a propensity to abuse alcohol. She inherited another aspect of the parents' "moral" state at conception—her father's frequent beatings of her mother—in the form of a misshapen right leg that makes her limp. (We learn in *Fortune of the Rougons* that the leg was not damaged in the womb but rather formed poorly because of the circumstances.) From Josephine she also inherited a capacity for hard work.[47] Soon abandoned by Lantier, she resumes her old occupation as a laundress and ironer and marries Coupeau, a roofer who lives in the quarter. Coupeau falls from a building, abandons his trade, and gradually takes to drink. Gervaise, fulfilling a long-standing dream, opens her own laundry in the courtyard of an immense tenement known as the "Grande Maison." The shop's back rooms house the family. Business goes well until Gervaise's easygoing ways overtake her. Lantier returns and turns the household into a ménage à trois; burdened with supporting two men, Gervaise decides she can indulge herself too; as her work becomes shoddy, the shop collapses, and the work that others give her dries up. Now drinking heavily, she and Coupeau sell their possessions to survive. (Lantier, still in the shop, is living off one of Gervaise's neighborhood rivals, Virginie, who has opened a grocery there.) Coupeau dies in Sainte-Anne Hospital, the city's principal mental asylum, in a fit of delirium tremens. Gervaise goes more quietly: reduced to living in a niche under a stairway in the Grande Maison, she dies "bit by bit" of "the filth and fatigue of her wasted life." One morning neighbors discover her body, "already green," after several days' absence (*L'Assommoir*, 513).

Gervaise's end is finely plotted: six chapters tell her aspirations and rise, six her disappointment and fall. The two sets are separated by a pivotal chapter in which Gervaise throws a bacchanalian feast—marking both her success and the point where indulgence overtakes work—and Lantier worms his way back into her life. The entire arc is presaged and reprised several times.[48] Through free indirect style, working-class slang becomes ubiquitous not only in the characters' speech and thoughts but in the narrative itself, gradually erasing the textual boundaries between Gervaise and her milieu while also allowing neighborhood opinion to emerge as a judgmental chorus alongside the narrative voice. (Zola's knowledge of slang came from *Dictionnaire de la langue verte: Argots Parisiens comparés* or *Dictionary of Slang: Parisian Argots Compared*, 1866, compiled by Alfred Delvau; and *Le Sublime, ou, Le travailleur comme il est en 1870 et ce qu'il peut être* or *The Sublime, or the Worker in 1870 and What He Can Be*, 1870, a half-ethnographic, half-reformist tract by Denis Poulot.) In the next-to-last chapter Gervaise revisits her entire life as she walks the neighborhood on a winter night, her reflections given in a tour de force of free indirect style.[49] In the final chapter Gervaise witnesses Coupeau's hallucinatory death throes—a description relying on *On Alcoholism, the Diverse Forms of Alcoholic Delirium and Their Treatment* (*De L'alcoolisme, des diverses formes du délire alcoolique et de leur traitement*, 1874) by Valentin Magnan, a doctor and researcher at Sainte-Anne—and begins to "do Coupeau" for the neighborhood's amusement (*L'Assommoir*, 503–4). The puppet-like quality of her performance highlights once more her subjection to forces greater than her, symbolized by the novel's many animate machines, most notably the still that produces rotgut in her favored bar and the entire Grande Maison.

L'Assommoir tracks the state of Gervaise's body during her rise and fall. Two parts of the body—the arm and the leg—are freighted with meaning. Gervaise's "lovely blond arms" are associated with her skill and diligence as a laundress and by extension her capacity for hard work. Her limping right leg connotes all that brings her to ruin. Early on it is hardly noticeable except when she "lets herself go" out of fatigue.[50] Coupeau's spiteful sister-in-law names her "the gimp" (*la banban*), while the good worker Goujet admires her for coping with it. By the end, however, she limps so badly that no one can walk beside her; in her degradation she no longer is concerned with neighborhood opinion (*L'Assommoir*, 150, 437–38). In the course of the transformation her arms too change: the shoulders become fat and slick, while the elbows grow accustomed to resting on the table where she drinks (*L'Assommoir*, 187, 435). The limbs' connotations recuperate the reformist discourse on workers of Zola's time. Gervaise's arms figure the cliché of diligence and economy; the bad leg, the cliché of carelessness and intemperance.[51] The latter connection echoes in the novel's language through the often observed homophony of the verbs *boiter* and *boire*. *Elle boite, elle boit*; she limps, she drinks.

Gervaise's arms and leg are competing synecdoches within the scope of her body—which one will sum her up?—and metonymies for aspects of her personality. Remarkably, the figures extend beyond Gervaise's body to convey meaning onto the world around her.[52] To begin with the synecdoches: Gervaise's arms and bad leg each indicate something about her as a whole, but her internally conflicted nature is echoed in the working-class society of the quarter through contrasting characters. The blacksmith Goujet—whose sculpted arms seem "copied from those of a giant"—embodies the diligence and thriftiness of the good worker while Lantier—who gets fat "devouring" the businesses of Gervaise and Virginie—embodies the laziness and excesses of the bad (*L'Assommoir*, 207, 378, 510). If Gervaise is a synecdoche for the surrounding world, the world exerts its own force on her. A clique led by her in-laws mocks her, Goujet and his upstanding mother begin to spurn her, and neighborhood opinion turns clients against her—all creating the conditions for her mental and physical fall. That is, Zola projects the social milieu back into Gervaise's body in a figurative circle.[53] Maybe if Gervaise could escape the quarter she could escape her body, but she cannot. The circuit of synecdoches shows her trapped in a "closed horizon" (as Zola put it in *Germinal*), in which her milieu exerts its own fatality.[54]

Metonymies that originate in Gervaise's body reinforce the sense that she is trapped in a world which she can escape only in death. Metonymy, let us recall, is the trope of contiguity. Start with what is beneath the leg: when Lantier abandons Gervaise she is "thrown on the pavement" (*jetée sur le pavé*), but these are not streets she can negotiate. Zola reprises the plunge on her most desperate night, when she nearly "falls on the sidewalk" (*tomber au trottoir*, slip into prostitution), but falls short: there are no takers (*L'Assommoir*, 51, 481). Little wonder that when her will fails she drags her shoes across that pavement (*trainer les savates*, live carelessly), as she dragged her leg through their rooms on the morning she realized that Lantier was with another woman (*L'Assommoir*, 28, 437, 476). She was after all born with her leg "late" (*avec sa jambe en retard*); when she crosses Paris to visit Coupeau at Sainte-Anne, it lags behind the entire time (*L'Assommoir*, 58, 500). The metonymy of the street surface as a hostile social environment surely changes the simple equation of *boiter* and *boire*, limping and drinking: whether halting or able, all of Gervaise's responses to her world attach themselves to the thing that hits the pavement, her leg, whose history is her history.[55] By the end Gervaise herself seems to understand her limp in this way: as she shambles through the neighborhood in the penultimate chapter, revisiting the sites of her life, the gas lamps exaggerate her gait in proportion to her despair, her shadow turning a somersault with each step: "A real clown [or puppet, *guignol*]! . . . My God but she was funny and frightful. Never had she understood so well how she had sunk" (*L'Assommoir*, 488).

Curiously, when Coupeau falls from the roof he breaks his right leg, the one that afflicts Gervaise. The scene swarms with slang meaning "leg" and "foot": in addition to the common "paw" (*patte*, foot), Coupeau uses a compass to trace shapes on the zinc he uses in roofing (*compas*, legs), a concierge tells him she is out to buy a haunch for dinner (*gigot*, leg), Coupeau is angry because his assistant won't bring his soldering irons (*fers*, feet), and after the fall he is taken to the hospital on a stretcher (*brancard*, in the plural, legs).[56] Legs multiply and Coupeau becomes just one more pair ready for snapping. Coupeau habitually boasts that "it's the street that's afraid of him," but he is not the master of his environment he thinks he is: when Nana, his daughter with Gervaise, calls from the street he slips, and "like a cat with tangled paws," slides into the abyss. (Appropriately, for a washerwoman's husband, he hits the street with the thud of a bag of laundry; *L'Assommoir*, 142, 145–46.) In Coupeau's world it is not the healthy but the broken leg that is omnipresent.

The results of Coupeau's convalescence are as overdetermined as his fall. With his "pin" (*quille*, leg) "trussed and stiff as a sausage,"

Coupeau rails against the injustice of the world, develops a "muffled rancor" toward work, is overtaken by laziness, and gets a taste for alcohol.[57] These are all qualities associated with *Gervaise's* leg. Coupeau's limb curiously is a metonymy of hers. It too fails to meet the challenge of the pavement. The conjoint metonyms of leg and street illuminate not just Gervaise's nature but a social condition—at present called "precarity"—and responses to it that seem inevitable in the novel's semantic sociology. Consider the iron (*fer*), which is essential to both their trades, in the one for soldering, the other for smoothing wrinkles. By association with horseshoes (*fers à cheval*), a *fer* may be a foot (usually as *les quatre fers*, all fours), but a *fer* may also be a manacle. In popular slang "dragging the right" (*tirer la droite*) was the habitual walk of a convict, from dragging a *fer*.[58] And that is the walk of Gervaise and Coupeau: they are prisoners of all that their legs connote.

Ghoulishly, their one-way street ends in dancing: Coupeau's delirium tremens and Gervaise's imitation of it. The end is long-prepared: Gervaise's leg is called a "jig" (*gigue*) and Coupeau is known to "leg about" (*gigoter*, dance) when drunk.[59] The novel thus draws a semantic line from the leg to the names of dances scattered throughout: *branle*, *chahut*, *galop*, *rigodon*, *saute*, and *valse*, among many others.[60] Gervaise dances when she receives loans from Goujet's mother and a pawnbroker, the very rooms and streets "dance" when she is drunk, and Coupeau's hands do the same as his disease progresses (*L'Assommoir*, 215, 242, 398, 413). They spend many nights "dancing by the sideboard" (*danser avant le buffet*, go without a meal) when money is short (e.g., *L'Assommoir*, 384, 438). Coupeau subjects Gervaise and Nana to innumerable beatings (*danses*), while their neighbor, an alcoholic locksmith, dances his wife and daughter to death in the same way.[61]

One cannot deny the Dionysian quality of the motif of dance, which contributes to the thread of feast and potlatch that Jacque Dubois identifies in the novel. Just as often, however, the vocabulary of dance contributes to a mechanical image of the human body, its disjointed parts moving puppet-like in concert with the novel's animate machines.[62] The connection first appears in the immense laundry where Gervaise resumes her trade. Washerwomen move like marionettes in the haze created by a panting steam engine. Later visiting the forge where Goujet works, Gervaise sees the arms of blacksmiths and bolt-making machines moving in cadenced rhythm, indistinguishable one from the other (*L'Assommoir*, 32–33, 50, 209). The semantic dismemberment of the body reaches a gruesome peak in Coupeau's final days. In the dance of his delirium tremens he is a "real puppet" (*un vrai polichinelle*), with his legs, arms, hands, and feet seemingly tugged by strings. When the rest of him appears dead his feet still dance on their own. With the human body cut apart and mechanized, fatality returns in a different register. Goujet, imagining the day when bolt-making machines will put him out of work, says that "the flesh can't fight against iron [*le fer*]," but one might say too that in *L'Assommoir*, the *will* can't overcome the *leg* (*L'Assommoir*, 211, 506, 514).

From this perspective, what does it mean for Gervaise to "do Coupeau" by imitating his dance? Gervaise recoils from explaining Coupeau's "final gallop" (*galop*, originally a dance) to a watching intern because she sees the roofer reenacting parts of his life and their relationship.[63] Nonetheless, after returning from her first visit to Sainte-Anne, she demonstrates his dance to the incredulous neighbors. After her next visit she does so under duress, worried that by imitating Coupeau she too will become sick. Her fears may have been correct: later, people in the neighborhood see her spontaneously "doing Coupeau" alone, which they attribute to watching her husband too long (*L'Assommoir*, 503, 509, 516). The case of Coupeau's leg, however, already has shown how qualities of the body become qualities of the mind in *L'Assommoir*. If Gervaise finally becomes a puppet by imitating Coupeau, then fate and contingency are nearly interchangeable in the novel's peculiar metonymic causality. Gervaise's inherited qualities, physically manifested in the limp, become Coupeau's after a chance event leads his injured leg to imitate her malformed member. Another contingent event—imitating Coupeau—leads to her own puppetization. In the end she is not imitating Coupeau so much as giving corporeal representation to the situation faced by all inhabitants of the quarter, whether they recognize it or not.

Synecdoches and metonymies originating in Gervaise's body thus play a semantically critical role in Zola's description of his central character, other inhabitants of the quarter, their milieu, and its impact on them. Figurative language helps establish the novel's moral dichotomies, but also shows their limited relevance to understanding what happens when the leg meets the street. Body figures become a means of creating a social typology, but also for evoking the (supposedly) closed, inescapable quality of working-class society. Synecdoches do so through circuits from individual to milieu and back; metonymies by compounding the qualities of this world to the point that even chance events seem inevitable. The free semantic play that makes these figures so effective would not be possible if Gervaise's body remained tied to her grandmother

Dide's via the Rougon-Macquart family tree and its quasi-scientific causality. The passage from the cracked nerve to the malformed leg may be the novel's enabling, "axiomatic" metonymy, but otherwise Dide and her world withdraw, allowing the novel to develop its rich and strange semantic texture.

To be sure, Zola's formal choice to focus his novel about working-class life on one woman and the quarter she inhabits had its own consequences. The figurative circles in the novel's mimesis of individual and social life create a horizon that is as analytically closed as the world it describes. The machines that actually pull the strings were topics for other novels. This leaves *L'Assommoir* itself politically inert, despite the clamor it caused: for the reader as for Gervaise, there is no way out. Yet the response to this novel quickly made body figures a transposable technique of naturalist description and analysis. Although Gervaise is trapped, the techniques that created her world exited the novel and were adopted by other writers. These appropriations of *L'Assommoir* introduced its synecdoches and metonymies into new situations. As I argued in the previous chapter, such appropriations were one way of signaling an affiliation with naturalism and thus of claiming a position in the naturalist literary field, but they also developed the novel's techniques further by applying them "out of place." Given the complex hereditary framework for the Rougon-Macquart novels, it is worth recalling that *The Fortune of the Rougons* became well known abroad only *after* the scandal of *L'Assommoir*. In the same way that the semantic play inside *L'Assommoir* was possible because Gervaise's fate was not strictly tied to Dide's, we can say that its impact outside *L'Assommoir* was possible because the novel's reception was not strictly tied to the reception of *The Fortune of the Rougons*. That is, the granular history of the circulation of naturalist fiction—which novels became known when, and how—shaped the development of naturalist technique.

TRANSLATING GERVAISE

The clamor over *L'Assommoir* indeed was great. Because the controversy attracted international attention, it is one of the most consequential examples of how the transnational history of naturalist fiction was inseparable from transnational disputes among critics, authors, and readers. Criticism of the novel began as soon as its first installments appeared in *Le Bien Public* in 1876. The novel's language bothered critics the most, even though the newspaper cut the most daring parts. The conservative critic Albert Millaud famously charged: "This is not realism . . . this is pornography." The government threatened to intervene during serialization, and when the volume appeared in 1877, the state banned *L'Assommoir* from train stations on the grounds of obscenity. Meanwhile, the young writers Guy de Maupassant, Joris-Karl Huysmans, Henry Céard, Léon Hennique, and Paul Alexis organized a party to celebrate the novel—the so-called Trapp dinner discussed in chapter 1—to which they invited Zola, Flaubert, and Edmond de Goncourt (Jules having died). The poet Stéphane Mallarmé—hardly thought to be a naturalist—wrote in praise of Zola's experiments with language.[64]

As happened with many of the Rougon-Macquart novels, *L'Assommoir* was appropriated by parodists, moralists, and popular culture. (In the case of *Nana*, as I show in chapter 3, this kind of appropriation turned Gervaise's daughter into a figure with an international career.) The novel inspired songs, caricatures, postcards, and other derivatives that turned it into a media event. It was also subjected to moralistic rewriting. Achille Scondigné's *L'Assommé* (1877), one volume in a purported "History of a French Family in the Nineteenth Century," turned the workers of the neighborhood into a virtuous lot. The hero of *Pierre Blot* (1877) by Paul Féval dies of drink but finds faith on his deathbed. Zola himself agreed to moral clarification in the French theatrical version (1879), on which he worked secretly with William Busnach and Octave Gastineau. Several of the play's secondary characters—including one of the novel's hardest drinkers, Mes-Bottes—denounce the evils of alcohol, while Lantier and Virginie are straightforward traitors.[65] The attention made *L'Assommoir* France's first best-seller.[66]

It also made *L'Assommoir* the first work of French naturalism to be well known abroad. Although many European intellectuals would have read the novel in French, the speed with which translations appeared suggests its appeal: two in 1878 (English and Italian), then at least seven in 1879, and at least fifteen more by 1893. (By this time there were at least five English versions, three German ones, and three Italian.)[67] The theatrical adaptation was quickly translated as well. In some countries, such as Germany, Spain, and Hungary, *L'Assommoir* was the first of Zola's novels to be translated. (Translations of some stories and novellas had appeared earlier.)[68] In other countries its success set off a wave of translations of other works by him. (With the exception of a Russian version, *The Fortune of the Rougons* did not begin to be translated until after the publication of *L'Assommoir*.)[69] The translations typically were abridged and often self- or government-censored. Moral revision continued: in the first English version (*Gervaise, A Story of Drink*, condensed into five chapters) Gervaise marries Goujet and bans alcohol from the house; they raise Nana together. The Spanish theatrical version has Nicolás (Goujet) saving Gervasia and Juana (Nana) from Virginia and German (Lantier).[70] As in the French parodies and revisions mentioned earlier, these rewritings focused on individual characters and the plot, although other aspects of the novel also gained much attention.

In foreign literary circles *L'Assommoir* was both polarizing and catalyzing. To give only a few examples: in Italy, the novelist Luigi Capuana's 1877 article on *L'Assommoir* became a manifesto for *verismo*, the variety of realism that had been emerging since the 1860s.[71] The critic Francesco De Sanctis, a stalwart opponent of idealism in literature, initially wrote in praise of the first Rougon-Macquart novels. In 1879, perhaps with political ambitions in mind, he savaged *L'Assommoir*. Ironically, his about-face ensured that Zola was at the center of every Italian literary polemic for a decade.[72] In Hungary, where opinion of Zola had been overwhelmingly hostile, the translation of *L'Assommoir* in 1879 prompted critics to begin changing their views. There as in many countries, Zola's novels were agents of cultural and literary evolution.[73] In Poland, an older generation of critics was forced to acknowledge *L'Assommoir*'s achievements, despite disgust. The novel became a touchstone for differentiating between kinds of realism.[74] In Bohemia, after *L'Assommoir* was translated in 1885 critics began to present Zola's work as a *positive* model for literature in Czech, although they warned against passive imitation. The changing assessment deepened as younger writers seeking to renovate Czech literature came to the fore.[75] Italy, Hungary, Poland, Bohemia: *L'Assommoir* was controversial in many places, but the pattern of the novel's impact reflected the uneven geography of the naturalist novel as a whole. In the transnational landscape of rival realisms, its deepest effect seems to have been greatest where other French, English, and Russian varieties were not already dominant.

As *L'Assommoir*'s fame spread it became common for writers to cite specific scenes in the book. These intertextual shout-outs were both acts of homage and announcements of affiliation that contributed to the formation of the naturalist literary field. The most popular scenes were the feasts after Gervaise's marriage to Coupeau and on her saint's day. Traces of them have been found in Aluísio Azevedo's *The Mulatto* (*O Mulato*, 1881) in Brazil, Stephen Crane's *George's Mother* (1896) and Norris's *McTeague* (1899) in the United States, and Ivan Cankar's

On the Brink (*Na klancu*, 1902) in Slovenia, among other novels.[76] Other common episodes include a fight between Gervaise and Virginie, for example in Benito Pérez Galdós's *Fortunata and Jacinta* (*Fortunata y Jacinta*, 1886–87) and Vicente Blasco Ibáñez's *May Flower* (*Flor de Mayo*, 1895) in Spain; a visit that Gervaise's wedding party makes to the Louvre, in Galdós's *The Disinherited* (*La Desheredada*, 1881) and Crane's *Maggie, a Girl of the Streets* (1893); and her late-night streetwalking, in *Maggie* and Eugen Kumičić's *Olga and Lina* (*Olga i Lina*, 1881) in Croatia.[77]

Gervaise and the young Nana became points of departure for many characters. Literary historians see Gervaise in the alcoholic protagonist of Minna Canth's *Lopo the Peddler* (*Kauppa-Lopo*, 1889) in Finland, the laundress Piedade in Azevedo's *The Slum* (*O Cortiço*, 1890), and Francka, a servant in Cankar's *On the Brink*.[78] A number of characters recall the young Nana, such as Pombinha in *The Slum*, a sexually repressed girl who becomes a celebrated prostitute; and Brigita, Malči, and Lojzka in Cankar's *The House of Our Mother of Charity* (*Hisa Marije Pomočnice*, 1904), who observe their mothers in flagrante delicto.[79] Interestingly, it is not unusual to find the young Nana as the inspiration for a character's debased childhood and adolescence, and Gervaise for her mature years and decline. The amalgam continued to appear after the adult Nana got a novel of her own. Examples are Amparo, the working-class heroine of Emilia Pardo Bazán's *The Tribune* (*La Tribuna*, 1882) in Spain, Maggie in Crane's novella, and Tončka, the cigarette maker-cum-prostitute of Fran Govekar's *In the Blood* (*V krvi*, 1896) in Slovenia. (All in the family: Tončka's delinquent daughter recalls Nana again.)[80]

Some of these Gervaise-like characters show authors going beyond homage to respond to *L'Assommoir*'s themes and techniques. The central disagreement of such novels-in-dialog concerned the deterministic combination of hereditary and environmental forces from which Gervaise has no escape.[81] The protagonist of Canth's *Lopo the Peddler* leaves her husband and child by her own choice to take up a trade associated in Finland with sexual commerce. A hyper-erotic alcoholic, she seems typical of female characters created by male naturalist writers, yet in Päivi Lappailainen's view, Canth's insistence on Lopo's self-determination responded both to the idealization of women in Finnish romanticism and to its realist and naturalist reversal, in which fallen women were helpless victims of predatory social elites. In contrast, Lopo is a "complete physiological woman" who makes her own fate.[82] Cankar's *On the Brink*, a novel that Tone Smolej considers to both affirm and negate *L'Assommoir*, similarly uses a character inspired by Gervaise to respond to the determinism of Zola's novel. Francka, the protagonist, faces a hostile social environment which, like Gervaise, she surveys through an open window in the first scene. (Gervaise is waiting for her unfaithful lover; Francka glimpses hers for the first time.) Her path through a series of dwellings also parallels Gervaise's. Yet in a crucial episode when she collects her Coupeau-like husband from a bar, she resists the invitation to drink. "Higher illusions" allow her and other characters from Cankar's naturalist period to transcend the environments in which they live.[83]

In Pardo Bazán's *The Tribune*, an alternative Gervaise is part of a multi-front response to *L'Assommoir* that includes secondary characters and a painstakingly described milieu. Francisca Gonzalez-Arias argues that the "imaginative modification" of *L'Assommoir* allowed Pardo Bazán to refine the techniques and voice that created the distinctive naturalism of *The House of Ulloa* (*Los Pazos de Ulloa*, 1886) and the novels that followed. *The Tribune*'s heroine Amparo has obvious similarities to Gervaise (down to a Goujet-like worker who worships her from afar) and Nana (she comes of age in the streets). Her milieu, the fictional Calle de los Castros neighborhood of Coruña, resembles the Goutte d'Or quarter not simply as a "working-class district"—a ubiquitous setting after *L'Assommoir*—but in the detailed descriptions of lives and behaviors through which Pardo Bazán created it. (Like Zola, Pardo Bazán did extensive fieldwork.) Yet Amparo, who is seduced and abandoned by a young gentleman, is an essentially good if shallow woman, strong in religious faith and uncomfortable in the licentious atmosphere of the streets. Unlike *L'Assommoir*, moreover, the inhabitants of her neighborhood do not work toward her downfall but help her resist the moral degradation that could await her. Pardo Bazán's point-by-point engagement with *L'Assommoir*, then, allowed the author to work toward the "Catholic naturalism" of her later novels in which determinism is replaced by grace.[84]

Tracing novels in dialogue with *L'Assommoir* in naturalist circles and beyond could continue. Two further, compelling examples would be Giovanni Verga's *The Malavoglias* (*I Malavoglia*, 1881) and Galdós's *The Disinherited*, whose authors found solutions to narrative problems through their encounters with *L'Assommoir*. In the late 1870s Verga, the principal novelist of Italian *verismo*, discussed Zola's work extensively with Capuana when he was searching for a new style. Tullio Pagano and others argue that the discussions produced the remarkable free indirect style of *The Malavoglias*, which uses the vocabulary and rhythms of

Sicilian dialect to narrate the struggles of an eponymous family as their village is integrated into the new Italian state. (In an echo of *L'Assommoir*, the family name, which idiomatically connotes haplessness, could be translated literally as "The Gimps.")[85] In the late 1870s Galdós, for his part, was looking for a way to bring together the character-focused social analysis of his "contemporary novels" (*novelas contemporáneas*) and the historical perspective of his "national episodes" (*episodios nacionales*). In Stephen Gilman's view, a dialogue with *L'Assommoir* was key to Galdós's development of techniques of description, characterization, and narration that let him create characters in novels such as *The Disinherited* who experience the present as history while also representing the society in which they live. As in Verga's case, *L'Assommoir*'s use of spoken language in free indirect style was important in solving the impasse because it gave Galdós new ways to describe milieu, blur the division between central characters and their environments, and reduce the heavy presence of the narrator in his earlier work.[86]

To guard against the simple conclusion that *L'Assommoir* was "influential," let me point out that these examples show writers picking, choosing, and recombining aspects of Zola's novel. The prestige of French writers obviously was critical to the attention that *L'Assommoir* received. The novel did not circulate in a barrier-free space in which all writers had equal standing. Yet the history of *L'Assommoir*'s reception reveals invention and—importantly—counterargument, notably by two female writers, Canth and Pardo Bazán. This is not, then, a history of imitation. And while novels such as Azevedo's *The Mulatto* and Galdós's *The Disinherited* combined techniques developed in France with "local material" from the societies in which the writers worked, they are better seen as indictments of their worlds, not compromises. Finally, these examples show that the appropriation and adaptation of the topics, themes, and form of naturalist fiction proceeded by extracting characters, scenes, and motifs from novels like *L'Assommoir*. Writers did not emulate *L'Assommoir* so much as dismantle it, making the circulation of naturalist fiction a history of intentionally chosen fragments and pieces rather than the witless acceptance of literary hegemony.

JAWS AND FISTS, THE CHIN AND THAT HAIR

Body figures were part of writers' complex engagement with the methods of representation that gained international fame with *L'Assommoir*.

I turn now to two examples to explore through close reading how the literary form of naturalist fiction changed as it was practiced in other parts of the world, and to consider as well how some of the changes suggest a reflection on method. Writers adapted the figurative description of pathological behavior to a variety of historical circumstances, from the relation of labor, desire, and money in the United States at the turn of the century (Frank Norris's *McTeague*) to the human cost of civilizing projects in Japan in the Meiji era (Shimazaki Tōson's *Spring*). Characteristically, however, in these novels the closed circuit of individual and social pathology seen in the figure of the leg in *L'Assommoir* breaks apart. In the process contingency is uncoupled from fate. Not that they are happy stories: the eponymous McTeague, after killing his wife and best friend over gold, will die in the California desert. Tōson's Aoki—one of two central figures in *Spring*—hangs himself after a nervous crisis whose ultimate cause is the Meiji state. But body figures in each of these novels place individual and society—individual and social pathology—into a different relationship than they have in *L'Assommoir*. Their closed circuit broken, contingency returns as history. Indeed, the possibility of using body figures to represent a *pathological* but not *inevitable* here and now—which would be both for and against Zola's methods—seems to be the reason both for their appeal as a novelistic technique and for the ability of writers to deploy them in so many different circumstances.

At first glance Norris and *McTeague* (1899) seem utterly invested in the determining force of the body. The milieu surrounding characters such as McTeague, a gold miner turned dentist, and Trina, his Swiss-American wife, seems only to confirm and abet their inherited qualities. McTeague's propensity for alcoholism and violence goes back to the "third, fourth, and five hundredth generation" of his ancestors, while Trina's parsimony comes from instincts of saving and hoarding passed on through her "peasant blood" (*McTeague*, 22, 78–79). These qualities are indicated by physical features in the typical naturalist manner and reflect both Norris's reading of Zola (particularly *L'Assommoir* and *The Human Beast*) and an interest in atavism (in Norris's terminology, the return of the "brute") gleaned from Max Nordau and Cesare Lombroso.[87] Incessantly repeated phrases concerning physical features—McTeague's "mallet-like fists," Trina's "adorable little chin"—are part of the world of "the enormous, the formidable, the terrible" that Norris admired in Zola's work and strove to create in his own.[88] In *McTeague*, however, body figures introduce history alongside heredity. They become vehicles for an examination of the relationship between labor, money, and value in America's Gilded Age that begins in the novel's story and passes into its narrative discourse. McTeague and Trina develop pathologies specific to the time and place—signaled now by the relationship of meaning-laden parts of the body to each other—that expose money as a signifying system with only a communally agreed relationship to value. The true pathology may be belief in the meaning of money rather than the opposite.

Norris, the American writer most eager to associate himself with Zola, was a critical figure in the rejection of the genteel realism that was dominant in fiction at the time. He discovered Zola's work as a student at Berkeley and drafted two novels that reflected his enthusiasm during a year at Harvard in 1894–95: *Vandover and the Brute* and *McTeague*. A year later he wrote about Zola as an essentially "romantic" writer whose characters, "twisted from the ordinary," are flung into "the throes of a vast and terrible drama."[89] His view of Zola is not as much a departure as many Norris scholars imagine: we should recall that when Zola planned the Rougon-Macquart novels, he decided to create exceptional characters in the manner of Stendhal instead of generalizeable ones à la Flaubert. *Vandover and the Brute* (published posthumously in 1914) is about a moneyed young man in San Francisco whose hedonism triggers atavistic degeneration. He ends up mopping the floors of buildings that he once owned—a gesture to Gervaise's job mopping her former shop in *L'Assommoir*. *Vandover and the Brute* has much in common with the anatomical narrative of early naturalist novels such as *Germinie Lacerteux* and *Thérèse Raquin*, including a vocabulary of the nerves used to describe Vandover's decline. The return of the nerve in *Vandover and the Brute*'s system of mimesis reflected its role in nativist alarm about the supposedly declining position of Anglo-Saxons in American society, which was blamed on causes ranging from their contamination by primitive ethnic and class others to their greater susceptibility to "civilized" diseases such as neurasthenia, a new ailment popularized by the neurologist George Beard in *American Nervousness: Its Causes and Consequences* (1881) and enlisted in Nordau's argument on general social decay in *Degeneration*.[90]

McTeague, which was loosely inspired by a lurid murder in San Francisco, continues to employ a quasi-scientific language of the body, but more dynamically and on a different scale. The novel opens in a Polk Street neighborhood of San Francisco where McTeague, a man of massive proportions, has a dental parlor. (Gold makes the first of many appearances in the fillings he makes for his patients.) McTeague learned dentistry as a teenager by apprenticing with a "charlatan" who passed through the gold-mining camp where he grew up working as a car-boy (*McTeague*, 6). McTeague's friend Marcus introduces him to a diminutive cousin, Trina, who needs dental work. (The menagerie of the building where McTeague and Marcus live, which recalls *L'Assommoir*'s Grande Maison, is one of several gestures to Zola's novel.) During an appointment McTeague is uncontrollably aroused and kisses Trina while she is under gas. Although she is frightened by him, McTeague wins her affection and they become engaged. Before they are married Trina learns that she has won $5,000 with a lottery ticket that the building's peculiar maid, a Hispanic woman named Maria, forced her to buy. (Maria ceaselessly tells anyone who will listen that her family once owned a hundred-piece gold table service.) Trina invests her money with an uncle for whom she does piecework making toys, and plans their ascent to middle-class life. A series of dwellings tracks their social rise and fall. Trina makes one concession to McTeague's desire to spend the money—buying him a gilt tooth to hang outside his practice—but her windfall mainly inspires her to save, an instinct she concedes is "stronger than I" (*McTeague*, 119). She amasses coins in a locked trunk, and when alone, takes them out to cherish.

Marcus, who had imagined Trina as his wife, becomes convinced that he has a claim on the money and fights with McTeague; during one battle he bites through McTeague's ear and the enraged dentist breaks his arm—"the brute" having "leaped instantly to life" (*McTeague*, 132). Marcus notifies the authorities that McTeague is practicing without a diploma and then leaves town. Deprived of his trade, McTeague takes increasingly menial jobs and starts drinking with cronies while Trina is ever more obsessive about saving. Their increasingly tormented relationship is exemplified by ghastly scenes where McTeague grinds Trina's fingers between his teeth. He takes pleasure in brutally extracting money; she in the pain of withholding it (*McTeague*, 170–71). McTeague absconds with Trina's considerable stash just at the time she loses two fingers to blood poisoning. No longer able to make toys, she works as a scrubwoman in a school. She withdraws her $5,000 and changes it for gold coins; one evening she spreads them between her sheets and sleeps naked in their cool embrace. When McTeague returns to demand more money, he beats the uncooperative Trina to death. He flees with the coins into mining country and then toward Mexico. North of Death Valley he and a prospector find a vein of gold, but spooked, he flees again. A posse is on his trail and Marcus is one of the group. McTeague heads into Death Valley where Marcus alone pursues him. Trapped, he beats Marcus to death, but his ex-friend handcuffs them together with his last breath. McTeague has kept the gold, but he will die in the alkali wastes.

McTeague's and Trina's rise and fall is explained through coded parts of the body. McTeague is introduced as a "young giant" with enormous hands "hard as wooden mallets" and a square head whose jaw is "salient," that is, forward-jutting, "like that of the carnivora." The hands and jaw signal metonymically what McTeague is and will become as the "foul stream of hereditary evil" beneath "all that was good in him" rises to the surface (*McTeague*, 6, 22). Those massive hands: a corporeal index for the violence that erupts when slow-witted McTeague is awakened. They inevitably appear when the brute faces the challenges of life in society. The jaws with their "immense" teeth: instruments to satisfy appetites too primitive for finer mastication. They clench and clack in moments of anger and desire (e.g., *McTeague*, 20, 34). On her wedding night Trina is terrified of McTeague's hands and jaws alike; as the two settle into married life she contemplates seeing them day after dreary day (*McTeague*, 102–3, 105–6). Norris's epithetic diction—the hands always "mallet-like," the jaws ever "salient"—ensures that these parts of the body sum up McTeague for the reader as well.

The portrait of McTeague is a concatenation of nativist stereotypes and the latest scientific arguments on race and crime. Like both syllables of McTeague's name, the square skull and protruding jaw signal that he is Irish and thus subject to Irish "race impulses," in Norris's phrase.[91] The jaw also indicates an atavistic propensity for crime, according to criminological theories from Lombroso that Norris encountered through Nordau's *Degeneration* and Zola's *Human Beast*.[92] Supporting the arc of the plot, in which McTeague and Trina each revert to their racial types, is a broader discourse already noted in *Vandover and the Brute* on the threat that "primitives" posed to Anglo-Saxons.[93] Beyond the portraits of McTeague and Trina, the complex of ideas about race and "race impulses" supports the novel's typology of the Polk Street neighborhood and McTeague's building, whose inhabitants range down a supposed ethnic hierarchy from aged Anglo-Saxons to the junk-dealer Zerkow, whose particularly vile portrait features "cat-like lips" and "prehensile fingers" meant to connote a "Jewish" passion to possess gold (*McTeague*, 28). The invocation of scientific knowledge, a strategy Norris found in Zola, legitimates the normative position of the novel's narrative observer and thus these racist stereotypes.[94]

As McTeague's nature is indexed by his jaw and hands, Trina's is indicated by her chin, hair, and their relation to each other in her "economical little body." The "adorable" chin quivers at critical moments, among them her first experience of sexual desire for McTeague and her loss of possessions when the couple must auction their belongings (*McTeague*, 51, 107, 156). The qualities initially associated with the chin—sexual reticence and the "peasant" impulse to save—crowd out all others. In contrast to the parsimonious chin, Trina's hair is "heavy, abundant, odorous," a "sable tiara" that is frequently noted as absorbing all the vitality of her face. A signifier of sensuality at the time the novel was published, the hair's "sweet, heavy, enervating" "feminine perfume" first awakens the beast in McTeague.[95] She stops combing and braiding the locks as her mania for saving increases. Most revealing is the *relationship* of Trina's hair and chin: the hair's weight tips her head back and forces her chin forward, to McTeague's delight (*McTeague*, 47, 184). That is, the disorderly mass pushes Trina's chin—and thus the passions associated with it—into the jutting position, indicating atavism, which McTeague's jaw naturally assumes. Her "passion for her money" and "perverted love" for her husband become the two poles of her emotional life (*McTeague*, 171).

Fittingly, the jaw and the chin each frame the mouth, an organ for satisfying McTeague's and Trina's complementary appetites. Mark Seltzer's "thermodynamic" reading of *Vandover and the Brute* identifies a coordinated economy of expenditure and preservation in the protagonist's decline into a gibbering degenerate.[96] What Vandover embodies jointly is split in *McTeague* into the pleasure McTeague takes in consuming and taking and that which Trina takes in saving and withholding. Seltzer's argument for a coordinated equilibrium seems contradicted, however, by the important role of chance in Norris's fiction. The narrator of *McTeague* remarks that happenstance brought McTeague and Trina face to face, allowing their "mysterious" sexual instincts to knit together (*McTeague*, 53). Trina's similarly fortuitous win in the lottery tips their socially acceptable economic appetites into atavistic splurging and hoarding.[97] As in *L'Assommoir*, contingent events seem to confirm hereditary fate. But if the jaw of the one and the chin of the other are connected, what links McTeague's hands and Trina's hair?

McTeague's hands are a figure for his violent nature, but the "hands of the old-time car-boy" gained their shape when the young McTeague pulled rock from the earth for its transformation into gold (*McTeague*, 6). The impulses associated with them may be hereditary, but the hands' form and activity is historical, that is, they figure not only his urges but also the time and place in history in which they erupt. The moment is carefully chosen: whether extracting it from the earth or from Trina, McTeague's hands supply the jaws and mouth with a specific commodity—gold—that means all others. Nonetheless, McTeague and other characters are susceptible to a magical quality in money's expression of value, inherent in its role in transforming labor from a concrete, individual form to the abstract, externalized form in which the relationship of people to each other is expressed by things.[98] A primitive veneration of the material signifier abides in the social (hence historical) agreement over money's meaning, which is to say that in McTeague the brute will emerge, but how it emerges is contingent rather than eternal.

If McTeague's hands reveal the role of labor in money's signification of value, Trina's hair—the other term in the novel's paired pairs of body figures—reveals the role of desire. Trina's windfall disrupts the "normal" (capitalist) relationship of labor, money, and value. ("Why should I win?" Trina says to the gathered crowd, but then asks herself, in free indirect style: ". . . why shouldn't she? After all, it was not a question of effort or merit on her part"; *McTeague*, 65). As labor reverts to violence (those hands), parsimony reverts to the pure desire of possession (that hair). The problem is one of signification: Trina can no longer believe in the social fiction that money requires to exist. "She would look at the paper that Uncle Oelbermann had given her, and tell herself that it represented five thousand dollars. But in the end this ceased to satisfy her, she must have the money itself" (*McTeague*, 195). Trina's hoarding is ostensibly a regression to her peasant nature, but perhaps it is *money* that actually reverts, from a universal equivalent back to a thing to hold and cherish. The more primitive and unruly the hair, the greater the urge to possess this thing that no longer signifies value yet retains its magical attraction.

The novel's identification of the social, and pathological, nature of money through the rise and fall of McTeague and Trina is reinforced by Maria's stories about her family's gold plates, which she tells for her pleasure and to which Zerkow listens for his own. Zerkow marries Maria so that he can hear the stories every night, and eventually comes to believe that the gold service actually exists. After giving birth to a sickly, "hybrid" child Maria snaps out of her delusion and denies she even told such tales, leaving her husband convinced that she is hiding the treasure (*McTeague*, 135). He murders her after ransacking the house and is found drowned in the bay clutching a bag of tin plates and rusty utensils. For Zerkow, speaking of gold makes it exist, which may be the case for money too: its physical signifier means value because people say it does. Stories within a story, Maria's tales have a parallel in *McTeague*'s narrative discourse, where gold-colored images (from dental fillings and the gilt tooth to spots of light) proliferate to the point that "gold" as a linguistic signifier is disconnected from signification and finally refers only to other instances of itself. The semiotic confusion that *McTeague*'s characters experience bleeds into the text that creates them, extending its delirious pleasure to readers while also alerting them to their own participation in fictions of value.[99]

There is no evidence that Norris doubted the ethnic stereotypes he used to create characters in *McTeague*, but by this point in the novel we are well beyond protruding mandibles and peasant hoarding into something more troubling both for the world Norris describes and for naturalist mimesis. It is worth comparing the abundance of legs in *L'Assommoir* to the proliferation of gold in *McTeague*. The semantic play in the one is inverted in the other: in *L'Assommoir* too many things signify "leg"; in *McTeague*, "gold" signifies too much. The ubiquity of signifiers connected to Gervaise's bad limb figures the impossibility of escaping the determinisms of heredity and milieu. In *McTeague*, in contrast, the ubiquity of signifieds generated by a four-letter word reveals the fragility of a semiotic system that people must believe in for capitalism to operate. In both story and narrative discourse, the semiosis of value generates confusion about what money means and proves to be easily upset by its own contradictions. McTeague and Trina are not done in by the force of their milieu but by its failings, which resonate in the novel's depiction of their disaster.

In *McTeague*, then, figurative language concerning the body ultimately exposes the historicity of the capitalist organization, in turn-of-the-century California, of what Norris considered human nature. Violence and desire may be yoked to the production of value by the money-form, but through their transformation, not suppression. Body figures in *McTeague* break open the determinism of Zola's naturalism to show the reader the mutability of social forms. Pathologies of the body rooted in late nineteenth-century U.S. nativism meet the critical view of the pathologies of capitalism that Norris continued to develop in *The Octopus* (1901) and *The Pit* (1903), the first two volumes of his unfinished *Epic of the Wheat*. At the same time, the breakdown of the system of money through an excess of desire and a dearth of belief—which becomes part of *McTeague*'s linguistic fabric—works against the foundational assumption in naturalist mimesis that words have both a figurative and objective relationship to things. Without attributing too much importance to Norris's post-gold-rush California milieu, the use of body figures in new circumstances seems to have pushed naturalist methods into new, possibly self-reflective, epistemological terrain. Which is to say again that the history of form in naturalist fiction cannot be separated from the emergence, extension, and dissolution of the naturalist literary field.

THE CIVILIZED NERVE

Shimazaki Tōson's *Spring* (1908) also uses figurative language related to the body to expose the mutability of social forms, not to explore capitalist semiotics but rather the possibility and consequences of resisting ideologies of progress that naturalize the here and now. *Spring* offers an alternative to triumphalist histories of Japan's Meiji period (1868–1912), when a new state and civil-society reformers carried out projects of "civilization and enlightenment" (*bunmei kaika*) that resulted in such sweeping transformations of daily life that the historian Takashi Fujitani calls them "cultural terror."[100] The story of *Spring* is one of suffering youth that reflected a general reassessment of the state's goals and means after victory (as it was seen in Japan) in the Russo-Japanese War of 1904–05.[101] Through a quality of "double vision" first noted by Miyoshi Yukio, the novel presents a twofold critique of the actions of the Japanese state in the 1880s and Japanese society after the war.[102] The pathological nerve is a key trope, but with a different meaning than found in *The Fortune of the Rougons* or *Vandover and the Brute*. In the depiction of Aoki, one of a pair of characters at the center of the novel, the nerve is a figure for a critical view of state and society, while nervous illness figures the consequences of resistance. The story of the second of the pair, Kishimoto, dramatizes a shift by many writers in Tōson's generation from overt opposition toward the cultivation of a literature of the self that they imagined withstood instrumental appropriation. The form of *Spring* reflects the change and reveals a meta-literary reflection on the relationship of observation and expression which, like the exploration of the semiosis of value in *McTeague*, suggests a meditation on the techniques of naturalist mimesis.

Spring appeared at a turning point in naturalist fiction in Japan. As I explained in the previous chapter, the naturalist works that appeared around the turn of the century, by Kosugi Tengai, Tayama Katai, Nagai Kafū, and other writers known as "Zolaists," were founded on the exhaustively descriptive *shajitsu*—"realism"—that was a response to the sentimental fiction of the 1890s. In his early work Tōson was known as a poet, but his novel *The Broken Commandment* (*Hakai*, 1906), about discrimination against so-called *burakumin*, was the first contribution to naturalist fiction in Japan by a writer who had not been part of the Zolaist push.[103] It was more overtly critical than earlier naturalist works, but from a perspective that amplified their mutedly romantic depiction of oppressed individuals. Although Katai's novella *The Quilt* (*Futon*, 1907) came to be seen as the beginning of a turn toward egocentric naturalist fiction in Japan (the "I-novel"), it arguably built on the romantic individualism of *The Broken Commandment*.

The importance of the body in the Zolaist period of naturalist fiction in Japan can be seen in Katai's pivotal story "The End of Jūemon" ("Jūemon no saigo," 1902), about a middle-aged delinquent responsible for a string of arsons in a village that seems to breed misfits. The story's narrator—a visitor from Tokyo—ponders whether Jūemon's behavior has environmental or hereditary causes (there is a history of murder in the family), and finds Jūemon's character imprinted on his visage: "Across a red face with glaring eyes was cast the shadow of truly dreadful vice and abandon," the narrator recalls. "All the traces of the history of his miserable life seemed to be woven into its devious folds."[104] The problem of Jūemon's behavior has a figurative correlate in a deformity caused by a loop of his intestines that protrudes into the scrotum, swelling it grotesquely. The scrotum connotes massive sexual appetites but also their unsatisfiability because it is the cause of ostracism suffered since childhood. Such interplay between Jūemon's body's physical form and its figurative connotations reappears in an exchange that connects his predicament to the transformations of the Meiji period. A man from a nearby village urges Jūemon to remake himself in Tokyo: "Really, just apply yourself because you are certain to succeed," he says, using a Meiji-era phrase for success and self-advancement, *risshin*, which translates literally as "raising the body." "Not with this body," Jūemon replies. In its physicality it repels ideological imprecations.[105] The villagers ultimately drown Jūemon and the narrator's final glimpse is of a "face horribly bloated . . . eyes staring dreadfully, mucus trickling from nose to half-open mouth, huge scrotum dangling limply" ("Jūemon," 116).

Jūemon's end reflects the tendency that Iwasa Sōshirō notes in many works of early Japanese naturalism to depict a beast-like "nature within" erupting into disastrous conflict with society. After the Russo-Japanese War, Iwasa argues, the trope was replaced by representations of "nature" in states of pain, illness, or decomposition. Katai's story "One Soldier" ("Ippeisotsu," 1908), about a soldier in the Russo-Japanese War dying of beriberi, reflects the general shift in naturalist fiction as well as Katai's own experience as a war correspondent.[106] Other examples abound, including Tōson's *Broken Commandment*, which uses the rhetoric of illness in its ambiguous critique of discrimination, and *Family* (*Ie*, 1911), which makes the transmission of disease within two intermarried clans a metaphor for their difficulty adapting to the new society.[107] Indeed, from this time onward figurative connections between individual disease and social pathology became common in works of naturalism in Japan. Afflictions of the nerves such as neurasthenia, already present in early works such as Kafū's *Flowers of Hell* (*Jigoku no hana*, 1902), were especially favored in this kind of critique. Nervous diseases (*shinkei byō*) and problems caused by a nervous temperament (*shinkei shitsu*) had been connected to "civilization" in professional and popular medical discourse since Japanese neurologists and psychiatrists began to incorporate this part of the body into medicine in the 1880s.[108] (Nervous tissue was not part of the Chinese-derived system of medicine that was dominant in Japan until the Meiji period.) Although George Beard considered Americans to be especially susceptible to neurasthenia, in Japan it came to be called "Meiji disease" for its connection to the era's transformations.[109] In literature, the often morbid fascination with nerves was compounded by Nordau's contention in *Degeneration*, with which many Japanese writers were familiar, that the new European developments which they found most exciting, from naturalism to symbolism, were the result of nervous disorders.[110] Behind some of the new literature of nerves, then, lurked a self-image of writers as dysfunctional products of a pathological society.

Spring begins as a roman à clef whose characters are recognizably the young writers active in the journal *Literary World* (*Bungakukai*) in the 1890s, including the poet Kitamura Tōkoku (as Aoki) and Tōson himself (as Kishimoto). As Tōson examines the frustrations of his generation, which one observer in the novel calls "the youth of the new age, battling forward," he also takes a sympathetic position in contemporary debates over the generation that came of age after the Russo-Japanese War, which commentators considered materialistic and apathetic to national concerns. In one of the novel's most famous lines Aoki declares, "Japan today is nothing but a tomb for youth."[111] In the novel's double vision, Aoki's indictment also applies to the period after the war and ultimately to the Meiji civilizing project as a whole. Such a critical attitude toward Japanese modernity does not waver, but as the novel's form gradually shifts from a generational roman à clef to a third-person "I-novel" focused on the younger poet Kishimoto, the broad social critique of the early part of the novel narrows to a story of personal aesthetic struggles that are a markedly different response to the social changes of the Meiji period.

Spring is structured by a series of reunions of what the narrator refers to as "the group," opening with Kishimoto's meeting with Aoki and two other friends near Mt. Fuji after an extended journey to western Japan. Early in the novel the gatherings are dominated by literary debates and lamentations over the indifference of society toward the young men's ambitions. At one gathering Aoki shouts of sepulchral Japan, "There's no life! Or originality! Naive drivel, that's all the poetry you hear!" Another member tells Kishimoto that the present age doesn't tolerate the dreams of the young. He wonders if they were all born too early (*Haru*, 107, 186, 243). Over some three years the gatherings' energy wanes as enthusiasm cools and practicalities loom. The drift from aesthetic fraternity to nostalgic companionship is punctuated by two events. Midway through *Spring* Aoki commits suicide, and at its end Kishimoto departs Tokyo for a teaching position in the city of Sendai that will support his poetry. Up to Aoki's suicide the narrative focus moves from character to character, supporting the novel's depiction of "the group" as representative of a generation. Although the longest sections of this part of the novel focus on Kishimoto and Aoki, they are only the first among peers. After Aoki's disappearance Kishimoto, struggling to support his mother and the family of an imprisoned brother, gradually becomes the novel's sole narrative focus. Kishimoto's increasing distance from members of the group is highlighted by the fact that the narrative now focalizes their infrequent meetings through him. Although some critics argue that even in the beginning of *Spring* other characters only serve to reveal Kishimoto's personality and state of mind, the narrowing of the narrative focus in the later part indisputably changes the novel's themes, from the anguish of a generation to that of an individual.[112]

Tōson's examination of the quandary of youth in the Meiji era pairs Aoki and Kishimoto from an early point. Aoki's wife Misao remarks the similarity of their temperaments, each imagines himself in a metaphorical prison, and Aoki first attempts suicide with a dagger (he succeeds with a noose), a method that Kishimoto considers himself.[113] A portrait of Aoki in the first scene notes that his appearance and manner, from knitted brow, wan cheeks, and "intrepid, arrogant" forehead to a habit of glaring at things around him, revealed "an exceptionally sensitive nervous temperament" (*hijō ni kabin na shinkeishitsu*). The sum total seemed to say that this was a man "who would not stop until beaten and crushed." Aoki's decline, which is foreshadowed here, is tracked by the fraying of his nerves. Kishimoto remarks that Aoki's recent work reveals "unfathomable anxiety" and may show him on the way to madness (*Haru*, 6, 82, 85). Struggling against intense fatigue and losing the will to write, Aoki meditates ceaselessly on his situation: "It became a habit, and even when there was no need, he thought," the narrator explains. "He thought, he thought, even worn out he still thought. There was hardly a moment when his mind was at rest" (*Haru*, 136–37).

Tōson presents causes for Aoki's decline beyond his recent difficulty writing. In an old letter Misao finds after his death, Aoki intertwines his condition with the history of Japan in the Meiji period. According to the letter (drawn from one by Tōkoku), he inherited his nervous constitution from his mother, who also inculcated a desire for fame that became a "disease" (*yamai*) leading him astray in his teenage years (*Haru*, 204, 206, 207). The first of many periods of "melancholia" (*kiutsubyō*) came when his political ambitions were crushed by the government's suppression of campaigns for liberal democracy in the 1880s. Indignation and anger "as a youngster of nervous temperament" sent him to bed for several months (*Haru*, 208–9). Entering the university, he resolved to battle the philosophy of survival of the fittest spreading from Europe, and then to fight for justice through political fiction in the manner of Victor Hugo, only to face continuing despair as a result of his "brain disease" (*nōbyō*) and a final fall from the ladder of worldly ambition (*Haru*, 210–11).

The nerve in *Spring* carries the combination of physical and figurative meanings that is seen so often in naturalist mimesis. Its deterioration is the cause of Aoki's suicidal melancholia, and in this sense is a synecdoche for his physical-mental being, but it is also a metonym for his relationship to the world, particularly the collision of his idealism with the Meiji state. Tōson repeatedly underlines the connection between Aoki's "exhausted" nerves and the fatigue that comes from his "battles with the world" (*Haru*, 107, 132). If the nerve is a figure for resistance, the *ailing* nerve thus is a figure for its consequences. The status of the nerve in the novel is intentionally paradoxical: Aoki's body is both degenerate and "civilized," unlike the primitive, ethnic, proletarian bodies of *McTeague*. Unlike the vague origins of the family "crack" in *The Fortune of the Rougons*, moreover, the causes of Aoki's nervous "derangement," to use Zola's phrase, are the state and society. The ostensible triumph of the civilizing project is turned on its head: *bunmei kaika* destroys what it makes. Description of Aoki's body, then, is a means of pointed, political critique.

Although Aoki's counterpart Kishimoto contemplates suicide too, he arrives at an individualistic accommodation with the world. Kishimoto's face has a "melancholy" (*chin'utsu*) cast that reflects a "pitiful disposition" by turns "haughty yet meek, radical yet cowardly, excitable yet hesitant" (*Haru*, 10). The contradictions of his character reverberate throughout the novel. Although a poet he struggles to communicate, a problem highlighted by a counterpoise between description of his physical sensations and mental turmoil, as if he cannot transpose his worldly existence into words.[114] Suffering from uncertainty about his artistic ambitions and the frustrations of his love for a former student, he begins a pilgrimage to nowhere. Upon arriving at the coast he contemplates the sea, "a cold, meaningless tomb" where he might "bury his hopes, his love, his young life." Thinking it would be "pointless" (*tsumaranai*) to die when there is so much in the world that he does not know, however, he turns away (*Haru*, 100–101). It is not clear until after Aoki's death that such a commitment to experience, periodically reiterated, ultimately is a commitment to artistic creation. In his dark moments Kishimoto repeats to himself, "create, create," and as the life of the group becomes sterile he shuts himself up in pursuit of a "way" (*michi*) that would be his alone, a means to complete the work that Aoki left unfinished (*Haru*, 251, 253). He again considers suicide and emerges with a renewed commitment by reasoning that the obligation to "find his own way" is more important than even the obligation to his impoverished family. "Everyone must find his own way," he reasons. "Not knowing even why one lives as one does, where would be the filial devotion in that?" As he departs for Sendai, where he will teach and write while sending money to Tokyo, he "dreams of a fantasy world, not knowing when it would arrive," and thinks to himself, "Even as I am I want to live" (*Haru*, 285, 299).

Kishimoto considers himself Aoki's successor, but the denouement of Kishimoto's story shows that their responses to Meiji society differ fundamentally. Where Aoki's art was connected to political struggle, and in some ways memorialized its failure, Kishimoto's art is a personal undertaking. If Aoki's nervous exhaustion indicates a conflict with a misshapen society, and the difficulty of maintaining a critical view of it, we can say that Kishimoto's struggle is to find a desire to live (a "way") that such a society will condone. Significantly Kishimoto, regardless of his "depressive disposition" (*ukkutsushita seishitsu*), is never described in the novel with the vocabulary of nerves (*Haru*, 42). One might speculate that Tōson hesitated to have a character based on himself suffer from nervous illness. Regardless, the contrast between the somatic description of Aoki's nervous degeneration and the more conventionally "psychological" description of Kishimoto's struggles reproduces, in the novel's mimesis, the difference between Aoki's active, oppositional position and Kishimoto's passive, acquiescent one. The nerve may be crushed, but the mind can adjust.

The change in *Spring*'s techniques of mimesis corresponds to its change in form. The shift from roman à clef to I-novel is often attributed to the publication of Katai's *Quilt* while Tōson was working on *Spring*.[115] The change of genres underscores the difference between Aoki's and Kishimoto's responses to the predicament of a generation, however, and through the narrowing of the narrative focus it supports the elaboration of Kishimoto's individualistic solution. It thus seems far from coincidental. The change isolates Aoki's critique in both temporal and formal terms: his rejection of the society created by the Meiji state belongs to another time and another form, each left behind. Yet the discontinuity of genres, like the difference in descriptive techniques, blocks a reading of Kishimoto's resolution as a simple overcoming of Aoki's despair. What emerges is an ambivalent sense of belatedness: there was a time when people believed another society was possible, and suffered for believing so; Tōson's generation—in the 1890s *and* after the Russo-Japanese War—bears responsibility for it not seeming possible now.[116] The nerve's disappearance is a failure of nerve.

But isn't there another way we should *also* read such changes in form? The proposition that body, mind, and society can be observed and described with the same scientific techniques was fundamental to the naturalist mimesis that traveled the world after the appearance of *L'Assommoir*. Supporting this proposition was the combination of corporeal etiology and corporeal representation behind naturalist body figures: on the one hand, physiological theories of human behavior, and on the other, descriptions of personality, behavior, and ultimately social institutions through parts of the body. By the end of *Spring*, descriptions of body, mind, and society are decoupled. Each is described differently and the body loses its figurative function. The novel moreover *stages* observation in two different ways, with different formal qualities and vocabularies. "Observation" is exposed as a phenomenon of literary form. Formally, *Spring* seems to present naturalism's position that scientific observation legitimates literary expression, which is intact in the representation of Aoki's decline and death, as a proposition no less axiomatic—contrived—than Dide's "crack." In addition to being a generational story and a critique of the Meiji civilizing project, *Spring* is a meta-literary reflection on the techniques of naturalist mimesis.

Such a reflection extends to naturalism's contradictory politics. The bracketing of Aoki's ideals as both valid and impossible exposes the contradiction in naturalist fiction between reformist intent and deterministic theory.[117] The gap is present at the start, in the Rougon-Macquart novels: however much they mean to reveal the truth of late nineteenth-century French society, the closed circuit of hereditary and social determinism that is a basic part of their social analytic seems to exclude the possibility of change. We have seen such a contradiction reproduced in *McTeague* and *Spring*. They introduce history and contingency into the representations of their respective societies, yet they do so through deterministic theories of ethnic atavism and nervous degeneration. The contradiction also becomes a matter of form, with confusion over the meaning of money entering the narrative discourse of *McTeague* and the bifurcation of narrative form cordoning resistance off from "life" in *Spring*. As a vehicle for critique, the naturalist body is contradictory in many ways.

THE TRANSFORMATION OF MIMESIS

Taking pathological bodies as the keystone of social description was the foundation of a critical stance toward societies that naturalist writers considered to be pathological in themselves. Zola's work combined new scientific ideas with techniques drawn from earlier European realism to show the intersection of heredity and milieu in determining the lives and fates of characters, but ultimately, Zola believed, to show the origin and development of social forms. The synecdoches and metonymies of the physical body that I have called "body figures" were key to this project. Through the infamy of several novels—most importantly, *L'Assommoir*—naturalist techniques of social representation circulated around the planet. Writers appropriated these techniques to describe and analyze societies as different as Aluísio Azevedo's Brazil (in

The Mulatto), Minna Canth's Finland (in *Lopo the Peddler*), Norris's United States (in *McTeague*) and Tōson's Japan (in *Spring*). Preserving the premise that the naturalist text could connect individual and social pathologies both scientifically and figuratively, they identified sources of bodily-social derangement that often were more specific than the vaguely parallel "cracks" of Dide's brain and Louis-Napoléon's France in *The Fortune of the Rougons*. In doing so they interrupted the seamless relationship of hereditary and social determinism that made fate and contingency identical in *L'Assommoir*. Nonetheless, the contradictions found at the start of naturalism's travels remained: the proposition that figurative language was scientific; the notion that literary "observation" was objective social investigation; and the coexistence of determinism and reformism.

The history of naturalist body figures can offer several methodological lessons for studying literature and other forms of expressive culture on a large scale. A first lesson concerns chronologies. As a far-reaching *transnational* phenomenon, naturalism seems to have barely existed before *L'Assommoir*, even though the novel appeared more than a decade after early naturalist works in France such as *Germinie Lacerteux*, and seven volumes into Zola's Rougon-Macquart series. The chronology of naturalist fiction in transnational terms differs from its national chronologies in France, Argentina, Japan, or any other country. At the same time, we have seen that naturalism had a great, and uneven, impact in local contexts, with *L'Assommoir* becoming a rallying cry for establishing realism in some places but for rejecting it—or at least its naturalist version—in others. Either response shows that "local" literary histories shaped the reception of naturalism and thus are also part of its transnational history. Understanding this kind of messy history requires working at several different scales and giving up any expectation of uniformity.

Another lesson concerns the circulation of literary techniques. The history of circulation that was a key part of the history of the transnational field was undeniably a history of influential works. Perhaps more importantly, however, it was a history of influential techniques that could be detached from the works themselves. "Body figures" were one such technique, adaptable to many situations within the scope of the assumptions about the relationship between bodies and societies that underpinned them. The extraction of techniques from the works in which they appeared was aided by the programmatization of naturalism as a method through manifestos, prefaces, and other parts of the critical discourse that accompanied it as it traveled. In a broader perspective, the focus of our attention should be what writers *took* from works such as *L'Assommoir*, as much as the works themselves. Earlier, I said that the history of naturalism was a history of intentionally chosen fragments and pieces; one could also say it was a history of piracy and bricolage.

A third lesson concerns the cognate genres of social knowledge (including, in its early form, neurology) from which naturalism drew ideas and legitimation. The evolving relationship with such "fellow travelers"—Lucas succeeded by Lombroso, Beard, and Nordau, to cite examples given in this chapter—was a hallmark of naturalism as both a method and a literary phenomenon. Yet once the key proposition that Zola drew from Lucas—that a writer could objectively describe social relations by describing the body—became a technique of representation, writers did not need to read Lucas's two-volume *Treatise* to use the technique. One could say that such ideas were "folded into" naturalist form and traveled within it, something that undoubtedly helped the adoption of the techniques by writers for whom the ideas themselves might have been arcane, if not alien. In the early decades of naturalism, some such underlying ideas were widely accepted and thus the techniques themselves could be adapted without controversy, each iteration deepening the role of the techniques in naturalist fiction as a whole. As a consequence, however, contradictions that were rooted in naturalism's initial constellation of ideas, such as that between determinism and reformism, became contradictions of form.

Finally, the application of naturalist techniques such as body figures to new social conditions could force such contradictions to the surface, with unexpected results. The simple fact that conditions in turn-of-the-century California and Meiji-era Japan—to use examples from this chapter—differed from those in Third Republic France may in itself have forced history into Zola's deterministic identification of fate and chance. The differences are apparent in the stories of *McTeague* and *Spring* (needless to say), but they may also be a reason why the two novels use their explorations of the relationship between individuals and society to argue for the contingency of social structures. We also saw that the differences seem to have propelled changes in the two novels' literary form—the appearance of semiotic confusion in the narrative discourse of *McTeague* and the mutation of narrative form from roman à clef to I-novel in *Spring*. If so, adaptation was a formally generative process that realized possibilities in naturalist fiction that would not have emerged otherwise. At the same time, I have argued, we can see in these novels the traces of reflections on method of a kind quite different from the many naturalist manifestos, not trumpeting the program but rather acknowledging, perhaps unwillingly, where it stumbles. That *McTeague* and *Spring* responded to contradictions in naturalist method differently—the one grappling with problems of language, the other of observation—should lead us to recognize that the fact they responded to such contradictions was typical, while relinquishing the expectation that responses in different parts of the world should be the same.

Let's not over-celebrate naturalist multiplicity. As it traveled, naturalist fiction not only did not abandon the physiological determinism present at its origins and folded into its form, it embraced it in new guises. Yet the undeniability of social difference always posed a challenge to such determinism. As another consequence of naturalism's passage through the planet, then, the fault lines of naturalist mimesis inevitably reappeared: a form in confrontation with the world and with itself.

CHAPTER 3

The Unbound Woman

A journalist in Émile Zola's 1880 novel *Nana* describes its unrestrained heroine as a "golden fly" who spreads social rot, "corrupting and deranging Paris between her snowy thighs."[1] The same might be said of *Nana* itself, which was the second of Zola's novels to bring naturalism to international attention. In the decades after its release an epidemic of sexually and economically independent female characters who straddled the line between stage performance and prostitution appeared in naturalist fiction from North America to East Asia. The phenomenon of the "Nana figure" is the point of departure of this chapter. Opponents of naturalism might have agreed that naturalist fiction was a literary plague. For us, however, the Nana figure is an opportunity to turn from the roles that figurative language and the degenerate body played in naturalist mimesis to another set of issues that the history of naturalist fiction raises for large-scale literary study: the formal transformations that occur when a character with a complex relationship to one social environment is introduced into another.

Naturalist fiction is known, and sometimes reviled, for the female characters at the center of many of its narratives. We are already familiar with Edmond and Jules de Goncourt's Germinie, Zola's Gervaise, and Frank Norris's Trina, to whom we could add Luisa, the adulterous bourgeois wife in José Maria de Eça de Queirós's *Cousin Basilio* (*O Primo Basilio*, 1878) from Portugal; Katinka, the melancholic spouse of a railway clerk in Herman Bang's *By the Wayside* (*Ved Vejen*, 1886) from Denmark; Maggie, the misled daughter in Stephen Crane's *Maggie, A Girl of the Streets* (1893); Sonoko, the teacher raped by her school principal in Nagai Kafū's *Flowers of Hell* (*Jigoku no hana*, 1902) from Japan; and the rural innocent turned celebrated prostitute at the center of Federico Gamboa's *Santa* (1903) from Mexico. As this short list suggests, when women in naturalist fiction are central characters they are frequently prostitutes, wayward wives, nymphomaniacs, or in some way sexually deprived and yearning. Naturalist fiction often seems both fascinated and frightened by the idea of a woman who is self-liberated through her own labor, her resistance to conventional marriage, and her rejection of reproductive sexuality. Such characters were favorites for shocking the polite literary world, but they seem to have been too dangerous for writers to allow them to be truly free. Fatalistic plots and deterministic ideas about women's sexuality restrain them. The significant exceptions are to be found in the work of the few women naturalist writers, such as Victoria Benedictsson in Sweden, Minna Canth and Ina Lange in Finland, and Edith Wharton on the edges of naturalism in the United States.

Within this larger group, characters reminiscent of Zola's Nana were ubiquitous in naturalist fiction. The Nana figure, however, was not simply a character type. Nana herself did not come from nowhere but was assembled from bits and pieces of discourse on prostitution, public hygiene, and urban life; fiction about prostitutes; and popular clichés. The Nana figure was produced in turn through an engagement with *Nana* that included parodies, pirated sequels, and original works but extended to nonliterary forms such as songs and dances. Among the most important of the Nana figure's "sisterly resemblances" was an antagonistic relationship with the society that created her. Yet the nature of the antagonism varied with the society that was its target, making the Nana figure seem less like a traveling character than a social analytic that could be applied in many places.

The Nana figure raises questions that must be central to understanding naturalist fiction as a transnational phenomenon and thus to crafting methods for studying geographically extensive histories of literature, film, visual art, and other expressive forms. What role does circulation play in the extraction of a character from a novel? If a character like Nana was the product of a specific intellectual milieu, how does the character change when separated from its "constitutive discourses"? The plots in which Nana and her sisters appear depended on changes in the structures of family and labor that are fundamental to capitalist societies. Was the Nana figure a reflection of such changes, or did she contribute to the gendering of capitalist modernity, a process that scholars now see unfolding on a transnational scale?[2] Answering these questions requires resisting some tendencies in current studies of "world literature." Much of this scholarship—for example, on the "diffusion" of the European novel—focuses exclusively on the literary, in an implicit if not intentional step back from a view of fiction as the product of both literary and nonliterary discourses.[3] The history of the Nana figure, however, challenges us to examine naturalist fiction's changing relationships with fellow-traveling genres of social thought as it moved around the world. As I observed in chapter 1, "World Lit" arguments also tend to treat literary forms as essentially fixed when they depart their place of origin, leaving writers elsewhere in a position of imitating, rejecting, or working out compromises with (typically) European models.[4] The history of the Nana figure, in contrast, reveals a process of continual transformation that cannot be separated from the geographical circulation of naturalist fiction. As much as the Nana figure was a large-scale phenomenon, moreover, its variations show writers responding to local political and economic contradictions.

Comparing *Nana* to later "Nana narratives," including the Japanese writer Kosugi Tengai's *New Year's Finery* (*Hatsu sugata*, 1900) and the American Theodore Dreiser's *Sister Carrie* (also 1900), reveals a set of central qualities for the Nana figure: performance, contagion, and mobility. These characteristics emerge as the concepts of society and the techniques of representation at work in *Nana* shift in relation to each other, allowing a transposition of the novel's dense narrative discourse into qualities of character. The change opens the Nana figure to possibilities for social investigation beyond those available in Zola's novel. Recognizing the transformations that occur through travel demands that we reconsider the role of *Nana* in the process. If the novel's "originality" was to draw existing tendencies in social thought and representation together into a constellation that was consequential because it could travel widely, Zola's character may be less the progenitor of the Nana figure than one of its early iterations.

CIPHER ASSEMBLED

Anna Coupeau, as Nana was formally named, entered the world in *L'Assommoir* (1877) as the daughter of its alcoholic protagonist Gervaise. A girl "who took to vice like a fish to water," she was sent to work making artificial flowers, but by the end of the novel she already had a career trading affection for finery (*L'Assommoir*, 427). *Nana* (1880) opens in a Parisian theater where she is to make her debut in the titular role of a comic opera, *The Blond Venus*. The first scene introduces all of the novel's main characters, who are either on stage or in the audience. They include actors and actresses such as Nana's rival Rose; Mignon, Rose's husband, agent, and pimp; Fauchery, critic, playwright, and later author of the "golden fly" article; and a number of aristocrats, among them Muffat, a pious court official, his wife Sabine, and her father Chouard, who is prominent in court like his son-in-law but unlike him, a rake. The audience waits feverishly for the curtain to rise, its curiosity heightened by the "sing-song vivacity" of Nana's name, which has been the center of a publicity blitz. A sexual current running through the audience is echoed in the insistence of Bordenave, the play's entrepreneur, in calling the theater a "brothel" (*Nana*, 24, 26). When Nana finally appears she sings and acts horribly—as Bordenave predicted to Fauchery—and the show seems lost until a cherubic young man calls out: "So chic!" Nana swiftly takes possession of the audience and the premier is a success. She has "something else," as Bordenave puts it, that makes her lack of talent irrelevant (*Nana*, 25, 35).

Zola contrasts scenes of two salons in the days after the premier, at Muffat's mansion and Nana's apartment, to illustrate the collapse of boundaries between high society and the demimonde that is one of the novel's narrative lines. Many of the well-placed men at the first gathering whisper their plans to meet at the second one. Lifted by the success of her play and financial support from Muffat, whom she captivates, Nana rises in society. Harassed by creditors and besotted men, however, she disappears from the high life and sets up house with an actor who abuses her and steals her savings. She is scarcely able to pay the "aunt" from her childhood—actually her former employer—who takes care of her sickly son. Working on the street again, she completes her education with the discovery that polite folk like the "filthy stuff" more than anyone else (*Nana*, 275). She makes her comeback by reenchanting Muffat, who gets her a part in a drama that flops, thanks to her, but which lets her launch a new career as a "grande dame," dictating women's fashion and entertaining men in a mansion provided by her patron. She begins "devouring" men and fortunes in a "mania of consumption" (*Nana*, 312, 414). Scandal looms when the young man who saved *The Blond Venus* attempts suicide after finding Nana sleeping with his older brother. The ruined Muffat, for his part, discovers Nana in bed with his father-in-law and retreats into Catholicism. After appearing once more in the theater—in scenes where she need only pose—Nana sells everything and disappears, only to resurface when her son contracts smallpox. Catching the disease from him, she dies in a hotel surrounded by rivals and ex-lovers who slowly file out, leaving her corpse alone. Outside, the Franco-Prussian War has just started and crowds in the street are shouting "To Berlin!" (*Nana*, 475).

The language of the body is common in *Nana*. Zola refers often to Nana's skin, its blond coat (*poil*), and most of all her genitals (*sexe*), the ensemble having "total power" over men and thus society. All are on view in the third act of *The Blond Venus*, when she appears on stage nude.[5] In his article, Fauchery says that her family's "spoiled blood" (*sang gâté*) had created in Nana a "nervous derangement of her woman's genitals" (*un détraquement nerveux de son sexe de femme*), a phrase that could have come from the enumeration of hereditary traits in the first Rougon-Macquart novel, *The Fortune of the Rougons* (*La Fortune des Rougon*, 1877) (*Nana*, 224). Figures of the body in the manner of *L'Assommoir* obviously are at work here: Nana's skin, adjacent to a corrupt elite, is a metonymy for social decay, while her vagina is a synecdoche for the vice-ridden society's desires. Perhaps because Zola made the connections between Nana's body, her behavior, and the world around her so obvious, however, skin and genitals do not generate figures with the complex associations of Gervaise's gimpy leg in *L'Assommoir*. Nana's resonance comes rather from the way Zola combined his sources for the novel to create perfect reciprocity between Nana and the society that made her.

Like many of Zola's characters, Nana took shape in a thick weave of theories of society and techniques of social description that mixed empirical observation with normative judgment. Perhaps the most significant strand came from the surveys of Parisian prostitution carried out by Alexandre Parent-Duchâtelet in the 1820s and 1830s, which became fixed points of reference for new regimes of regulation, debates over the social effects of the sex trade, and representations of the prostitute herself. In the fluidity of her career—call girl, actress, streetwalker, and well-kept mistress—Nana exemplifies one of Parent-Duchâtelet's greatest fears, that women could move easily in and out of prostitution, thereby introducing acquired vices into decent society. Programs to identify and regulate the activities of sex workers targeted such mobility, which became an important feature of the Nana figure.

(When she is working the streets Nana narrowly avoids arrest under laws inspired by Parent-Duchâtelet's work.)[6] Parent-Duchâtelet's observations were turned into clichés in novels and plays about prostitutes that flourished in nineteenth-century France—the most evident literary contribution to *Nana*—which included Victor Hugo's *Marion de Lorme* (1831) and Honoré de Balzac's *Cousin Bette* (*La Cousine Bette*, 1847), and in naturalist circles, Joris-Karl Huysmans's *Marthe, Story of a Whore* (*Marthe, histoire d'une fille*, 1876) and Edmond de Goncourt's *The Whore Elisa* (*La Fille Elisa*, 1877).[7] Like Parent-Duchâtelet's "typical" prostitute, Nana has a lastingly childish personality and rejects the bourgeois values of order and economy, yet is prone to fits of charity and religious sentiment. Physically she shares with the type a plump figure and a squawking voice hardly suited to the stage.[8] Zola's description of the erotic rapport between Nana and her audience also tapped longstanding associations of actresses with prostitution, strengthened by the recent appearance of the *café-concert* singer, an entertainer who offered sexual services to men. That Georges, the teenaged innocent who becomes infatuated with Nana, first glimpsed her on the stage reflects the moral peril that actresses were thought to pose.[9]

Works of urban reportage written in the wake of the Commune, such as Charles-Jérôme Lecour's *Prostitution in Paris and London, 1789–1871* (*La Prostitution à Paris et à Londres, 1789–1871*, 1872) and Maxime du Camp's *Paris, Its Organs, Functions, and Life* (*Paris, ses organes, ses fonctions et sa vie*, 1872), magnified prostitution into a problem threatening to engulf society. Their examinations of urban life drew on theories of hygiene to add shades of contagion and epidemic to the connection that Parent-Duchâtelet drew between prostitution and problems of public health.[10] A sense of hygienic danger is clear in Fauchery's description of Nana as a gilded vector of disease. The rapidly rising incidence of syphilis, which is transmissible in the womb, compounded the "venereal anxiety" (as Alain Corbin puts it) that such works inspired. In turn it connected them to another body of thought that shapes Nana: the theories of hereditary degeneration behind the family tree of the Rougon-Macquart novels. In *Nana* they are glimpsed in comments that her nervous derangement is the result of "a long heredity of poverty and liquor" and that she is driven by an "unconscious family rancor, passed down in the blood."[11] Nana was thus made of many of the elements that contributed to the medical models of cultural crisis that proliferated in meditations on social dislocation in late nineteenth-century France.[12]

Nana of course has a narrative and symbolic structure that is more complex than an assembly of theories and empirical observations. (Zola referred to *Nana* as a "poem of male desires.")[13] Although Zola applied theories of heredity directly to explain Nana's rancor toward her patrons, for example, the conceit of the golden fly also draws hereditary determinism into a metaphorical argument on social destruction. In the novel's ghastly ending, when Nana dies of smallpox as the crowd calls for the war that brought down the Second Empire, the narrator reprises and expands Fauchery's declaration that Nana poisoned men into the charge that she had poisoned "a people" (*Nana*, 224–25, 475). The notion of infection, initially derived from discourse on public health, thus becomes a master metaphor for social relations during the Second Empire. The metaphor is strengthened by Nana's mobility, which is coded as both cause and symptom of the diseased state of the society in which she moves.[14] The stress on vision in many of the novel's key scenes adds a dialectical quality to the hygienic metaphor by identifying the viewer as a willing participant in the epidemic (and muddying the issue of Nana's responsibility).

The epidemiological view of social relations is also supported by a series of correspondences that critics observe, through which social distinctions disappear in the crowd of men around Nana, female characters increasingly resemble her, and binary sexual difference begins to erode through episodes of cross-dressing and Nana's sexual relations with women.[15] Indeed, the infection that Nana spreads already seems pervasive at the beginning of the novel, when the audience responds to her stage debut with a uniformity which suggests that the virus of uncontrollable desire has been passing among its members for some time. The collective "fever" that seizes the Parisian crowd at the novel's end is only the most explicit example of self-destructive, yet happily contracted, mass infection (*Nana*, 462). Nana remains "the central flesh" of the hygienic metaphor, in a phrase from Zola's notes, but it is never clear whether she is the primary source of the infection racing through French society or simply its most visible embodiment.[16]

The difficulty establishing blame for what happens around Nana undeniably can be read as a misogynistic cliché, the all-destroying woman who cannot take responsibility for her acts because she has no subjectivity. From the perspective of the emergence of the Nana figure, however, it is also worth considering whether the novel is *unable* to assign her a fixed meaning. As men and their fortunes crumble around her, Nana maintains that she has done nothing which others did not want her to do—"They go after the women, when it's the men who demand things"—and Zola finally kills her with a disease having no relation to the rest of the novel (*Nana*, 456). (Despite the possibility of semantic displacement between *la petite vérole* and *la vérole*—smallpox and syphilis—it is difficult to see Nana's demise as an end that follows from her crimes.)[17] The final chapter's allegory of war fever likewise fails to contain her symbolic excess. On the contrary, the circumstances of Nana's death suggest not narrative closure so much as a deus ex machina that puts an end to a character who resists meaning and represented "the edge of the known world" to Zola, in Bernice Chitnis's phrase.[18] The novel's final image of "Venus decomposing," with hair the color of the sun streaming out from a slowly liquefying face, suggests more than anything horror over what she might mean (*Nana*, 474). If Nana's demise indicates both her resistance to meaning and Zola's turn away from it, however, the ambiguities of her end lend the character an openness to reinterpretation. It should not be surprising that Nana's final solitude, a sign of her ambiguity, became a characteristic motif of the Nana figure.

THE BIRTH OF THE NANA FIGURE

Nana began to be detached from *Nana* even before the novel was published. In 1877 Édouard Manet exhibited a painting titled *Nana* inspired by her depiction in *L'Assommoir*, which featured a woman in petticoats contemplating herself in a mirror and a top-hatted man gazing avidly from the side of the frame. Manet's tableau in turn was the basis for an infamous scene in *Nana*, in which she undresses and caresses herself in front of a mirror as a disheartened Muffat looks on.[19] Such kaleidoscopic mediations of Nana continued in the advance publicity for the novel. The launch began in May 1879 with a front-page announcement in the newspaper *Le Voltaire*, where *Nana* would be serialized, of a sensational sequel to *L'Assommoir*, and ended with posters bearing Nana's name plastered across Paris. On October 7, nine days before serialization started, *Le Voltaire* published a front-page excerpt that Zola said conveyed the novel's "moral and philosophical views."[20] The extract comprised the passage immediately preceding the scene before the mirror, which presents Fauchery's article on the golden fly in a style of "free indirect reading" as Muffat browses the piece. The *mise en abyme* epitomized Nana's already specular existence by offering Muffat's apprehension of the article on Nana as a précis of *Nana*. Henry Céard, one of the young writers in the "Médan group" that met at Zola's country house, wrote him the day before serialization commenced: "There is an enormous curiosity about *Nana*. The name is on every wall of Paris, as far as the eye can see. It verges on obsession and nightmare."[21] Even before the first installment arrived in kiosks, Nana's ubiquity had created a paradoxical uncertainty about who she was. The question frequently posed in the novel itself—"Who is Nana?"—was already being bruited in the world.[22]

The public curiosity about Nana, which made the novel about her Zola's most profitable one, quickly spread abroad. In 1880, the year *Nana* was released as a volume in France, it was translated into at least eight languages: Bengali, English, Italian, Modern Greek, Portuguese, Russian, Spanish, and Swedish. By 1883 there were translations into at least five more—Czech, Danish, German, Hungarian, and Serbo-Croatian—joined by 1890 by a growing number of retranslations and a version in Yiddish.[23] (By the turn of the century *Nana* had been translated into English at least four times, German three.) The history of translation reflects the prestige that Zola and French naturalism increasingly enjoyed around the world. Aspects of it also recall the complexities of the circuits through which naturalism traveled. A Bengali publisher, physically distant from European salons, released a translation in the same year that *Nana* appeared as a volume in France. Because of gaps in copyright protection, competing German translations appeared in Grossenhain and Budapest, while the first American translation appeared four years before the British one.[24] (Francophiles were not scarce among Bengali intellectuals, but if the Bengali edition was a double translation via English, the American edition would have been the intermediary.) That a Portuguese translation appeared in Brazil four years before the first one in Portugal reflected the tendency of educated Portuguese to read in French on the one hand, and the close eye that Brazilian intellectuals kept on developments in France on the other. Jewish emigration to the United States, with its unfamiliar language, was probably the only reason a Yiddish translation was made, since Jewish readers in Europe were likely to read the novel in the dominant language of the country in which they lived, if not in French. (For the same reason a Hebrew translation, for which there was hardly any market in the late nineteenth century, did not appear until 1930.)[25]

The early translations were often expurgated, sometimes with Zola's consent; many were abridged or even, like Nagai Kafū's 1903 Japanese version, essentially summaries.[26] Even relatively sanitized versions were subject to seizure by the authorities on grounds of obscenity, their publishers and translators put on trial and fined.[27] In some places such as Greece, however, the translation of *Nana* at all was the occasion for critical controversies that contributed to the rise of the realistic novel as a dominant literary form.[28] Like *L'Assommoir*, *Nana* was an "inciter, unifier, catalyzer" (to recall Yves Chevrel's phrase) that upset local literary fields whether it was praised or denounced. Pieces written in its defense, such as the foreword that Ayissalaos Yannopoulos Ipiriotis wrote when the Greek translation was published as a volume, became part of the critical discourse on naturalism that accompanied and sometimes preceded its arrival in different parts of the world.[29]

As the fame of *Nana* and Nana surged, Zola's character became a crossover product. In France, "Nana-tomical" caricatures appeared in the press, offering her the praise of mockery.[30] A parodic operetta, *Nana and Company* (*Nana et Cie*), joined the theatrical adaptation written by Zola and William Busnach, which premiered in 1881. Nana's musical career continued in a "Nana Polka" and the comical song "Nana's Donkey" ("L'Ane à Nana").[31] Her name was used to sell sweets and hats in Greece, and to describe a manner of dressing.[32] In the United States, other novels by Zola were marketed to stress their connection with her. One American publisher released its translation of *Nana* in 1880 with the subtitle *Sequel to "L'Assommoir,"* to associate it with Zola's first overseas sensation, but the renown of Gervaise's daughter seems to have been so profitable that the publisher re-released *L'Assommoir* two years later with the subtitle *Nana's Mother*. When the same press published its version of *Germinal* in 1885, the novel was called *Nana's Brother: Son of "Gervaise" and "Lantier" of "L'Assommoir."*[33] The commercial possibilities that Nana offered, which were all too appropriate considering the time she spends consuming goods and men, encouraged the separation of the character from the novel that bore her name.

Some of the most notable products to derive from Zola's novel were the *Nana*-inspired works that abounded in the decades after its publication. These ranged from pirated sequels and evident knockoffs, through original works that acknowledged their ties, to novels with indirect connections but in which traces of *Nana* and Nana seem clear. It was from these works that what I am calling the "Nana figure" emerged, aided by the way that commerce and the popular imagination had already extracted her from Zola's novel. The process began scarcely a week after the start of serialization with *Nana's Daughter, a Potty-Loving Novel by Mr. Émile Zola* (*La Fille à Nana, Roman orduraliste par M. Émile Zola*), a piece in the newspaper *Le Figaro* that purported to be the first installment of a story about Nana's offspring. The author, Albert Millaud, had recognized himself as Zola's model for Steiner, the lover of Nana's rival Rose.[34] In 1880 Cletto Arrighi, an inspiration for Italian *veristi* such as Giovanni Verga, moved Zola's heroine south in *Nana in Milan* (*Nanà a Milano*). The novel uses several months Nana is said to have spent in the city to criticize the political class of post-unification Italy.[35] The following year Alfred Sirven and Henri Leverdier followed Millaud's lead in France with a full-length sequel, *Nana's Daughter: A Novel of Parisian Manners* (*La Fille de Nana: Roman de moeurs Parisiennes*), which attempts to re-right the moral conventions that *Nana* inverts.[36] Like the retitled American editions mentioned earlier, these early descendants of *Nana* located themselves in the branches of the Rougon-Macquart family tree. (Some readers in the United States mistook the English translation of Sirven and Leverdier's riposte—which had the subtitle *A Continuation of and Sequel to Émile Zola's Novel of "Nana"*—for a new work by Zola.)[37]

Works less directly derivative of *Nana* announced their connection through references to the character and her novel. As I argued in chapter 1, such citations should be considered both acts of homage and efforts to legitimate authors' positions in local literary fields. *Olga and Lina* (*Olga i Lina*, 1882), by the Croatian novelist Eugen Kumičić, tells the story of a half-Hungarian prostitute (Lina) who enthralls an aristocrat happy to lose his fortune to her; she goes so far as to kill his wife (Olga) to take her place. Kumičić, who modeled several scenes on episodes in *Nana*, defended Zola in the Croatian press and proposed adapting naturalist methods to local mores. The target of *Olga and Lina*, a Germanized aristocracy happy to betray itself and the people, suggests that Kumičić saw in naturalism a method for exposing hypocrisy.[38] (The xenophobic tropes on which he relied recall the ethnic stereotypes at work in Norris's *McTeague*, 1899.) The Spanish novelist Eduardo López Bago, whose work drew inspiration from *Nana* and other novels by Zola, also seems to have regarded naturalism as a way to hone fiction for ideological combat. Estella, the central figure of López Bago's *The Prostitute* and *The Pale Woman* (*La Prostituta* and *La Pálida*, both 1884), the first two works of a naturalist tetralogy, is a girl from the Madrid slums who enters prostitution when her virginity is sold to a syphilitic marquis who is the secret owner of a chain of brothels. Later sleeping with his son, who already suffers syphilis in congenital form, she stimulates the full development of the disease. Supporting the parallels between Estella and Nana as vectors of corruption in societies enjoying their ruin is the revelation that the doctor who treats father and son is a devoted reader of Claude Bernard's *Introduction to the Study of Experimental Medicine* (*Introduction à l'étude de la médecine expérimentale*, 1865), the pretext for Zola's theory of the "experimental novel."[39]

The ways that some of these novels signal their ties to Zola illustrate the role that names play in many Nana narratives. While the "sing-song vivacity" of Nana's name contributed to her fame in- and outside *Nana*, as the novel moved through the world the name's vacant quality seems to have contributed to the Nana figure's indeterminate social identity. A character in *"The Worst Sort of People"* (*"Sämre folk,"* 1885), by the Finnish novelist Ina Lange, is a half-Russian girl named Nadja, in reflection of her Russian father but also, according to Riikka Rossi, in a reference to Nana. She migrates from the southwestern archipelago of Finland to Helsinki to work as a servant, later becomes a prostitute, and finally breaks into the theater world as a choir girl, corrupting those who come in contact with her as she cuts a path to St. Petersburg and Moscow. When her career as a singer turns sour she takes shelter in a home for fallen women run by Finnish nationalists, and rebuilds her life as a humble servant known by the Finnophone name Maja.[40] Nadja may signify the threat of Russian domination, and Maja the possibility of a response, but the mutability of the name underscores the more fundamental connection the novel draws between the unrestrained woman and social chaos. Another example is the eponymous heroine of Chilean novelist Augusto D'Halmar's novel *Juana Lucero* (1902), a disillusioned prostitute whom the narrator describes as "the Zolanian fly" (*la mosca Zolaniana*). At the moment of her greatest disgust with the life that circumstances have forced her to lead she rechristens herself "Naná," a name suggested by a friend who has heard about Zola's book. Henceforth she refers to the innocent girl she had been as "the other" (*la otra*).[41] Through the change of name she acknowledges, and even embraces, her irredeemability in defiance of the society that made her so. Alongside a gendered social chaos, the mutability of names in Nana narratives signifies a willful independence that even the examples of the genre most dependent on the stereotype of the independent woman as whore seem loath to deny.[42]

The tour of works with features plausibly connected to *Nana* could continue, to include for example Eugenio Cambaceres's *Sentimental*

Music (*Musica sentimental*, 1884), Norris's *The Pit* (1903), Gamboa's *Santa*, and well into the twentieth century, Cyprian Ekwensi's *Jagua Nana* (1961), about an aspiring prostitute in postcolonial Nigeria.[43] The examples given so far, however, reveal several recurring qualities of the Nana figure. She often occupies a shifting position between prostitute and entertainer. Indifferent toward procreation and marriage, she skillfully calculates what the men around her desire. She commonly is described in shades of infection, through association with disease or sinister influence. She moves unimpeded through the society that made her, underscoring its hypocrisy, while taking a blithely unrepentant view of her own behavior. The plots in which she appears frequently serve as social diagnostics—"medical-social novel" is the subtitle of many works by López Bago, a onetime medical student—but plot structures seem unable to solve the riddle of her identity. Instead they restrain her through mechanisms that are remarkably brutal, such as the demise of Estella, murdered by the marquis's son, and Nadja's nationalist reeducation. Typically she ends up alone, if not dead.

As we saw in the previous chapter, characters recalling Gervaise also appeared after the publication of *L'Assommoir*. It is worth considering, then, the differences between the history of naturalist body figures and that of the Nana figure. The relentless fall of Gervaise attracted much attention, but *L'Assommoir*'s use of figurative language to connect Gervaise's degenerate body with the pathological society around her was more important than the doomed character for the development of naturalist technique. When writers lifted this method from the novel, moreover, they used it in similar fashion even when, as we saw in *McTeague* and Shimazaki Tōson's *Spring* (*Haru*, 1908), they broke apart Zola's deterministic circles. What writers took from *Nana*, in contrast, were precisely motifs associated with Nana as a character—performance, mobility, contagion, and a certain moral ambiguity—yet their use of these motifs in new works did not simply reproduce her. As we will see in *New Year's Finery* and *Sister Carrie*, the Nana figure and her position in the novels in which she appeared differed in important ways from Nana and *Nana*, and in this sense what we can recognize now as the Nana figure emerged on the supposed "periphery" of the naturalist literary field rather than originating in the work of Zola. While writers' adoption of the technique of body figures contributed to the expansion of the naturalist field, in this case the relationship is reversed: the expansion of the field was critical to the appearance of the Nana figure. *New Year's Finery* and *Sister Carrie*, to which I turn now, show moreover that Nana narratives transform the ideas and techniques that intersect in the narrative discourse of *Nana* in ways that open new possibilities for the character and analysis of her milieu. That is, the Nana figure cannot really be predicted from *Nana*.

ENCLOSING AN ENIGMA

Kosugi Tengai's novel *New Year's Finery* (1900) announces its ties to *Nana* by reproducing key elements of Zola's novel. Like *Nana*, *New Year's Finery* introduces all of its major characters in a scene at the beginning of the novel set in a theater. Its heroine Oshun is a singer of *kiyomoto bushi*, a type of narrative music derived from kabuki, who rose from a humble background. Her performance in the opening of *New Year's Finery*, much like Nana's first appearance on stage, transforms her into an object of desire. Assumed to be a woman of easy morals because her art is associated with brothels, Oshun negotiates social expectations regarding sex and marriage as Nana defies them. Finally, Oshun like Nana suffers what seems both social and narrative retribution for her assertion of independence. The novel differs from *Nana* in important ways, however—Oshun is both talented and chaste, for example—and we thus should consider these explicit parallels not so much things borrowed from Zola but rather the foundation for a further exploration of the possibilities of the Nana figure. Rather than jointly inviting and embodying social corruption, as Nana does, Oshun exposes ideological contradictions in late Meiji Japan regarding women, labor, and sexuality.

Tengai began his career in the early "Zolaist" period of naturalism in Japan, when he and other writers such as Tayama Katai and Nagai Kafū explored the work of Zola in search of a way forward from the sentimental "novels of misery" (*hisan shōsetsu*) that dominated Japanese fiction in the mid-1890s. He was a satirical writer of modest fame, on the edge of the prominent novelist Ozaki Kōyō's circle, when he discovered an English translation of *Nana* in a used bookstore in Tokyo in 1898. Although he had heard of Zola's work, by his account reading *Nana* was an experience of enormous insight into problems of mimesis with which he had struggled for several years, particularly the lingering, moralistic authorial presence in Japanese prose that he thought impeded the direct representation of social reality.[44] As he put it in the preface to his novel *Popular Song* (*Hayari uta*, 1902), a naturalist manifesto that I have quoted earlier: "Nature is nature. It is not good, bad, beautiful, or ugly." Rather than judging the world, authors should try to make the reader feel as if his faculties had been touched by it (*Hayari uta*, 4). Inspired by the precise descriptions of characters and their environs that he found in *Nana* and subsequently in Zola's *The Earth* (*La Terre*, 1887), Tengai began a series of documentary sketches. (One from 1900, "Yōkyūba no ichijikan" or "An Hour in a Cabaret," consists almost solely of description, without any unifying narrative or authorial presence.) *New Year's Finery*, one of the first full-length naturalist narratives in Japan, continued the documentary enterprise through careful attention to details of interior spaces, urban geography, dress, and manners. It was the first of four novels Tengai planned on Oshun's life and loves.[45] Unlike many naturalist writers in Japan, Tengai did not follow the turn toward fictions of the self in naturalist fiction in Japan at the end of the decade, and instead wrote in his exhaustively mimetic mode until the end of his career in the 1940s.

New Year's Finery opens as the audience at the Haruki-za (an actual theater in Tokyo) exchanges gossip about Oshun, of whom hardly anything is known. In the crowd are Takiyama, a banker; his friend Kasada, a journalist; Onooka, an aristocratic moneylender; Tamae, an heiress rumored to be a nymphomaniac; and Ryūtarō, a young man attending with his aunt. As in *Nana*, the audience is rapt by the end of the performance (although Oshun stays clothed). As in *Nana* too, shouting matches break out in the theater: some call Oshun a "goddess," others a "man-killer" and "whore queen."[46] The arguments are the first act in a story that is essentially driven by struggles between different characters—including Oshun—to define her. We learn that Oshun has taken to the stage because her father, an alcoholic painter, is unable to support her family. She had worked in a factory, where she and Ryūtarō developed a mutual crush, but the lecherous advances of a supervisor drove her into the still more morally perilous world of the theater. Takiyama (assisted by Oshun's accompanist Kiyoju) and Onooka (helped by a comedian named Bun'yū) compete to become Oshun's patron, a financial arrangement that would come with sexual favors. She accepts gifts from both but rebuffs their sexual overtures. Meanwhile Ryūtarō is under pressure from a relative to succeed him as priest in a Buddhist temple, but his greedy aunt, sensing a more lucrative option, considers a proposal from Tamae to make him her plaything. Oshun's world thus is one of sexual-financial transactions in which all are assumed to participate. The seeming impossibility that someone like Oshun would not take part leads to a false arrest for prostitution, triggering events leading to a denouement in which she arranges her fate from the limited options available to her and cuts a bargain with Onooka.

Literary, moral, legal, and social-scientific discourses concerning women and sexuality contributed to the production of Oshun. The literature of prostitution of the eighteenth and early nineteenth centuries offered many examples of figures caught between the demands of profession, family, and love.[47] Beginning in the 1870s, when the Meiji state began its program of "civilization and enlightenment" (*bunmei kaika*), independent and destructive women became ubiquitous figures in literature, from the "poison women" (*dokufu*) who appeared in stories of sexually tinged murders, through the girl student Osei in Futabatei Shimei's *The Drifting Cloud* (*Ukigumo*, 1886–89), to the aspiring writer Yoshiko in Katai's novella *The Quilt* (*Futon*, 1907).[48] In many of these characters the appearance of "modernity," the freedom to move outside of the home, and uncontrolled sexuality were linked. *New Year's Finery* also taps into the ambiguous fame of female musicians during the period. Women began performing in venues outside the so-called pleasure quarters in 1877, after a long-standing ban on public performances by female musicians was lifted. By the end of the century female performers of narrative music were selling out halls in Tokyo, including the Haruki-za where Oshun makes her debut. Their fans included competing groups of young men, a real-world source for the arguments that erupt during Oshun's performance. The sexual virtue of such performers was a matter of constant doubt and their popularity alarmed the authorities, who considered them a threat to the moral health of the audience.[49]

New ideas regarding virginity, monogamy, and prostitution, rooted in regimes of public and national hygiene, contributed as well to Oshun and the plot of *New Year's Finery*. Beginning in 1876 and continuing to the turn of the century, new arguments on public health supported the development of a system for licensing and regulating prostitutes that included medical examinations, police monitoring of brothels, and surveillance of women suspected of engaging in unlicensed sex work. (The system was based mainly on the French one developed by Parent-Duchâtelet.) An overlay of Confucian views of filial piety in the new regime established family poverty as the only acceptable reason to apply for a license, a noteworthy provision considering that Oshun takes to the stage and later marries herself to Onooka in order to support her parents and sister.[50] Regulated sexual labor was distinguished not only from unlicensed activity but also from marital monogamy and premarital virginity (the latter now defined by sexual inexperience rather than age or demeanor). The idealization of monogamy and virginity was part of a redefinition of family relations involving law, hygiene, and the extension of Confucian moral norms from social elites to the populace as a whole, an establishment of modern "tradition" that pervades Oshun's efforts to pursue her art while resisting sexual advances and showing the expected devotion to her parents. Many of the new norms and structures were codified in the 1890 Civil Code.[51]

Like Nana, Oshun thus incorporates aspects of several familiar social types, including entertainer, prostitute, and virgin daughter. Yet the constitutive discourses that establish these types do not define who Oshun *is* but who she can *become*. The seemingly subtle departure from the pattern in *Nana* reveals what we will see is a significant shift from narrative discourse toward character when the Nana figure is extracted from Zola's novel. As in *Nana*, a number of characters ponder the question "Who is Oshun?" early in *New Year's Finery*, including Onooka, Takiyama, and Tamae. The discussions of Oshun, which begin with her first public performance, turn frequently to the anomaly that she is pretty and talented yet unattached to a man as wife or mistress, and is apparently a virgin.[52] The journalist Kasada thus observes that she is "a contradiction from beginning to end," while Bun'yū, the comedian helping Onooka pursue Oshun, says that she will not be able to continue so for long (*Hatsu sugata*, 20–21, 51–52). The ambiguity of Oshun's identity also appears in the gap between her public and domestic lives, as sensational performer and dutiful daughter. (Invited to perform privately for Onooka after her show at the Haruki-za, Oshun demurs, on the grounds that her mother is waiting at home.) The competition over Oshun, involving not just Takiyama and Onooka but also Tamae, who feeds Ryūtarō sexual rumors about Oshun to try to break their bond, ultimately is a struggle to ascribe a social identity to her as she moves between the home and various professional venues. Such attempts are frequently accompanied by the activity of looking, a visual objectification of Oshun that helps focalize the narrative.[53] Vision continues to connote obsession, as in *Nana*, but gains an additional meaning of projected social expectations. Not only the characters of *New Year's Finery* but also its narrative, we can say, fixes its gaze on Oshun so as to fix her identity. (The novel's title, which could be translated literally as *First Glimpse*, underscores the importance of such acts of looking.)[54]

As with other Nana figures, Oshun's name contributes to her social ambiguity, in her case through the way it is inscribed in the text.

Written Japanese uses Chinese ideographs and two phonetic syllabaries, with numerous combinations able to designate the same sounds. When characters in *New Year's Finery* who know Oshun in the context of her family (such as her mother) speak her name it appears in the text as お俊—"Oshun." When characters who know her as a performer (such as Takiyama and Kasada) speak it, the name appears as 小しゆん—again "Oshun," in a different inscription.[55] The two ways of writing the name are plausible variations on each other, with the latter having faint connotations of the brothel districts and their associated arts. The only characters in whose dialogue both inscriptions appear are Bun'yū, Kiyoju, and Tamae.[56] Appropriately so: the performers working for Onooka and Takiyama and the heiress with her eyes on Ryūtarō are the characters most actively trying to transform Oshun's social identity from young innocent into sexually bound woman, that is, to turn お俊 into 小しゆん. The first two try to persuade Oshun's mother to sell her daughter as a mistress, while Tamae tries to drive Ryūtarō away from Oshun so that she can have her way with him. Although the figure of Oshun focalizes the narrative of *New Year's Finery*, moreover, both forms of the name appear in the narration, in keeping with the fact that her social position remains unsettled until the end of the novel (e.g., *Hatsu sugata*, 36, 84). In comparison to Lange's *"The Worst Sort of People,"* where Nadja's transformation into Maja marks her rehabilitation, or D'Halmar's *Juana Lucero*, where Juana announces her defiance by adopting the name Naná, *New Year's Finery* uses the possibilities of written Japanese to incorporate the dispute over Oshun's identity into the linguistic fabric of the novel itself.

Oshun does not have complete liberty to defy such ascriptions of identity. Instead, she negotiates a position in the progressively tightening web of ideas and institutions through which others (and the narrative) try to define her. One evening Oshun and Ryūtarō discover that they have been taken to the same inn by Takiyama and Tamae; they flee to a restaurant in their neighborhood. A policeman bursts in as they share a chaste moment and arrests them for engaging in prostitution. (Presumably the charge is working without a license, for which Nana barely escapes arrest.) Oshun's fate unfolds dramatically following the intervention of the law. She is able to avoid scandal because Kasada, the journalist, suppresses the news about her arrest. When Oshun dines with him to express her gratitude, he forces her to drink to the point of unconsciousness, then rapes her. To his blithe apology she responds, "because of you, my entire life is a waste," a reference to the loss of the virginity that was the only proof she was not the prostitute many assumed her to be (*Hatsu sugata*, 133). With her chastity gone she faces increasing pressure to become Takiyama's mistress. By chance Oshun learns that she is adopted and thus bears an especially deep obligation to her impoverished parents. She uses the remnants of her freedom to arrange a marriage with Onooka under terms that provide a comfortable home for them. On the day of her marriage she secretly watches Ryūtarō take vows at his uncle's temple and then walks pensively out into the countryside, seemingly defiant despite her fate, a scene that by reproducing Nana's final solitude alludes once more to Zola's novel.

Even in the context of the restraints on her identity that Oshun faces, the rape that signals the beginning of her enclosure seems out of proportion to her transgressions, suggesting in its symbolic excess a variety of narrative retribution reminiscent of *Nana*. The discourses that shape Oshun's fate play roles in *New Year's Finery* which are fundamentally different from those that helped produce Nana, however. Nana's behavior is determined by the world that made her. Contemporary ideas of hygiene, heredity, and sexuality contribute to a social metaphor to which she is subordinate (or meant to be). In *New Year's Finery*, in contrast, Oshun begins free of such determinations. Her sole fundamental trait is her ability to create music. (The only moment Oshun speaks her own name, near the end of the novel, it is to declare she is "Oshun the *kiyomoto* singer"—*kiyomoto no Oshun*—in an embrace of her skills and reputation. Here the name is written 小しゆん, as it is when other characters know her as a performer [*Hatsu sugata*, 149]). The contemporary discourses on female independence, prostitution, and marriage that contribute to Oshun thus do not explain why she does what she does—as in the case of Nana—but why her search for independence is doomed. The arc of her story is nearly the opposite of that of Nana, who shrugs off restraint with increasing ease and finally is eliminated from the world through an illness that has little to do with her crimes. Oshun, in contrast, begins in freedom and ends bound by social conventions crafted precisely to block the aspirations that she harbors. The contemplation of social decay in *Nana* gives way to a fundamental conflict between the economically and sexually independent woman and society.

Two essential changes allow the creation of Oshun, a figure of brutally thwarted ambitions, out of Nana, a rancorous agent of social decay. The theories of heredity and the overt hygienic metaphors that define Nana in Zola's novel all but vanish in Tengai's. Although Oshun's adoptive father is an alcoholic and the entire family lives in poverty, the revelation of her adoption severs any hereditary connection of her disposition to such circumstances. (This seems the only reason for the odd detail.) While theories of hygiene contribute to the sexual regime that binds her, moreover, she is not a symbol of disease. As I argued in the previous chapter, constitutive discourses such as the surveys of prostitution that Zola drew on when creating Nana may be folded into naturalist figures and travel silently with them. Although Tengai need not have read Parent-Duchâtelet, his work remains present in Oshun—with important consequences, as we will see. At the same time, it is not altogether surprising that these overt aspects of *Nana* disappear because Tengai was primarily interested in Zola's techniques of mimesis, not his efforts to deploy natural and social science in fiction.[57]

As such deterministic explanations of behavior recede, Oshun's capacity as a performer comes to the fore. It is not just that she is as good at singing *kiyomoto bushi* as Nana is bad at singing operettas. In a broader sense, until others succeed in defining her, she is only what she does. In contrast to Nana, whose clash with the society that created her only reveals its hypocrisy, Oshun's troubles speak of a basic conflict between the freedom to create one's identity and a social order hostile to such self-invention. Such a romantic and tragic view of the individual, which is common in Japanese naturalism, responds not only to changes in the gendered organization of social relations in Japan, but also to a broad political and ideological consolidation at the turn of the century that can be found in other fiction from the time.[58] Thus while *New Year's Finery* signals its filiations with *Nana*, it uses the competing attempts to assign identity to its Nana-like character to address ideological fault lines in the society in which Tengai worked. The transformation of Nana into Oshun allows *New Year's Finery* to realize possibilities untapped in Zola's novel.

INDIVIDUALITY WITHOUT CONTENT

The stress on performance that appeared when Tengai turned the theatrically inept Nana into a talented singer can be found in Nana narratives that appeared elsewhere, including Theodore Dreiser's *Sister Carrie* (1900) in the United States. Although Dreiser said he had not read any of Zola's work before writing the novel, its parallels with *Nana* have intrigued critics for decades. Like Nana, Carrie is of modest origins but is repelled by the manual labor that seems to be her lot; she finds material comfort as a kept woman; she attracts admirers when she takes to the stage; her story is told as a series of relationships with men; and she ends the novel alone. H. L. Mencken speculated that Zola could have influenced Dreiser through an intermediary. A "second-degree" genealogy would be plausible because as we saw in chapter 1, works of French naturalism were well known—and intensely debated—in the United States by the time Dreiser composed *Sister Carrie*. One candidate for intermediary is a colleague of Dreiser's at the *St. Louis Globe-Democrat*, who lent him an unpublished novel with elements reminiscent of *Nana* and the central section of Balzac's *Lost Illusions* (*Illusions perdues*, 1837–43). By Dreiser's account, the manuscript was his introduction to realism in literature.[59] From a less insistently genealogical perspective, *Sister Carrie* is undeniably part of the break with the existing American realism that naturalist writers like Crane and Norris were leading. It also is a novel with similarities not only to *Nana* but to other fiction with Nana-like characters—such as *New Year's Finery*, *Santa*, and *"The Worst Sort of People"*—which are compelling enough to view it as part of the phenomenon of the Nana figure. In this transnational context the question that *Sister Carrie* directs us to, then, is what large- and small-scale economic and political forces supported the appearance of Nana figures and ultimately the naturalist literary field.

In an often-recounted story Norris, the most Zolaist of American writers, ensured the publication of *Sister Carrie*. Letters indicate that after a publisher rejected *Sister Carrie* Dreiser submitted it to Doubleday, Page, because its predecessor firm had published *McTeague* and three other novels by Norris. (Dreiser read *McTeague* while his manuscript was at the first publisher.) The novel was accepted on the recommendation of Norris, who was a reader for Doubleday, Page, at the time. There are many versions of what followed (some, from Dreiser, presenting himself as a moral crusader), but it is certain that after one of the firm's principals tried to drop the novel on moral grounds, Norris and the friend who helped Dreiser edit the draft of *Sister Carrie* prevailed on him to honor the initial agreement. Although the publisher did not stick the book in the cellar (as some stories say), it sold poorly and Dreiser did not return to fiction for a decade, when he published *Jennie Gerhardt* (1911).[60] With the publication in short order of *The Financier* (1912), *The Titan* (1914), and *The Genius* (1915), critics came to see him as the chief representative of American naturalism.

Sister Carrie, which was loosely inspired by an episode in the life of one of Dreiser's sisters, opens with the heroine on a train from Wisconsin to Chicago. She meets a traveling salesman, Drouet, and on arriving goes to the flat of her parsimonious sister and brother-in-law. Looking for work the next day, Carrie is intensely conscious that others see her as a "wage-seeker." Shortly after, in a department store for the first time, she feels "each trinket and valuable" making a "claim" on her, simultaneously sensing how poorly she compares to the clerks. Her "longing for dress and beauty" is the first strong indication of a propensity to fashion herself through the eyes of others.[61] Carrie finds work in a shoe factory but soon reunites with Drouet, who gives her money and later rents an apartment where they live together. When Drouet is away she takes up with a friend of his, Hurstwood, who manages a posh saloon. With Drouet's encouragement she plays a role in amateur theatrics at his chapter of the Elks and experiences the intense pleasure of controlling how others—including her two lovers—see her. (Hurstwood, his eyes riveted on her, "caught the infection"; *Sister Carrie*, 135.) The infatuated Hurstwood steals money from his employer, leaves his wife and children, and tricks Carrie into going to Montreal, where they marry. They travel on to New York, where Dreiser coordinates Hurstwood's fall and Carrie's rise in the meticulously described metropolis. Hurstwood ends up killing himself in a flophouse on the Bowery; Carrie, through a series of increasingly prominent roles, reaches the heights of Broadway theater.

The many discordant voices in *Sister Carrie*—the source of much critical interest, and sometimes irritation—offer a way to begin exploring Carrie's resemblance to other Nana-like naturalist heroines. The novel's narrator speaks at various times as a sentimental moralist, hard-nosed reporter, social historian, and chronicler of high-society glitz.[62] The different voices echo turn-of-the-century debates about women, including consumption and work; the challenge that unmarried, sexually active women posed to norms of domesticity; and the nature of subjective identity. In the background was a general sense of alarm in which the sexuality of women was treated as a problem illuminating every other.[63] Carrie was born from the intersection of these debates and the various modes of representing women and the city that supported them, including many that contributed to Nana and Oshun. Some elements, such as the language of hygiene in *Nana* and Confucian filiality in *New Year's Finery*, are absent here, while new ones such as sociological theories of imitation play an important role. Carrie may show kinship with Nana and Oshun not because of a direct line of influence from Zola to Dreiser, but because the confluence of intellectual, political, and economic currents that produced her are similar to those that produced other Nana figures, keeping in mind that many of these currents had increasing geographic reach.

Cautionary novels about young women negotiating the moral hazards of the world were one source for a character like Carrie, who passes briefly through the household of her sister but soon is at large in Chicago. Although such books were a target for naturalist writers in the United States, the novels of Laura Jean Libbey, sentimental tales of girls who fend off amorous men as they struggle to make a living in the city, and those of Bertha Clay and Albert Ross, frequently about poor brides proving their worth in rich families, provided Dreiser with elements of the plot, characters, and tone of *Sister Carrie*.[64] (Carrie has read Clay's 1883 novel *Dora Thorne*, and she hears guests at a dinner party discuss Ross's 1891 *Moulding a Maiden*; *Sister Carrie*, 78, 236–37.) Moralistic fiction had a social-scientific counterpart in efforts to monitor and reform working-class women. As industrial capitalism created new opportunities to earn wages, women increasingly worked and socialized outside of the parental home before marrying, leaving them vulnerable, in commentators' views, to unmarried pregnancy, venereal disease, and prostitution.[65] This spectral "unattached woman," as Priscilla Wald calls her, was more anonymous than the politically active New Woman and her behavior more difficult to determine.[66] Efforts to establish and study the social type were inseparable from the moral panic she occasioned. Like the young woman who worried reformers, Carrie seeks factory work as soon as she arrives in the city. Alerted to the attractions of the nighttime city by a glimpse from her train, she soon asks her sister about the theater, a commercialized entertainment favored by working-class youth. The narrator explains that her interest springs from a "craving for pleasure" that is "so strong it was the one stay of her nature," completing the association of wage work, the city, and unrestrained sexuality (*Sister Carrie*, 6–7, 23–24). In contrast to the mythically proportioned Nana (whom the Catholic Muffat calls "the monster of the scriptures"; *Nana*, 226), Carrie's individuality thus effectively merges with a social type that was hotly debated at the time.

The enterprise of social investigation underlay other techniques of representation and theories of behavior that helped create Carrie. The work of social philosophers to whom Dreiser overtly refers—such as Herbert Spencer—was less important than reportage on urban poverty.

Documentary works such as Jacob Riis's *How the Other Half Lives* (1890) and Robert Woods's *The Poor in Great Cities* (1895) built a rhetoric of urban degradation that appears in the sections of *Sister Carrie* concerned with the fall of Hurstwood. Other remarkable scenes operate in a style that Carrie Bramen calls the "urban picturesque," which Dreiser practiced as a journalist in the 1890s.[67] Dreiser places his heroine in chic restaurants and on fashionable streets that are venues for self-display. While walking on Broadway she finds herself "stared at and ogled." Longing to feel "the delight of parading here as an equal," she vows to transform herself (*Sister Carrie*, 226–27). A "naturally imitative" personality assists the self-transformation, revealing the contribution of new sociological theories to the proposition of Carrie (*Sister Carrie*, 79). The work of Gabriel Tarde, introduced from France to the United States in the 1890s by James Mark Baldwin, held that imitation was a universal faculty explaining psychology and social relations. In his influential *Mental Development in the Child and the Race* (1894) Baldwin argued that imitation is "the soul of our social relationships," and indeed it is the soul of Carrie's.[68] Finally, Carrie's intuitive understanding of the role of jewelry and clothing in self-transforming imitation recalls commentary on the emerging culture of consumption, particularly the theory of "pecuniary emulation" elaborated by Thorstein Veblen in *The Theory of the Leisure Class* (1899).[69] The dynamic relationship between Carrie and her environment compounds the sense that she lacks fixed qualities and relativizes norms of behavior, which she chooses depending on whether they are enabling or restrictive rather than moral.

Carrie's rise to theatrical fame is no coincidence. When Dreiser's novel appeared, acting was both a common metaphor for identity and a profession through which highly visible women fought for economic and social independence.[70] Yet her career also recalls an aspect of *New Year's Finery*: as in Tengai's novel, a relatively unimportant part of Nana—her comical attempt to be an actress—becomes a central quality of Carrie. Carrie's existence as a performer on and off stage likewise inspires numerous attempts to fix her social identity. They have a different meaning than in *New Year's Finery*, however, where the vise-like diminishment of possible identities signals the death of Oshun's freedom. From the moment Carrie encounters Drouet on the train she seems willing to be almost anyone someone asks her to be. The rare cases when she refuses reveal the principle at work. Carrie rejects identities that would prevent her from changing again, such as the thrifty wage-earner that her sister wishes her to be in Chicago, or the self-sacrificing wife that Hurstwood demands after their flight to New York. In this light her rejection of the town of her birth, unseen in the novel, suggests less a decision to be *someone* else than a desire for the freedom to be *anyone* else. If this essentially prospective quality leads Carrie to embrace a "cosmopolitan standard of virtue" (as the novel's opening passage warns), doing so does not necessarily make her worse (as it predicts).[71] The fluid relationships of seeing and being seen through which Carrie creates herself are the very basis of the freedom she seeks, in contrast to the symptoms of social disease or acts of interpellation that they are in *Nana* and *New Year's Finery*. While there is no "real" Carrie—the association of acting with female inauthenticity is one of the novel's many sexist clichés—she remains free, for the same reason, from the many false identities around her.

Carrie's acceptance of nearly all identities but attachment to none makes names a problem in this novel too. Unlike *Nana* and *New Year's Finery*, no one asks "Who is Carrie?"—perhaps not because her identity is self-evident, but because there are many Carries that are separately acceptable to her interlocutors. The question of who Carrie is may not even be poseable for lack of a stable referent. Her original surname Meeber appears only at the beginning of the novel. Afterward she moves under the surnames Drouet; Murdock, the name Hurstwood uses in Montreal; Wheeler, his name in New York; and Madenda, from her stage name for the amateur production in Chicago, which she revives when she gets a role as a chorus girl on Broadway. On stage she is Laura, Katisha the Country Maid, and the Little Quakeress, among other roles, while in the narrative she receives epithets including "the little toiler," "the little dramatic student," and the unusually judgmental "little soldier of fortune" (*Sister Carrie*, 37, 45, 120). Names proliferate until the difference between them disappears. All are roles for Carrie, a situation illustrated by her delight when she discovers her first, "long-hoped for" notice in the papers: an item saying Carrie Madenda will take a role in a play previously filled by another actress. With a stage name taking on a part, Carolyn Meeber has finally vanished.[72] "Nana" names a physical body that entrances the world with its genitals, not its acting, as Zola's narrator often observes. Although the name is meaningless, Nana's ghastly death shows that she remains confined to the body that bears it. In *New Year's Finery* and *Sister Carrie*, in contrast, escaping names per se means the difference between social confinement and the possibility of self-determination. While Oshun ultimately is defined as 小しゆん, Carrie frees herself from naming. The enigma and danger of the Nana figure, we can say, is her resistance to names that are understood to be not just linguistic but social designations.

The long-disputed closing scene of *Sister Carrie*—in which the recurring motif of Carrie in a rocking chair, looking out the window at the street, reappears—suggests a final failure to name her. The last image of Carrie, alone, resembles the final scenes of solitude in *Nana* and *New Year's Finery* and recalls the varieties of narrative retribution that the heroines of those novels suffer. The voice of the sentimental moralist that dominates the opening of *Sister Carrie* returns in force, asserting that a misguided "longing for that which is better" directed the steps of Carrie's "erring," and insinuating that she is unhappy and disillusioned (*Sister Carrie*, 368–69). Keeping in mind the ways that the contradictory constellation of discourses in the novel create a character without content, however, Carrie is clearly not susceptible to conventional condemnation. The novel's final lines, addressed directly to her—"Know, then, that for you is neither surfeit or content . . . In your rocking-chair, by your window, shall you dream such happiness as you may never feel"—emphasize the prospective orientation of Carrie's self at the same time they withdraw fulfillment from her, leaving her free even if not yet anyone (*Sister Carrie*, 369). Like the final scene of *New Year's Finery*, then, the end of *Sister Carrie* associates solitude with defiance. In both cases, the dangerous ambiguity of the Nana figure appears by shifting the episodes of performance that are occasional parts of the story of *Nana* into the character of the Nana figure, to the point that in *Sister Carrie* performance is the defining quality of the heroine's imitative personality. Carrie's increasingly conscious desire to invent herself, which drives the novel to its conclusion, becomes the sole index of her content-free being. The final obstacle to her self-invention, in fact, does not appear in the story of *Sister Carrie*—as Nana's smallpox and the machinations trapping Oshun appear in the stories of *Nana* and *New Year's Finery*—but in its narrative discourse, through the rhetoric of turn-of-the-century moralistic novels that resurfaces in the last lines. Perhaps for this reason, the narrative retribution that Carrie suffers is more histrionic in expression than what Nana and Oshun experience, yet less consequential for her. In contrast to Nana's death or Oshun's rape, the loneliness that the narrator declares to be a curse upon her is an inward component of self-consciousness, not a consequence arriving from without. In the context of industrialization, urbanization, and moral alarm over young female wage-earners and the emerging culture of consumption in the United States, we can see in *Sister Carrie* an ambivalent exploration of the reflexive creation of identity. In the transnational context of the Nana figure we can see that like *New Year's Finery*, *Sister Carrie* pursues possibilities that are only implicit in Zola's *Nana*.

FORMAL TRANSPOSITIONS AND MINIMAL SCHEMAS

The resemblances among Nana, Oshun, and Carrie show that the Nana figure is not a fixed type but a cluster of qualities in a shifting relationship to each other. Among the most important traits in common are an urban existence, disinterest in reproductive sexuality linked to an instrumental attitude toward marriage, a magnetic effect on male admirers, and, despite varying degrees of moral hesitation, an ultimately unrepentant view of one's acts. Related qualities of the narrative discourse surrounding the Nana figure are a heightened visuality in descriptive language (and indeed in narration), the ending motif of solitude, and the instability of names. From the range of characteristics one can distill three that are fundamental: performance on stage and in public, the ability to inspire contagious infatuation, and a social mobility that lets the Nana figure resist ascriptions of identity. That these qualities could combine and recombine with others explains why the Nana figure could address matters as different as the moral hypocrisy of the Second Empire, the reorganization of marriage and sexual labor in Japan's Meiji period, and the emergence of a culture of consumption and the transformation of domesticity during the Gilded Age in the United States.

The Nana figure's malleability resulted from specific changes that allow Nana to take flight from her novel. Some aspects of Nana and *Nana* recede while others come to the fore in new form. The discourse of heredity behind the family tree of the Rougon-Macquart novels fades as a determining factor in *New Year's Finery* and *Sister Carrie*. Hereditary explanations of Oshun's behavior in *New Year's Finery* are cast aside (because she is adopted), and they are completely absent in *Sister Carrie*. (Carrie's imitative personality is the opposite of hereditary determination.)[73] The Lamarckian view of heredity that Zola espoused was discredited in the last decades of the century, no doubt speeding the disappearance of issues of heredity from many novels inspired by his work. The language of hygiene in *Nana* also disappears from *New Year's Finery* and *Sister Carrie*, but with different effect. The association of Nana with contagious social disorder, which the language of hygiene establishes, remains a durable quality of the Nana figure but is expressed by other means, such as the obsession of fans in *New Year's Finery* or the imitative dynamics of crowds in *Sister Carrie*. The explicit (and thus limiting) discourse of hygiene is shed while leaving the association intact. The trope of mobility, in contrast, is consistently associated with the city while its meaning changes significantly. Nana's ability to move freely through Second Empire Paris is primarily an indication of its decadence, but Oshun's and Carrie's mobility lends itself to the sexualization of their refusal to perform unpaid domestic labor on the one hand, and wage labor on the other. The moral connotations of mobility become more ambiguous, the economic connotations, more explicit.

The most important change in the qualities of Nana, the Nana figure's emphasis on performance, becomes a central characteristic precisely as deterministic theories of behavior disappear. The transformation of Nana's inept attempt to become an actress into the actual talent of Oshun and Carrie puts them in more dynamic relationships with the societies around them and allows their novels to raise questions about their social identities. Nana scarcely has any subjectivity beyond what is expressed in the phrase "I want." The conflicts between individual and society in *New Year's Finery* and *Sister Carrie*, in contrast, provide their heroines with a self-consciousness that strengthens their resistance to attempts to fix their identities. Such a sense of self—which might be phrased as "I am not"—is repeatedly connected to the Nana figure's gender through her rejection of marriage, domesticity, and reproduction. Her capacity to perform is presented as both content-free and essentially feminine, a cliché and a contradiction in the proposition of the Nana figure as empty of meaning. I do not want to downplay the potentially anti-woman politics that are folded into the Nana figure and retrievable at any time. Note, however, that because of the changes I am describing, the Nana figure assumed an oppositional position toward the world around her that could have many different meanings.

Indeed, amid changes that seem common to the Nana figure per se, we can see shifts which show that individual versions of her were always connected to specific contexts. The regulation of women's sexual activity, which is an important foundation for *Nana*, contributes crucial elements of the plot of *New Year's Finery*. In *Sister Carrie* it is only the source of minor intrigues such as Carrie's bigamous marriage to Hurstwood. Conversely, conspicuous public consumption serves mainly to highlight decadence in *Nana* and is absent from *New Year's Finery*. In *Sister Carrie*, however, it is an important part of Dreiser's treatment of social relations. Thus, in the proposition of Oshun we can see changes in social norms and laws regarding women's behavior in Japan; in that of Carrie, the growth of a culture of consumption in the United States. Such specific contexts informed different versions of the Nana figure and at the same time were the object of social analysis carried out through her. Around the Nana figure's central qualities of performance, contagion, and mobility, then, there was a changing constellation of other elements. The latter, however, were not incidental: it was precisely through variations responding to specific contexts that the Nana figure emerged.

Such observations still do not explain what made the shifting composition of the Nana figure possible. The structuralist poetics that has informed much work on Zola since the 1970s tends to treat characters like Nana as manifestations of the novels' organic structure.[74] If this were the case, it should have been difficult to remove Nana from the structure that produced her, much less change her qualities. Yet versions of the Nana figure began to be extracted from *Nana* even before serialization commenced, and quickly became ubiquitous in mass culture. One reason is that Nana was not wholly original. She was the product of theories of social behavior and techniques for representing it that circulated in and around Zola's novel. Their dissemination and ongoing evolution aided her separation from it. Because the figure that emerged differed from Zola's heroine, however, this explanation is not enough. The Nana figure was not simply lifted free of *Nana* by the constellation of ideas around it.

We might ask instead whether the Nana figure traveled widely because certain aspects of *Nana*'s dense narrative discourse, where the novel's descriptive and figurative social anatomy is centered, could be transposed into aspects of the Nana figure as character. Such "formal transpositions" would proceed through the shifts in the theories and techniques of representation that I have just discussed. Performance becomes a quality of the Nana figure when several episodes in *Nana*, important as illustrations of the corrupt state of her audience, are turned into a basic trait of Oshun's and Carrie's personae. Contagion and mobility become fundamental qualities through similar transpositions. The overt hygienic metaphors of *Nana*—according to which society *wants* to be infected—disappear from *New Year's Finery* and *Sister Carrie*, only to highlight their heroines' abilities to inspire contagious behavior. The collapse of social boundaries illustrated by Nana's ability to roam between heights and depths becomes a morally ambiguous aspiration to self-determination in Oshun and Carrie. Each of the three central qualities of the Nana figure shows features of the narrative discourse of *Nana* moving into the Nana figure herself. The Nana figure assumes qualities that structure *Nana* as a whole.

Are Oshun and Carrie then characters in the conventional sense? Despite their self-consciousness, positive expressions of who they are and what they want are scarce. Performance, contagion, and mobility, moreover, are qualities of activity, not psychology, which indicate the heroine's relationship to others. We may see here the legacy of the emphasis on description of the visible in early naturalist fiction such as the Goncourt brothers' *Germinie Lacerteux* (1864). Nonetheless, it is striking that the plots such qualities propel are concerned with the assertion, rather than the content, of individuality. These core traits remain after a sorting and winnowing of possibilities internal to Zola's novel. The formal transposition that creates the Nana figure thus establishes what could be called a "minimal schema" of qualities. It bears several proper names—Oshun, Carrie, Nadja, Lina—but really operates as a peripatetic social diagnostic. The transposition that establishes it undeniably flattens the complex relationship between Nana and her milieu, in which her desires join seamlessly with others' desires to satisfy them. The Nana figure has a more simply adversarial relationship to society. Yet the reduction leaves the Nana figure more dynamic—not less—as demonstrated by the variety of plots she generates and the range of social criticism to which she can lend herself. It was in this form that Nana traveled widely.

Certain qualities of the Nana figure—particularly contagion, which always smacks of public hygiene—show that traces of the genres of thought which contributed to the creation of Nana remain after the transposition of narrative discourse into character. Folded into the Nana figure, they travel with it. Their presence helps explain the consistency of the Nana figure's minimal schema even in situations where the specific complex of ideas behind Nana is not evident. It may also explain why the Nana figure's combination of qualities remained generative. They are indeed a schema, not just an assortment, because the potential for the Nana figure to assume different meanings follows from her central qualities' relation to each other. What I am calling the Nana figure, then, ultimately is not the character but this mobile, flexible assemblage. To return to Fauchery's metaphor, the "golden fly" was neither *Nana* nor Nana but the minimal schema—the social diagnostic—that writers deployed around the world.

The specific qualities of the Nana figure are not coincidental. Rather, they tell us something about why she appears in certain contexts, or what she diagnoses. In turn, they allow us to see what makes her different from competing icons such as the New Women and rebellious daughters—think Henry James's Daisy Miller—who also populated late nineteenth-century intellectual culture, or later figures such as the Modern Girl. The Nana figure, as *New Year's Finery* and *Sister Carrie* attest, is frequently associated with contradictions in the social treatment of female labor. (Recall that Nana, Oshun, and Carrie all performed manual labor before embarking on their careers.) The qualities of the Nana figure make her particularly suited to expressing such contradictions, in contrast to the problems of education associated with the New Woman or those of mass culture with the Modern Girl. Oshun's and Carrie's talents provide them with the economic means to move freely outside of the parental household while remaining unmarried. In others' eyes, however, their mobility is morally congruent with prostitution. Paid female labor is assumed to be sexual labor, in contrast to the unpaid domestic labor of daughter and wife. The ambiguity of Oshun's and Carrie's aspirations to independence follows from the implicit dichotomy between male and female labor that emerges as a contradiction in capitalist social relations when the abstraction of labor through its commodification obscures its continuously embodied form. By seeking compensation for their work Oshun and Carrie each act as a self-interested economic subject, the ideal actor of liberal political economy, but to do so as a woman is a scandal.

The situation is different in Zola's novel, where society cannot fully reject Nana's assertions of independence because it wants to submit to her rebellion. What *New Year's Finery* and *Sister Carrie* identify as a contradiction in liberal ideology is, in *Nana*, as yet only a social pathology of the Second Empire. (The theories of heredity in *Nana*, which undercut liberal views of the subject, are one obstacle to the contradiction appearing.) The properly ideological problem emerges in *New Year's Finery* and *Sister Carrie* because the formal transposition that creates the Nana figure moves the conflict between freedom and restraint, and therefore the contradiction in the gendered organization of labor, to the novels' centers. The Nana figure's final solitude marks the desire for independence as both aberrant and genuine. The source of the conflict is the refractory structure of social relations and cannot be resolved by eliminating an individual or a social type. Thus, while the ubiquity of the Nana figure might suggest she is an all-purpose female demon, clearly she expresses a form of moral panic that is specific to capitalist societies. Recognizing this, one nonetheless should not ignore the divergent outcomes of Carrie's and Oshun's defiance. Given these novels' attention to the problem of labor, one might consider the differences in plot on the one hand in light of different degrees of the transformation of social relations by the commodification of labor *in general*—relatively advanced in the United States at the time, incipient in Japan—and on the other, of differing systems for regulating *women's* labor, with the far more paternalistic regime in Japan founded on precisely the changes in law and social norms that are in the background of *New Year's Finery*.

The Nana figure thus provided authors with an opportunity to explore social and philosophical problems that remained submerged in Zola's novel. What at first seems derivative is in fact the opening of new possibilities. The career of the Nana figure therefore demands that we reconsider conventional ideas of originality when thinking about the movement of works or genres outside their place of origin, ideas that we have seen lead to logical cul-de-sacs in theories of "World Literature" that measure new works against European models. Because the new possibilities for investigation found in *New Year's Finery* and *Sister Carrie* appeared through the formal transposition that created the Nana figure out of *Nana*, it is unlikely they would have surfaced if Nana had remained in *Nana*, or *Nana* in France. The movement of Zola's novel around the world made the extraction of the Nana figure from *Nana* possible, and by putting her into different circumstances, promoted the appearance of versions of her that could not be predicted from *Nana* itself. The possibilities of the Nana figure are manifest when she is abroad in the world.

Nana did not instigate the emergence of the Nana figure because the process involved more than just the reproduction of a heroine. The process included the critical "literary" matter of creating a minimal schema that passed for a character, but also the ongoing transformation of the theories and techniques for representing the social on which *Nana* drew, the circulation of these theories and techniques to ever greater parts of the world, and the large- and local-scale economic and political conditions that made them not only available but perhaps also useful to writers. The process did not begin with the publication of *Nana*. Rather, the novel put its own sources into a combination that was consequential for the naturalist field because it could be flattened and transformed into the Nana figure. *Nana* does not contain all of her possibilities, some of which are blocked by the theories of heredity and hygienic metaphors in the novel. Nor does it determine her later variations, which arose from differing political and economic conditions. In a certain sense, the

Nana-like heroines that appeared after the publication of *Nana* were variations without an original. Reversing the perspective and considering Nana in light of the characters that followed, one might recognize her as the first such variation, in that she shares the qualities of the minimal schema, albeit in a less explicit configuration.

The causes of the Nana figure's emergence are therefore complex. In addition to the constellation of elements that went into *Nana*, the circulation of Zola's novel, and the formal transpositions that created the Nana figure's minimal schema, we must also consider some characteristics of naturalism as a transnational phenomenon. We saw in the first chapter that shared references to a central group of works—primarily Zola's—was an important factor in the appearance of the naturalist literary field. Writers could signal their affiliation through dedications and prefaces, but the reproduction of motifs from Zola's fiction was another common means. The nature of the naturalist field thus made something like a series of variations on Nana especially likely. But if the Nana figure was also a figure of social contradictions, then perhaps beyond a simple string of iterations we can see a form of structural causality by which the unevenness of the capitalist world system promoted the appearance of versions of the Nana figure that expressed, symptomatically, economic and ideological fault lines in different locales.[75] Naturalism was not the only way of writing realistic fiction that could make such contradictions visible, but the confluence of naturalism as a movement and specific material conditions makes the appearance of the Nana figure seem overdetermined.

The history of the Nana figure should be instructive, then, for the study of other expressive forms on the move. We saw in the previous chapter that the adoption of a technique from early naturalist works—synecdoches and metonymies of pathological bodies—contributed to the geographical extension of the naturalist field. So too did the Nana figure. The appearance of Nana-like characters around the world that allows us to discern the minimal schema common to them—and thus to recognize the Nana figure—would not have been possible, however, without the field's growth through the participation of more and more writers. To recall an earlier point, from a transnational perspective the history of the naturalist literary field is more fundamentally the history of its figures than of novels and stories. The phenomenon of the Nana figure shows that the expansion of the field played a key role in the development, not just the circulation, of such figures. The history of the Nana figure thus puts into relief some points that might be applied to the study of other forms of expressive culture on a large scale. Instead of searching for origins (or originality), trace combinations and recombinations of ideas and techniques. Watch for formal transformations that happen on the move, such as the transpositions of aspects of narrative discourse into qualities of character examined in this chapter, because they are a way that aspects of one work may be extracted and incorporated into others. Do not mistake the appearance and reappearance of tropes, characters, and fragments of plot for free-floating expressive fun (Nana here, there, everywhere) but dig into the material forces, local and global, behind the variations. Which is to say, above all, ground investigations of expressive forms circulating through the world in the political and economic history of the planet.

CHAPTER 4

Plains, Boats, and Backwaters

August Strindberg's novel *The Red Room* (*Röda rummet*, 1879), often thought to be the first volley of naturalist fiction in the Nordic countries, opens with a famous panorama of Stockholm. Beginning from a terrace in Mosebacke, the narrative eye roams across the metropolis, out into the archipelago, and returns to circle through the city's political, commercial, and cultural center. The bird's-eye view ends with an allusion to Honoré de Balzac's *Old Goriot* (*Le Père Goriot*, 1835): like that novel's Rastignac, *The Red Room*'s protagonist, a would-be writer named Falk, raises his fist in challenge to the city. Ironically, Falk is hapless. The novel follows him as he stumbles through a corrupt and cynical world, in the process creating, in Strindberg's words, "a panorama of a society I don't love and which has never loved me."[1] The city as society: Strindberg's novel is an example of naturalist fiction's penchant for creating spatial analogues for social relations. *The Red Room*'s geographic panorama launches its social one, but fundamentally they are the same. "Stockholm" organizes a representation of society that is at once descriptive, narrative, and figurative.

From the role of the body in mimesis and the ways the character of the self-liberated woman functioned as a social diagnostic in naturalist fiction, I turn now to how naturalist fiction modeled social relations. The aspiration behind naturalism's "social figures" was not only to describe elements of society, but to show their relationship to each other and the social whole by depicting the ensemble in action. Social figures are perhaps the point where empirical investigation, literary representation, and social thought intersect most fundamentally in naturalist fiction. As grand as many naturalist projects were, there seems always to have been a tacit acknowledgment of the impossibility of exhaustively describing something whose totality could only be imagined. Many naturalist writers resorted to other means, from creating concrete symbols for abstract forces to the contradictory enterprise of narrating synchronic social structures. The representations of society that resulted are distillations of naturalism's continually evolving social imaginaries. Like all social imaginaries they have factual and normative sides, evident on the one hand in naturalism's fealty to documentation, and on the other, first of all, in the belief that "documentary" fiction would be objective ipso facto.[2] Far more than the observations of Émile Zola on heredity or Theodore Dreiser on "the cosmopolitan standard of virtue," the social figures of naturalism reveal writers' most basic assumptions about what society is and should be.

Strindberg's spatialization of society as city was not the only approach naturalist writers took to creating social figures. In *Bel-Ami* (1885), Guy de Maupassant's method was biographical: the career of an opportunist and his successive lovers as the concupiscent intersection of politics, business, and the press in Third Republic France. Giovanni Verga's *The Malavoglias* (*I Malavoglia*, 1881) and Shimazaki Tōson's *The Family* (*Ie*, 1911) used the declining fortunes of families in post-unification Sicily and Meiji Japan to examine the transformations of the world around them. In *The Call of the Wild* (1903), Jack London's favored figure for social relations was the wolf-pack. Spatial figures, however, were ubiquitous. Many writers favored the city: the tripartite geography of Plassans in Zola's *Fortune of the Rougons* (*La Fortune des Rougon*, 1871), the predatory Bowery in Stephen Crane's *Maggie, A Girl of the Streets* (1893), and the entropic Tokyo in Masamune Hakuchō's "Dust" ("Jin'ai," 1907). The countryside was also a useful microcosm, as seen in Herman Bang's *By The Wayside* (*Ved Vejen*, 1886), set in a village in northern Jutland; Clorinda Matto de Turner's *Birds without a Nest* (*Aves sin Nido*, 1889), in an Andean mining town; and Frank Norris's *The Octopus* (1901), in California's San Joaquin Valley. Whatever the means, these works have in common the ambition to create synthetic representations of how societies are organized and function through a bounded milieu that is both part of and stands in for the whole.

The phenomenon of the social figure not only shows the great appeal of naturalism as a method for investigating—and explaining—

changing societies, but also its limits. *Germinal* (1885), the third of the novels by Zola most responsible for widening the adoption of naturalist methods, illustrates key elements of the approach to social figuration that emerged in metropolitan France. This novel about a mining strike turns a plain in northern France into a spatially delimited, structurally integrated figure for a capitalist society governed by a homogeneous developmental temporality. As writers in other parts of Europe and the world adopted and adapted naturalist methods, they created social figures that responded to local conditions ranging from economic to ideological ones. Two central examples in this chapter are a sealing ship in London's *The Sea-Wolf* (1904) and a rural district in Tayama Katai's *The Country Teacher* (*Inaka kyōshi*, 1909). We will also see, however, that addressing the local led writers to break with assumptions implicit in the social figures of French naturalism, particularly regarding the relationship of social structure and time. In some cases the single social figure of metropolitan naturalism fractured into several, while in others its unitary temporality multiplied. In the history of naturalist social figures we can read on the one hand the uneven political and economic history of the planet and on the other the history of the naturalist literary field, in which different formal responses to new social realities proliferated. While the phenomenon of the social figure continues to help us understand why and how the field expanded, it also reveals reasons for the field's eventual dissolution.

NARRATIVES OF STRUCTURE

In a famous attack on naturalism, the Marxist critic Georg Lukács compared realist writers who "narrate"—preeminently, Balzac—to naturalist writers who merely "describe." Novelists who narrate depict society in the throes of its transformation by capitalism. Protagonists such as Lucien of Balzac's *Lost Illusions* (*Illusions perdues*, 1837-43) participate in the upheavals of their times, and through them, so do readers. Novelists who narrate establish proportion among details, so that even a minor aspect of decor or dress can reveal the direction and inexorability of the historical process, which for Lukács was the conflict of classes.[3] Novelists who describe, such as Zola and Gustave Flaubert (both naturalists to Lukács), accomplish none of this. Virtuoso scenes such as the country fair in Flaubert's *Madame Bovary* (1857) and the horse race in Zola's *Nana* (1880) are "mere filler" in plots that present static portraits of society. Unconnected to narratives that reveal history at work, the details in such novels are undifferentiated and overwhelming. Characters are observers of the world rather than participants in it, or even worse, only picturesque elements in fictional tableaux. Novelists who describe only give meaning to specific details by forcibly turning them into symbols. In their episodic plots, the organization of social relations by capitalism is not a process but a social fact. In aesthetic terms, naturalism inevitably becomes formalist; in political terms, it becomes disillusioned and acquiescent. Led along this path, Lukács says, readers of naturalism adopt passive positions as spectators of their worlds.[4]

Readers of Flaubert and Zola may not quite recognize the novelists Lukács is criticizing. Yes, they favored episodic plots, and yes, their symbols could be blunt—but they were not narrators? Norris's view of Zola as a writer of "vast and terrible" dramas reminds us that many of the Rougon-Macquart novels are page-turners.[5] Will La Lison, a locomotive, crash in *The Human Beast* (*La Bête humaine*, 1890)? Will Denise, a shop clerk, best the department-store maestro Octave in *Ladies' Paradise* (*Au Bonheur des Dames*, 1883)? The issue may not be whether naturalism narrates or describes, but what it narrates: "history," or something else?

Jacques Dubois, writing about Zola's relationship to the social sciences, argues that the Rougon-Macquart novels do not produce knowledge of society through their overt, often doctrinaire commentary but through their fiction. The novels may begin with phantasmal ideas, but through narrative, symbol, characterization, *and* description they create new interpretive representations of the social structure. By their nature such new understandings of society are concrete rather than theoretical and thus remain somewhat latent (i.e., readers have to draw them out).[6] Nonetheless, individual novels and the Rougon-Macquart series as a whole show Zola intent on revealing the horizontal differentiation and specialization of late nineteenth-century France. Their stories are concerned with the classing and declassing of individuals within these structures, rather than the movement of entire classes.[7] If one is looking for a Marxian dialectic of history, the novels offer a static view of society. In the social figures that result, however, institutions and the individuals associated with them *are* in conflict. The protagonists' stories reveal the relationship of parts and the forces pitting them against each other.

One could say that Zola's novels narrate *structure* rather than History, as Lukács wanted. The social figures of naturalism are a narrative sociology. The Zolean novel's episodic chapters, which Lukács so disliked, are typically of two types. One uses setting to describe an element of the figure, as a chapter of *Germinal* uses a compound of miners' barracks to describe the lives of industrial workers. A second type presents conflict between elements, as when the miners visit company headquarters to demand fair pay. The favored metaphor is spatial, as these examples show: in *Germinal*, the various parts of the socioeconomy of mining are spread across "a great plain" (*une plaine immense*) (*Germinal*, 118). Their relationship is coordinated by novelistic space as the narrative coordinates the episodes presenting each of them. The typical Zolean social figure thus is integrated and coherent. Its readable social organization is held together by forces that characters exploit—as Aristide Rougon exploits Haussmanization in *The Kill* (*La Curée*, 1872)—but rarely change. Spatially the social figure is closed, a bounded milieu in the manner of the Goutte d'Or neighborhood of *L'Assommoir* (1877) or the department store of *Ladies' Paradise*. The strategy of describing the organization of such spaces by *narrating* it reflected Zola's interest in showing how social structures change, but also reveals the role that a particular assumption about "social time" plays in his social figures. Change happens on the scale of the structure, affecting all of its parts, if not equitably so. The Rougon-Macquart series shows the strategy at work on a grand scale: the parts of society that are the topics of individual novels have distinct locations that are coordinated in a twenty-volume array.

Although Zola did not invent multivolume realism—his agonistic model was Balzac's *Human Comedy*, after all—the Rougon-Macquart novels inspired many similar projects. In Spain, Eduardo López Bago wrote a tetralogy of "medico-social novels" about prostitution (1884–85); in Puerto Rico, Manuel Zeno Gandía wrote one collectively called *Chronicles of a Sick World* (*Crónicas de un mundo enfermo*) which he began in 1894 and finished in 1922. Amalie Skram planned five volumes on *The People of Hellemyr*, a family on the Norwegian coast, finishing four (*Hellemyrsfolket*, 1887–98). In Germany, Michael Georg Conrad planned ten volumes on the life of Munich, completing three, and Arno Holz a series of plays about Berlin, completing just one. In Japan, as noted in the last chapter, Kosugi Tengai's *New Year's Finery* (*Hatsu sugata*, 1900) was to be the first of four volumes on the life of the musician Oshun, although Tengai stopped at the third.[8]

To understand how naturalist social figures changed in new circumstances, some series that conspicuously failed may be more instructive than those that succeeded. Verga's *The Malavoglias* was to be the first of a five-volume cycle on Italian society with the upbeat title *The Vanquished* (*I Vinti*). He completed the second one, *Mastro-don Gesualdo* (1889), about a bourgeois social climber, but abandoned the rest.[9] Aluísio Azevedo likewise planned a series, *Brazilians Old and Modern* (*Brasileiros antigos e modernos*), which was to begin with *The Slum* (*O Cortiço*) followed by *The Brazilian Family* (*A Familia Brasileira*) and three more volumes. It was meant to do for Imperial Brazil what the Rougon-Macquart novels did for Second Empire France. After several years of research for the series, Azevedo used some characters intended for *The Brazilian Family* in an entirely different novel, *The Man* (*O Homem*, 1887), and incorporated others into *The Slum*, published three years later. The rest of the series disappeared.[10] *The Malavoglias* and *The Slum* are remarkable novels, however. It seems doubtful that Verga and Azevedo were not up to the task of completing four more. What, then, was the obstacle?

An explanation by the eminent Brazilian critic Antônio Cândido highlights the conditions in which a writer like Azevedo undertook a Zolean plan. The structure of the Rougon-Macquart series, Cândido argues, reflected the relatively great social and economic differentiation in the French society of Zola's time, in which the worlds of politics, finance, industrial labor, shopkeepers, and so on were distinct and distant from each other. Zola could write a novel on each segment, the better to treat it in its own terms. Such a *specialization of novels* was impossible in Brazil, where the capitalist and the worker were tightly attached—first of all by slavery, which affected the position of free and enslaved laborers alike. *The Slum* encompasses parts of Brazilian society spread among different novels in Zola's series—drawing on *L'Assommoir*, as noted in chapter 2, but also on *The Kill*, *Nana*, *Pot-Bouille* (1882), and *The Joy of Life* (*La Joie de vivre*, 1884)—while putting them in an entirely new relationship. Thus the beehive of shacks where the novel's poorest, racially diverse characters live is adjacent to, and just below, the mansion of the richest character, a Portugal-born importer named Miranda initially conceived as the central character in the unwritten *Brazilian Family*.[11] Azevedo did not just rearrange categories established by Zola, but revised and added new ones, notably race. That is, *The Slum* adopts some essentials of Zola's method—a spatial arrangement whose structure is revealed through narrative—while creating a figure specific to the social reality of Azevedo's here and now. One could say that in abandoning that novel and the series—collapsing some parts together while junking the rest—Azevedo arrived at his own method of figuring Brazilian society. Put another way, what "failed" was *Zola's* way of doing it—and the failure was productive. Without digging into Verga's aborted cycle, one might apply a similar logic: not because the society of post-unification Sicily was like that of Imperial Brazil, but because their respective differences from metropolitan France resulted in the impressive, and impressively different, *Slum* and *Malavoglias*.[12]

Examples from Japan may clarify what is at stake here. Iwasa Sōshirō observes that many naturalist stories and novels of the 1900s took so-called *shinkaichi* as their settings, "newly opened areas" that were no longer rural because of the expansion of cities, but nonetheless not urban. Critics sometimes explain fiction from the 1880s and 1890s set in *shinkaichi* as allegories of modernization. In such readings, the space of the *shinkaichi* is a temporally liminal area where the premodern and modern meet.[13] In the 1900s, Iwasa argues, naturalist writers used such settings to describe not the process but the consequences of the transformation of Japanese society. In Mayama Seika's story sequence *South Koizumi Village* (*Minami koizumi mura*, 1907–09), for example, a town is putrefying literally and figuratively: located on a river that drains the sewers of the city of Sendai, it experiences all the harm of "modernity" without the benefits.[14] The neighborhood of *The Slum*, we might observe, is also a kind of *shinkaichi*: sandwiched between a quarry and the higher land occupied by Miranda, it was built by an avaricious and socially ambitious grocer. It seems that in some parts of the world the uneven transformation of social relations became the focus of naturalist social figures, in marked contrast to the figures of an integrated if oppressive order common in others. In comparing Zola's *Germinal*, London's *The Sea-Wolf*, and Katai's *The Country Teacher* I will suggest some reasons for this fault line in naturalist method. The figure of the plain in *Germinal* coordinates social space and social development, but *The Sea-Wolf* ultimately creates three figures, each elaborating a different social order, in an ambiguous critique of capitalism, while the figure of the countryside in *The Country Teacher* foregrounds the lived experience of unevenness in Meiji-era Japan.

THE HORIZONS OF STRUGGLE

The origins of *Germinal* (1885), set in the area of a fictional town in the Valenciennes coal basin, reflect Zola's changing plans for narrating the social, political, and economic history of nineteenth-century France. Zola's 1869 scheme for the Rougon-Macquart series included a novel about workers that became *L'Assommoir*, but after a ferocious reaction to the Paris Commune he decided to add a novel about an insurrectionary worker that would lead up to the 1871 rebellion. Following criticism of his depiction of the working class when *L'Assommoir* was published, he decided that the second worker novel would focus on workers' social and political lives and would center on a strike, not a revolt.[15] (Parts of the insurrectionary novel eventually appeared in *La Débâcle* or *The Debacle*, 1892.) Gervaise's son Étienne, the only character available in the family tree published in *A Page of Love* (*Une page d'amour*, 1878), would be the Rougon-Macquart representative. In the original plan of family traits Étienne was to be prone to alcoholism and homicidal mania, which posed a problem that was both structural and political if Zola wanted to take the worker's movement seriously. How to turn a born criminal into a labor militant? Paul Leroy-Beaulieu's book *The Worker's Question in the Nineteenth Century* (*La Question ouvrière au XIXe siècle*, 1872), which characterized socialist militants as quasi-religious fanatics, provided a solution. Étienne, although not free of his impulses, would become a political zealot—and thus an acceptable leader of the strike—while homicidal mania would be the topic of still another novel, *The Human Beast*, featuring a newly invented brother, Jacques.[16] As with other novels, *Germinal*'s tenuous connection to the Rougon-Macquart clan enabled a more complex investigation that mingled the histories of the Second Empire and the Third Republic, particularly the mining strikes in 1869 at La Ricamarie and Aubin, which were violently suppressed, and a fortuitously timed strike at Anzin in 1884 that Zola visited during his research. The novel's other sources included journalism and fiction on the working conditions and lives of miners, recent work on political economy, and books on contemporary socialism.[17]

The scholarship on—and political criticism of—*Germinal* frequently turns to Zola's representation of the strike, which finally collapses, and the workers' roles in it. Some defend the novel on the grounds that the topic and documentation were radical in themselves and forced Zola to take a critical view of capitalism regardless of his intentions.[18] Others have stressed the radicalization of the miners, through which they gain a voice to articulate their own history and grievances. The stirring ending—when Étienne imagines the germination of seeds sown during the strike—rings false to many, however, considering that the plot's basic message is that radical programs fail. While the miners gain a voice, they use it ineffectively.[19] Moreover, the novel can be read as naturalizing capitalism through the correspondences it creates between the human and nonhuman worlds and its ample use of myth.[20] Sandy Petrey says that the novel can support all of these readings, pro and con, because it is essentially dialogic in its presentation of political discourses in conflict.[21] Point taken, but note that the whole range of arguments concerns how Zola represents conflict in a world whose social relations, from horizon to horizon, bottom to top, are wholly organized by industrial capitalism. Such a social figure may have been plausible in Zola's part of the world, but not everywhere. For the purposes of understanding how naturalist social figures changed as the technique was used in other parts of the world, the more fundamental question is not how Zola treated class conflict, but how he created the plain where he staged the clash between classes.

Germinal begins with Étienne's arrival at Le Voreux, a mine near Montsou where he gets work on a team led by Maheu, a fourth-generation miner, which includes his daughter Catherine and a brute named Chaval toward whom Étienne feels an instinctual, reciprocated enmity. Despite the miners' evident misery, Étienne resolves to stay and finds lodging with a former miner and cabaret owner, Rasseneur, who knows Étienne's old foreman in Lille, a leader in the International. Étienne begins a political education through his conversations with Rasseneur and Souvarine, a Russian anarchist who also lodges there. Later taking a spare bed at the Maheus, he begins to lecture the family on socialism. Jealousy impels Chaval to abduct Catherine, which the family accepts. After a long-rumored change in pay, the miners strike and present their demands to the company director. Étienne and Rasseneur, who advocates the long game, quarrel over strategy, but in a nighttime gathering in the nearby forest Étienne triumphs with a messianic speech. The next day he leads a growing, uncontrollable crowd across the plain from mine to mine—damaging many—and finally into Montsou, where a riot ends in the death and castration of a shopkeeper aligned with the company. The company takes advantage of damage to the last independent mine to buy it for a song and recruits Belgian scabs to reopen the pits. When the miners descend on Le Voreux, soldiers on guard open fire and kill fourteen of them, including Maheu. Étienne is disgraced and many miners return to work. A spectacular cave-in at Le Voreux, the result of sabotage by Souvarine, wrecks the mine's machinery and traps many miners underground. Étienne, Catherine, and Chaval are confined in a collapsed passage, the way out blocked by slowly rising waters. Tensions rise over the course of days and Étienne kills Chaval in a fight to possess Catherine. The two finally consummate their relationship, but Étienne alone survives to be rescued. With his education complete, he decides to go to Paris to begin a political career with his former foreman. In the last scene he watches miners on their way to the pits, seemingly with a new resolve they have gained from the struggle. As he walks back out of the plain, in the culmination of a series of metaphors of fertility, he imagines the earth sown with seeds of resistance that will sprout and reach the surface from below: it is April, or in the calendar of the French Revolution, the month of Germinal.

The plain in which the action of *Germinal* takes place, routinely described as "flat," "great" (*immense*), and "vast," is defined by sites and relations between them that jointly create a political-economic geography.[22] The plot is, in one sense, the characters' transformation of this abstract space into a space of political experience. Its surface is dotted with emblematic places. A first set consists of "the mine," where Étienne finds employment; "the compound," where the Maheu family lives; and "the Directory," the regional headquarters of the mining company, which doubles as the director Hennebeau's home. The miners routinely move between the mine and the compound, while company officials, such as the engineer Négrel, move between the mine and the Directory. Two other sites exist primarily in relation to the company headquarters: the rentier house of the Grégoires, who live off the company's extraction of surplus value (and who rarely meet the miners except as mendicants); and the entrepreneurial house of Deneulin, which doubles as the headquarters for the independent mining concession that is the only obstacle to the domination of the plain by "big business" (*les gros capitaux*) (*Germinal*, 442). Completing the primary sites are Hennebeau's bourgeois dining room and Rasseneur's cabaret. A trio of political positions on the Right and Left is associated with each site. The Orleanist Grégoire (i.e., an economic liberal), the Bonpartist Deneulin (who fears the Emperor is too easy on labor), and the tepid republican Négrel talk politics in the dining room. The "possibilist" Rasseneur (i.e., a pragmatic gradualist), the anarchist Souvarine, and the budding revolutionary Étienne discuss it in the cabaret.[23]

Connecting these sites and others on the surface—such as nearby factories—are roads that allow the movement of goods and people and make the entire plain an "industrious city" (*Germinal*, 137). The roads are economically enabling, but they are also a means of political control. At the company's request, the state blocks them at key moments in the strike. Underground, *Germinal* creates another network: the passages that allow the movement of miners and coal. As the months pass, Étienne becomes as familiar with these as with the roads and streets above. Several of the company's mines are connected underground, making it possible to move great distances through these self-cut paths. The contrast between the openness of the surface and the claustrophobia of the mine emphasizes the difference between the parallel planes, although as we will see, in the end Zola inverts the relation between the seemingly free surface and the constricted depths. The miners' constant movement between the two creates a vertical axis that complements the horizontal one.

Scattered throughout *Germinal*'s space are sites with mythical resonance. Le Voreux is both mine and animate machine, a "gluttonous beast, crouching there to devour the world," the miners whom it gobbles in mouthfuls of twenty or thirty during the morning descent.[24] Above the coal-bearing stratum of the depths is an aqueous layer of fine sand known as "the Torrent," an underground sea with its own storms and shipwrecks. (When it is undammed by Souvarine, the Torrent causes the cave-in that pulls the "beast" into the abyss.) One of the area's oldest mines has been burning underground for centuries and is said to entomb the damned. Its name, Le Tartaret, recalls Tartarus, where the Olympian gods confined the Titans. Its heat has created the "Green Swathe" (*la Côte-verte*), a perpetually verdant expanse on the surface that symbolically connects subterranean exploitation to a fertile future. The forest clearing where Étienne engineers mass mobilization is a similarly utopian locale, an "outside" inside the plain which the company aims to control. Finally, those in the plain speak of "down there" (*là-bas*), Paris, where the company's directors manage the events of this world. In their meeting with Hennebeau, however, the miners' delegates ask themselves just where that is: "down there" is beyond their ken (*Germinal*, 277).

Étienne learns the geography of this economically, politically, and socially interconnected space by roaming it. Ultimately, however, control of the plain depends on understanding what surrounds it. The physical and epistemological boundary of *Germinal*'s plain has a name: *l'horizon*. The word bears many meanings in the novel, not all shared with its English cognate, among them the geographical limit of vision and a view or prospect, that is, the sight of everything up to that limit. The interrelation of the sites within the plain goes hand in hand with the line drawn around it, the two together gesturing to a totality ("society") that they create more symbolically than descriptively, Zola's painstaking documentation notwithstanding. The word *horizon* may also mean expectations of the future, matters of subjective belief rather than geographical knowledge, which change through the education that Étienne and the miners gain during the strike.

Zola stages the entire problem of the horizon through Étienne's arrival in the plain and his ascent after his first day in the mine. *Germinal* begins with Étienne walking "under a night without stars and the darkness and thickness of ink," able to sense the "great expanse" (*horizon immense*) around him only from the gusts of the March wind (*Germinal*, 49). He arrives at Le Voreux amid furnace flare-ups and the mysterious groaning of the steam engine. Maheu's father Bonnemort, unloading cars of coal, gestures to "invisible points" as he describes the area (*Germinal*, 53). At the end of the day, back on the surface, the young man considers whether to remain: "As Étienne debated with himself, his eyes, which were wandering across the great plain, gradually made it out. He was surprised, he hadn't imagined a prospect [*horizon*] like this, when old Bonnemort had pointed it out to him in the depths of the shadows." The often-quoted visual survey, which carefully indicates what is to the left and right, in front of and behind Étienne, ends with a realization: "It was no longer the unknown of the shadows, the inexplicable claps of thunder, the flashing of unknown stars" (*Germinal*, 118–20). That this realization comes at the end of a day of initiation and education reinforces the sense that Étienne's new knowledge is experiential, not simply geographic. The passage moreover has a proleptic quality: through repeated descents and ascents, what is unknown will become known. Étienne's education begins with the elements of the plain, continues with their relationships to each other, and finally, through the failure of the strike, extends to the forces dictating the relationships.

The miners' collective story too is an experiential education about the nature of the horizon.[25] The narrator attributes the miners' initial resistance to Étienne's preaching to the "vague malaise" of a "closed horizon" (*horizon fermé*) (*Germinal*, 219). The condition is both epistemological and temporal. On the one hand, the miners are unable to see beyond the present in order to imagine a different future. On the other hand, time itself seems dysfunctional. Its passage is only the "eternal recommencement of poverty" for the miners. Human fertility is twisted into repetition: young couples steal moments of pleasure in the precincts of an abandoned mine, but the "revenge of creation" only produces miners-to-be who will share their parents' "hereditary ideas of subordination" (*Germinal*, 93, 175, 221). Conditions underground in fact encourage regression: the miners work "like true animals" (*en varies brutes*) and share the "destiny of livestock." Maheu's youngest son Jeanlin is a "human runt" returning to his "original animality" (*Germinal*, 218, 221, 241). Time may be not just at a standstill, but actually running backward.

Fittingly, Zola describes the beginning of the miners' radicalization as a change in the perception of the horizon. As a result of Étienne's lectures to the Maheus "the closed horizon was bursting" (*c'était l'horizon fermé qui éclatait*), letting light shine into their gloomy lives. When his ideas "sprout" around the compound others become impatient to have their share of the happiness "on the other side of this horizon of poverty" (*au-delà de cet horizon de misère*), which has been as "closed as a tomb" (*Germinal*, 221, 237). The miners' use of space changes as they are convinced they can cross the horizon to get to the "other side," a new society that will "sprout in one day." The Maheu house and the compound become sites of political discussions that previously were limited to a few men in Rasseneur's cabaret. After the forest meeting the miners fill the roads and then overflow their banks in a "flood" that races across the "interminable plain," rejecting the present state of society as they reject the constraints imposed by the plain's geography (*Germinal*, 221, 388, 392). *Germinal* associates such an experience of space with political delirium that reaches a peak of "religious exaltation" under the influence of Étienne, an "apostle bearing the truth" who has given the miners a messianic view of time (*Germinal*, 340, 343). The idea that they need only cross the horizon is a misunderstanding of time whose consequence is the regression not just of "runts" like Jeanlin but of the entire marching crowd, whose jaws lengthen atavistically into those of "wild beasts" in the eyes of the frightened bourgeoisie.[26] Despite the sacking of Montsou, "the closed horizon would not open" (*l'horizon fermé návait pas voulu s'ouvrir*) and the authorities once again block the roads (*Germinal*, 458). In the rhetoric of *Germinal* the miners' misunderstanding of the nature of the horizon is a misunderstanding of strategy, and the liberation promised by the experience of space without constraints is an illusion.[27]

Moving across the surface of the plain accomplishes nothing because the source of the miners' strength is underground. As much as Zola may have wanted to be sympathetic to strikes in the abstract, in *Germinal* he has the miners set back their cause of equitable pay by refusing to work.

They must descend and retake the surface from below. The company, intent only on regaining control of the surface, scarcely understands the danger posed by its success.[28] The novel's last scene, in which Étienne imagines the germination of the true struggle, thus inverts the symbolic investment of the plain. Constraint becomes a condition of freedom; the inhospitable land becomes fertile soil. Étienne's and the miners' perception of the horizon changes to suit: now it is neither closed nor open but "glorious." It is not the horizon, which remains all-enclosing, but rather the earth that will "burst" (*Germinal*, 590, 594). One could say that the miners have resolved to work within time, having given up the supposedly deluded idea of a revolutionary escape from the present. Although Étienne leaves the plain, they will transform it.

The plain in *Germinal* thus is simultaneously a figure for a synchronic theory of social organization and a diachronic theory of politics. If the mistake of believing there is an "other side" of the horizon shows that one cannot leap ahead in history, then the singular totality of the plain as a spatialized network of social relations goes together with a unitary quality of the time operating within it. Change happens on the scale of the entire plain, affecting not just one or several elements but all of them, individually and in relationship to each other.[29] *Germinal* is anti-revolutionary, then, not just in its depiction of the strike but in its figurative creation of the space that subtends all possible outcomes of conflict. Immediate political considerations aside, *Germinal* illustrates essential qualities of the social figures that can be found in many of Zola's novels, beginning with the town of Plassans in *The Fortune of the Rougons*: bounded space, integral internal organization, and homogeneous developmental time. There is a more fundamental politics in this triumvirate—the proposition of "history" as a unitary, inexorable process—that comes into question in London's *The Sea-Wolf* and Katai's *The Country Teacher*.

GERMINAL'S SPROUTS

Any novel by Zola published after *L'Assommoir* and *Nana* received instant attention abroad, but the impact of *Germinal* differed from that of the other two novels that pushed Zola and French naturalism into the international arena in ways that reflected both the era and *Germinal* itself. Translation now was immediate. A German version ran simultaneously in six newspapers while *Germinal* was still in serialization in France.[30] Seven foreign book editions appeared in 1885, the year Charpentier published the novel as a volume in French: one each in German, Italian, Portuguese, and Spanish, and three in English. (A Chicago edition was titled *Germinal*, one in London added the subtitle *Or Master and Man*, and as noted in the previous chapter, another in Philadelphia connected all the Rougon-Macquart dots by calling the novel *Nana's Brother: Son of "Gervaise" and "Lantier" of "L'Assommoir."*) By 1900 there were at least twenty-two translations, including six each in English and German.[31] Many of the translations only had a family resemblance to the French *Germinal* and each other, as the Slovenian critic Josip Stritar, who knew the novel in French, realized while arguing with a colleague who had read a German version.[32] Often muted or missing were not just the sex scenes, but also the political discussions, critical references to the Catholic Church, and even the strike itself.[33]

Diluted or not, *Germinal* became an immediate point of reference. In the dedication to his story collection *Wicked Society* (*Schlechte Gesellschaft*, 1885), the German writer Karl Bleibtreu raised his hat to the "poet of *Germinal*." A young writer in Hermann Conradi's story "His First Book" ("Sein erstes Buch," 1889) complains that *Germinal* is everything for his friends, who cannot talk of anyone but Henrik Ibsen, Georg Brandes, and Zola.[34] The heroine of William Edwards Tirebuck's *Miss Grace of All Souls* (1895), set during the lockout of English and Welsh coal miners in 1893, invokes the subtitle of the English translation mentioned earlier when she asks a pit owner why he will not admit that "masters and men are, after all, one in their interdependence on each other."[35] The title of *The Seeds She Sowed* (1891), Emma Leslie's novel about the London dock strike of 1889, gestures to *Germinal*'s governing metaphor, although with the opposite message: a young girl saves proletarian families from ruin through virtue, not revolt.[36] The attention *Germinal* received was great enough that Camille Lemonnier's preface to *The Flesh-Eater* (*Happe-Chair*, 1886) informed readers that he was already working on his strike novel when Zola's book was published.[37]

As with *L'Assommoir* and *Nana*, elements of *Germinal* began to appear in the work of other naturalist writers. The most evident element is documentary description of the conditions in which the working class lived and labored—a feature of many of Zola's novels and other varieties of European realism, to be sure. Elements more specific to *Germinal* include a contrast between a proletarian and a bourgeois family, echoing that between the Maheus and the Grégoires in *Germinal*. The dyads had descriptive functions, establishing the gap between the laboring poor and the leisured rich, and narrative ones, allowing the creation of parallel narrative paths through different parts of society. Examples can be found in the miner family of the Ockleshaws and the mine-owning Brooksters in Tirebuck's *Miss Grace of All Souls*, and the Puerto Rican coffee-growing family of Leandra and the plantation-owning del Saltos in Zeno Gandía's *The Pond* (*La Charca*, 1894). (Leandra's fertility ensures the reproduction of the workforce, in an echo of Maheu's fecund wife.)[38] Tirebuck compares miners' collective hunger to the sumptuous dinners of the bourgeoisie, reprising the lavish lunch underway at the Hennebeaus' when the miners' delegation arrives in *Germinal*. Norris does the same in *The Octopus*, a novel about a battle between farmers and an avaricious railroad, when an officer of the Pacific and Southwest Railroad throws a feast while a destitute farmwife and her daughter wander the roads. (In the well-appointed dining room, which remarkably resembles the Hennebeaus', guests pepper their conversation with French.)[39]

Aspects of *Germinal*'s characters too began to appear. Self-educated radicals recalling Étienne have central roles in *Miss Grace of All Souls*, in which a third-generation Ockelshaw, Sam, espouses a vague but passionate socialism; *The Octopus*, whose Presley, radicalized by a saloonkeeper, preaches to farmers; and the Slovenian writer Fran Saleški Finžgar's *From the Modern World* (*Iz modernega sveta*, 1904), where Rožman, injured in a factory accident, educates himself in the hospital and then rallies his fellow workers to strike.[40] Zeno Gandía's *The Pond* features two love triangles, in parallel to *Germinal*, one among a plantation owner, Leandra, and her Catherine-like daughter Silvina, and the other among Silvina and two plantation workers, Ciro and Gaspar, the latter reminiscent of Chaval in his bestiality.[41] In "The Pit" ("El Pozo"), a story in the Chilean writer Baldomero Lillo's collection of coal-mining stories *Underground* (*Sub Terra*, 1904), characters recalling Chaval and Étienne vie for the affection of a female miner, the one seeming to succeed until he is killed by the other.[42] In Tirebuck's *Miss Grace of All Souls* the shooting of a Maheu-like father by soldiers sent to suppress the strike propels it forward, while the death of a father in a mine collapse in Lillo's "Juan Fariña" pushes the son to take revenge against the mine itself, in an echo of *Germinal*'s Souvarine flooding Le Voreux, by setting off explosives in a tunnel reaching under the Pacific. (Unlike Souvarine, he dies in the process.)[43] In many of these works the introduction of an outsider provides the opportunity to describe working and living environments, a device not unique to Zola or naturalism but that in the presence of other elements from *Germinal* also recalls the novel.[44] Finally, we should note the important function of setting in many of these works, as the immediate site of struggle and a microcosm of greater conflicts: the mines, dockyards, factories, and plantations we have seen, to which could be added the Andean town at the center of Matto's *Birds without a Nest*.

The most important element that these works share with *Germinal*, however, certainly must be the theme of workers gaining class consciousness and trying to change the world without assistance. This is not to say that Zola invented the strike novel, but that *Germinal* stood out for depicting a worker revolt as a justified and self-guided response to economic oppression, Zola's gradualism notwithstanding. From this point of view, the endings of novels sharing elements of *Germinal* are instructive. In *Miss Grace of All Souls* strikers led by Ockelshaw father and son are victorious, and a marriage between Sam and Grace, a vicar's daughter, portends an alliance between workers and enlightened parts of the middle class. Tirebuck's radicalized family, like Zola's Maheus, is both a metaphor for and an instrument in the collective radicalization of the miners. Class awakening similarly is a theme and plot point in Finžgar's *From the Modern World* and Norris's *The Octopus*. Political optimism was not required: while the strike in *From the Modern World* culminates in an agreement with management, the revolt against the railroad in *The Octopus* ends in defeat with no promise of what Maheu's wife calls "the big one" (*le grand coup*) (*Germinal*, 589). (Instead, *The Octopus* was followed in 1903 by *The Pit*, about wheat speculation on the Chicago Board of Trade.) In Lillo's "Juan Fariña," collective suffering concludes with an aggrieved son's individualistic attack against the mine, not its owners. Zeno Gandía's *The Pond* describes the collective suffering of Leandra's family and Puerto Rican plantation workers as a group, but features no collective response. At the end the epileptic Silvina, suffering a seizure, pitches off a cliff and breaks her skull at the edge of the pond where her mother washes their meager clothing. From Tirebuck's tale of coal workers in industrialized England to Zeno Gandía's account of coffee workers in colonial Puerto Rico, one finds both collective action and its absence: for the moment, note that the range of endings amounts to a collective meditation on the conditions of possibility for revolt.

At this point we should also pause, however, to observe that while there was certainly a wave of literature that gestured to *Germinal*—which could also include, to step briefly away from prose, the German playwright Gerhart Hauptmann's *Before Dawn* (*Vor Sonnenaufgang*,

1889) and *The Weavers* (*Die Weber*, 1892)—the number of such works was smaller than those appearing in the wake of *L'Assommoir* and *Nana*, with parodies notably few. Although characters sharing some elements of Étienne appeared, moreover, there was no genre of "Étienne figures" like the Nana figures that appeared after *Nana*. On the contrary, it was common to split the descriptive function of the outsider from the theme of the self-radicalized worker. Examples are Grace and Sam in Tirebuck's *Miss Grace of All Souls* and the newly arrived doctor Sluga and Rožman in Finžgar's *From the Modern World*. *Germinal* also did not have the stylistic impact that *L'Assommoir* had on writers such as Benito Pérez Galdós in Spain and Verga in Italy. Some critics and publications which had loudly debated Zola's earlier work were conspicuously silent about *Germinal*.[45] Although *Germinal* cemented the international reputations of Zola and French naturalism, the response to it was fundamentally different.

There were formal and political reasons for the difference. Formally, while Gervaise and Nana are the undisputed centers of their novels, in *Germinal* the role of Étienne oscillates between charismatic leader and one worker among many.[46] The novel's closing passages, moreover, signal a definitive shift from an individual to a collective proletarian subject that will not need anyone's help to launch "the big one." *Germinal* thus did not lend itself to the extraction of a single character as *L'Assommoir* and *Nana* did. By the same token, the need to coordinate multiple, equally significant characters made the novel as a whole harder to emulate. One can also say that setting aside a central pathological character in favor of a constellation of characters, each responding to the pressures upon them, represented a formally different approach to the relationship of individual and milieu than that found in *L'Assommoir*, where Zola used free indirect style to collapse the distance between Gervaise and the Goutte d'Or, or *Nana*, where Nana's mobility was one of many ways Zola showed that society had created its perfect enabler. The difference made *Germinal* philosophically and politically more complex, but stylistically less interesting. Finally, while the setting and story of *Germinal* take on mythical tones, the plain is not a "generic" locale like *L'Assommoir*'s working-class quarter, making it less transposable, while for a bourgeois reader a mythified man-eating economic system surely would have been less titillating than the mythified man-eating woman of *Nana*.

Politically, lifting elements from *Germinal* was risky in a way that reprising characters or scenes from the morally scandalous *L'Assommoir* and *Nana* was not. (As noted, even translators were wary of the novel's political speeches.) Nonetheless, at a moment when trade unions were rising in the industrialized world the novel did have "extraordinary resonance," in Sylvain Barreur's view. At Zola's funeral in 1902, a group of miners from the northern French city of Denain chanted "Germinal! Germinal!"[47] Although *Germinal* was essentially anti-revolutionary in its treatment of the horrors of the strike and intended to frighten the bourgeois reader (as Zola said in his plans), it effectively was received as a socialist novel.[48] The protagonist of the socialist novelist Margaret Harkness's *George Eastmont: Wanderer* (1905) reports that *Germinal* was his guide to the mines of Scotland. The publishing arm of the social democratic party Népszava issued the first Hungarian translation, which was stocked by union libraries, and Zola's novels were favorites with proletarian readers in Germany, to critics' dismay.[49] A leftist journal of the "Generation of 1890" in Spain adopted the novel's title (as did several in France), the writers associated with it being known as *Germinalistas*. An abridged translation of *Germinal* into Japanese in 1906, serialized in the journal *Studies in Socialism* (*Shakai shugi kenkyū*), was meant to explain socialist ideas.[50] *Germinal*'s place in the socialist literary canon was strong enough that some twentieth-century socialist critics took it for granted that Zola was on their side.[51]

That *Germinal* could be received as a socialist, revolutionary novel makes it all the more important to ask what happened to its method of figuring society, posited on self-enclosed structure and temporal homogeneity, when it was transposed to places with positions in the world political economy different from that of metropolitan France. The examples of Zeno Gandía's *The Pond* and Lillo's stories in *Underground* are already evidence that *Germinal*'s strike story was difficult to reproduce in places where, for socioeconomic rather than literary reasons, novels about self-organized worker revolts would not have resonated as they did in heavily industrialized parts of the world. Jack London's *Sea-Wolf* and Tayama Katai's *Country Teacher* show ways that the method, not simply the content, of the naturalist social figure exemplified by *Germinal* changed as the naturalist novel traveled.

THE VIEW FROM THE CROSSTREES

The Sea-Wolf (1904) tells the story of Humphrey Van Weyden, a San Francisco rentier who is pressed into work on a sealing boat captained by a brutal Norwegian, Wolf Larsen. Like *Germinal* and many naturalist novels and stories, the novel relies on a social figure—a bounded space, internally integrated, with a specific temporality—to reflect on the society of its time. Van Weyden narrates the structure of Larsen's "hell-ship," the *Ghost*, which is organized by the forces of capital and race.[52] Although London, like Stephen Crane, rejected the label of naturalist, the novel appears to gesture to Zola and *Germinal*. Larsen manipulates his crew with the "cruel hand of a vivisectionist," echoing Zola's 1868 preface to *Thérèse Raquin*, while a Cockney member of Larsen's crew exhibits "hereditary servility" in the manner of *Germinal*'s Maheu family (*Sea-Wolf*, 492, 540). Also contributing to the novel's story and the social figure of the *Ghost* are the popularized philosophy of the survival of the fittest seen in other work by London such as *The Call of the Wild*; ideas about race and evolution gleaned from reading Ernst Haeckel, Thomas Huxley, and other scientists and philosophers; and turn-of-the-century critiques of capitalism. At a critical point in *The Sea-Wolf*'s story and refutation of the view of the world that Van Weyden brings on board the *Ghost*, however, two other social figures appear, a rival steam-powered sealer and a Bering Sea island where Van Weyden remakes himself, in the company of a female castaway, before rejoining society. The multiplication of social figures, each with its own organization and claims about the "natural" order of society, is a break with the method of social figuration found in *Germinal* that is meant to expose the historical—and unnatural—character of capitalism. At the same time the fracturing of one figure into three, I will argue, reflects an unwillingness to reconcile London's hostility to capitalism with the evolutionary racism he endorsed, and shows how the changes in form that occurred as naturalist methods were used in new places could reflect the political contradictions of writers and the societies in which they worked.

Van Weyden's first-person narrative in *The Sea-Wolf* begins on a fogbound ferry from Sausalito to San Francisco, as he muses on the division of labor that relieves him of the need to understand tides and navigation so that he can pursue a career as an authority on Edgar Allen Poe. A ship rams the ferry, and in the ensuing chaos Van Weyden is swept into the open ocean where he is rescued by the *Ghost*. Rather than return him to San Francisco, Larsen impresses Van Weyden to work as a cabin boy, renaming him "Hump" and telling him "it will be the making of you" (*Sea-Wolf*, 500). The succeeding chapters are filled with Hump's observations of the "little floating world" of the *Ghost*, which he discovers is a racialized hierarchy organized by "force, nothing but force," moral suasion being unknown (*Sea-Wolf*, 516, 523–24). Hump and Larsen have long debates pitting the former's idealism against the latter's materialism, in which Larsen maintains that the big eat the little in order to keep moving and the lucky simply eat most and move longest. Already having criticized Hump for standing on "dead men's legs"—his father's wealth—Larsen attacks him for being unwilling to recognize that his comfort has come from the labor of others who work to survive (*Sea-Wolf*, 500). Hump comes to see the captain as so purely primitive that he recalls men who lived before the development of the "moral nature," but Larsen suffers debilitating headaches that sometimes confine him to his cabin for days (*Sea-Wolf*, 557). For his part, Hump worries that he is being mentally and morally tainted by the environment on the *Ghost*. When the ship's mate disappears under suspicious circumstances Hump unwillingly succeeds him, and having discovered his own "legs," learns to operate the ship (*Sea-Wolf*, 596–97).

The character and pace of the narrative, which up to this point has focused on Hump's observation of the shipboard world, change when the *Ghost* picks up the survivors of a sunken mail steamer, among them an East Coast poet, Maud Brewster, whose presence incites rivalry between Hump and Larsen. The tension is interrupted by the appearance of the *Macedonia*, a steam-powered sealing ship captained by Larsen's brother, a "lump of an animal" untroubled by philosophical matters, whom Larsen momentarily outmaneuvers in pursuit of their prey (*Sea-Wolf*, 560). Larsen tries to rape Maud—with Hump powerless to stop him—but is overcome by his mysterious cerebral malady. Hump and Maud escape in a boat and eventually drift to an island inhabited only by seals. As they prepare for winter, Hump feels the "youth of the race" burgeoning in him and Maud too discovers an unknown resourcefulness (*Sea-Wolf*, 711). One morning, in one of the novel's improbable turns, they wake to find that the *Ghost*, masts and rigging in shambles, has drifted into their cove. On board is an increasingly disabled Wolf Larsen. His brother had lured his crew away with higher pay and one man slashed the lines as he left, leaving the captain alone and adrift. The new Hump teaches himself basic engineering and is able to repair the ship with Maud's help despite Larsen's enfeebled attempts at sabotage. A day after they set sail for Japan, Larsen, now unable to move, see, or speak, succumbs; moments after they bury him at sea, a U.S. Coast Guard cutter appears on the horizon. With rescue at hand, the chaste survivors kiss at last.

Like *Germinal*, *The Sea-Wolf* narrates structure, using Hump's experiences on the *Ghost* to construct a figurative world with a jointly economic and racial order. Through Hump's observations London maps a spatialized division of labor, in which captain and mate occupy the *Ghost*'s cabin, seal hunters the quarters in steerage, and sailors the forecastle. Qualities that London attributes to race and ethnicity reinforce the crew members' positions in the division of labor. The sailors, of English and Scandinavian stock, mainly acquiesce to their place in the order of things. (A Scandinavian and a young sailor of Irish descent are defiant, but resistance is futile: Larsen lets them drown when they try to escape.) The hunters, a "superior breed" whose faces have hard lines and marks of the "free play of passions," are predators by nature and occupation (*Sea-Wolf*, 497, 506). They willingly enforce a shipboard order based on the harvesting of seals and the sailors' labor. Larsen, whose massive visage reveals the "immense vigor or virility of spirit" behind it, incites and is the victor in such evolutionary struggle.[53] Early on, when Larsen and the mate send a green sailor aloft to shift a sail, Hump sees the element of force in the economic organization. "The callousness of these men, to whom industrial organization gave control of the lives of other men, was appalling," he remarks. Onboard, life was only "a cipher in the arithmetic of commerce" (*Sea-Wolf*, 531). Racial hierarchy justifies and reinforces the economic order in the typical Social Darwinist ruse.

The social order defined by the rails of the *Ghost* is all-encompassing. Hump's references to the ship as a "little world" are amplified poetically when Larsen sails into a fog bank in flight from the *Macedonia*: "The mind recoiled from contemplation of a world beyond this wet veil which wrapped us around," Hump recalls. "This was the world, the universe itself, its bounds so near one felt impelled to reach out both arms and push them back" (*Sea-Wolf*, 669). Implicit in the bounded quality of novelistic space is the assertion that the conditions of economic and evolutionary competition prevail homogeneously across it. The self-enclosed world serves both to refute Hump's received ideas about the world he left and to expose its real organizing principles. Larsen mercilessly points out the contradictions in Hump's views, arguing that the system which allows people like Hump to live off the labor of others is simply one "piggishness," and Larsen's own forthright creation of such a system is just another (*Sea-Wolf*, 520–21). The world he has created shows that might is right, the soul an illusion, and beauty an irrelevant effect of utility. The only thing that might be called sin is one being's rejection of the inborn impulse to devour another. As voiced by Larsen, the novel's negation of genteel views of the world is Social Darwinist and Nietzschean, with the beast driven by survival rolled together with the superman.[54] (Larsen's demise puts his views in a different light, but that is a matter for later discussion.)

Hump's captivity on the *Ghost* forces him to "look more closely at life as it was lived," an experience that he says "opened up for me the world of the real." His newcomer's position on the ship, like Étienne's in the plain, is a narrative conceit that allows London to expose "the concrete and objective phases of existence," as Hump calls them. (The phrase reflects the Marxian—rather than Nietzschean—aspect of this presentation of the *Ghost*.)[55] The conditions he discovers are the foundation of an economic division of labor, and therefore a structure of of social relations, rooted in force and biology. The "goodness" of specialization on which he meditated during the trip across San Francisco Bay was only a class-based obfuscation of social reality (*Sea-Wolf*, 481). Hump's self-observed transformation while in the world of "the real" includes a recognition of the true order of things. Stripped of ideological apology and observed in its concrete reality, the *Ghost* is both an inversion and a reduction of the world Hump left behind. He realizes that he finds Larsen's philosophy a better explanation of the world than his own and concludes that the brutality around him is having a "degenerative" effect (*Sea-Wolf*, 575–76). A doubled point of view fittingly appears in the narrative discourse of *The Sea-Wolf*, in which Hump, as narrator, observes both the *Ghost* and retrospectively his own transformation. The double perspective is dramatized when Hump climbs the ship's fore crosstrees to look for sealing boats in a storm: from his perch he looks down "as though outside the *Ghost* and apart from her," while noting his own giddy trajectory as the ship rolls in the sea (*Sea-Wolf*, 608).

The primitivization of life that Larsen carries out on the *Ghost* does not reduce the social order to its organizing principles, however, so much as assert new ones. As Larsen reveals reality to Hump, so *The Sea-Wolf* reveals it to the reader. Larsen may be "the perfect type of the primitive man" and believe that the order of the *Ghost* is the world as it always has been and always will be, but it is not an anachronism: the *Ghost* is the world as it actually exists (*Sea-Wolf*, 540). In this novel, however, ideological exposure is also ideological enchantment. The social reality that *The Sea-Wolf* "reveals" is replete with late nineteenth-century nativist views of the natural order of races and the parallel discourse on the subservient position of women in society. These too are part of the "nature" that Hump discovers. As in Norris's work, contemporary fears of the proletarianization and ethnicization of Anglo-Saxons lurk in the spectacle of a coupon-clipper with "Puritan" ancestry working as a cabin boy.[56] They are reinforced by Hump's effeminate state when he is pulled out of the sea: he had already "shrieked aloud as the women had shrieked" during the wreck of the Sausalito ferry, and now the "sensitiveness" of his "nervous organization" is shocked by the first events on the *Ghost* (*Sea-Wolf*, 487, 503).

Here we can see the other face of primitivization in *The Sea-Wolf*: stripping Hump of his overcivilized ways as a means for his re-masculinization and racial revitalization. He arrives on the *Ghost* enervated, unfit for life outside his study, and "not amative to any considerable degree," but he rises to his hereditarily legitimated position at the top, for the moment subordinate only to the "magnificent atavism" of Larsen himself (*Sea-Wolf*, 557, 582). The temporality of such nativist evolutionism, which reflects London's on-and-off endorsement of the ideology of Anglo-Saxonism in the United States, is typically contorted: his crewmates will never advance beyond their natural positions in forecastle or steerage, but Hump is both over-evolved and not evolved enough.[57] Hump's re-masculinization is similarly ambiguous. Although Lee Clark Mitchell has shown that standing erect becomes a gendered prerogative in *The Sea-Wolf*'s allegory of the rise of *Homo erectus*, the re-righting of gender relations is not evident until Hump and Maud are alone on Endeavor Island.[58] On board the *Ghost*, Hump believes that his "toughening or hardening . . . could not be anything but wholesome for 'Sissy Van Weyden,'" but his appraisal of Larsen's physique is increasingly erotic. He finds the captain's body below the neckline "fair as the fairest woman's" and cannot tear his eyes from its magnificent biceps. His gaze is met with Larsen's demand that Hump become his, that is the ship's, mate (*Sea-Wolf*, 593–94, 603). Hump's re-masculinization unexpectedly undermines sexual difference.

By this point, Larsen's and London's zeal to reduce the *Ghost* to a world of force has reached a dangerous point not only in the story—with the presentiment of a fight for racial and sexual dominance—but also, I would say, in London's willingness to expose the world as he sees it. Three things intervene: the rescue of Maud—seemingly conjured to prevent male sexual union—the sighting of the *Macedonia*, and an unexpected change of genre. The social figure of the *Ghost* splits into two—the *Macedonia* and Endeavor Island—the one concerned with capitalism and the other with race. They are separated not only as physical spaces or sociological problematics but also through different plot conventions, those of the adventure novel that *The Sea-Wolf* has been up to this point and those of the sentimental novel, including the expectation of a happy ending, which begin to assert themselves along with Maud.[59] The change reveals symmetries in what in many ways is an ungainly narrative architecture. Maud appears after a shipwreck, and the appearance of the *Macedonia* leads to the wrecking of the *Ghost*. Framing the wreckage of the middle of the novel is the sinking of the ferry at the start and Hump's and Maud's abandonment of the *Ghost* at the end. The bracketing of the novel by marine disasters and the bifurcation of form associated with the pair of them in the middle is perhaps an unwilling indication of contradictions that the novel will not resolve.

The contrast between the *Ghost* and the *Macedonia* is one of sail and steam, but in light of London's presentation of the *Ghost* as a microcosm of capitalism, we can also see the two ships as figures for rival forms of it. The *Macedonia* as ship and social organization has different means of extraction, processing, and locomotion. More maneuverable and carrying more boats, it "hogs" the sealing grounds and bests the *Ghost* through economic, not physical violence.[60] (An offstage bargain over pay, not fratricide, spells the end of the *Ghost*.) Considering Wolf Larsen's hyperindividualism and his brother's brutal rationalism, the *Ghost* and the *Macedonia* can be read as figures for capitalism in its liberal and Fordist forms.[61] The contrast between the two ships' organizations for extracting profit from ocean and crew suddenly thrusts Wolf Larsen's beliefs about the timeless order of things into history, as an ideology legitimating the order of the *Ghost* which must compete with his brother's apparent belief in the "natural" rationalization of the work process.[62] The *Macedonia* did not evolve from the *Ghost*, it is its rival.

It is common to see the victory of the *Macedonia* over the *Ghost* as inevitable, and indeed the fog bank that Larsen steers into to escape the *Macedonia* recalls the fog at the beginning of the novel, through which Van Weyden drifts with a false sense of security. Neither man knows the disaster ahead.[63] It is worth observing, however, that in the ocean where *Ghost* and *Macedonia* collide there are no fixed boundaries, no fixed relationships, and no inevitabilities. For the socialist London, if the outcome of the collision of liberal and Fordist capitalism was not foreordained, neither too was the existence of capitalism itself. Another vessel was and is possible. The appearance of the *Macedonia* thus deepens and extends *The Sea-Wolf*'s critical examination of capitalism and the social relations on which it depends.

On Endeavor Island, in contrast, the critique of capitalism that began with the *Ghost* and continued with the *Macedonia* disappears. The story of racial rejuvenation through regression, however, continues: the space of the island is a stage for the reinvigoration of Anglo-Saxons, and thus for re-creating the "proper" racial foundations for American society. The process is safely heteronormative. As he builds shelter, kills seals, and re-rigs the ship, Hump experiences "the old hunting days and forest nights of my remote and forgotten ancestry" (*Sea-Wolf*, 711). As on the *Ghost*, racial "nature" reasserts itself, although in this case neither Hump nor London are interested in exposing the ruse. In the process, the specialization of Hump's and Maud's former world is reorganized to create a gendered division of labor. Hump learns all manner of manly skills, while Maud learns to be his helper. (He comes to think of her as his "mate-woman"; *Sea-Wolf*, 750.) In the evolutionary philosophy that underpins the novel, the couple's ability to cooperate, and their scrupulous sexual morality, reflect a developmental superiority over a ruthless individualist and would-be rapist like Larsen.[64] Although there is no racial hierarchy within the division of labor on the island, London's proposition of it thus is premised on a racial difference that is also a difference of class. That the entire episode presumes a rescue (once Maud arrives, they must be able to marry) reinforces the point: implicitly, the Anglo-Saxon reinvigoration is staged with respect to competing, inferior races. When Hump and Maud reenter the world, they will transform their race-class and preserve its naturally superior place in society. If the appearance of the *Macedonia* shows London thinking historically about capitalism, the temporality of Endeavor Island is evolutionary fantasy.

The splitting of the *Ghost* into three social figures allows *The Sea-Wolf* to avoid reconciling London's opposition to capitalism with his endorsement of race philosophy. The critique of capitalism finally is confined to the *Macedonia* (and the adventure novel); the solution to racial "enervation" is limited to Endeavor Island (and the sentimental novel). To really keep the two apart, however, a last structural problem remained: Wolf Larsen, who plays a role in both issues for most of *The Sea-Wolf*. He is shown to be unable to compete on both economic and racial grounds. His heroic capitalism is no match for the rationalized one associated with his brother, and lacking a "moral nature," he is incapable of the higher cooperation of Hump and Maud. London's supermen always fail, a point that he was distressed that readers did not grasp.[65] Yet Larsen's "brain breakdown," like Nana's smallpox, has nothing to do with these reasons for his demise (*Sea-Wolf*, 746). June Howard argues that Larsen's malady is both a contingent circumstance and an "inevitable fatality," structurally necessary because it allows moral closure.[66] It is also necessary, I would argue, because it keeps capital and race in separate philosophical and political compartments.

In examining novelistic space in *Germinal*, we saw that the novel's economic and political conflicts are staged in a single bounded space composed of individual sites meant to be symbolically meaningful and a set of relations between them proposed as a synecdoche for broader social relations. A single linear temporality applies to the entire plain. The politics of the plain as social figure inheres particularly in the last quality—its temporality—which disqualifies revolution in favor of "sober" progress toward justice. *The Sea-Wolf* adopts the method, but unexpectedly social figures multiply in the novel. Moreover, while *The Sea-Wolf*'s three social figures have distinct internal organizations, each is—in the inhabitants' views—timeless. Rather than being governed by a single temporality, they combine in two contradictory historical and political arguments. Through the *Ghost*, and in its collision with the *Macedonia*, London crafted an inventive way of showing the historicity of capitalism and the supplanting of its liberal form by its Fordist one. Through the *Ghost* too, and continuing on Endeavor Island, he presented an argument for "rectifying" the racial and patriarchal foundation of American society. Ultimately, the politics of social figures in *The Sea-Wolf* inheres in the multiplication of figures, not in any single one of them. In the multiplication of figures we see London's own unwillingness to resolve the conflict between his opposition to capitalism and the doctrines of racial hierarchy that he fitfully supported. (The conflict, not limited to *The Sea-Wolf*, is especially apparent in his 1903 book of reportage on poverty in London, *The People of the Abyss*.) Beyond London's own political contradictions, however, we can see the unwillingness—strong now as it was then—to recognize the role of race and racism in the history of capitalism in the United States, and how that role was changing as post-Reconstruction laws directed at African Americans combined with nativist arguments against immigration. The fracturing of the social figure when London brought the technique to bear on the late nineteenth-century American economic and political moment tells us that as naturalist methods evolved in different parts of the world, so did the politics of its "truth-telling" (including truths not to be mentioned), which are to be found not only in the stories naturalist writers told, but in the form in which they told them.

LIVING UNEVENNESS

We might think of the multiplication of social figures in *The Sea-Wolf*—and the competition among them—as an argument against the way that metropolitan naturalist writers such as Zola bounded social space. From this perspective, we could think of Tayama Katai's *The Country Teacher* (1909) as an argument against a different quality of the social figures found in metropolitan works like *Germinal*: their internal integration. Katai's novel confronts the unevenness of development that haunted the "progress" of the Meiji era: planned backwardness in the economy, incomplete penetration of the state's political projects, and the persistence of "outdated" habits and customs in everyday life. Like *Germinal* and *The Sea-Wolf*, *The Country Teacher* uses a newcomer—the teacher Seizō—to lead the reader through the setting that provides material for its social figures. Seizō's peregrinations, however, do not reveal an integrated order. Instead, the novelistic space of *The Country Teacher* is composed of heterogeneous, only partially integrated human histories, the human everyday, and the nonhuman world.

Katai is notable as the only writer who contributed to both the early Zolaist period of naturalism in Japan and the later, "egocentric" period when the field was joined by other writers such as Shimazaki Tōson and Iwano Hōmei. Alongside "The End of Jūemon" ("Jūemon no saigo," 1902), his manifesto "Plain Description" ("Rokutsu naru byōsha," 1904) did much to push naturalism in Japan into wider literary circles. Even after the appearance of his autobiographical novella *The Quilt* (*Futon*, 1907), however, Katai continued to produce both novels based on research and fieldwork such as *The Country Teacher* and autobiographically inspired works such as *Life* (*Sei*, 1908). For decades critical arguments about *The Country Teacher* have centered on its style, either to fault Katai for practicing a naive objectivism or to save him from the charge. His portmanteau manifestos such as "Plain Description" and "On Mimesis" ("Byōsharon," 1911), however, belie a more complex project. Viewed in the context of the transnational history of naturalist fiction, we can see Katai developing a method of social figuration adequate to his perception of turn-of-the-century Japan that we might call the "mimesis of unevenness." The figure of the countryside re-creates "in the surface of the prose" (as Katai put it) the social reality and subjective experience of heterogeneous patterns of social relations mingling in one present. Like *The Sea-Wolf*, *The Country Teacher* sets out to overturn an ideological ruse—but it is the ruse of "development," which as we have seen was a basic assumption behind social figures like the plain in *Germinal*.

At the beginning of *The Country Teacher* Hayashi Seizō, who has just graduated from what was called middle school (a fairly high achievement), is walking from his parents' home in Gyōda to begin work as an elementary-school teacher in an agricultural village, Miroku, in what is now urbanized Saitama prefecture. As he walked "a new life was being unrolled," we learn. "He felt as if whatever it would be, a new life had meaning and hope" (*Inaka kyōshi*, 5). The short life that follows is based on the diary of a teacher that Katai received from a writer and Buddhist priest in a temple near Hanyū, midway between Gyōda and Miroku. In addition to providing most of *The Country Teacher*'s story, passages from the diary appear in the novel itself, along with Katai's own documentary observations of the area, which was not far from where he grew up.[67] Seizō and a group of friends in the novel are identifiably "literary youths" like the characters in Tōson's novel *Spring* (*Haru*, 1908), which I discussed in chapter 2, but rusticated and bound for obscurity.[68] Over the next three years, Seizō's expectations are ground inexorably down. Unable to contemplate high school because his father is a serial bankrupt, he tells a friend that he feels the job in Miroku is the first step to being "buried in the countryside" (*inaka ni uzumoreru*) (*Inaka kyōshi*, 32). He rents a room from a local priest (modeled after Katai's friend) and fitfully attempts to write or study for exams that would let him move to a bigger school, but he feels "buffeted by circumstances" and increasingly withdraws (*Inaka kyōshi*, 126). Roaming the area, he begins writing impressionistic prose sketches (*shaseibun*) of a kind in vogue since the 1890s, discovers the hard lives of farmers and textile workers, and observes the repetitions of the seasons and the everyday. He starts frequenting a nearby brothel district—amassing debts that destroy his reputation—and goes to Tokyo to take the entrance exam for the national music college, failing utterly because he could only practice on his school's small organ.

Seizō turns over a new leaf in late 1903, resolving to dedicate himself to school and revive relations with his friends, but he develops tuberculosis. Meanwhile, in a carefully crafted convergence, construction extends a Tokyo rail line into the area and the Japanese and Russian states begin a march to war.[69] Seizō moves to a house in Hanyū with his aged parents and follows the war closely after he is unable to teach. His final decline corresponds to Japan's victory at Liaoyang, which presaged the fall of Port Arthur and was a turning point in the conflict. His parents, doctor, and a friend gather around Seizō's body as a parade passes outside, in the first of what I will argue are three endings for *The Country Teacher*. It is followed by a ceremony held at night—to avoid the cost of a service—in which Seizō literally *is* buried in the countryside, and then by a bleak glimpse of the temple graveyard, which is visited from time to time by a young woman thought to be a former student and is buffeted by autumn winds and the roar of passing trains.

By beginning a novel called *The Country Teacher* with Seizō's journey to the village of Miroku and ending it with the din of the new railway, Katai would seem to frame Seizō's life in dichotomies with a familiar ring: country and city, backwardness and modernity, to which we can add banality and success (*heibon* and *seikō*), and being buried in the countryside versus "rising in the world" (*risshin*). Seizō may die too soon to see it, but a certain kind of "now" eventually does arrive in the provinces. While it is possible, however, to read the arc of the story as the arrival of modernity, one wonders if Katai does not encourage us to dismiss that frame as a cliché by having Seizō, just arrived from the marginally larger town of Gyōda, ask himself condescendingly whether Miroku deserves even to be called a village.[70] Seizō's frequent comparison, during his first several months, of the village at hand to the Tokyo he imagines elsewhere, and of the vulgarity of its inhabitants to his friends' self-cultivation, ends up revealing Seizō's initial view of the countryside to be a projection of his own resentment. The distance Katai maintains from Seizō's first impression is a first indication that he is casting doubt on conventional ways of describing the "countryside" and its relationship to the metropolis.

Like the plain in *Germinal* and the ship in *The Sea-Wolf*, the landscape revealed by Seizō's wanderings in *The Country Teacher* is dotted with symbolically resonant sites. Seizō's school, the post office in Hanyū where a former classmate works, and eventually the stations of the train line evoke the projects of Meiji-era "civilization" (*bunmei*). These projects' ability to compel changes in human behavior can be seen in processions of children to school and young men to call-up points for the draft when the war with Russia begins.[71] The clanging of looms and the singing of young women operating them—audible traces of the Meiji period, when the government promoted textile exports to fund industrial development—also cross the landscape. Scattered among these signs of recent transformations, however, are remnants of old castles and boundary markers for defunct feudal domains (*Inaka kyōshi*, 10, 21, 22). This is not a space of abstract social relations, nearly devoid of history like the plain of *Germinal*, but one in which old patterns of relations are coeval with new ones. The graveyard of the temple where Seizō lives is emblematic: amid the weathered graves, many abandoned, he finds tombstones for a man who served the new state in the Meiji Restoration, the entrepreneur who built the area's first mechanized silk filature, and a soldier who died in the first Sino-Japanese War (1894–95). On one evening stroll Seizō hears the songs of factory girls, observes reeds sprouting at the edge of a pond, and walks through a cluster of decaying but still occupied samurai houses (*Inaka kyōshi*, 57–58, 99). Heterogeneous traces of the past are concatenated in and with the present in what Ernst Bloch called the non-contemporaneity of the contemporaneous.[72]

Katai's creation of a world in which social practices with different historical origins commingle in one present recalls Marx's argument on "formal subsumption," his term for the way that capitalism, in its initial development, takes over labor practices that emerged in earlier eras without changing the process of production itself. (Formal subsumption changes the scale of production to increase the extraction of surplus value; "real subsumption" changes the process, and as a consequence the social relations that support it.)[73] Although Marx's interest was in real subsumption, some later analysts such as Rosa Luxemburg drew attention to formal subsumption to explain the heterogeneous character of social relations that results when practices of production are uncoupled from the social context in which they emerged and are directed to different ends.[74] Such practices retain traces of their historical identities and thus are reminders of other eras and modes of production. The inhabitants of the area that Seizō roams seem to be living the results. In contrast to *Germinal*'s plain, which is wholly organized for the industrial extraction of surplus value, in their world mechanized silk-reeling shops are planted among farmers and cottage weavers. On his walks Seizō ponders the money a friend's father made buying land after the Meiji Restoration on the one hand, and the frequent rape of factory girls on the other (*Inaka kyōshi*, 68, 142).

Katai's treatment of the human everyday and the nonhuman world in *The Country Teacher* further highlights the lived experience of unevenness. The rhythms of communal life and the cycles of the seasons mix with "eventful" history to create a temporal unevenness that Harry Harootunian argues is typical of formal subsumption.[75] At school the children fête the Emperor's birthday—a celebration created in 1873—while the village still observes New Year's on the old lunar calendar (*Inaka kyōshi*, 112, 124). The seasons affect other patterns of life. During Seizō's first autumn in Miroku:

> On clear days, winnowing fans spun busily in the courtyards of farmhouses. Carts stacked high with bundles of rice came one after another. Finish reaping the late rice while it's still not cold, harvest the buckwheat too, and sow the wheat. With this on their minds all the farmers worked their hardest. From late October to the start of November the cold autumn wind of the Kantō plain already began to blow. Morning frost whitened the thatched roofs.

When the harvest is complete towns and villages suddenly become lively: music seeps from restaurants, farmers bring their daughters to fabric shops, and villagers offer sweet rice cakes to Seizō at school (*Inaka kyōshi*, 113–14). Later passages enumerating events from the war with Russia and the new habits it brought—children now play soldier in the fields—are interrupted with observations on the flowering of plants and trees.[76] The novel's description of the uneven transformation of social relations thus is met by a parallel emplotment of discrepant temporalities, in which the linear eventfulness of "success," industrialization, and the Russo-Japanese War competes with the repetition of the everyday and the cyclical quality of the seasons. The new, the habitual, and the nonhuman world are neither assimilated to each other nor fully distinct.

Katai supported his presentation of the social and temporal unevenness of late-Meiji Japan with a distinctive prose style. The descriptions in *The Country Teacher* rarely subordinate one detail to another, whether through overt explanation, shift of tone, or the use of conjunctives. Many descriptive sentences have an enumerative form: . . . *mo areba* . . . *mo atta*, literally "If there was . . . there was also . . ." Of Seizō's students, for example: "If there were some who could read, there were also some who could not." Of the outskirts of Gyōda, where Seizō walks with his father: "If there were rich houses surrounded by high hedges of evergreen oak, there were also houses facing ditches fouled with algae whose crude walls were collapsing" (*Inaka kyōshi*, 41–42, 46). As the second passage shows, Katai also emphasizes the visual in his descriptions, frequently using the verb *mieru* in its past tense of *mieta*, "could be seen." (Auditory details are common too, accompanied by *kikoeta*, "could be heard.")[77] Like the sections of free indirect style in *L'Assommoir*, such passages often mingle Seizō's perceptions with the narrative discourse, diminishing the presence of a narrator. Katai accomplishes something similar in striking passages that widen their view to include Seizō in the field of perception, again using a characteristic diction: *sugata*, "figure" or "profile." On his first day of classes: "In the next period the figure of the new teacher appeared before the table in classroom number three." On his first trip home: "For a while Seizō's figure could be seen between the rows of old houses in the backstreets, but suddenly he opened the wooden sliding door of a small house and went in" (*Inaka kyōshi*, 23, 44). Passages like these imply a point of view other than Seizō's, perhaps that of a narrative observer but just as plausibly, depending on the occasion, Seizō's students, townspeople, or some other collective bystander.[78]

Describing his method in the period when he wrote novels such as *The Country Teacher* and *Life*, Katai said his goal was "painting," not "description."[79] In the autobiographical *Life* he wanted to depict phenomena "just as I had seen them, heard them, and felt them." He called the technique *heimen byōsha*—usually translated as "flat description"—and said it was inspired by the Goncourt brothers' ability to describe phenomena "indifferently" (*heiki ni*).[80] A more literal if ungainly translation of the phrase would be "uni-planar." Katai explained that he did not want to penetrate into the "interior" of "objective phenomena" or the "inner spirit" (*naibu seishin*) of characters. Rather, the goal was to re-create "in the surface of the prose" (*bun no men ni*) scenes as they had passed from eyes to brain. He considered mimesis (*byōsha*) thus pursued to be fundamentally different from sketch literature of the kind that Seizō pens in *The Country Teacher*, which emphasized the writer's subjective response to a scene.[81] We should heed warnings such as Sōma Tsuneo's against treating the phrases Katai coined to explain his techniques as more precise than he intended them to be.[82] Nonetheless, the contrast between the dialectic of surface and depths in *Germinal* and Katai's "flat" approach to novelistic space, the one positing homogeneous developmental time, and the other multiple temporalities, is striking. (Plain vs. plane: a coincidence of English translation, but still.) Like other naturalist writers on the then-periphery, Katai took social and temporal unevenness as a given, and in response he devised methods of social figuration that departed from those found in the work of writers like Zola not just in content but in the language used to make them.

It seems fitting that a novel of multiple temporalities should have three endings. They amplify Katai's critique of late-Meiji society by giving the lie in turn to the eventfulness of the state, the project of "civilization," and success. In the last quarter of the novel the rhythms of the everyday and the seasons which have been part of Seizō's world are all but overwhelmed by the progress of the Russo-Japanese War, the construction of the rail line, and the advance of his tuberculosis, that is, the death of his aspirations. None of these, however, become the determining frame for his demise. In the lead-up to the novel's first ending—Seizō's death—the bedridden teacher feels it is "pitiful" that he cannot die for the country. Even corpses on the battlefield are happier than he is (*Inaka kyōshi*, 233–34, 237). Some critics read Seizō's torment as an appeal by Katai on behalf of those left out of the nation and its glories, but the way Katai stages Seizō's death suggests it is a mistake to read *The Country Teacher* as an argument for national inclusion.[83] Katai's most notable departure from the diary that was the novel's main source is the date of Seizō's death, which he moved some three weeks earlier to coincide with a parade in Hanyū to celebrate the Japanese victory at Liaoyang, a turning point in the war as noted earlier. Seizō's parents, doctor, and a friend encircle his corpse as townspeople outside shout "Long live the Empire!" ("Nippon teikoku banzai!").[84] Surprisingly, critics have not noticed the allusion to the last scene of *Nana*, when Nana's lovers and rivals encircle her body while Parisian crowds shout "To Berlin!" in their enthusiasm for the war with Prussia. In Zola's novel the chant is historically ironic: the crowd has no idea that the society which nurtured the "golden fly" will soon be humiliated in a disastrous war. In Katai's scene the irony is aimed more directly at Seizō's fantasy of belonging, which has done nothing for him and, circumstances differing, would do nothing for those celebrating the nation's accomplishments.

The novel's second and third endings similarly dispatch the ideologies of material progress and individual success. In the second, Seizō is buried after a brief graveside ceremony at night, to save the cost of a daytime funeral in a temple. The sutras are read by a novice in the temple where Seizō once lived because the priest's fee would be too great. Yoshida Seiichi's reading, that the rites show the final collapse of a petit bourgeois family under the force of capital, may be heavy-handed, but Katai's emphasis on the actual poverty of an era of "civilization" is clear.[85] As if to underscore the response to eventful fables of national development, the nonhuman world, which has largely been absent in the description of Seizō's final months, reappears. As the small party walks to the cemetery, "the chirping of insects in the hedges could be heard like rain," while "the rusty water moving in a ditch could be seen faintly in the lamplight" (*Inaka kyōshi*, 239). The sensorial richness itself, indifferent to human wealth or poverty, seems to condemn the era's proud projects.

The resurgence of other temporalities continues in *The Country Teacher*'s third ending, which Katai said was inspired by Ivan Turgenev's *Fathers and Sons* (*Ottsy i deti*, 1862).[86] *The Country Teacher* is well known for its final passage: "At the end of autumn the wind off Mount Akagi always came down and the forest behind the temple roared like the tide. Trains from the Tōbu line running along the forest's edge as far as Ashikaga passed by morning and night making a frightful din" (*Inaka kyōshi*, 242). Into the seeming struggle between the seasons and the timetable, however, a third temporality of habit and memory intrudes. The narrator of *Fathers and Sons* tells of visits by the protagonist Bazarov's aged parents to the village graveyard where he lies, a habit that reappears in *The Country Teacher* in visits by Seizō's mother to the temple cemetery. (Bazarov meant to make his mark on the world through anarchism; Seizō, when he arrived in Miroku, through literature.) In *The Country Teacher*, direct narrative observation of the mother is followed by hearsay about another periodic visitor. The priest is told by his wife, who has heard it from someone else, that the young woman who appears from time to time is a former student of Seizō's teaching at a primary school in Hanyū.[87] Although Seizō and his aspirations are buried in the countryside, the memory of him lives on in individual habit and the collective discourse of everyday life. The presence of the train—what more linear a symbol could there be—tells us that the return of the seasons and the everyday have not banished the promises of progress. Like the nonintegrated social figure of the countryside, however, the three endings of *The Country Teacher* dramatize the ever-incompleteness of the transformation of society by state and capital.

SOCIAL FIGURES AND SOCIAL DIFFERENCE

Had Lukács known Katai's work, he might have judged *The Country Teacher* an especially egregious example of a novel that only "describes," and as a consequence is filled with undifferentiated detail that fails to illuminate the historical dialectic. Perhaps, however, the undifferentiating style *is* the illumination, not of a singular History but of the commingling of multiple patterns of social relations and the histories that created them. The social figure that Katai created using this style is strikingly different from the figures found in *The Sea-Wolf* and *Germinal* (never mind Balzac), with the figures in London's and Zola's novels being strikingly different from each other as well. The social figures and the differences among them can tell us a great deal about how a transnational field such as that of naturalist fiction develops.

The most fundamental quality that *Germinal*, *The Sea-Wolf*, and *The Country Teacher* have in common is their creation of a bounded social space that is revealed through a roaming narrative focalizer. In *Germinal*, what the narrative "reveals" (i.e., creates) is a structure defined by sites and their interrelation: the mine, the compound, and the company headquarters, for example, and the political, economic, and social relations among them that contribute to the organization of the plain. "Depth" connotes the integration of seemingly dissimilar elements of society: novelistic space in *Germinal* is deep in proportion to the complexity of the division of labor on the surface. The integration of the structure of the plain is both synchronic and diachronic. Sites in the plain form a single structure that is subject to a single developmental time. The miners must succeed not by trying to get out of the plain, but by exploiting their superior understanding of it.

If one were to see the differences among naturalist social figures as an argument about the nature and development of societies, *The Sea-Wolf* and *The Country Teacher* would disagree with *Germinal* on the figurative relationship of bounded milieu, internal organization, and temporality. *The Sea-Wolf* produces three bounded social spaces, the ships *Ghost* and *Macedonia* and the island where Hump and Maud are stranded. Each has an internal structure which the inhabitants perceive to be natural rather than historical. The shifting ocean, however, puts the three figures in a historically contingent relationship with each other. *The Country Teacher* produces a single social space, but this structure is not integrated in the manner of the plain in *Germinal* or the *Ghost* in *The Sea-Wolf*. Multiple temporalities—of eventful history, the everyday, and nature—jostle in it. In an interesting contrast to Zola's concern with depth, Katai described the prose style he used to create the figure of the countryside as "flat." Politically, *The Sea-Wolf* challenges the inescapability of the order of capital, while *The Country*

Teacher challenges ideologies of progress, national glory, and success. A more basic political disagreement in their social figures, however, is with the assertion in novels like *Germinal* of a singular, unalterable relationship between social structure and developmental time. The social figures of *The Sea-Wolf* and *The Country Teacher* present different views both of structure and its relation to time, and they would therefore "disagree" with each other as well as with *Germinal*. If we were to examine additional novels and stories we would find more ways of figuratively representing social structure and social change—that is, more disagreements—and certainly would reach additional conclusions about the creation and politics of naturalist social figures. Nonetheless, we can draw out some points from the comparison of *Germinal*, *The Sea-Wolf*, and *The Country Teacher* that are instructive for the naturalist field as a whole.

The social figures of naturalist fiction are always both descriptive and normative, even if at first glance an author like Katai put more emphasis on the first, and one like London on the second. The imperative to describe, however, seems the main force behind changes in how writers narrated the structure of social relations and the assumptions underlying their methods. The challenge of describing new social conditions provoked multiple, dissimilar revisions to the techniques that crystallized in France. As I have argued throughout this book, innovations in form were driven by social difference. From this perspective, the changes in form in *The Sea-Wolf* and *The Country Teacher* would have different "local" causes. This is an opportune moment, then, to consider the role that unevenness on a *transnational* scale also played in the plural evolution of naturalist techniques of social figuration. Again, it would be foolish to search for a "global" etiology of formal change in naturalist fiction. We can ask, however, if the social figures found in naturalist fiction might reflect the global situation in addition to the local.

None of the examples of social figures that I have given in this chapter—from *Germinal*, *The Sea-Wolf*, and *The Country Teacher* to *The Slum*, *The Malavoglias*, *South Koizumi Village*, and *The Pond*—are "about" the global in the immediate and mediated ways that Debjani Ganguly and Pheng Cheah, for example, have traced in later twentieth- and twenty-first century fiction about globalization and postcoloniality.[88] Nonetheless, the world political economy reverberates in them. If the plain in *Germinal* is concerned with the form that the struggle between labor and capital takes in industrialized economies, it also reflects a time when the economic, political, and social development of several European countries was treated as a universal pattern. The plain is in France, but it is meant to figure "society" in a generalized sense. If the social figure of the ship in *The Sea-Wolf* contemplates a transition in metropolitan capitalism from liberal to monopoly forms—the destruction of the *Ghost* by the *Macedonia*—it also stages, perhaps unwillingly, the roles that race and racism played in the expansion of capitalism in the United States and the world. If the countryside in *The Country Teacher* becomes a figure for unevenness and non-contemporaneity, Katai's novel about the periphery of the periphery may also be a displaced meditation on the relationship of politically, economically, and culturally peripheral Japan to metropolitan centers. In the connection it makes between the disorientations of rural life and the Russo-Japanese War, his novel may also interrogate the dependent relationship of different varieties of capitalism on different varieties of empire. These novels are not *about* their global moment but they certainly are *of* it. Unevenness and asymmetries in the transnational political economy, not only local social differences, underlay differences in the social figures of naturalist fiction. We have seen such differences too in the Nana figures and body figures found in novels and stories from different parts of the world. The late nineteenth- and early twentieth-century shape of the world is reflected not only in the organization of the naturalist literary field, but also in its aesthetic history.

The unevenness both of the world and the transnational literary field resonates in these novels in another way, through what Benedict Anderson called "specters of comparison" that appeared as metropolitan methods came into contact with political, economic, and social conditions in different parts of the planet.[89] The fracturing of the single social figure in *The Sea-Wolf*, I have suggested, followed in part from London's use of methods from French naturalism to model social relations in the United States. Similarly, the conspicuous non-integration of social practices and their associated temporalities in *The Country Teacher* is the inverse of social figures that assume a deep and legible relationship of elements of society to each other and the whole. Each novel is shadowed, not so much by the incommensurability of conditions in Japan or the United States with those in France, but by the incommensurability of local conditions with the ways of representing social organization and social change propagated through naturalism's travels. Viewed as an ensemble, moreover, these social figures and the many others one might examine are shadowed by an incommensurability with each other in that each adaptation of naturalist methods, compelled by distinct challenges of description, differed from the others. At the same time, the social figures of naturalist fiction *can* be compared through the history of the transnational literary field itself, in that the history of the field's expansion is also the history of writers' confrontation with social difference and thus of the successive, discrepant revisions of method that resulted. But if this is the case, we have reached a point where we can see that one of the organizing principles of the field—the legitimating role played by French naturalism, especially the work of Zola—was in conflict with the necessity of adapting naturalism to new conditions. The history of naturalist social figures shows us one reason why the transnational field thinned and finally disappeared, a topic that I will discuss further in the conclusion of this book.

For the moment, however, there are three more lessons of method that we might take from the history of social figures for the study of other transnational, "large-scale" phenomena in expressive culture. For one, pay attention to failures, because failure to follow a received model may be as instructive as fidelity to one. I do not mean calamitous failures so much as "generative" ones that led to manifest breaks in method. That Arno Holz only was able to complete one of his series of plays about Berlin is a shame; that Tayama Katai, a doctrinaire Zolaist at the start of his career, devised a prose style suited to the mimesis of unevenness is something to ponder. For another, look for both the immediate and mediate—or mediated—reasons for changes in topic, theme, and form. The multiplication of social figures in *The Sea-Wolf* reflected at once London's interest in refuting the inevitability of capitalism, the contradictions in how its American apologists and critics saw the role of race in its development, and the large-scale changes in the extraction of surplus value through which Fordist capitalism supplanted its liberal form. Finally, consider the possibility that the reasons for the emergence of a transnational phenomenon may also be among the reasons for its disappearance.

CONCLUSION

Figures in and of the World

Tayama Katai's *The Country Teacher*, in which the pursuit of naturalist goals led to a radical revision of naturalist technique, brings the dissolution of the transnational literary field into sight. It is not that naturalism "ended" as a transnational phenomenon in a specific year, because the field changed shape constantly as writers in different parts of the world entered or dropped out. The cumulative effect of successive adaptations, each in response to different conditions, however, was that naturalist technique dispersed to the point that the many different naturalisms resembled each other less and less. Although writers such as Theodore Dreiser and Kosugi Tengai continued to ply their own versions, the careers of some of the last naturalisms directly connected to the emergence and extension of the field, in China and Korea at the start of the 1920s, were brief. Yet there were as many naturalist afterlives as there were naturalisms. In the United States a number of African American writers, including Richard Wright and Ann Petry, began working in a naturalist mode around 1940 to depict the impact of racism and racist social structures on individuals and communities.[1] In Japan, the so-called I-novel—the egocentric descendant of the naturalism of the 1900s—was revived after 1945 by young writers such as Yasuoka Shōtarō and Shimao Toshio to depict the degradations of life after the Asia-Pacific War.[2] Critics agree on the impact naturalism had on the novels of the Egyptian writer Naguib Mahfouz, notably the *Cairo Trilogy* (1956–57), although he persistently denied it.[3] Scholars of African literature find a critical engagement with naturalism in the depiction of war (Ngũgĩ wa Thiong'o's *Weep Not Child*, 1964), urban poverty in Kenya (Meja Mwangi's *Going Down River Road*, 1976), and the rural everyday in Botswana (Bessie Head's stories in *The Collector of Treasures*, 1977), among other topics.[4] While acknowledging the risk of collapsing together quite different works, one may observe that one thing naturalism appeared to offer these writers was the means to depict the force that social environments exert on individual behavior. They eschewed, however, the emphasis on the power of heredity in so much naturalist fiction, a point to which I will return.[5]

Critics' views of naturalist writers also changed in the years after naturalism subsided as a transnational phenomenon. Studies of naturalism are a thriving field—or fields, since work on naturalism in Japan is quite different from work on naturalism in Brazil, for example. Different naturalist writers, however, experienced different national fates. Outside of research on naturalism as a movement, Émile Zola is studied most for his use of free indirect style—at its most inventive in *L'Assommoir*—and his documentary depiction of nineteenth-century France, which is of lasting interest to historians. In the 1920s Katai retroactively was made the founder of the I-novel, his "confessional" novella *The Quilt* henceforth overshadowing stylistically inventive fiction such as *The Country Teacher*. Outside the United States Jack London was enthusiastically received—and widely translated—as a socialist writer. In the United States he was excised from literary anthologies during the Cold War and now effectively is a writer of fables about individualistic dogs.[6] There were as many afterlives of naturalist writers as there were afterlives of naturalism.

The reasons for naturalism's ends illuminate the history that we began examining in the first chapter of this book and pursued in the following chapters through the transformations of form found in three "figures" associated with degenerate bodies (the body figure), self-liberated women (the Nana figure), and bounded social milieus (the social figure). Through the body figure we examined the role of the decaying body in naturalist mimesis, finding that metonymies and synecdoches of the body became means to represent the relationship between individual behavior and large social forces. In *L'Assommoir*, figurative language related to the leg supported an argument by Zola that the working class is unable to escape its socially determined fate. Metonymies and synecdoches of body parts in Frank Norris's *McTeague*—McTeague's jaw and fists, Trina's chin and hair—reprised the codes of American nativism but also explored the psychology and semiosis of money. In Shimazaki Tōson's *Spring*, the nerve and contemporary discourse on nervous maladies became vehicles for a critical analysis of the civilizing projects of the Meiji state. The history of the body figure, which included the "folding in" of many of the ideas that were the scaffold of the Rougon-Macquart novels, showed writers successively adapting a common technique in naturalist fiction to address their here and now.

The history of the Nana figure showed the contribution of a ubiquitous character—the self-liberated woman—to naturalist social analysis. Zola's character Nana was one of many examples of topic, theme, and form intersecting in naturalist fiction to create a constellation of qualities that could travel. While Nana was the vector and embodiment of the corruption of Second Empire society, the multiplication of Nana-like characters through parodies, pirate sequels, and so on allowed the character to be detached from *Nana* and become a mobile diagnostic. In Dreiser's *Sister Carrie* the Nana figure was an expression of anxiety about young working-class women, and more broadly about the supposed instability of women's identities, while in Tengai's *New Year's Finery* she exposed fault lines in new discourses about family, marriage, and female sexuality. The history of the Nana figure reveals a cluster of recurring qualities—performance, contagion, mobility—that moved from the narrative discourse of *Nana* into the character herself. This "formal transposition" lent the Nana figure a malleability that allowed writers to tap into possibilities that were unrealized in *Nana*. At the same time, ideas from Zola's era that were critical to the creation of Nana—ideas derived from studies of prostitution and public hygiene, for example—remained part of the Nana figure as it moved through the world.

Examining the narrative—not simply descriptive—function of setting in much naturalist fiction showed that naturalist writers frequently narrated social structure by creating a third kind of figure, bounded social spaces composed of emblematic sites. Such social figures modeled the structure of writers' worlds and advanced arguments about the nature of social change. Through the plain in *Germinal*, Zola revealed the dynamic organization of industrial society as he saw it, and inveighed against revolutionary "delusion," yet predicted the victory of—literally—deep forces over superficial ones. London, addressing the conflicts of his time in *The Sea-Wolf*, created a floating world that was the ideological unmasking of the world of his readers. The novel's three social figures call into question the inevitability of capitalism while also advancing a contradictory, racist view of social order. In *The Country Teacher*, Katai's "flat" description of the countryside produced a figure of uneven social transformation and temporal heterogeneity that evoked the Meiji period's political economy of underdevelopment and cast doubt on common ideas about progress. Social figures in naturalist fiction emerged through a common tendency to narrate structure, but also most clearly reveal the limits of adapting techniques developed in metropolitan France to describe different societies.

What are some broader lessons we can learn from this history? As I said at the start of this book, one reason that I began writing about naturalism was frustration with the lengthy discussions of how one *might* study literary forms on a big scale. In that spirit I see this book as an example of a method developed by "doing it," whose critical features I have drawn out at the end of the individual chapters. Having set the example before you—and to be sure, it is only one of the ways scholars have been approaching the problem—I am loathe to inject more "global babble" into discussions of literary studies and the future of the humanities. Nonetheless, to add to what I have tried to show by example in the preceding pages, I would like to make a few more observations on what the history of naturalist fiction can tell us about studying other expressive forms—speculative fiction, "haiku," minimalist music (the possibilities are abundant)—that have geographically extensive histories. I want to draw together several qualities of naturalist figures that are common in the histories of expressive forms when viewed on a large scale; turn to some of the material, political, and intellectual conditions of possibility that allowed naturalism to become a transnational phenomenon, including naturalist writers' attitudes toward language; and then consider the reasons the transnational naturalist field dissolved.

First, naturalist figures only appeared through a process of detachment and adaptation. A character such as Zola's Nana was created in specific social conditions and with specific extra-textual legitimation. While Zola created Nana as both the cause and consequence of the fraudulent society around her, her symbolic force depended on moral alarm over sexual hygiene, a medicalized sense of cultural crisis, and a history of prostitutes as characters in fiction. When Nana was appropriated for other purposes—in Eugen Kumičić's *Olga and Lina*, to indict the Germanized Croatian aristocracy, and in Tengai's *New Year's Finery*, to indict the contradictions in an invented moral tradition—she was detached from *Nana* and adapted to other circumstances. New conditions prompted the successive adaptations that turned a man-eating character from Zola into a social analytic. What this means, however, is that Nana was not a "figure" until she was extracted from Zola's novel and repurposed. Getting "out of place" was essential, to borrow Roberto Schwarz's phrase once more (although not to use it as he intended). Naturalist figures existed only in their variations. They certainly have genealogies, but if we approach the genealogies not as family trees but as series created through repeated detachment and reproduction, then what one reluctantly calls the source becomes, retroactively, only the first variation. Originality is a red herring for something like the history of naturalist fiction, along with the arguments about imitation and catching-up of which Casanova's claims about "Literary Mean Time" are only a recent, attention-grabbing example.

Second, the production of figures was a source of heterogeneity, not uniformity, in the transnational field. One reason for this is that naturalist figures reflect what writers *took* from works in circulation such as Zola's novels rather than something they received through influence. Writers in different parts of the world may have shared common means, but they had different ends. Another reason is that naturalist figures were always created in the material medium of language. The chains of metonymies and synecdoches that tie together the social pathologies of the Goutte d'Or quarter in *L'Assommoir*—which begin with Gervaise's bad leg and ultimately reveal her and her husband as puppets of circumstance—exist only through words and idioms: *jambe*, *patte*, *tomber au trottoir*, the whole list of dances in the novel. Figurative chains evoking social pathologies appear in *McTeague*, *Spring*, and other naturalist novels and stories frequently enough to see the body figure as a typical naturalist technique. The same is true of the other figures examined in this book. But even though Norris knew *L'Assommoir* well, McTeague's *jaw* is not a "translation" of Gervaise's *jambe* save in a rather loose (and therefore unproductive) sense of the word. Naturalist figures were realized in specific languages, and their etiology and resonance differed in every case, first of all because of the differing qualities and histories of rhetoric of the languages in which writers worked.

Third, the emergence of the transnational naturalist field cannot be separated from the production and reproduction of figures. In the first chapter of this book we saw that naturalist fiction moved around the world through multiple, dissimilar circuits. The history of the field is to be found in part in the history of such circulation. We saw too that "Zola"—perhaps more the name to which one paid tribute than the author himself—was a legitimating principle that could be invoked by intertextual allusion and paratextual homage. Such shout-outs were another factor in the creation of the field. The emergence of clusters of shared figures, which were alike in being variations, reveals that the field also took shape and grew through the development of literary form. The coherence of the field—what made naturalism a transnational phenomenon instead of a collection of national schools—was largely due to the variations in form that appeared as writers in different parts of the world revised naturalist technique. That is, naturalism was a transnational phenomenon because of invention, not imitation. There were limits to how far adaptation could go before the family resemblance among naturalist writers disappeared. Yet asking "Is this naturalism too?" misses the point: if we only look for the identical, then maybe the only naturalist was Zola, as Jules Lemaître said in 1891. Such a conclusion would tell us nothing, however, about why Júlio Ribeiro, Ina Lange, Nagai Kafū, and Frank Norris all thought they were writing naturalist fiction.

The process of detachment and adaptation that produced naturalist figures did not happen in a vacuum. It depended on certain conditions of possibility, some related to the era when naturalism emerged and some to naturalism itself. First, obviously, were the material conditions that allowed the circulation of texts: changes in printing technology and transportation, the industrialization of publishing, and so on. Closely related were the conditions that allowed "Zola" to become the legitimator and organizing principle of the naturalist field: the prestige of French and French literature, and behind them, the power of France in Europe and the world. In an acerbic argument on literature and underdevelopment, Antônio Cândido said that the distinction French literature enjoyed among writers in Latin America—which was as much a matter of political as literary history—was little more than an opportunity to transfer their cultural dependency from Spain and Portugal to France.[7] While I have argued that writers gained more than an illusory sense of independence by declaring their affiliation with naturalism, naturalist figures undeniably reflected their geopolitical moment.

The figures employed in naturalist fiction also reflected their more local political and economic moments, in the plural. If naturalist figures and the entire naturalist field existed because of successive adaptations of method, then the conditions to which individual writers responded shaped the field as a whole. It was essential that metropolitan techniques got out of place, but essential too were conditions in the places they got into. It would be folly to attempt a "global" morphology of local adaptation which would require, among other things, accounting for the history of written and oral expression in each place where naturalist fiction appeared. (Recall that one of the premises of this book is that totalizing, "World Lit" explanations are a mistake.) A more thorough materialist analysis than has been possible here—tracing, for example, the relation of the Nana figure to the economics of women's labor—might tell us more about the political and economic conditions where naturalism could flourish, and thus also where it could not. In a sense, however, the monumentality of the task is the message: naturalisms proliferated because of the multiplicity of human social life.

A different condition of possibility was the intellectual context in which naturalist fiction circulated. Throughout this book we have seen the ways that "fellow travelers," particularly from the biological and social sciences, contributed to naturalist fiction. The most important of these companions were mid-nineteenth century ideas about the role of heredity in behavior, but they also included theories of social development and regimes of hygiene. Many of these "fellow travelers" were also circulating around the world. Naturalism stood out among nineteenth-century realisms for appealing to such nonliterary sources in an effort to establish quasi-scientific authority. While I have argued that such "constitutive" ideas did not have to go everywhere that naturalism went—because some were folded into naturalist figures as they were detached from specific novels—there is no doubt that the presence of fellow travelers assisted the circulation and amplified the resonance of the figures that were one of the notable qualities of naturalist form.

Finally, the production and reproduction of naturalist figures relied on shared assumptions about the relationship of language to social reality. The history of naturalist fiction shows that its writers did not believe naively in the transparency of language, as is commonly charged. The commingling of description and figuration in Gervaise's gait in *L'Assommoir*, Wolf Larsen's ship in *The Sea-Wolf*, and the confinement of お俊 as 小しゆん in *New Year's Finery*, all realized in language, are evidence to the contrary. We might rather say that in naturalist fiction figures mediate between the internal worlds of novels and stories and the external worlds of writers, between the means of analysis and its object. Of course, this would be true of realism generally. (To recall an example from chapter 2, Balzac's portrait of Madame Vauquer in *Old Goriot* both explains the little society she has created in her boarding house and identifies her as a social type familiar to the reader.) What distinguished naturalism was the assertion that the relationship mediated by the figure was both rhetorical and scientifically objective. To naturalist writers, language could figure social reality.

To draw these points together: the emergence of the body figure, the Nana figure, and the social figure was not only the result of the formation and growth of the transnational naturalist field but also a contributor to it. The same was true of the development of form in naturalist fiction more broadly. The production and reproduction of figures, propelled by adaptation to new circumstances and realized in language, contributed to the field's fundamental heterogeneity. The process of detachment and adaptation would have been impossible without specific material and political conditions, and it was mutually imbricated with the histories of naturalist fellow travelers. The circulation of naturalist figures was not a matter of translation, but it did depend on a characteristic view of language. And in the largest sense, the history of naturalist form cannot be separated from material, political, and intellectual histories that were not simply "parallel" to literary history but really should be considered part of the history of naturalism per se.

The qualities of naturalist figures and the conditions that supported their appearance and circulation can help us better understand the reasons why the naturalist field dissolved. Although confrontation with different political, economic, and social conditions pushed writers to revise naturalist techniques, and thus was an essential part of the appearance and extension of a naturalist field outside France, it led to a multiplication of techniques of social description and analysis that were not always reconcilable with each other. If naturalism was essentially a method—as many of its adherents thought it was—then the embrace of the method in different parts of the world paradoxically was naturalism's undoing as a transnational phenomenon. I want to emphasize that the problem was different from changes in literary fashion—and views that naturalism was "out of date"—which doubtless too were a factor. Adaptation put more pressure on some aspects of naturalist form than on others. Malformed limbs, atavistic jaws, and decayed nerves have much in common as figures explaining the relationship of individual behavior and social environment. The plain in *Germinal*, the ship in *The Sea-Wolf*, and the countryside in *The Country Teacher* likewise show similarities of technique such as the creation of an enclosed milieu and the use of an outsider to describe its structures and mechanisms. Yet if Zola's internally integrated, temporally homogeneous plain was plausible in industrialized France—and to the French bourgeois reader—it was not so elsewhere and to all, as we can see when London, by creating multiple figures for social relations, insisted on the contingency of social forms and Katai, taking a "flat" approach to describing human and nonhuman life, brought into question conventional ideas of social change. Such divergence in how writers used naturalist methods ultimately followed from the shared aspiration to limn social structures in their entirety. Some aspects of the naturalist project, then, inevitably undermined the coherence of the naturalist field.

The cumulative invalidation of ideas associated with naturalism, both those on which it overtly relied and those folded into its figures, also contributed to the collapse of naturalism as a transnational movement. We have seen that naturalism's relationship to fellow travelers changed as they too evolved. In keeping with developments in neurology, for example, the "clinical" observation of nervous derangement in *Germinie Lacerteux* eventually was supplanted by the discourse of neurasthenia as an explanation for the social causes of Aoki's suicide in *Spring*. Some propositions, however, were so fundamental as to move with naturalism wherever it went. Surely the most important of these was the Lamarckian principle of the inheritance of acquired characteristics that was the linchpin of naturalist ideas about the force that heredity exerted on individuals. Although Zola considered the nervous "crack" of the matriarch of the Rougon-Macquart clan to be only an axiom, the logic of the crack and the structure of the Rougon-Macquart series was Lamarckian. Zola recapitulated the hereditary scheme in the final volume, *Doctor Pascal*, even though by 1893 the acquisition of inherited characteristics was a dubious proposition. As such ideas lost credibility, so too did the aspects of naturalist method that relied on them. It is not surprising, then, that later writers such as Petry and Mahfouz who adopted some naturalist techniques went out of their way to reject others, including heredity as an explanation of character and a mechanism of plot.

The credibility of naturalist approaches to language similarly weakened as decades passed after the 1860s, when the foundational work of the Goncourt brothers and Zola appeared. Again, I would caution against the simple explanation that realist writers—naturalists foremost among them—regarded language as a transparent medium. This modernist shibboleth explains little. If we recognize instead that naturalism proposed to "figure" social reality with scientific objectivity, then first of all the negation of principles on which naturalist figures relied—such as Lamarckian heredity—negated the pretense of precision. But one might also observe the ways that some naturalist fiction cast doubt on its own assumptions about language. In the bacchanalian supper in *L'Assommoir* and the proliferation of images of gold in *McTeague*, signification seems to become its own end. In the problem of the *meaning* of gold in *McTeague* and the flux of unsubordinated detail in *The Country Teacher*, signification seems to become a critique of its own purpose. Even within naturalist texts we find writers occasionally exploiting rather than resisting the ways that language may be used to signify only itself. The play of language in naturalist fiction was restrained by a purpose, but such purposes could—and did—change.

Finally, we should note the ways that the basic structure of the naturalist field was unsustainable. The geopolitical conditions that supported the emergence and expansion of the field remind us that a transnational movement that legitimated itself by references to Zola and his work belonged to an era when a writer from the most powerful part of Europe could play that kind of role without serious dispute. The challenge to such asymmetries, mounted in different places at different times, was not only political. It was also structural. The field organized by "Zola" was basically monocentric, created through unidirectional citations of a French writer by writers elsewhere. The paucity of "peripheral" writers' citations of each other was significantly less only in a few places such as East Asia, where a variety of naturalism that developed in Japan became regionally influential, and the Nordic countries, where a first generation of naturalist writers provided intraregional inspiration for a second. Such local complexity was not truly a challenge to the basic organization of the naturalist field, however, since French naturalism still lurked as a legitimating—if secondhand—point of reference. Organized as it was, the naturalist field could truly accommodate neither relations between writers unmediated by the work of Zola, nor the multidirectional citations that such relations would support, without coming apart.

A few comparisons to what is now called "global modernism" help put these observations on the end of naturalism into relief. Differences in attitudes toward language were obviously great—the possibility of language to figure itself being seen as an advantage, not a liability—but such differences have been well understood for quite some time. One achievement of modernist studies more recently, however, has been to show the polycentric quality of the modernist moment, created by multidirectional and reciprocal literary relations.[8] The argument is not that the modernist field was suddenly level. Rather, it is that modernist practice had the potential to expose and challenge both the economic and political asymmetries organizing the world and those organizing relations between writers.[9] The dual challenges that modernism could pose certainly reflect a political and economic conjuncture different from the conjuncture when naturalism first appeared.[10] But if we recall an argument from the first chapter of this book—that on a large scale, literary tendencies conventionally treated as sequential "eras" may be coeval—we can see that modernism did not just appear at a different time, but also offered a different principle for transnational literary relations. Even if the true realization of modernism's polycentric possibility remained out of reach, that principle was strikingly different from that of the naturalist field. More than matters of technique, intellectual affiliations, or attitudes toward language, the structure of the naturalist field may have been the anachronism that brought naturalism to an end as a transnational phenomenon.

Finally, in addition to the methodological lessons that one can draw from the history of naturalist fiction, I would like to offer four more thoughts about responding to current challenges for "large-scale" studies of culture. Foremost at the present moment, I would say, is to begin with history and let theory follow after. The history of naturalist fiction shows that specific paths of circulation, for example, mattered a great deal in how it developed in different parts of the world. While geopolitical conditions facilitated naturalism's travels, moreover, the ways that writers adapted naturalist method were always shaped by the political and economic situation at hand. Their work was also informed by the literary pasts of the locales and languages in which they worked. One cannot understand the phenomenon without tracing out the paths, exploring the conditions in which writers worked, and learning the history of expression in their languages. Premises and teleologies derived from the history of western European literature and arts—which are still the basis of most theory in the humanities now—easily obscure rather than clarify the unexpected turns and untidy complications of genres and forms that were conjointly evolving in several dissimilar parts of the world. So too do a priori definitions, which as we have seen make it difficult to grasp the range of creative practices that such a far-flung phenomenon may comprise. Rather than insisting on them, proceed inductively, anticipate contradiction, and embrace the unexpected.

Next, perhaps, is to approach geographically extensive phenomena such as naturalist fiction as synchronically organized, diachronically evolving transnational fields rather than as the history of individual writers and their work. Having escaped the scale of the nation, however, do not jump reflexively to the imaginary scale of the globe. Recognize that such fields have both large-scale and local conditions of possibility and that their organizing principles reflect economic and political circumstances, mechanisms of writerly self-identification and position-taking, and immanent aesthetic possibilities. Their chronologies may be quite different from the chronologies conventionally accepted in national contexts. (The "Manifesto of Five" from 1887, in which several young writers denounced Zola, caused a stink in France but was a minuscule event in naturalism's transnational history.) Accept that several transnational fields may exist at a given time, with different, perhaps overlapping geographies. Coeval fields may be rivals or they may intermingle. Acknowledge that writers, artists, filmmakers, and so on may work simultaneously in fields of different scale, from local to regional to "big." They may have much to gain by using their positions in one to strengthen their positions in the other, the character of local fields thus affecting the character of transnational ones, and vice versa. Approaching a phenomenon like naturalism as a transnational field thus requires a commitment to working on multiple scales and understanding the immediate and mediated connections between them.

If a history of something like the rise and demise of naturalist fiction is to be more substantial than a history of names, titles, and plot summaries—of which I have given many—it must also be a history of form. To accomplish that, a third point: the necessity of close analysis. Transnational fields are made of successive formal interventions, or one might say, of form in motion. One simply can't understand such changes from a distance, and thus at least part of large-scale research in the humanities should be devoted to close-up examination of individual works. Yet I think that my analysis of novels and stories from France, Japan, and the United States in this book also shows that what we need may not be close reading as commonly practiced, but rather a way of reading (or watching or listening) that looks for what a writer (or composer or game designer) has taken from earlier works in the field, how he or she signals a position with respect to them, and how the resulting intervention changes the character of the field as a whole. It is a kind of analysis that looks for productive mismatches between received form and at-hand social context and considers failures, especially generative ones, to be part of the story. It is also a kind of analysis that requires developing expertise in at least some of the geographical areas encompassed by the field—learning languages, the history of visual idioms—while recognizing that expertise in one or a few areas does not grant expertise in them all. It thus requires, as I have said before, a kind of argumentation that acknowledges its limits and opens to the work of others.

Finally, in thinking again about the current conjuncture in the humanities, whether one calls it their crisis or their global turn: new challenges provoke much anxiety. "There's so much to read." "How could I ever know enough to write about that?" One never does know enough, and if one can't read it all one can still read a lot. The problem is not volume so much as uncertainty. So: accept that one can't plan where an investigation like this will lead. One can choose the points of departure, and one should choose them well. Not every way through a complicated, transnational history will shed equal light on the entire phenomenon. Even if one can choose where one begins, moreover, it is impossible to know where one will arrive. Yet in the present moment—when understanding how cultural forms evolve on a large scale ultimately is an urgent political task—caution can seem like a cop-out. The challenge is to develop methods adequate to the problem, and the only way to do it is to do it. I would say this is true not only of transnational studies of culture but also of many fields in the humanities, including my own discipline, comparative literature, which are laboring to overcome the parochial terms in which they were conceived. Relinquish the security of the familiar, and welcome the tumult of the world: the most important encounters don't happen at home but on the road.

Notes

PREFACE

1. Dipesh Chakrabarty, *Provincializing Europe: Postcolonial Thought and Historical Difference* (Princeton, N.J.: Princeton University Press, 2000), 27.

2. Notable work that has appeared since then includes the special issue of *Modern Language Quarterly* on "peripheral realisms" (see the editors' introduction by Jed Esty and Colleen Lye, "Peripheral Realisms Now," *Modern Language Quarterly* 73, no. 3 [2012]: 269–88); Debjani Ganguly's *This Thing Called the World: The Contemporary Novel as Global Form* (Durham, N.C.: Duke University Press, 2016); Michael Allan's *In the Shadow of World Literature: Sites of Reading in Colonial Egypt* (Princeton, N.J.: Princeton University Press, 2016); and the collection *Territories and Trajectories: Cultures in Circulation*, ed. Diana Sorensen (Durham, N.C.: Duke University Press, 2018) (see Sorensen's introduction, "Alternative Geographic Mappings for the Twenty-First Century," in *Territories and Trajectories*, 13–19).

3. As Stefan Helgesson succinctly puts it: "Studying the circulation of literary texts across spaces and languages is a fully legitimate (and difficult) endeavor which can by no means just be reduced to an ideological function." Helgesson, "The World-Literary Formation of Antonio Candido," in *Re-Mapping World Literature: Writing, Book Markets and Epistemologies between Latin America and the Global South*, ed. Gesine Müller, Jorge J. Locane, and Benjamin Loy (Berlin: De Gruyter, 2018), 227.

4. Erich Auerbach, "Philology and Weltliteratur," trans. M. Said and E. W. Said, in *Princeton Sourcebook in Comparative Literature*, ed. David Damrosch, Natalie Melas, and Mbongiseni Buthelezi (Princeton, N.J.: Princeton University Press, 2009), 135. To be clear: my examination of "figures" in naturalist fiction has nothing to do with Auerbach's much-lauded work on the *figura* and figural interpretation in European literature. For the latter, see *Mimesis: The Represen-*

tation of Reality in Western Literature, trans. Willard R. Trask (Princeton, N.J.: Princeton University Press, 1953), 73ff.; and Auerbach, "Figura," trans. Jane O. Newman, in *Time, History, and Literature: Selected Essays of Erich Auerbach*, ed. James I. Porter (Princeton, N.J.: Princeton University Press, 2013).

5. For Schwarz's classic examination of the question, see "Misplaced Ideas," trans. Edmund Leites and Roberto Schwarz, in *Misplaced Ideas: Essays on Brazilian Culture* (London: Verso, 1992), 19–32.

6. Aamir Mufti, *Forget English! Orientalisms and World Literatures* (Cambridge, Mass.: Harvard University Press, 2016), 241. For Moretti's first statement of the problem, see "Conjectures on World Literature," *New Left Review* 1 (2000): 55. (This work will be cited parenthetically in text.) The quantitative problem is not only a specter in "global" studies. Margaret Cohen addressed it decades ago in French literary history. See *The Sentimental Education of the Novel* (Princeton, N.J.: Princeton University Press, 1999), 21–22.

7. See my *National History and the World of Nations: Capital, State, and the Rhetoric of History in Japan, France, and the United States* (Durham, N.C.: Duke University Press, 2008), 14–16.

8. This is true even though France was expanding its overseas empire and was also a destination for intra-European migration at this time. One can ultimately trace the absence of any prominent role for race and immigration in French naturalist texts to the absence of immigration from that country's discourses of nation and society. See Gérard Noiriel, *The French Melting Pot: Immigration, Citizenship, and National Identity*, trans. Geoffroy de Laforcade (Minneapolis: University of Minnesota Press, 1996), 6–7.

9. The relationship of French and German naturalist fiction was the topic of Yves Chevrel's earliest pioneering work, "Le Roman et la nouvelle naturaliste française en Allemagne," doctoral thesis, Université de Paris-Sorbonne, 1979.

10. I discuss Casanova's *World Republic of Letters* in chapter 1.

11. Arjun Appadurai, "Disjuncture and Difference in the Global Cultural Economy," *Public Culture* 2, no. 2 (1990): 5. See also Arif Dirlik, *Global Modernity: Modernity in the Age of Global Capitalism* (Boulder, Colo.: Paradigm, 2007), 20.

CHAPTER 1

1. See Georg Lukács, "The Zola Centenary," in *Studies in European Realism* (London: Merlin, 1972); and Georg Lukács, "Narrate or Describe?" trans. Arthur D. Kahn, in *Writer and Critic and Other Essays* (New York: Grosset and Dunlap, 1974). I discuss Lukács's critique in chapter 4.

2. F. W. J. Hemmings, "Origins of the Terms Naturalisme, Naturaliste," *French Studies* 8 (1954): 109–10, 111, 113. Responding to charges that he cooked up the term "naturalism" to make his work seem heftier, Zola claimed that French and Russian critics had used it earlier. The terms *natural'naya shkola* (natural school) and *naturalizma* (naturalism) had been used by Vissarion Belinsky and other Russian critics since the late 1840s, but to refer to Nikolai Gogol and some other writers. Nonetheless, the resemblance of *naturalisme* and *naturalizma* has caused lasting confusion (Hemmings, 115–17).

3. On the dinner as a "founding event," see David Baguley, *Naturalist Fiction: The Entropic Vision* (Cambridge: Cambridge University Press, 1990), 16–20.

4. Jules Huret, *Enquête sur l'évolution littéraire* (Paris: Charpentier, 1891).

5. "Naturalisme pas mort. Lettre suit." Quoted in Baguley, *Naturalist Fiction*, 2.

6. Yves Chevrel, *Le Naturalisme: Étude d'un mouvement littéraire international* (Paris: Presses Universitaires de France, 1982), 45.

7. The subtitle of Chevrel's *Le Naturalisme* is one example of the phrase.

8. Jobst Welge, *Genealogical Fictions: Cultural Periphery and Historical Change in the Modern Novel* (Baltimore, Md.: Johns Hopkins University Press, 2015), 129.

9. Paul Barnaby, "Nana in Milan: Cletto Arrighi and the Italian Reception of Zola," *New Comparison* 35–36 (2003): 164; Olga Ragusa, "The Study of Literary Relations: France and Italy in the Nineteenth Century," *Symposium: A Quarterly Journal in Modern Literatures* 47, no. 2 (1993): 149.

10. Jacques Marx, "Émile Varhaeren et la poésie naturaliste en Belgique," *Excavatio* 6–7 (1995): 36; Romain Debbaut, "Esthétique naturaliste et définition du naturalisme dans la littérature d'expression néerlandaise," in *Le Naturalisme en question*, ed. Yves Chevrel (Paris: Presses de l'Université de Paris-Sorbonne, 1986), 69, 73.

11. Florence Gacoin-Marks, "Les Débuts du naturalisme en Croatie et en Slovénie," *Cahiers Naturalistes* 77 (2003): 239–41.

12. Jelena Novaković, "La Réception d'Émile Zola en Serbie," in *Zola en Europe centrale*, ed. Norbert Bachleitner, Tone Smolej, and Karl Zieger (Valenciennes: Presses Universitaires de Valenciennes, 2011), 236–40.

13. Lucile Arnoux-Farnoux, "Ambiguïtés et singularités du naturalisme grec," *Cahiers Naturalistes* 77 (2003): 190–93. Other literary historians find elements of naturalism in the "ethographic" writing of the 1880s. See, for example, Pieter Borghart, "(Greek) Naturalism in European Perspective: A Comparative Approach," *Excavatio* 19, no. 1–2 (2004): 320.

14. Niels Ingwersen, "The Modern Breakthrough," in *A History of Danish literature*, ed. Sven Hakon Rossel (Lincoln: University of Nebraska Press, 1992), 268; James McFarlane, "Norwegian Literature 1860–1910," in *A History of Norwegian literature*, ed. Harald S. Naess (Lincoln: University of Nebraska Press, 1993), 151, 156–57, 161–62; Birgitta Steene, "Liberalism, Realism, and the Modern Breakthrough: 1830–1890," in *A History of Swedish Literature*, ed. Lars G. Warme (Lincoln: University of Nebraska Press, 1996), 233–34; Kai Laitinen, "The Rise of Finnish-Language Literature," in *A History of Finland's Literature*, ed. George C. Schoolfield (Lincoln: University of Nebraska Press, 1998), 87–91; and George Schoolfield, "A Sense of Minority," in *A History of Finland's Literature*, 386–88.

15. Ingwersen, "Modern Breakthrough," 280.

16. On the charge of "shoemaker realism" from the Swedish poet and novelist Verner von Heidenstam, see Steene, "Liberalism, Realism," 244.

17. See Mary Elizabeth Leighton and Kirsten MacLeod, "The Trials of Naturalism: Zola in the British Literary and Cultural Imagination of the Fin de Siècle," *Excavatio* 15, no. 3–4 (2001): 322–36.

18. I am distinguishing between "naturalism" as a variety of realism that emerged in France in the 1860s and what Belinsky called the "natural school" (*natural'naya shkola*). See note 2 (above) on this point. On Russian Zolaists and the response to Zola, see Marianne Gourg, "Quelques aspects de la réception des thèses naturalistes en Russie," *Cahiers Naturalistes* 65 (1991): 32–36.

19. John Stubbs Brushwood, *Genteel Barbarism: Experiments in Analysis of Nineteenth-Century Spanish-American Novels* (Lincoln: University of Nebraska Press, 1981), 16–17.

20. Donald Pizer, "Backgrounds and Sources," in Theodore Dreiser, *Sister Carrie*, ed. Donald Pizer, 2nd ed. (New York: Norton, 1991), 443.

21. Ribeiro, *The Flesh* (*A Carne*, 1888); Kafū, *Flowers of Hell* (*Jigoku no hana*, 1902); Maupassant, "Butterball" ("Boule de suif," 1880); Cambaceres, *Potpourri* (1882); Bang, *Generations without Hope* (*Haabløse Slægter*, 1880); Verga, *The Malavoglias* (*I Malavoglia*, 1881).

22. Strindberg, *The Red Room* (*Röda rummet*, 1879); Kondylakis, *Les Misérables of Athens* (*Oi áthlioi ton Athinón*, 1894); Zeno Gandía, *The Pond* (*La Charca*, 1894); Katai, *The Country Teacher* (*Inaka kyōshi*, 1909).

23. Eça, *Cousin Basilio* (*O Primo Basilio*, 1878); Skram, *Constance Ring* (1885); Pardo Bazán, *The Tribune* (*La Tribuna*, 1882); Azevedo, *The Slum* (*O Cortiço*, 1890).

24. Gamboa, *Santa* (1903); Kim, "Potatoes" ("Kamcha," 1925); Zola, *The Human Beast* (*La Bête humaine*, 1890); Norris, *McTeague* (1899); Lillo, "Juan Fariña" (1903); Finžgar, *From the Modern World* (*Iz modernega sveta*, 1904); Matto de Turner, *Birds without a Nest* (*Aves sin nido*, 1889); Dreiser, *The Financier* (1912).

25. Setty Moretti Alaoui, "Zola en Espagne: Horizon d'attente et réception," *Excavatio* 18, no. 1–2 (2003): 184–85.

26. Paul Arrighi, "Zola et De Sanctis," *Revue de la Littérature Comparée* 27 (1953): 439–45; Silvia Disegni, "La Diffusion de l'oeuvre de Zola en Italie," *Cahiers Naturalistes* 79 (2005): 111.

27. Arnoux-Farnoux, "Ambiguïtés et singularités," 190–92; Polyxène Goula-Mitacou, "La Traduction grecque de Nana," *Cahiers Naturalistes* 79 (2005): 143.

28. Alexander Coleman, *Eça de Queirós and European Realism* (New York: New York University Press, 1980), 45–47; Haroldo Ceravolo Sereza, "Machado de Assis and the Problem of 'Realism-Naturalism,'" in *Re-Reading Zola and Worldwide Naturalism*, ed. Carolyn Snipes-Hoyt, Marie-Sophie Armstrong, and Riikka Rossi (Newcastle upon Tyne, Eng.: Cambridge Scholars, 2013), 377–78.

29. Yoshida Seiichi, *Shizen shugi no kenkyū* (Tokyo: Tōkyōdō Shuppanbu, 1955), vol. 1: 132–35.

30. Kang U Wŏng-yong, "Nihon to Chōsen hantō ni okeru shizen shugi bungaku," *Hōsei daigaku daigakuin daigakuin kiyō* 52 (2004): 247; Bonnie S. McDougall, *The Introduction of Western Literary Theories into Modern China, 1919–1925* (Tokyo: Centre for East Asian Cultural Studies, 1971), 158–59.

31. Several examples from central, eastern, and southeastern Europe are Arnoux-Farnoux, "Ambiguïtés et singularités," 190–92; Florence Gacoin-Marks,

"Eugen Kumičić et la première réception d'Émile Zola en Croatie," in *Zola en Europe centrale*, ed. Norbert Bachleitner, Tone Smolej, and Karl Zieger (Valenciennes: Presses Universitaires de Valenciennes, 2011), 225; Sándor Kálai, "La Réception de Zola en Hongrie," in *Zola en Europe centrale*, 173; Jovanka Sotolova, "Émile Zola à la tchèque," in *Zola en Europe centrale*, 135–67; and Janina Kulczycka-Saloni, "Émile Zola en Pologne," *Cahiers Naturalistes* 32 (1966): 151.

32. Yves Chevrel, "Peut-on proposer une périodisation du naturalisme en tant que mouvement international?" in *Le Naturalisme en question*, ed. Yves Chevrel (Paris: Presses de l'Université de Paris-Sorbonne, 1986), 16. See also *Le Naturalisme en question*, 29–32. This work will be cited parenthetically in the text.

33. Marzia Finocchiaro, "De la Sicile à Milan: Itinéraire italien des réceptions du Naturalisme français," *Excavatio* 12 (1999): 179; Yves Chevrel, "Germinal en Allemagne," *Europe* 678 (1985): 95.

34. Monica Lebron, "Naturalism in New Climes: Argentina and Brazil," *Excavatio* 4–5 (1994): 133; Antonio Benítez-Rojo, "The Nineteenth-Century Spanish American Novel," in *Cambridge History of Latin American Literature*, ed. Roberto González Echevarría and Enrique Pupo-Walker (Cambridge: Cambridge University Press, 1996), vol. 1: 471.

35. Lars Åhnebrink, *The Beginnings of Naturalism in American Fiction* (New York: Russell and Russell, 1961), 112.

36. Tayama Katai, *Inaka kyōshi* (Tokyo: Iwanami Shoten, 1993), 238; Tone Smolej, "La Réception d'Émile Zola chez les Slovènes à l'époque de l'Autriche-Hongrie," in *Zola en Europe centrale*, ed. Norbert Bachleitner, Tone Smolej, and Karl Zieger (Valenciennes: Presses Universitaires de Valenciennes, 2011), 196; Manuel Prendes, "El personaje y sus libros en la novela naturalista hispanoamericana," *Excavatio* 18, no. 1–2 (2003): 403.

37. Herman Bang, *As Trains Pass By*, trans. W. Glyn Jones (Sawtry, Eng.: Dedalus, 2014), 42.

38. Camille Lemonnier, *Happe-Chair* (Paris: E. Monnier, De Brunhoff, 1886), i.

39. Quoted in Yves Chevrel, "De Germinal aux Tisserands," *Revue d'Histoire Litteraire de la France* 85, no. 3 (1985): 457.

40. For Lemaître's comment, see Huret, *Enquête sur l'évolution*, 11.

41. Guillermo Ara, *La novela naturalista hispanoamericana* (Buenos Aires: Eudeba, 1965), 9; Jean-Yves Mérian, "Les Débuts du naturalisme au Brésil," *Recherches et Études Comparatistes Ibéro-Françaises de la Sorbonne Nouvelle* 3 (1981): 35; Sōma Tsuneo, *Nihon shizen shugi ron* (Tokyo: Yagi Shoten, 1970), 22; Sunyoung Park, *The Proletarian Wave: Literature and Leftist Culture in Colonial Korea, 1910–1945* (Cambridge, Mass.: Harvard University Asia Center, 2015), 178.

42. A position that two eminent scholars of naturalist fiction, Yves Chevrel and David Baguley, each take. See Chevrel, *Le Naturalisme en question*, 32; and Baguley, "The Nature of Naturalism," in *Naturalism in the European Novel: New Critical Perspectives*, ed. Brian Nelson (New York: Berg, 1992), 17.

43. Schwarz, "Misplaced Ideas."

44. David Damrosch, *What Is World Literature?* (Princeton, N.J.: Princeton University Press, 2003), 4.

45. David Damrosch, "World Literature in a Postcanonical, Hypercanonical Age," in *Comparative Literature in an Age of Globalization*, ed. Haun Saussy (Baltimore, Md.: Johns Hopkins University Press, 2006), 45–46.

46. On the imagination of barrier-free space in scholarship on "world literature," see Mufti, *Forget English!* 8–9.

47. For the gamut of ecologies, see Alexander Beecroft, *An Ecology of World Literature: From Antiquity to the Present Day* (New York: Verso, 2015), 33–36. This work will be cited parenthetically in text.

48. On translation failures and untranslatability, see Emily S. Apter, *Against World Literature: On the Politics of Untranslatability* (New York: Verso, 2013), especially chapter 1. This work will be cited parenthetically in text.

49. For the history, see Mufti, *Forget English!* chap. 1; for the phrase, 240.

50. Lydia H. Liu, *Translingual Practice: Literature, National Culture, and Translated Modernity—China, 1900–1937* (Stanford, Calif.: Stanford University Press, 1995), 227–38; Allan, *In the Shadow of World Literature*, 80–87.

51. Two discussions of Moretti's work that I have found useful are Jonathan Arac, "Anglo-Globalism?" *New Left Review* 16 (2002): 35–45; and John Frow, "Thinking the Novel," *New Left Review* 49 (2008): 137–45.

52. Moretti, "Conjectures on World Literature," 58, 59, 60. For the proposition of distant reading, a study-of-studies approach analogous to some projects in the social sciences, see 57–58. In some subsequent work Moretti turned from diffusion to study of the comparative "rises" of the novel in Europe and elsewhere. Here, perhaps to avoid the earlier problem of categories, he broadens the definition of the novel to effectively include any long fictional narrative, but finds differences so great as to suggest that the generic label loses sense when applied in this way. See Franco Moretti, "The Novel: History and Theory," *New Left Review* 52 (2008): 117–18.

53. Eric Hayot discusses the way critical categories reproduce teleologies of literary development in *On Literary Worlds* (New York: Oxford University Press, 2012), 2–6.

54. Mariano Siskind, *Cosmopolitan Desires: Global Modernity and World Literature in Latin America* (Evanston, Ill.: Northwestern University Press, 2014), 31–32. While Siskind's argument on the globalization of the novel is only one part of a richer study of Latin American *modernismo*, it has gotten much attention since its presentation in an article in 2010.

55. Pascale Casanova, *The World Republic of Letters*, trans. M. B. DeBevoise (Cambridge, Mass.: Harvard University Press, 2004), 108. This work is cited parenthetically in the text.

56. On naturalism, see Casanova, *World Republic of Letters*, 97–103.

57. On this logic, see Kristin Ross, "Translator's Introduction," in *The Ignorant Schoolmaster*, by Jacques Rancière (Stanford, Calif.: Stanford University Press, 1991), xi–xii. From this perspective, Jaime Hanneken's observations on the ability of writers to instrumentalize the prestige of Paris are especially acute. See Hanneken, "Going *Mundial*: What It Really Means to Desire Paris," *Modern Language Quarterly* 71, no. 2 (2010): 132, 135–36.

58. Chevrel, *Le Naturalisme en question*, 33, 37.

59. The concentric scheme is still clearer in some of Chevrel's later work. See for example Yves Chevrel, "Le Naturalisme à l'étranger: Croatie, Grèce, Slovénie," *Cahiers Naturalistes* 77 (2003): 183.

60. On the impact of European and U.S. romanticism, see, for example, Antônio Cândido, *Formação da literatura brasileira: Momentos decisivos* (São Paulo: Martins, 1959), 115–17; Benítez-Rojo, "Spanish American Novel," 429; and Doris Sommer, *Foundational Fictions: The National Romances of Latin America* (Berkeley: University of California Press, 1991), 26–27, 52–56.

61. Sommer, *Foundational Fictions*, 7, 24; Cândido, *Formação da literatura brasileira*, 115.

62. Benítez-Rojo, "Spanish American Novel," 429; Brushwood, *Genteel Barbarism*, 4; Cândido, *Formação da literatura brasileira*, 115; Sommer, *Foundational Fictions*, 14, 16–17.

63. On Latin American *modernismo* in the broad and narrow senses, see Siskind, *Cosmopolitan Desires*, 103–5 and 277 n. 2.

64. On the challenge of these developments to existing aesthetics, see Eva Paulino Bueno, *Resisting Boundaries: The Subject of Naturalism in Brazil* (New York: Garland, 1995), 3.

65. Dorothy Scott Loos, *The Naturalistic Novel of Brazil* (New York: Hispanic Institute of the United States, 1963), 66.

66. Ceravolo Sereza, "Machado de Assis," 377–78; Mérian, "Débuts du naturalisme," 30–31; Coleman, *Eça de Queirós*, 45–47.

67. Jean-Yves Mérian, *Aluísio Azevedo: Vida e obra (1857–1913)*, trans. Claudia Poncioni, 2nd ed. (Rio de Janeiro: Garamond, 2013), 265, 267, 297–300; Loos, *Naturalistic Novel*, 41–42.

68. Leonardo Mendes, "Sordid Literature: Naturalism and Sexuality in Brazil," *Excavatio* 21, no. 1–2 (2006): 58, 60; and Loos, *Naturalistic Novel*, chap. 4.

69. José Guilherm Merquior, *De Anchieta a Euclides: Breve história da literatura brasileira* (Rio de Janeiro: Livraria J. Olympio Editora, 1977), quoted in Bueno, *Resisting Boundaries*, 30.

70. See, for example, Bueno, *Resisting Boundaries*, 25–26; Antônio Cândido, *O discurso e a cidade* (São Paulo: Livraria Duas Cidades, 1993), 125; Mérian, "Débuts du naturalisme," 35.

71. On the problem of slavery in Brazilian Positivism, see Isabel DiVanna, "Reading Comte across the Atlantic: Intellectual Exchanges between France and Brazil and the Question of Slavery," *History of European Ideas* 38, no. 3 (2012): 454–55.

72. Mérian, *Aluísio Azevedo*, 293. See also Bueno, *Resisting Boundaries*, 25–28. On the "whitening solution," see Thomas E. Skidmore, "Racial Ideas and Social Policy in Brazil, 1870–1940," in *The Idea of Race in Latin America, 1870–1940*, ed. Richard Graham (Austin: University of Texas Press, 1990), 8–9.

73. Brushwood, *Genteel Barbarism*, 9–10.

74. Benítez-Rojo, "Spanish American Novel," 430; Manuel Prendes, *La novela naturalista hispanoamericana: Evolución y direcciones de un processo narrativo* (Madrid: Cátedra, 2003), 57–58.

75. Prendes, *Novela naturalista*, 50; John Paul Spicer-Escalante, "Civilización y barbarie: Naturalism's Paradigms of Self and Nationhood in Eugenio Cambaceres' Sin rumbo," *Excavatio* 13 (2000): 301; Brushwood, *Genteel Barbarism*, 9.

76. Prendes, *Novela naturalista*, 60–63.

77. Benítez-Rojo, "Spanish American Novel," 471–72.

78. Spicer-Escalante, "Civilación y barbarie," 301; Brushwood, *Genteel Barbarism*, 15–16.

79. David W. Foster, *The Argentine Generation of 1880: Ideology and Cultural Texts* (Columbia: Missouri University Press, 1990), 118–20, 139–41.

80. On Cambaceres's critique, see Benítez-Rojo, "Spanish American Novel," 471–72.

81. On the acceptance of Cambaceres, see Prendes, *Novela naturalista*, 64. Although Foster considers this position in defense of the status quo a peculiar "inversion" of naturalism in Argentina, one finds it elsewhere too, for example in the work of Kumičić in Croatia and Jack London in the United States (see chapters 3 and 4, respectively). Foster, *Argentine Generation*, 91.

82. Prendes, *Novela naturalista*, 74–77.

83. Zeno Gandía added two more novels to the series in the 1920s. On Zeno Gandía and Zola, see Gilbert Darbouze, *Dégénérescence et régénérescence dans l'oeuvre d'Émile Zola et celle de Manuel Zeno Gandía: Étude comparée* (New York: Peter Lang, 1997), chap. 1.

84. Prendes, *Novela naturalista*, 84–85; Oswaldo Voysest, "Clorinda Matto and Mercedes Cabello: Reading Émile Zola's Naturalism in a Dissonant Voice," *Excavatio* 11 (1998): 195–97.

85. Prendes, *Novela naturalista*, 80–81; Brushwood, *Genteel Barbarism*, 20.

86. Gamboa, "Historia de *Aparencias*," quoted in Prendes, *Novela naturalista*, 82 and 83 n. 32.

87. Cândido sees a "realism of romantics" and a "romanticism of naturalists" in Brazil, while Benítez-Rojo compares "romantic realism" and "naturalistic realism" in Spanish America (borrowing phrases from Fernando Alegría). Cândido, *Formação da literatura brasileira*, 111; Benítez-Rojo, "Spanish American Novel," 429–30. Simon Gikandi argues that a sense of political vocation in colonial and postcolonial Africa led some writers to adopt the "anachronistic" aesthetics of the romance and realism as they sought a way of writing suited to the realities they faced. See Gikandi, "Realism, Romance, and the Problem of African Literary History," *Modern Language Quarterly* 73, no. 3 (2012): 311–13, 320–21.

88. Brushwood, *Genteel Barbarism*, 20–21.

89. The canon of realism in the United States has been successively revised and expanded. Elizabeth Ammons presents a thoughtful reflection in "Expanding the Canon of American Realism," in *Documents of American Realism and Naturalism*, ed. Donald Pizer (Carbondale: Southern Illinois University Press, 1998), 435–52.

90. William C. Frierson and Herbert Edwards, "The Impact of French Naturalism on American Critical Opinion 1877–1892," *PMLA* 63, no. 3 (1948): 1011–16. (The charge against *L'Assommoir* is from a review in *Harper's*,

quoted on 1010.) On the "realism war," which is said to have begun with an appreciative piece on Henry James by Howells in 1882, see chapter 2 of Edwin H. Cady, *The Realist at War: The Mature Years, 1885–1920, of William Dean Howells* (Syracuse, N.Y.: Syracuse University Press, 1958).

91. Louis J. Budd, "The American Background," in *The Cambridge Companion to American Realism and Naturalism: Howells to London*, ed. Donald Pizer (New York: Cambridge University Press, 1995), 43.

92. Minimizing the connection to French naturalism has been the trend since the 1950s, although criticism before World War II readily acknowledged it. The denials typically rely on comparisons of American works to Zola's manifesto *The Experimental Novel* rather than to his fiction. I am looking deliberately to earlier scholarship such as the work of Åhnebrink and Albert Salvan. For an argument trying to minimize the connections, see Eric Carl Link, *The Vast and Terrible Drama: American Literary Naturalism in the Late Nineteenth Century* (Tuscaloosa: University of Alabama Press, 2004), 6–10. An example of the prewar view is Malcolm Cowley, "'Not Men': A Natural History of American Naturalism," in *Documents of American Realism and Naturalism*, ed. Donald Pizer (Carbondale: Southern Illinois University Press, 1998), 225–38.

93. *The Girl in Scarlet*, trans. John Stirling (Mary Neal Sherwood) (Philadelphia: T.B. Peterson and Bros., 1882); *Wedded in Death*, trans. unknown (New York: F. Tousey, 1884); *La Belle Lisa*, trans. John Stirling (Philadelphia: T.B. Peterson and Bros., 1882).

94. Albert J. Salvan, *Zola aux Etats-Unis* (New York: Kraus Reprint, 1967), 32; Åhnebrink, *Beginnings of Naturalism*, 47.

95. Crane quoted in Thomas Beer, *Stephen Crane: A Study in American Letters* (Garden City, N.Y.: Garden City Publishing, 1927), as cited by Åhnebrink, *Beginnings of Naturalism*, 96.

96. Åhnebrink, *Beginnings of Naturalism*, 112; Frank Norris, *McTeague: A Story of San Francisco*, ed. Donald Pizer, 2nd ed. (New York: Norton, 1997), 111. All parenthetical citations of *McTeague* in text will be to this edition.

97. Åhnebrink, *Beginnings of Naturalism*, 96, 105.

98. On Norris's role in the publication of *Sister Carrie,* see Pizer, "Backgrounds and Sources," 443; on the attempt to identify intermediaries between Dreiser and Zola, see Salvan, *Zola aux Etats-Unis*, 179–83. Dreiser acknowledged reading Zola after he wrote *Sister Carrie.*

99. On the contribution of Midwestern realism to naturalism in the United States, see Åhnebrink, *Beginnings of Naturalism*, chaps. 4–5.

100. Frank Norris, "Zola as a Romantic Writer," in *McTeague: A Story of San Francisco*, ed. Donald Pizer, 2nd ed. (New York: Norton, 1997), 273. June Howard observes that it is impossible to separate naturalism from the realism that it meant to oppose. Howard, "Sand in Your Mouth: Naturalism and Other Genres," in *Oxford Handbook of American Literary Naturalism*, ed. Keith Newlin (New York: Oxford University Press, 2011), 98.

101. Quoted in Åhnebrink, *Beginnings of Naturalism*, 61, from an undated letter.

102. On Howells's views, see Link, *Vast and Terrible Drama*, 45; for Norris's views, see "Zola as a Romantic Writer" and "A Plea for Romantic Fiction,"

in *McTeague: A Story of San Francisco*, ed. Donald Pizer, 2nd ed. (New York: Norton, 1997), 277–80.

103. Donald Pizer, *Realism and Naturalism in Nineteenth-Century American Literature* (Carbondale: Southern Illinois University Press, 1966), 15, 21, 25, 34–35. On naturalism and romanticism in the United States, see also Link, *Vast and Terrible Drama*, 64–65.

104. Cathy N. Davidson and Arnold E. Davidson, "Carrie's Sisters: The Popular Prototypes of Dreiser's Heroine," *Modern Fiction Studies* 23, no. 3 (1977): 395.

105. On conceptions of the self in romanticism, realism, and naturalism, see Lee Clark Mitchell, *Determined Fictions: American Literary Naturalism* (New York: Columbia University Press, 1990), 33.

106. Tsubouchi Shōyō, *Shōsetsu shinzui*, in *Tsubouchi Shōyō shū*, Nihon kindai bungaku taikei 3 (Tokyo: Kadokawa shoten, 1974), 40–42.

107. Tomi Suzuki, *Narrating the Self: Fictions of Japanese Modernity* (Stanford, Calif.: Stanford University Press, 1996), 26 and 196 n. 59.

108. Kawauchi Kiyoshi, *Zora to Nihon shizen shugi bungaku* (Matsudo: Azusa Shuppansha, 1990), 131.

109. Oka Yasuo, "Zoraizumu no jubaku," in *Nihon bungaku no rekishi*, ed. Yoshida Seiichi and Shimomura Fujio (Tokyo: Kadokawa Shoten, 1968), vol. 10: 118.

110. Yoshida, *Shizen shugi*, vol. 1: 131; Kawauchi, *Zora to Nihon*, 147–50. Ōgai's article, initially titled "On the Novel" ("Shōsetsuron"), later was reprinted as "On Novels Inspired by Medical Theories" ("Igaku no setsu yori idetaru shōsetsu ron").

111. Shōyō and Ōgai enunciated their positions multiple times. Representative examples are Tsubouchi Shōyō, "Sheekuspiya kyakuhon hyōchū," in *Meiji ki I*, Kindai bungaku hyōron taikei 1 (Tokyo: Kadokawa Shoten, 1971), 188–93; and Mori Ōgai, "Waseda bungaku no botsu risō," in *Meiji ki I*, 193–99.

112. Kawauchi, *Zora to Nihon*, 144–50, 153–54. See also Suzuki, *Narrating the Self*, 24–25.

113. Yoshida, *Shizen shugi*, vol. 1: 130.

114. Wada Kingo, *Byōsha no jidai—hitotsu no shizen shugi bungaku ron* (Sapporo: Hokkaidō Daigaku Tosho Kankōkai, 1975), 17.

115. Kunikida Doppo is sometimes placed among these early naturalists, although his work was inspired by the descriptions of nature he found in Wordsworth and the "sketch literature" (*shaseibun*) of the poet Masaoka Shiki.

116. Tayama Katai, "Rokotsu naru byōsha," in *Meiji ki II*, Kindai bungaku hyōron taikei 2 (Tokyo: Kadokawa Shoten, 1972), 363.

117. Yoshida, *Shizen shugi*, vol. 1: 144; and Kenneth G. Henshall, *In Search of Nature: The Japanese Writer Tayama Katai (1872–1930)* (Leiden: Global Oriental, 2013), 90–91, which notes the impact of Sudermann's *The Cat's Bridge* (*Der Katzensteg*, 1890) on Katai's "The End of Jūemon."

118. Suzuki, *Narrating the Self*, 48–52, 70–75.

119. Wada, *Byōsha no jidai*, 20. On the rejection of *shajitsu*, see Suzuki, *Narrating the Self*, 79.

120. On protest in naturalist fiction, see Suzuki, *Narrating the Self*, 81; and William F. Sibley, "Naturalism in Japanese Literature," *Harvard Journal of Asiatic Studies* 28 (1968): 165–68. While the attention to conflict between individuals and society commonly is attributed to Rousseau, a more proximate source is the Nietzschean individualism of the aesthetician Takayama Chogyū. See Irmela Hijiya-Kirschnereit, *Rituals of Self-Revelation: Shishōsetsu as Literary Genre and Socio-Cultural Phenomenon* (Cambridge, Mass.: Council on East Asian Studies, 1996), 27–28.

121. Hasegawa Tenkei, "Genjitsu bakurō no hiai," in *Meiji ki III*, Kindai bungaku hyōron taikei 3 (Tokyo: Kadokawa Shoten, 1972), 118.

122. Suzuki, *Narrating the Self*, 91. See also Edward Fowler, *The Rhetoric of Confession: Shishōsetsu in Early Twentieth-Century Japanese Fiction* (Berkeley: University of California Press, 1988), 6–10.

123. Marston Anderson, *The Limits of Realism: Chinese Fiction in the Revolutionary Period* (Berkeley: University of California Press, 1990), 28.

124. Anderson, *Limits of Realism*, 3–4, 25, 76–77.

125. McDougall, *Introduction of Western Literary Theories*, 158–59.

126. McDougall, *Introduction of Western Literary Theories*, 149. For a panoramic view of the role of students in the circulation of literary forms in East Asia, see Karen Laura Thornber, *Empire of Texts in Motion: Chinese, Korean, and Taiwanese Transculturations of Japanese Literature* (Cambridge, Mass.: Harvard University Asia Center, 2009), 34–46.

127. Dewei Wang, *Fictional Realism in Twentieth-Century China: Mao Dun, Lao She, Shen Congwen* (New York: Columbia University Press, 1992), 70. I thank Xiaobing Tang for discussing the distinction between the terms.

128. Wang, *Fictional Realism*, 25, 71.

129. McDougall, *Introduction of Western Literary Theories*, 183–84. For the phrase, see Wang, *Fictional Realism*, 49. Two other major sources for Mao Dun's ideas about naturalism were books by American scholars: William Lyon Phelps's *Essays on Modern Novelists* (New York: Macmillan, 1910) and Frank Wadleigh Chandler's *Aspects of Modern Drama* (New York: Macmillan, 1914). Wang, *Fictional Realism*, 71.

130. David Der-wei Wang, "Mao Tun and Naturalism: A Case of Misreading in Modern Chinese Literary Criticism," *Monumenta Serica* 37 (1986): 177–80. See also Jaroslav Průšek, *The Lyrical and the Epic: Studies of Modern Chinese Literature* (Bloomington: Indiana University Press, 1980), 133–34.

131. Wang, *Fictional Realism*, 70.

132. Wang, *Fictional Realism*, 37; Wang, "Mao Tun and Naturalism," 172.

133. For a detailed account, see Xiaobing Tang and Michel Hockx, "The Creation Society (1921–1930)," in *Literary Societies of Republican China*, ed. Michel Hockx and Kirk A. Denton (Lanham, Md.: Lexington Books, 2008), 104–7. Japanese naturalism also had a career in the Japanese colony of Taiwan that I will not cover here. On this topic, see Nai-huei Shen, "The Age of Sadness: A Study of Naturalism in Taiwanese Literature under Japanese Colonization," doctoral dissertation, University of Washington, 2003.

134. Christopher T. Keaveney, *The Subversive Self in Modern Chinese Literature: The Creation Society's Reinvention of the Japanese Shishōsetsu* (New

York: Palgrave Macmillan, 2004), 27; Průšek, *Lyrical and the Epic*, 166; Thornber, *Empire of Texts*, 243.

135. On ideas of individualism in the May Fourth era, see Liu, *Translingual Practice*, 87–88, 94–95.

136. Cheng Fangwu, "Realism and Trivialism" ("Xieshi zhuyi yu yongsu zhuyi," 1923), quoted in Tang and Hockx, "Creation Society," 114–15.

137. Keaveney, *Subversive Self*, 28, 72, 89–90.

138. Keaveney, *Subversive Self*, 146 n. 54.

139. Tang and Hockx, "Creation Society," 119–21; Keaveney, *Subversive Self*, 19. See also Liu, *Translingual Practice*, 97–98.

140. Tang and Hockx, "Creation Society," 123–24, 127.

141. Thornber gives many examples of the ongoing engagement with Japanese naturalism; see, for example, *Empire of Texts*, 306–11, on Ba Jin and Shimazaki Tōson.

142. Heekyoung Cho, *Translation's Forgotten History: Russian Literature, Japanese Mediation, and the Formation of Modern Korean Literature* (Cambridge, Mass.: Harvard University Asia Center, 2016), 23–24; Kang U, "Nihon to Chōsen hantō," 247.

143. Ki-Hwan Yu, "Le Manifeste naturaliste de Corée et Le Roman expérimental: Yeom Sang-Seob et Émile Zola," in *Re-Reading Zola and Worldwide Naturalism: Miscellanies in Honour of Anna Gural-Migdal*, ed. Carolyn Snipes-Hoyt, Marie-Sophie Armstrong, and Riikka Rossi (Newcastle upon Tyne, Eng.: Cambridge Scholars, 2013), 315. On Yi's project, see Ann Sung-hi Lee, *Yi Kwang-su and Modern Korean Literature, Mujŏng* (Ithaca, N.Y.: East Asia Program, Cornell University, 2005), 40–48.

144. Sunyoung Park, "The Colonial Origin of Korean Realism and Its Contemporary Manifestation," *Positions* 14, no. 1 (2006): 176. On the political and cultural climate, see also Kim Yoon-shik, "KAPF Literature in Modern Korean Literary History," *Positions* 14, no. 2 (2006): 406–8.

145. Yu, "Manifeste naturaliste," 314; Kang U, "Nihon to Chōsen hantō," 247.

146. Park, "Colonial Origin," 175; Thornber, *Empire of Texts*, 242–43.

147. Kim, "KAPF Literature," 407; Yu, "Manifeste naturaliste," 314.

148. Kim Tong-in, "The World Created by Self," trans. Jae-Yon Lee, *Acta Koreana* 16, no. 1 (2013): 257, 260. On the essay, see Jae-Yon Lee, "On Kim Tong-in's 'The World Created by Self' and Yŏm Sang-Sŏp's 'Individuality and Art,'" *Acta Koreana* 16, no. 1 (2013): 254–55.

149. On Hyŏn's story, see Park, *Proletarian Wave*, 106–7.

150. Yŏm Sang-sŏp, "Individuality and Art," trans. Jae-Yon Lee, *Acta Koreana* 16, no. 1 (2013): 262–63. On the essay, see Yu, "Manifeste naturaliste," 316–17.

151. Jiwon Shin, "Recasting Colonial Space: Naturalist Vision and Modern Fiction in 1920s Korea," *Journal of International and Area Studies* [Seoul] 11, no. 3 (2004): 69.

152. Kang U, "Nihon to Chōsen hantō," 239. In Yŏm's view, art expressed both the character of the artist and the ethnic people (*minjokchŏk*). Yŏm, "Individuality and Art," 267.

153. Park, "Colonial Origin," 176.

154. Yŏm Sang-sŏp, "On the Eve of the Uprising," trans. Sunyoung Park, in *On the Eve of the Uprising and Other Stories from Colonial Korea* (Ithaca, N.Y.: Cornell University East Asia Series, 2010), 35. Park gives an insightful reading of the novel and its place in the literature of the 1920s in *Proletarian Wave*, 178–83.

155. Yu, "Manifeste naturaliste," 315; Park, "Colonial Origin," 178, quoting Pak's essay "New Tendency Literature and Its Place in the Literary World" ("Sin'gyŏnghyangp'a munhak kwa kŭ mundanjŏk chiwi," 1925). On the turn to New Tendency literature, see Park, *Proletarian Wave*, 127–33; on Mao Dun's views, see Anderson, *Limits of Realism*, 42–43.

156, My thanks to Youngju Ryu for this information. The phrase is Kim's.

157. See, for example, Thornber's discussion of Yŏm's novel *Three Generations* (*Samdae*, 1931) and Shimazaki Tōson's *The Family* (*Ie*, 1911) in *Empire of Texts*, 311–14.

158. Yu, "Manifeste naturaliste," 316.

159. Michael Denning, *Culture in the Age of the Three Worlds* (New York: Verso, 2004), 55–60.

160. On serial contextualism, see David Armitage, "What's the Big Idea? Intellectual History and the Longue Durée," *History of European Ideas* 38, no. 4 (2012): 497–99. Like Armitage too, I consider the concrete connections between contexts to be the ultimate justification for the approach.

161. See Jacques Revel, "Multiple Narratives: Scale and Discontinuity in History," in *Unsettling History: Archiving and Narrating in Historiography*, ed. Sebastian Jobs and Alf Lüdtke (New York: Campus Verlag, 2010), 59; and Wai-Chee Dimock, *Through Other Continents: American Literature across Deep Time* (Princeton, N.J.: Princeton University Press, 2006), 77–80.

162. Here I am relying on Pierre Bourdieu's theory of literary fields. See "The Field of Cultural Production, or The Economic World Reversed," trans. Richard Nice, in *The Field of Cultural Production*, ed. Randal Johnson (New York: Columbia University Press, 1993), 30–31, 35–36.

163. Edmond and Jules de Goncourt, *Germinie Lacerteux* (Paris: Union Générale d'Éditions, 1979), 23, 24. All parenthetical citations of this novel in text will be to this edition.

164. Kosugi Tengai, *Hayari uta* (Tokyo: Iwanami Shoten, 1954), 4. (Parenthetical citations of this novel in text are of this edition.) On critics' views of *Nanà a Milano,* see Barnaby, "Nana in Milan," 165; on Cabello, see Prendes, *Novela naturalista*, 85. Barnaby considers Arrighi's preface to be partly satirical. On the concept of paratext, see Gérard Genette, *Paratexts: Thresholds of Interpretation*, trans. Jane Lewin (New York: Cambridge University Press, 1997), 1–2.

165. Welge, *Genealogical Fictions*, 89–90.

166. Ingwersen, "Modern Breakthrough," 266–67, 281.

167. In addition to the long piece that gave the volume its title, the essays "Money in Literature" ("L'Argent dans la littérature") and "Naturalism in the Theater" ("Le Naturalisme au théâtre") were especially influential.

168. For Taylor's definition, see *Modern Social Imaginaries* (Durham, N.C.: Duke University Press, 2004), 23–25. Taylor was elaborating ideas advanced by Cornelius Castoriadus in *The Imaginary Institution of Society*.

169. On Morel, see Daniel Pick, *Faces of Degeneration: A European Disorder, c. 1848–c. 1918* (Cambridge: Cambridge University Press, 1989), 50–52.

170. On Lombroso's intellectual sources, see Mary Gibson, *Born to Crime: Cesare Lombroso and the Origins of Biological Criminology* (Westport, Conn.: Praeger, 2002), 20; on his increasing reliance on the idea of degeneration, see p. 25.

171. Émile Zola, *La Bête humaine* (Paris: Gallimard, 2001), 65, 86; George L. Mosse, "Introduction," in *Degeneration,* by Max Nordau (Lincoln: University of Nebraska Press, 1993), xx; Nordau, *Degeneration*, 166, 176, 232, 475–76.

172. Frank Norris, "A Case for Lombroso," in *The Apprenticeship Writings of Frank Norris*, ed. Joseph R. McElrath and Douglas K. Burgess (Philadelphia: American Philosophical Society, 1996), vol. 2: 129; Donald Pizer, *The Novels of Frank Norris* (Bloomington: Indiana University Press, 1966), 58.

173. For a short overview of the transnational history of neurasthenia, see my "Exhausted by Their Battles with the World: Neurasthenia and Civilization Critique in Early Twentieth-Century Japan," in *Perversion and Modern Japan: Experiments in Psychoanalysis*, ed. Nina Cornyetz and Keith Vincent (London: Routledge, 2009), 243–45. Nordau uses the term "hysteria," but its etiology follows Beard's explanation of the causes of neurasthenia. On Nordau and neurasthenia, see *Degeneration*, 36–40.

174. Gibson, *Born to Crime*, 29.

175. Prendes, *Novela naturalista*, 17; Bueno, *Resisting Boundaries*, 15; Michael Bourdaghs, *The Dawn That Never Comes: Shimazaki Tōson and Japanese Nationalism* (New York: Columbia University Press, 2003), 51.

176. For Brandes's call for a literature of problems, see his "Inaugural Lecture, 1871," trans. Evert Sprinchorn, in *The Theory of the Modern Stage*, ed. Eric Bentley (London: Penguin, 1992), 388–90.

177. Ingwersen, "Modern Breakthrough," 276–77. On Bang's attack on Brandes, see 266–67.

178. Yoshida, *Shizen shugi*, vol. 1: 136.

179. Tracing the impact of these writers is far beyond the scope of this book, but for selected examples from two European literary "peripheries," see Antun Barac, *A History of Yugoslav Literature* (Ann Arbor: Michigan Slavic Publications, Dept. of Slavic Languages and Literatures, University of Michigan, 1976), 138, 154–56, 161–62, 167–68, 174; Zdenko Skreb, "Le Naturalisme dans les littératures yougoslaves," in *Le Naturalisme en question,* ed. Yves Chevrel (Paris: Presses de l'Université de Paris-Sorbonne, 1986), 53–57; Ingwersen, "Modern Breakthrough," 264; McFarlane, "Norwegian Literature," 145, 150; Laitinen, "Rise of Finnish-Language Literature," 86, 90–91; Schoolhouse, "Sense of Minority," 370–71.

180. Skreb, "Le Naturalisme," 53–57; Barac, *History of Yugoslav Literature*, 154–56, 162, 167, 174.

181. Laitinen, "Rise of Finnish-Language Literature," 85–86, 90–91; Schoolfield, "Sense of Minority," 360, 364–65, 370–72.

182. Christophe Charle, *Paris fin de siècle: Culture et politique* (Paris: Seuil, 1998), 179–85.

183. The idea of a realist moment is broadly inspired by Raymond Williams's idea of "realist intention" in literature, which he presents as a "method" in distinction from the "fundamental attitude" exemplified by the classical European realist novel. See Williams, "A Lecture on Realism," *Screen* 18, no. 1 (1977): 62–63.

184. Sven Hakon Rossel, *A History of Scandinavian Literature, 1870–1980*, trans. Anne C. Ulmer (Minneapolis: University of Minnesota Press, 1982), 35; Barac, *History of Yugoslav Literature*, 153; Åhnebrink, *Beginnings of Naturalism*, 88. On the history of national romanticism on the peripheries of the British Empire, see Katie Trumpener, *Bardic Nationalism: The Romantic Novel and the British Empire* (Princeton, N.J.: Princeton University Press, 1997).

185. In stressing writers' announcements of affiliation over immanent aesthetic qualities as a criterion, I am broadly indebted to Bourdieu. See "Field of Cultural Production," 42.

186. I owe the idea of multidirectional citation to the Modern Girl Around the World project. See Modern Girl Around the World Research Group, "The Modern Girl as Heuristic Device: Collaboration, Connective Comparison, Multidirectional Citation," 4–6; and "The Modern Girl Around the World: Cosmetics Advertising and the Politics of Race and Style," in *The Modern Girl Around the World: Consumption, Modernity, and Globalization*, ed. Alys Eve Weinbaum et al. (Durham, N.C.: Duke University Press, 2008), 26.

187. On reciprocity in center-periphery relations, see Stefan Nygård and Johan Strang, "Facing Asymmetry: Nordic Intellectuals and Center-Periphery Dynamics in European Cultural Space," *Journal of the History of Ideas* 77, no. 1 (2016): 76, 80–81.

188. On this period in Azevedo's career and the nonfiction book he planned, *Japan As It Is* (*O Japão como ele é*), see Mérian, *Aluísio Azevedo*, 555–58, 571–73.

189. On the non-encounter of Azevedo and Katai, see my "Haven't We Met? On the Scales of Connection," *Verge: Studies in Global Asias* 3, no. 2 (2017): 86–89. On the mediation of relations through the field, see Bourdieu, "Field of Cultural Production," 46. The most important vehicle for "nonaligned" literary relations during decolonization was the trilingual journal *Lotus*. For its history, see Hala Halim, "Lotus, the Afro-Asian Nexus, and Global South Comparatism," *Comparative Studies of South Asia, Africa and the Middle East* 32, no. 3 (2012): 568–83.

190. Roberto Schwarz, "National Adequation and Critical Originality," trans. R. Kelly Washbourne and Neil Larsen, *Cultural Critique* 49 (2001): 18, 20. I discuss Cândido's reading of *O Cortiço* in chapter 4.

191. Schwarz, "National Adequation," 20.

192. Michel Foucault, "What Is an Author?" trans. Josué V. Harari, in *The Essential Foucault*, ed. Paul Rabinow and Nikolas Rose (New York: New Press, 2003), 388–89.

193. Nygård and Strang, "Facing Asymmetry," 85–87.

194. This is a point I owe to Georg Brandes's famous observations on the literatures of large and small countries. See Brandes, "World Literature," trans. Haun Saussy, in *Mapping World Literature: International Canonization and*

Transnational Literatures, by Mads Rosendahl Thomsen (New York: Continuum, 2008), 144.

195. Pierre Bourdieu, "Les Conditions sociales de la circulation internationale des idées," *Actes de la Recherche en Sciences Sociales* 145 (2002): 5.

196. I borrow the phrase "double frame" from Nygård and Strang, whose demonstration of the ways intellectuals could play one scale against the other contradicts Casanova's belief that peripheral writers must be either "international" or "national" (seeking autonomy by looking to Paris on the one hand, or accepting a sullied, heteronomous position on the other). See Nygård and Strang, "Facing Asymmetry," 88–90; and Casanova, *World Republic of Letters*, 94.

197. Harsha Ram, "The Scale of Global Modernisms: Imperial, National, Regional, Local," *PMLA* 131, no. 5 (2016): 1374–75.

198. For an example of Moretti's view of the novel as a transhistorical form that "rises" independently in different parts of the world, see "The Novel."

199. Appadurai, "Disjuncture and Difference," 3.

CHAPTER 2

1. Kelly Basilio Bénoudis, *Le Mécanique et le vivant: La Métonymie chez Zola* (Geneva: Droz, 1993), 36.

2. Honoré de Balzac, *Le Père Goriot* (Paris: Gallimard, 1971), 28–29. Parenthetical citations of this novel in text will be to this edition.

3. Philippe Hamon, *Du descriptif* (Paris: Hachette, 1993), 105–6.

4. Hamon, *Du descriptif*, 111.

5. Émile Zola, "Documents et plans préparatoires des Rougon Macquart," in *Les Rougon-Macquart V*, ed. Henri Mitterand (Paris: Gallimard, 1967), 1736–37. Parenthetical citations of these documents in text are to this edition.

6. Henri Mitterand describes the craze, and writers' special interest in neurology, in *Zola* (Paris: Fayard, 1999), vol. 1: 575–77.

7. Gustave Flaubert, *Correspondance* (Paris: Charpentier, 1887), vol. 2: 370.

8. Quoted in Margaret Gilman, "Two Critics and an Author: 'Madame Bovary' Judged by Sainte-Beuve and by Baudelaire," *French Review* 15, no. 2 (1941): 139.

9. Hippolyte Taine, "Balzac," in *Nouveaux essais de critique et d'histoire*, 2nd ed. (Paris: Hachette, 1866), 118.

10. Patrick O'Donovan, "The Body and the Body Politic in the Novels of the Goncourts," in *Spectacles of Realism: Body, Gender, Genre*, ed. Margaret Cohen and Christopher Prendergast (Minneapolis: University of Minnesota Press, 1995), 217, 221–22.

11. Émile Zola, "'Germinie Lacerteux' par MM. Edmond et Jules de Goncourt," in *Oeuvres critiques I*, ed. Henri Mitterand, Oeuvres complètes 10 (Paris: Cercle du Livre Précieux, 1968), 62. The Goncourts returned the favor by defending *Thérèse Raquin* as an "admirable autopsy of remorse." Quoted in Susan Harrow, "Thérèse Raquin: Animal Passion and the Brutality of Reading," in *The Cambridge Companion to Emile Zola*, ed. Brian Nelson (Cambridge: Cambridge University Press, 2007), 105.

12. Émile Zola, *Thérèse Raquin* (Paris: Garnier-Flammarion, 1970), 60. All parenthetical citations of this novel in text will be to this edition. I use "derangement" to translate *détraquement*, which more literally would be "untracking." On the associations of *détraquement* with Zola's machinic metaphors—especially common in female characters—see Jean-Louis Cabanès, *Le Corps et la maladie dans les récits réalistes (1856–1893)* (Lille: Klincksieck, 1991), vol. 1: 315–16. "Putrid literature" was the title of an 1868 article by the critic Louis Ulbach condemning *Thérèse Raquin*, *Germinie Lacerteux,* and other works of a recent "monstrous school" of novelists (reproduced in Zola, *Thérèse Raquin*, 39–44).

13. Character description is the key means for classifying characters through external discourses such as medicine, Hamon points out. Hamon, *Du descriptif*, 111.

14. The gruesome scenes are among the novel's many gothic elements, examined by Colette Becker in "De la Vénus de Gordes à la Vénus du Pont-Neuf: Jeux de réécriture," in *Lire/Dé-lire Zola*, ed. Jean-Pierre Leduc-Adine and Henri Mitterand (Paris: Nouveau Monde, 2004), 91–95.

15. See, for example, Zola, *Thérèse Raquin*, 157–58. On free indirect style as "represented speech and thought," see Ann Banfield, *Unspeakable Sentences: Narration and Representation in the Language of Fiction* (London: Routledge, 1982), 69–70.

16. The letter, from early 1868, is reproduced in Zola, *Thérèse Raquin*, 53–54.

17. See Hippolyte Taine, *Histoire de la littérature anglaise* (Paris: Hachette, 1863), vol. 1: xxii–xxxi. Taine's use of the word *race* is near that of late nineteenth-century social science but retains meanings of "nation" and "people."

18. Zola, "Documents et plans," 1743–45. On Zola juggling Taine, Flaubert, and Stendhal, see Pierluigi Pellini, "Archéologie d'une 'maison de verre': Sur Zola et la folie," *Compar(a)ison* 2 (2003): 6–8.

19. Charles Letourneau, *Physiologie des passions* (Paris: Germer Baillière, 1868), 4–5.

20. Robert A. Nye, "Degeneration and the Medical Model of Cultural Crisis in the French Belle Époque," in *Political Symbolism in Modern Europe*, ed. Seymour Drescher, David Sabean, and Allan Sharlin (New Brunswick, N.J.: Transaction, 1982), 20.

21. Robert A. Nye, *Crime, Madness and Politics in Modern France: The Medical Concept of National Decline* (Princeton, N.J.: Princeton University Press, 1984), 143; Nye, "Degeneration and the Medical Model," 20.

22. Pick, *Faces of Degeneration*, 73.

23. Pellini, "Archéologie d'une 'maison de verre,'" 8–9. On Zola's discovery of Lucas, see Mitterand, *Zola*, vol. 1: 235, 345–46, 710.

24. Mitterand, *Zola*, vol. 1: 723; Cabanès, *Le Corps et la maladie*, vol. 1: 402–3; Auguste Dezalay, *L'Opéra des Rougon-Macquart: Essai de rythmologie romanesque* (Paris: Klincksieck, 1983), 204–8.

25. Carlos López-Beltrán, "In the Cradle of Heredity: French Physicians and L'Hérédité Naturelle in the Early 19th Century," *Journal of the History of Biology* 37, no. 1 (2004): 50.

26. Prosper Lucas, *Traité philosophique et physiologique de l'hérédité naturelle dans les états de santé et de maladie du système nerveux* (Paris: Baillière, 1847), vol. 1: 7–8. Given the range of meanings of *morale*, I translate it as "mental" or "moral" according to context.

27. Lucas, *Traité philosophique*, vol. 1: 96, 191.

28. Lucas, *Traité philosophique*, vol. 2: 376–77.

29. Lucas, *Traité philosophique*, vol. 1: 4–6.

30. Such cases appear throughout the *Treatise*; the last 400 pages of the second volume are devoted solely to them.

31. On the permutations of characteristics, see Zola, "Documents et plans," 1710–12, 1726–28, 1732–34; on behavioral pathologies, see 1701–03, 1724. Zola relied on these notes throughout the series. Mitterand, *Zola*, vol. 1: 726.

32. Cabanès discusses the role of medical knowledge in portraits in the Rougon-Macquart novels in *Le Corps et la maladie*, vol. 1: 405. More evidence of Lucas's impact on Zola can be found in *The Experimental Novel* (*Le Roman expérimental*, 1880), the manifesto Zola published to explain the method of the Rougon-Macquart novels, where he paired "physical life" (*vie physique*) and "the life of the passions and intellect" (*vie passionnelle et intellectuelle*) and said that study of the one leads to study of the other along a single "line" (*voie*) from chemistry through physiology to anthropology and sociology. Émile Zola, "Le Roman expérimental," in *Anthologie des préfaces de romans français du XIXe siècle*, ed. Herbert S. Gershman and Kernan B. Whitworth, Jr. (Paris: Julliard, 1964), 258, 273.

33. Jean Borie points out this critical difference between the work of Balzac, in which body and society are metaphorically related but distinct, and that of Zola, in which body and society are one. Borie, *Zola et les mythes; ou, De la nausée au salut* (Paris: Livre de Poche, 2003), 27–29.

34. Nicholas White, "Family Histories and Family Plots," in *The Cambridge Companion to Emile Zola*, ed. Brian Nelson (Cambridge: Cambridge University Press, 2007), 25, 33.

35. On myth, see especially Naomi Schor, *Zola's Crowds* (Baltimore, Md.: Johns Hopkins University Press, 1978); and Borie, *Zola et les mythes*; on rhythm, see Dezalay, *L'Opéra des Rougon-Macquart*.

36. White, "Family Histories," 23. For examples of Lucas's terminology and reasoning, see Émile Zola, *La Fortune des Rougon* (Paris: Gallimard, 1981), 73 (Antoine), 96 (Pascal), 91 (Eugène), 92 (Aristide), 233 (Silvère). The first two versions of the Rougon-Macquart family tree, prepared in 1869, are annotated using Lucas's scheme. Zola, "Documents et plans," 1777–79. Hereafter, all parenthetical citations of *La Fortune des Rougon* in text are of the 1981 Gallimard edition.

37. Zola, "Documents et plans," 1742. The axiomatic quality may be one reason why Gilles Deleuze, writing about *The Human Beast*, says the *fêlure* transmits nothing but itself. Deleuze, "Zola et la fêlure," in *Logique du sens* (Paris: Éditions de Minuit, 2002), 373.

38. On the abstract social relations that are characteristic of capitalist societies, see Moishe Postone, *Time, Labor and Social Domination* (Cambridge: Cambridge University Press, 1993).

39. Colette Becker, "Zola, un déchiffreur de l'entre-deux," *Études Françaises* 39, no. 2 (2003): 16–17.

40. White, "Family Histories," 28.

41. The classic examples are Émile Durkheim, *De la division du travail social: Étude sur l'organisation des sociétés supérieures* (Paris: Félix Alcan, 1893); and Gabriel Tarde, *Les Lois de l'imitation: Étude sociologique* (Paris: Félix Alcan, 1890).

42. For one such interpretation, see Susan Harrow, *Zola, the Body Modern: Pressures and Prospects of Representation* (London: Legenda, 2010), 147–49.

43. On the revisions, see Henri Mitterand, "Étude [La Fortune des Rougon]," in *Les Rougon-Macquart I* by Émile Zola (Paris: Gallimard, 1960), 1537–39.

44. Norris, "Zola as a Romantic Writer," 274.

45. Pellini, "Archéologie d'une 'maison de verre,'" 9–10.

46. Émile Zola, *L'Assommoir* (Paris: Gallimard, 1978), 17. Parenthetical citations of this work in text will be of this edition. On the book's title, see Jacques Dubois, *L'Assommoir de Zola*, 2nd ed. (Paris: Belin, 1993), 51–52; and David Baguley, *Emile Zola: L'Assommoir* (Cambridge: Cambridge University Press, 1992), 73.

47. Zola, *Fortune*, 162; Zola, *L'Assommoir*, 58.

48. On these stagings of Gervaise's life, see Dubois, *L'Assommoir de Zola*, 115; and Baguley, *Emile Zola*, 73.

49. Dubois, *L'Assommoir de Zola*, is the essential study of free indirect style in the novel; see chaps. 5 and 6.

50. Zola, *L'Assommoir*, 28, 34. Harrow sees the limp as the structuring trope of the novel (Harrow, *Zola*, 80).

51. Henri Mitterand, *Le Regard et le signe: Poétique du roman réaliste et naturaliste* (Paris: Presses Universitaires de France, 1987), 220.

52. I am indebted to Basilio's arguments on metonymy in *L'Assommoir* and *Ladies' Paradise* (*Au Bonheur des Dames*, 1883), although Basilio neglects the polysemic quality of metonymies in Zola's work, as seen in the case of Gervaise's leg. See Basilio, *Le Mécanique et le vivant*, part 2, chap. 1.

53. Harrow, *Zola*, 159.

54. Émile Zola, *Germinal* (Paris: Gallimard, 1978), 219. Parenthetical citations of this work in text are of this edition.

55. Harrow, *Zola*, 80.

56. Zola, *L'Assommoir*, 142, 144, 145, 146; Alfred Delvau, *Dictionnaire de la langue verte: Argots parisiens comparés*, 2nd ed. (Paris: E. Dentu, 1866), 59, 107, 226.

57. Zola, *L'Assommoir*, 151–54; Delvau, *Dictionnaire*, 405.

58. Delvau, *Dictionnaire*, 471.

59. Zola, *L'Assommoir*, 183, 500; Delvau, *Dictionnaire*, 226.

60. I borrow this list from Yvonne Bargues Rollins, "Une 'Danse macabre': L'Assommoir de Zola," *Nineteenth-Century French Studies* 9, no. 3–4 (1981): 244.

61. Zola, *L'Assommoir*, 387, 397, 430, 435; Delvau, *Dictionnaire*, 128.

62. Dubois, *L'Assommoir de Zola*, 59–63; Rollins, "'Danse macabre,'" 239–41, 245.

63. Zola, *L'Assommoir*, 510–15. On the scene at the hospital, see Naomi Schor, "Sainte-Anne: Capitale du délire," *Cahiers Naturalistes* 52 (1978): 101–5; on *galop*, see Rollins, "'Danse macabre,'" 244 n. 8.

64. Henri Mitterand, "Étude [L'Assommoir]," in *Les Rougon-Macquart II* by Émile Zola (Paris: Gallimard, 1961), 1556–66.

65. Baguley, *Emile Zola*, 104–5. Mitterand lists a number of parodies in "Étude [L'Assommoir]," 1567.

66. Mitterand, "Étude [L'Assommoir], 1560.

67. 1878: *Gervaise, a Story of Drink*, trans. Henry Llewellyn Williams (London: Edward Ashman); *Lo scannatoio*, trans. Emmanuele Rocco (Milan: Treves);

1879: *L'Assomuar*, trans. Policarpo Petrocchi (Milan: Pavia); *Dovbnja*, trans. O. Roškevyč (L'viv: Dribnaja) (Ukrainian); *Az emberirtó*, trans. László Nyári (Budapest: Pfeifer); *Fällan*, trans. unknown (Stockholm: Alb. Bonnier); *Gervaise*, trans. Edward Binsse (New York: Carleton); *Nana's Mother*, trans. John Stirling (Philadelphia: Peterson); *La taberna*, trans. Miguel de Toro y Gómez (Madrid: A. Flórez);

1880: *Das Assommoir*, trans. Willibald König (Berlin: Freund & Jeckel); *Zapadnya*, trans. unknown (Moscow: L.F. Snegireva);

1881: *L'assommoir*, trans. Al Schumacher (Copenhagen: A.W. Henningsens); "Nevolja, olomak iz Assommoira" (excerpt), trans. unknown (*Radnik* [Dubrovnik], nos. 120–27); *Der Totschläger*, trans. Fritz Wohlfahrt (Grossenhain: Baumert & Ronge);

1882: *Der Totschläger*, trans. Roderich Rode (Grossenhain: Baumert & Ronge);

1883: *Krčna*, trans. Josef Černý (Prague: Nákladem Aloise Hynka);

1884: *The "Assommoir,"* trans. unknown (London: Vizetelly);

1887: *Faldgruben*, trans. unknown (Oslo: Verdens Gang); *I Tavérna*, trans. Giánnis Kótsikas (Athens: Zikáki);

1888: *L'Assommoir*, trans. unknown (Chicago: Laird);

1890: *L'Assommoir*, trans. Arthur Symons (Philadelphia: G. Barrie);

1893: *L'Assomuar*, trans. Policarpo Petrocchi (Naples: Bideri); *Der Totschläger*, trans. Willibald König (Budapest: Grimm); *Der Totschläger*, trans. unknown (Berlin: S. Frankl).

68. Alaoui, "Zola en Espagne," 184; Joseph Jurt, "The Reception of Naturalism in Germany," in *Naturalism in the European Novel: New Critical Perspectives*, ed. Brian Nelson (New York: Berg, 1992), 101; Kálai, "La Réception de Zola," 177.

69. *Karera Rugonov*, trans. unknown (St. Petersburg: Balasev, 1873). The next translation of *La Fortune des Rougons* appears to be *The Rougon-Macquart Family*, trans. John Stirling [Mary Neal Sherwood] (Philadelphia: Peterson, 1879).

70. Baguley, *Emile Zola*, 102, 106; Terry Hale, "The Imaginary Quay from Waterloo Bridge to London Bridge: Translation, Adaptation, and Genre," in *On Translating French Literature and Film II*, ed, Myriam Salama-Carr (Amsterdam: Rodopi, 2000), 235.

71. Tullio Pagano, *Experimental Fictions: From Emile Zola's Naturalism to Giovanni Verga's Verism* (Madison, N.J.: Fairleigh Dickinson University Press, 1999), 57–58.

72. Arrighi, "Zola et De Sanctis," 439–41, 445.

73. Kálai, "La Réception de Zola," 173, 177.

74. Jolanta Rachwalska von Rejchwald, "Apologie et aversion de Zola en Pologne," in *Zola en Europe centrale*, ed. Norbert Bachleitner, Tone Smolej, and Karl Zieger (Valenciennes: Presses Universitaires de Valenciennes, 2011), 97–99.

75. Sotolova, "Émile Zola à la tchèque," 136–37.

76. Åhnebrink, *Beginnings of Naturalism*, 274–76; Loos, *Naturalistic Novel*, 74; Tone Smolej, "L'Assommoir et l'oeuvre romanesque d'Ivan Cankar," *Cahiers Naturalistes* 77 (2003): 259.

77. Åhnebrink, *Beginnings of Naturalism*, 262–64; Thomas R. Franz, "Early Spanish Intertexts with 'L'Assommoir,'" *Horizontes: Revista de la Universidad Catolica de Puerto Rico* 32, no. 63–64 (1988): 5–6, 10; Gacoin-Marks, "Eugen Kumičić et la première réception," 211.

78. Païvi Lappailainen, "Seduced Girls and Prostitutes: The Character of the Fallen Woman in Finnish Naturalist Fiction," *Excavatio* 23, no. 1–2 (2008): 163; Loos, *Naturalistic Novel*, 77; Smolej, "L'Assommoir et l'oeuvre romanesque," 256–58.

79. Loos, *Naturalistic Novel*, 76; Smolej, "L'Assommoir et l'oeuvre romanesque," 260–61.

80. Åhnebrink, *Beginnings of Naturalism*, 257–61; Gacoin-Marks, "Débuts du naturalisme," 149–50; Francisca Gonzalez-Arias, "Parallels and Parodies: Emilia Pardo Bazán's Response to Émile Zola (La Tribuna and L'Assommoir)," *Bulletin of Hispanic Studies* 67, no. 4 (1990): 371–72.

81. I take the phrase "novel-in-dialog" from Stephen Gilman, who sees Galdós's *The Disinherited* in a "massive novel-to-novel dialog" with *L'Assommoir*. Gilman, *Galdós and the Art of the European Novel, 1867–1887* (Princeton, N.J.: Princeton University Press, 1981), 93.

82. Lappailainen, "Seduced Girls and Prostitutes," 157, 160–63.

83. Smolej, "L'Assommoir et l'oeuvre romanesque," 255–58, 261.

84. Gonzalez-Arias, "Parallels and Parodies," 370–73, 376. See also Welge, *Genealogical Fictions*, 89–90.

85. Pagano, *Experimental Fictions*, 60–61, 71–75. I thank Valentino Piazzi for explaining the connotations of the name.

86. Gilman, *Galdós*, 89, 92–98, 106–7, 113. For a slightly different genealogy (or arborology) of free indirect discourse, see Franco Moretti, *Graphs, Maps, Trees: Abstract Models for Literary History* (London: Verso, 2005), 81–91.

87. Mark Seltzer finds the brute to be the "generative principle" of American naturalism and the source of its aesthetic. Seltzer, *Bodies and Machines* (New York: Routledge, 1992), 38.

88. Norris, *McTeague*, 20, 150; Norris, "Zola as a Romantic Writer," 274.

89. Norris, "Zola as a Romantic Writer," 274.

90. Gina M. Rossetti, *Imagining the Primitive in Naturalist and Modernist Literature* (Columbia: University of Missouri Press, 2006), 27, 41; Rebecca Nisetich, "The Nature of the Beast: Scientific Theories of Race and Sexuality in McTeague," *Studies in American Naturalism* 4, no. 1 (2009): 15–17. Their arguments on ethnicity and class in American naturalist fiction are indebted to June Howard, *Form and History in American Literary Naturalism* (Chapel Hill: University of North Carolina Press, 1985); see chap. 3. On the history of neurasthenia in the United States, see F. G. Gosling, *Before Freud: Neurasthenia and the American Medical Community, 1870–1910* (Urbana: University of Illinois Press, 1987), chap. 1.

91. Hugh J. Dawson, "McTeague as Ethnic Stereotype," *American Literary Realism* 20, no. 1 (1987): 36, 40–41. Norris uses the phrase in "The Novel with a 'Purpose'" (1902).

92. On Norris's encounter with Nordau and Lombroso, see Pizer, *Novels of Frank Norris*, 58–60. Mosse discusses Nordau's use of Lombroso in his introduction to *Degeneration*, xx–xxi.

93. Rossetti, *Imagining the Primitive*, 92–95, 98. Nisetich notes the conjunction of ethnic inferiority and sexual perversity in "The Nature of the Beast," 1–2.

94. Daniel Schierenbeck, "Is There a Doctor in the House? Norris's Naturalist Gaze of Clinical Observation in McTeague," in *Twisted from the Ordinary: Essays on American Literary Realism*, ed. Mary E. Papke (Knoxville: University of Tennessee Press, 2003) 65, 71.

95. Norris, *McTeague*, 17, 20. On the hair's symbolism, see Pizer, *Novels of Frank Norris*, 68.

96. Seltzer, *Bodies and Machines*, 37.

97. On the role of chance in the novel, see Pizer, *Novels of Frank Norris*, 67–69. In *Vandover and the Brute,* chance plays a similar role when Vandover's virtuous friend Dolly is infected with syphilis.

98. Karl Marx, *Capital: A Critique of Political Economy*, trans. Ben Fowkes and David Fernbach (New York: Penguin Books, 1976), vol. 1: 187.

99. I am indebted to Karatani Kōjin's *Marukusu sono kanōsei no chūshin* (Tokyo: Kōdansha, 1990) for this understanding of money as a signifying system. Although it is obligatory to cite Walter Benn Michaels's *The Gold Standard and the Logic of Naturalism: American Literature at the Turn of the Century* (Berkeley: University of California Press, 1987) here, the book offers unexpectedly little insight into *McTeague*'s exploration of money. Michaels's constant effort to reduce a thing to its opposite (the miser is a spendthrift, gold is junk) does not demonstrate the "logic of naturalism" so much as regurgitate variations on his "post-oppositional" view that the system of representation fostered by capitalism produces expressions of both approval and disapproval of it which the critic cannot possibly evaluate. Michaels, *Gold Standard*, 19, 141, 153. On the post-oppositional turn in studies of American literature, see Seltzer, *Bodies and Machines*, 134–35.

100. T. Fujitani, *Splendid Monarchy: Power and Pageantry in Modern Japan* (Berkeley: University of California Press, 1996), 19.

101. A classic examination of the trend is Oka Yoshitake, "Generational Conflict after the Russo-Japanese War," in *Conflict in Modern Japanese History:*

The Neglected Tradition, ed. Tetsuo Najita and Victor Koschmann (Princeton, N.J.: Princeton University Press, 1982).

102. Miyoshi Yukio, *Shimazaki Tōson ron* (Tokyo: Shibundō, 1966), 243–44. On the novel's historical vision, see also Uryū Kiyoshi, "Tōson no shin-jidai ishiki to Haru," *Fukuoka kyōiku daigaku kiyō dai-ichi bu bunka hen* 48 (1999): 4.

103. The term *burakumin* refers to people who were historically associated with leather tanning and other occupations that are considered unclean in Buddhism.

104. Tayama Katai, "Jūemon no saigo," in *Tayama Katai shū*, Nihon kindai bungaku taikei 19 (Tokyo: Kadokawa Shoten, 1972), 90, 109. The parenthetical citations of "Jūemon" in text are to this edition.

105. Katai, "Jūemon," 101–2. On the coinage of the term *risshin,* see Earl Kinmonth, *The Self-Made Man in Meiji Japanese Thought: From Samurai to Salary Man* (Berkeley: University of California Press, 1981), 55–59.

106. Iwasa Sōshirō, *Seikimatsu no shizen shugi—Meiji yonjūnendai bungaku kō* (Tokyo: Yūseidō, 1986), 139–41.

107. On disease and hygiene in *The Broken Commandment,* see chapter 2 of Bourdaghs, *The Dawn That Never Comes*; on disease and social change in *The Family*, see Nakayama Hiroaki, "Kettō no monogatari—'Ie' no 'yamai' ron," in *Shimazaki Tōson: Bunmei hihyō to shi to shōsetsu to*, ed. Hiraoka Toshio and Kenmochi Takehiko (Tokyo: Sōbunsha Shuppan, 1996), 182–97.

108. Kawamura Kunimitsu, *Genshi suru kindai kūkan—meishin, byōki, zashiki rō, arui wa rekishi no kioku* (Tokyo: Seikyūsha, 1990), 102–5. On the changing meaning of *shinkei,* see Arao Yoshihide, "Shinkei," in *Kōza Nihongo no goi 10* (Tokyo: Meiji Shoin, 1983), 236–40.

109. Morishita Yūdō, *Shinri ōyō nōshinkeisuijaku hitsujisaku* (Tokyo: Hakubunkan, 1909), 3.

110. On the complex reception of Nordau in Japan, see Kamakura Yoshinobu, "Shizen shugi bungaku to Makkusu Norudau—'Daraku ron' no yomare kata," *Kokubungaku gengo to bungei* 119 (2002): 68–73.

111. Shimazaki Tōson, *Haru* (Tokyo: Iwanami Shoten, 2000), 106, 107. Parenthetical citations of this work in text are of this edition. On criticism of the younger generation, see Oka, "Generational Conflict," 206–11.

112. On other characters as foils for Kishimoto, see Kōno Kensuke, "'Seishun' to iu tekusuto: Shimazaki Tōson Haru o megutte," in *Bungaku ni okeru nijūdai*, ed. Satō Yasumasa (Tokyo: Kasama Shoin, 1990), 126–32.

113. On their temperaments, see Tōson, *Haru*, 61–62, 110; visions of prison, 145, 269; suicide by dagger, 153, 285.

114. On the problem of communication and the focus on Kishimoto's physical sensations, see Ōida Yoshiaki, "Haru ni okeru komyunikeishon no mondai," *Bai* 7 (1991): 38–40. I disagree with the arguments of Ōida and others such as Konaka Nobukata that Kishimoto is described only in terms of his body, since descriptions of his mental state abound. See Konaka, "Kesareta shintai—Tayama katai 'Futon' no jidai," *Kokugakuin zasshi* 105, no. 11 (2004): 124–27.

115. On the impact of Katai's novella, see, for example, Miyoshi, *Shimazaki Tōson*, 166–67.

116. On the expression of belatedness in late-Meiji narrative form, see Jonathan E. Zwicker, *Practices of the Sentimental Imagination: Melodrama, the Novel, and the Social Imaginary in Nineteenth-Century Japan* (Cambridge, Mass.: Harvard University Asia Center, 2006), 201–5.

117. I owe this point to Bueno's observations about naturalism in Brazil. See *Resisting Boundaries*, 28.

CHAPTER 3

1. Émile Zola, *Nana* (Paris: Gallimard, 2002), 224–25. Parenthetical citations of this novel in text are of this edition.

2. For a compelling argument, see Modern Girl Around the World Research Group, "Modern Girl Around the World." Rita Felski's *The Gender of Modernity* (Cambridge, Mass.: Harvard University Press, 1995) remains an essential study of European examples; see chapter 1 in particular.

3. An early example is Moretti, "Conjectures on World Literature."

4. For the argument on imitation, see Casanova's explanation of "literary dependency" in *World Republic of Letters*, 10, 81, 93–94; on compromise, see Moretti, "Conjectures on World Literature," 60, 65. I have discussed Casanova and Moretti in greater detail in chapter 1.

5. Among many examples, see Zola, *Nana*, 25 (*peau*), 47 (*poil* and *sexe*), and 41 (*toute-puissance*).

6. Alain Corbin, *Women for Hire: Prostitution and Sexuality in France after 1850*, trans. Alan Sheridan (Cambridge, Mass.: Harvard University Press, 1990), 4, 5, 7.

7. Corbin, *Women for Hire*, 5–7; Colette Becker, "Introduction," in *Nana*, by Émile Zola (Paris: Dunod, 1994), vi, xxvii–xxviii.

8. Zola, *Nana*, 35, 71, 317, 386–87, 457; Corbin, *Women for Hire*, 7–9.

9. Mary Louise Roberts, *Disruptive Acts: The New Woman in Fin-de-Siècle France* (Chicago: University of Chicago Press, 2002), 54–56; Corbin, *Women for Hire*, 171–72.

10. Corbin, *Women for Hire*, 17–24.

11. Zola, *Nana*, 224, 447; for the phrase "venereal anxiety" see Corbin, *Women for Hire*, 251.

12. Nye, *Crime, Madness and Politics*, 134–49.

13. Zola's notes for the novel, quoted in Henri Mitterand, "Étude [Nana]," in *Les Rougon-Macquart II* by Émile Zola (Paris: Gallimard, 1961), 1665.

14. Larry Duffy, *Le Grand Transit Moderne: Mobility, Modernity and French Naturalist Fiction* (Amsterdam: Rodopi, 2005), 178–80. Zola draws on a history of infection as a theme that goes back at least to plague stories; a nineteenth-century precedent is Thomas Carlyle's *French Revolution* (1837). See Jonathan Arac, *Commissioned Spirits: The Shaping of Social Motion in Dickens, Carlyle, Melville, and Hawthorne* (New Brunswick, N.J.: Rutgers University Press, 1979), 129–30. Priscilla Wald examines the theme in the United States in *Contagious: Cultures, Carriers, and the Outbreak Narrative* (Durham, N.C.: Duke University Press, 2007).

15. Dezalay, *L'Opéra des Rougon-Macquart*, 105, 106, 108; Schor, *Zola's Crowds*, 103. My understanding of crowd scenes in the novel is indebted to *Zola's Crowds*, 83–86.

16. Zola's notes, quoted in Mitterand, "Étude [Nana]," 1667.

17. For such interpretations, see Schor, *Zola's Crowds*, 103; and Charles Bernheimer, *Figures of Ill Repute: Representing Prostitution in Nineteenth-Century France* (Durham, N.C.: Duke University Press, 1997), 218. On *la petite vérole* and *la vérole*, see *Figures of Ill Repute*, 224.

18. Dezalay, *L'Opéra des Rougon-Macquart*, 121; Bernice Chitnis, *Reflecting on Nana* (London: Routledge, 1991), 87.

19. Becker, "Introduction," v. See also Robert Lethbridge, "Zola and Contemporary Painting," in *The Cambridge Companion to Emile Zola*, ed. Brian Nelson (Cambridge: Cambridge University Press, 2007), 68. Mitterand sees the influence of the painting in an earlier scene, when the "Prince of Scotland" and Muffat watch Nana put on her makeup and dress during their backstage visit. Mitterand, "Étude [Nana]," 1663.

20. Quoted in Becker, "Introduction," lxvii. On the publicity campaign, see lxvi–lxix.

21. Quoted in Becker, "Introduction," lxv–lxvi.

22. Zola, *Nana*, 26–27; Chitnis, *Reflecting on Nana*, 1–2.

23. 1880: *Nana*, trans. unknown (Calcutta: Orient Book and Co.) (Bengali); *Nana (Sequel to "L'Assommoir")*, trans. John Stirling [Mary Neal Sherwood] (Philadelphia: T.B. Peterson and Brothers); *Nana*, trans. Flox [Ioannis Kambouroglou] (pub. unknown) (modern Greek); *Nanà*, trans Petrocchi and Standaert (Milan: G. Pavia & c.); *Náná, romance*, trans. unknown (Rio de Janeiro: F. Ferreira); *Nana: Roman*, trans. unknown (St. Petersburg: I.V. Vernadskago); *Nana*, trans. Tomás Tuero (Madrid: Alfredo de C. Hierro); *Nana: Roman*, trans. T. Wilson (Stockholm: G. J. Leufstedt);

1881: *Nana*, trans. Al. Schumacher (Copenhagen: A.W. Henningsens); *Nana: Roman*, trans. Fritz Wohlfahrt (Grossenhain: Baumert & Ronge); *Nana*, trans. Armin Schwarz (Budapest: G. Grimm) (German); *Nana: Regény*, trans. Julius (Budapest: G. Grimm) (Hungarian);

1882: *Nana: Roman*, trans. Fr. Schuller and Louis Schmidt (Prague: Hynek);

1883: *Nana*, trans. unknown (Belgrade: publisher unknown);

1884: *Nana: A Realistic Novel*, trans. unknown (London: Vizetelly and Co.); *Nana: Roman*, trans. unknown (Zurich: Frick-Vogel); *Naná: Versão livre*, trans. unknown (Porto: Folha de Hoje);

1888: *Nana: A Realistic Novel*, trans. Edith Wharton Chalmers (Chicago: Laird and Lee);

1890: *Nana: A realistishe shilderung fun Parizer aristokratishen leben*, trans. B. Gorin (New York: Hibru Poblishing Kompani);

1895: *Nana*, trans. Victor Plarr (London: Lutetian Society).

A longer list can be found in my "Nana in the World: Novel, Gender, and Transnational Form," *Modern Language Quarterly* 72, no. 1 (2011): 75–105.

24. On English translations, see David Baguley, "Les Oeuvres de Zola traduites en anglais 1877–1968," *Cahiers Naturalistes* 40 (1970): 200; on Ger-

man translations, see Aurélie Barjonet, "'Le Mieux est de rester volé et content': Armin Schwarz et Gustav Grimm, pirates des oeuvres de Zola," *Cahiers Naturalistes* 81 (2007): 186–89.

25. Alfred Kahanov, "Les Traductions hébraïques des oeuvres d'Émile Zola," *Cahiers Naturalistes* 65 (1991): 113.

26. *Joyū Nana*, trans. Nagai Kafū (Tokyo: Shinseisha, 1903).

27. Becker, "Introduction," lxxi; Norbert Bachleitner, "La Traduction de Zola à Vienne: Marché littéraire, censure et goût bourgeois," *Cahiers Naturalistes* 81 (2007): 169, 173–75; Leighton and MacLeod, "Trials of Naturalism," 325.

28. Goula-Mitacou, "Traduction grecque," 141–44.

29. Chevrel, "Peut-on proposer," 16; Arnoux-Farnoux, "Ambiguïtés et singularités," 190–92; Goula-Mitacou, "La Traduction grecque," 143; as cited in chapter 1.

30. Examples are collected in John Grand-Carteret, *Zola en images* (Paris: Félix Juven, 1908), 108, 112, 113.

31. Becker, "Introduction," lxxviii.

32. Goula-Mitacou, "La Traduction grecque," 141–42; Borghart, "(Greek) Naturalism," 328 n. 23.

33. *L'Assommoir, Nana's Mother*, trans. John Stirling [Mary Neal Sherwood] (Philadelphia: T.B. Peterson and Bros., 1882); *Nana's Brother: Son of "Gervaise" and "Lantier" of "L'Assommoir,"* trans. John Stirling (Philadelphia: T.B. Peterson and Brothers, 1885).

34. Becker, "Introduction," xxxi, lxxi.

35. Barnaby, "Nana in Milan," 163.

36. David Baguley, "La Fille de Nana: Palingenesis, Palimpsest?" *Romance Studies* 4, no. 1 (1986): 134–36.

37. Sirven and Leverdier, *Nana's Daughter; A Continuation of and Sequel to Émile Zola's Novel of "Nana,"* trans. John Stirling [Mary Neal Sherwood] (Philadelphia: T.B. Peterson and Brothers, 1881); Salvan, *Zola aux Etats-Unis*, 79.

38. Gacoin-Marks, "Débuts du naturalisme," 240, 243, 248.

39. Erika Sutherland, "Death in the Bedroom: Eduardo López Bago and His Suspect Syphilitics," *Excavatio* 18, no. 1–2 (2003): 278, 284.

40. Riikka Rossi, "Le Naturalisme en Finlande," *Excavatio* 17, no. 1–2 (2002): 278–80.

41. Prendes, "Personaje y sus libros," 402–3.

42. Fittingly, by the middle of the twentieth century *nana* had passed in French usage from a proper to a common noun, as a prejudicial reference to a young woman. Chitnis, *Regarding Nana*, 2.

43. I thank Maria Lujan Tubio and Pablo Picatto for bringing *Santa* to my attention, and Patrick Manning and Mark Sanders for telling me about *Jagua Nana*. Ekwensi's heroine too had offspring; he published a sequel, *Jagua Nana's Daughter*, in 1986.

44. Mori Eiichi, "Kosugi Tengai to Zora," *Nihon kindai bungaku* 18 (1973): 96–97.

45. He finished only two: *Love and Love* (*Koi to koi*, 1901) and *Imitation Purple* (*Nise murasaki*, 1905).

46. Kosugi Tengai, *Hatsu sugata* (Tokyo: Iwanami Shoten, 2000), 24–27. Parenthetical citations of this novel in text are of this edition.

47. For an overview of the literature of prostitution in the Edo period, see Kayanuma Noriko, "Geisha to jorō no shokugyō ishiki—kinsei bungaku ni miru irokoi no sekai," in *Bai-baishun to Nihon bungaku*, ed. Okano Yukie, Hasegawa Kei, and Watanabe Sumiko (Tokyo: Tōkyōdō Shuppan, 2002), 71–80.

48. Christine L. Marran, *Poison Woman: Figuring Female Transgression in Modern Japanese Culture* (Minneapolis: University of Minnesota Press, 2007), 1–5; Indra Levy, *Sirens of the Western Shore: The Westernesque Femme Fatale, Translation, and Vernacular Style in Modern Japanese Literature* (New York: Columbia University Press, 2006), 49–55.

49. A. Kimi Coaldrake, *Women's Gidayū and the Japanese Theatre Tradition* (London: Routledge, 1997), 14, 20–21.

50. Sheldon Garon, *Molding Japanese Minds: The State in Everyday Life* (Princeton, N.J.: Princeton University Press, 1997), 92–95; Sabine Frühstück, *Colonizing Sex: Sexology and Social Control in Modern Japan* (Berkeley: University of California Press, 2003), 42–46; Tengai, *Hatsu sugata*, 50–51.

51. William Johnston, *Geisha, Harlot, Strangler, Star: A Woman, Sex, and Morality in Modern Japan* (New York: Columbia University Press, 2005), 31–32; Ueno Chizuko, "Modern Patriarchy and the Formation of the Japanese Nation State," in *Multicultural Japan: Palaeolithic to Postmodern*, ed. Donald Denoon et al. (Cambridge: Cambridge University Press, 1996), 215; Sharon H. Nolte and Sally Ann Hastings, "The Meiji State's Policy Toward Women, 1890–1910," in *Recreating Japanese Women, 1600–1945*, ed. Gail Lee Bernstein (Berkeley: University of California Press, 1991), 171–72.

52. For such discussions, see Tengai, *Hatsu sugata*, 8–9, 18–21, 29–30, 48–49.

53. Goi Makoto, "Kankei toshite no 'miru' koto—Kosugi Tengai 'Hatsu sugata' no kōzō," *Rikkyō daigaku Nihon bungaku* 77 (1996): 17–18.

54. *Hatsu sugata* refers to clothing worn during the New Year's holiday, that is, one's first appearance of the year.

55. For example, Tengai, *Hatsu sugata*, 98–99 and 18–19, respectively.

56. For example, Tengai, *Hatsu sugata*, 46, 150 (Bun'yū); 37 (Kiyoju); and 79, 106 (Tamae).

57. Wada, *Byōsha no jidai*, 14–17.

58. Zwicker, *Practices of the Sentimental Imagination*, 202–4.

59. Salvan, *Zola aux Etats-Unis*, 179–80. Dreiser recounted reading the novel, whose similarities to the work of Zola and Balzac he did not grasp until later, in *A Book about Myself* (1922).

60. Pizer, "Backgrounds and Sources," 443, 464–65.

61. Theodore Dreiser, *Sister Carrie*, ed. Donald Pizer, 2nd ed. (New York: Norton, 1991), 13, 17. Parenthetical citations of this novel in text are of this edition.

62. Alan Trachtenberg, "Who Narrates? Dreiser's Presence in Sister Carrie," in *New Essays on Sister Carrie*, ed. Donald Pizer (Cambridge: Cambridge University Press, 1991), 90.

63. Carroll Smith-Rosenberg, *Disorderly Conduct: Visions of Gender in Victorian America* (New York: Oxford University Press, 1985), 180–81.

64. Davidson and Davidson, "Carrie's Sisters," 398–401.

65. Mary E. Odem, *Delinquent Daughters: Protecting and Policing Adolescent Female Sexuality in the United States, 1885–1920* (Chapel Hill: University of North Carolina Press, 1995), 1–3.

66. Wald, *Contagious*, 90–91.

67. Carrie Tirado Bramen, *The Uses of Variety: Modern Americanism and the Quest for National Distinctiveness* (Cambridge, Mass.: Harvard University Press, 2000), 160, 182–87.

68. Susan A. Glenn, *Female Spectacle: The Theatrical Roots of Modern Feminism* (Cambridge, Mass.: Harvard University Press, 2000), 89–91; Baldwin quoted on 91.

69. See Clare Virginia Eby, *Dreiser and Veblen: Saboteurs of the Status Quo* (Columbia: University of Missouri Press, 1998), 6, 123, on the affinities of the two.

70. Glenn, *Female Spectacle*, 2–4; Jennifer Costello Brezina, "Public Women, Private Acts: Gender and Theater in Turn-of-the-Century American Novels," in *Separate Spheres No More: Gender Convergence in American Literature, 1830–1930*, ed. Monika M. Elbert (Tuscaloosa: University of Alabama Press, 2000), 225.

71. Dreiser, *Sister Carrie*, 1. On the prospective quality of the self in *Sister Carrie,* see Philip Fisher, *Hard Facts: Setting and Form in the American Novel* (New York: Oxford University Press, 1985), 159.

72. Dreiser, *Sister Carrie*, 322. On names in *Sister Carrie,* see Fisher, *Hard Facts*, 160–62.

73. The minimization of discourses of heredity was also common in other parts of the world. See Gacoin-Marks, "Débuts du naturalisme," 243–44; and Borghart, "(Greek) Naturalism," 332–33.

74. An example is Schor's structuralist reading of *Nana*, which argues that the novel reenacts a *pharmakos* (scapegoat) myth. Schor, *Zola's Crowds*, 4–5, 103.

75. On the concept of structural causality, see Fredric Jameson, *The Political Unconscious: Narrative as a Socially Symbolic Act* (Ithaca, N.Y.: Cornell University Press, 1981), 35–43.

CHAPTER 4

1. Quoted in Peter Graves, "Afterword," in *The Red Room: Scenes from the Lives of Artists and Authors,* by August Strindberg (London: Norvik, 2009), 309, from an 1879 letter to Rudolf Wall.

2. On the factual and normative aspects of social imaginaries, see Taylor, *Modern Social Imaginaries*, 24.

3. Lukács, "Narrate or Describe?" 116, 128–29.

4. Lukács, "Narrate or Describe?" 110, 115–16, 131, 134, 146.

5. Norris, "Zola as a Romantic Writer," 274.

6. Jacques Dubois, "Zola et les sciences humaines," *Excavatio* 19, no. 1–2 (2004): 174–75.

7. Dubois, "Zola et les sciences humaines," 177–80.

8. Chevrel, *Le Naturalisme en question*, 109–10; José Antonio Galaos, "Manuel Zeno Gandía y sus Crónicas de un mundo enfermo," *Cuardernos Hispanoamericanos* 59 (1964): 416; McFarlane, "Norwegian Literature 1860–1910," 154; Sutherland, "Death in the Bedroom," 278, n. 2; Yoshida, *Shizen shugi*, vol. 1: 154–55.

9. Jonathan Smith, "Naturalism and Anti-Naturalism in Italy," in *Naturalism in the European Novel: New Critical Perspectives*, ed. Brian Nelson (New York: Berg, 1992), 163–65.

10. Mérian, *Aluísio Azevedo*, 503–8.

11. Cândido, *O Discurso e a cidade*, 126–27.

12. Unlike the comparison I am suggesting, Cândido's discussion of *I Malavoglia* and *L'Assommoir* focuses on the problem of popular language. See *O Discurso e a cidade*, 106–8.

13. Maeda Ai's work on Higuchi Ichiyō is an example. See *Text and the City: Essays on Japanese Modernity*, ed. James Fujii (Durham, N.C.: Duke University Press, 2004), 109–43.

14. Iwasa, *Seikimatsu no shizen shugi*, 151–53.

15. Henri Mitterand, "Étude [Germinal]," in *Les Rougon-Macquart III*, by Émile Zola (Paris: Gallimard, 1964), 1815–16, 1822–23; David Baguley, "Germinal: The Gathering Storm," in *The Cambridge Companion to Emile Zola*, ed. Brian Nelson (Cambridge: Cambridge University Press, 2007), 138–39.

16. Mitterand, "Étude [Germinal]," 1827–29, 1850–51.

17. On Zola's sources, see Mitterand, "Étude [Germinal]," 1832–41, 1847–49, 1852; and for an exhaustive investigation, see Richard H. Zakarian, *Zola's "Germinal": A Critical Study of Its Primary Sources* (Geneva: Droz, 1972).

18. Baguley, "Germinal," 147–48, citing Jean Fréville, *Zola, semeur d'orages* (Paris: Éditions Sociales, 1952).

19. Baguley, "Germinal," 148–49, citing Irving Howe, "Zola: The Genius of *Germinal*," *Encounter* 34 (1970); and Claude Duchet, "Le Trou des bouches noires," *Littérature* 24 (1976).

20. Henri Mitterand, *Le Discours du roman* (Paris: Presses Universitaires de France, 1980), 144–46.

21. Sandy Petrey, *Realism and Revolution: Balzac, Stendhal, Zola, and the Performance of History* (Ithaca, N.Y.: Cornell University Press, 1988), 183–94.

22. For descriptions of the plain, see, for example, Zola, *Germinal*, 49, 118, 279. On the coordination of sites and their relations, see Denis Bertrand, *L'Espace et le sens: Germinal d'Émile Zola* (Paris: Hadès, 1985), 58–59.

23. For example, Zola, *Germinal*, 192–96, 258–67.

24. Zola, *Germinal*, 52; Mitterand, *Discours du roman*, 143–44.

25. On the parallel stories, see Mitterand, *Discours du roman*, 145–46.

26. Zola, *Germinal*, 409. Petrey and others are right to insist that the voice describing the miners belongs to the bourgeois bystanders, not the narrator, but there is little difference from the narrator's vocabulary of atavism found else-

where in the novel. Petrey, *Realism and Revolution*, 190–91. On the elongated jaw in the discourse of atavism, see my discussion of *McTeague* in chapter 2.

27. In light of the way some critics see *Germinal* as a re-narration of the Paris Commune from the point of view of its "failure," the contrast with the Communards' liberating experience of space is revealing. See Kristin Ross, *The Emergence of Social Space: Rimbaud and the Paris Commune* (Minneapolis: University of Minnesota Press, 1988), 36–38, 41–42, and more broadly the first chapter of her *Communal Luxury: The Political Imaginary of the Paris Commune* (London: Verso, 2015). On *Germinal* and the Commune, see Roger Ripoll, "Zola et les communards," *Europe* 46, no. 468 (1968): 23–24; and Paul Lidsky, *Les Écrivains contre la Commune* (Paris: Francois Maspero, 1970), 111–16.

28. Bertrand, *L'Espace et le sens*, 135–36.

29. I examine the logic of such historical "interiority" in part 1 of *National History and the World of Nations*.

30. Chevrel, "Germinal en Allemagne," 90.

31. 1885: *Germinal*, trans. Carlynne (Chicago: Belford, Clarke); *Germinal; or Master and Man*, trans. Albert Vandam (London: Vizetelly); *Nana's Brother, Son of "Gervaise" and "Lantier" of "L'Assommoir,"* trans. John Stirling [Mary Neal Sherwood] (Philadelphia: Peterson); *Germinal*, trans. Ernst Ziegler (Dresden: Minden); *Germinal*, trans. Luigi Mercatelli (Rome: La Tribuna); *Germinal*, trans. Eduardo de Barros Lôbo (Lisbon: Empresa Litteraria Luso-Brasileira); *Germinal*, trans. Angel de Luque (Madrid: El Cosmos Editorial);

1886: *Germinal*, trans. unknown (Budapest: Népsava) (Hungarian);

1888: *Germinal; or Master and Man*, trans. Albert Vandam, ed. Ernest Vizetelly (London: Vizetelly) (further expurgation of the 1885 edition);

1890: *Nana's Brother, Germinal*, trans. unknown (Chicago: Laird and Lee, 1890);

1891: *Germinal*, trans. unknown (London: Przedswit) (Polish);

1892: *Germinal*, trans. Jana Třebický (Prague: Casopis Ceského Studentstva);

1894: *Germinal*, trans. Havelock Ellis (London: Lutetian Society); *Germinal*, trans. Armin Schwarz (Budapest: Grimm) (German);

1895: *Germinal*, trans. Zemplényi P. Gyula (Budapest: Deubler) (Hungarian);

1896: *Germinal*, trans. H. Rosé (Berlin: J. Gnadenfeld);

1897: *Zherminal*, trans. S. M. Bazhinoi (St. Petersburg: Tipografiia br. Panteleevykh);

1898: *Die Kohlengräber von Le Voreux*, trans. G. Gärtner (Berlin: Teistler); "Strajk," trans. Hámor (*Slovenské noviny* 13, no 82) (excerpt, Slovakian);

1899: *Germinal*, trans. C. Wallerstein (Dresden: Max Fischer);

1900: *Germinal*, trans. Hedda Moeller-Bruck (Leipzig: Leipzig Reclam); *Zsherminal, oder Nana's bruder*, trans. unknown (New York: Hibru Poblishing Kompani) (Yiddish).

32. Tone Smolej, "Germinal en Slovénie," *Cahiers Naturalistes* 83 (2009): 290.

33. For examples in English and German, see Denise Merkle, "Germinal en Grande-Bretagne de 1884 à 1895," *Cahiers Naturalistes* 81 (2007): 203–4; and Bachleitner, "La Traduction de Zola," 175–76.

34. Chevrel, "Germinal en Allemagne," 95.

35. Quoted in Ingrid von Rosenberg, "French Naturalism and the English Socialist Novel: Margaret Harkness and William Edwards Tirebuck," in *The Rise of Socialist Fiction, 1880–1914*, ed. H. Gustav Klaus (New York: St. Martin's Press, 1987), 168.

36. For a discussion, see H. Gustav Klaus, "The Strike Novel in the 1890s," in *The Rise of Socialist Fiction, 1880–1914*, ed. H. Gustav Klaus (New York: St. Martin's Press, 1987), 75–78.

37. Lemonnier, *Happe-Chair*, i, as cited in chapter 1.

38. Von Rosenberg, "French Naturalism," 165; Darbouze, *Dégénérescence et régénérescence*, 39, 49–50.

39. Von Rosenberg, "French Naturalism," 165; Åhnebrink, *Beginnings of Naturalism*, 295–98.

40. Klaus, "Strike Novel," 89; Åhnebrink, *Beginnings of Naturalism*, 295; Smolej, "Germinal en Slovénie," 291–92.

41. Darbouze, *Dégénérescence et régénérescence*, 39–40.

42. Donald F. Brown, "A Chilean Germinal: Zola and Baldomero Lillo," *Modern Language Notes* 65, no. 1 (1950): 51–52.

43. Von Rosenberg, "French Naturalism," 165; Brown, "Chilean Germinal," 47.

44. See, for example, Åhnebrink, *Beginnings of Naturalism*, 295, on Norris; Brown, "Chilean Germinal," 49, on Lillo; and Smolej, "Germinal en Slovénie," 290–91, on Finžgar.

45. Setty Alaoui-Moretti, "La Traduction espagnole de Germinal: Variation de sujet libre?" *Cahiers Naturalistes* 81 (2007): 211–13; Chevrel, "Germinal en Allemagne," 94–95.

46. Chevrel, "De Germinal aux Tisserands," 450–56.

47. Sylvain Barreur, "Zola en Hongrie," *Europe* 30, no. 83–84 (1952): 179; Mitterand, "Étude [Germinal]," 1868.

48. Zola: "il faut que le lecteur bourgeois ait un frisson de terreur." Quoted in Mitterand, "Étude [Germinal]," 1825.

49. Von Rosenburg, "French Naturalism," 153; Barreur, "Zola en Hongrie," 179; Hans-Joachim Schulz, *German Socialist Literature, 1860–1914: Predicaments of Criticism* (Columbia, S.C.: Camden House, 1993), 75–78, 109–12.

50. S. Saillard, "La Première Traduction espagnole de Germinal," *Cahiers Naturalistes* 75 (2001): 242; Sakai Kosen, "Hashigaki," in *Ki no medachi*, by Émile Zola (Tokyo: Arusu, 1921), 1–2.

51. See, for example, von Rosenberg, "French Naturalism," 154.

52. Jack London, *The Sea-Wolf*, in *Novels and Stories* (New York: Library of America, 1982), 595. Parenthetical citations of this novel in text are of this edition.

53. London, *Sea-Wolf*, 498. On London and evolutionary thinking, see Jeanne Campbell Reesman, *Jack London's Racial Lives: A Critical Biography* (Athens: University of Georgia Press, 2009), 48–54; and Lawrence I. Berkove, "Jack London and Evolution: From Spencer to Huxley," *American Literary Realism* 36, no. 3 (2004): 243–55.

54. On London's use of Nietzsche, see Rossetti, *Imagining the Primitive*, 58–59.

55. London, *Sea-Wolf*, 603–4; Rossetti, *Imagining the Primitive*, 61.

56. London, *Sea-Wolf*, 599. On such fears, see Howard, *Form and History*, 96–97; and Rossetti, *Imagining the Primitive*, 6–7.

57. On London's inconsistent embrace of Anglo-Saxonism, see Reesman, *Jack London's Racial Lives*, 34–37.

58. Lee Clark Mitchell, "'And Rescue Us from Ourselves': Becoming Someone in Jack London's The Sea-Wolf," *American Literature* 70, no. 2 (1998): 321–22.

59. Howard, *Form and History*, 173–74.

60. London, *Sea-Wolf*, 656; James A. Papa, Jr., "Canvas and Steam: Historical Conflict in Jack London's Sea-Wolf," *Midwest Quarterly* 40, no. 3 (1999): 277, 283.

61. On London's critique of individualism, see Rossetti, *Imagining the Primitive*, 59. On capitalism and the conflict between the brothers, see also Eric Carl Link, "The Five Deaths of Wolf Larsen," *Studies in American Naturalism* 5, no. 2 (2010): 156–58.

62. On this point I disagree with David Heckerl, who sees Larsen reducing social relations to a pre-liberal state of nature. See Heckerl, "'Violent Movements of Business': The Moral Nihilist as Economic Man in Jack London's The Sea-Wolf," in *Twisted from the Ordinary: Essays on American Literary Realism*, ed. Mary E. Papke (Knoxville: University of Tennessee Press, 2003), 204.

63. Papa, "Canvas and Steam," 280–81.

64. The contrast reflects London's basic agreement with Huxley's argument against Herbert Spencer, that humans must respond to evolution ethically. See Reesman, *Jack London's Racial Lives*, 52–54; and Berkove, "Jack London and Evolution," 245–47. Link finds London's connection of morality and evolution in his reading of Haeckel, not Huxley. See "Five Deaths," 162.

65. Link, "Five Deaths," 153–54, 155–56.

66. London, *Sea-Wolf*, 753; Howard, *Form and History*, 113.

67. On the novel's sources, see Maeda Akira, "Kaisetsu," in *Inaka kyōshi*, by Tayama Katai (Tokyo: Iwanami Shoten, 1993), 243–46; on how Katai transformed his observations, see Kobori Yōhei, "Tayama Katai 'Inaka kyōshi' ni okeru fūkei byōsha no keisei: Utsusu koto to amu koto no aidagara," *Kokugo to kokubungaku* 92, no. 12 (2015): 59–65. Parenthetical citations of Katai's *Inaka kyōshi* in text are to the 1993 edition of this work.

68. Sōma Tsuneo, *Nihon shizen shugi saikō* (Tokyo: Yagi Shoten, 1981), 122.

69. Hiraoka Toshio, *Nichiro sengo bungaku no kenkyū* (Tokyo: Yūseidō, 1985), vol. 1: 330.

70. Katai, *Inaka kyōshi*, 9–10. For a reading of *The Country Teacher* as the arrival of modernity, see Timothy J. Van Compernolle, *Struggling Upward: Worldly Success and the Japanese Novel* (Cambridge, Mass.: Harvard University Asia Center, 2016), 55–57.

71. Katai, *Inaka kyōshi*, 20, 193–94. On transformations of daily life by the state and capital in the Meiji period, see Yasumaru Yoshio, *Bunmeika no keiken* (Tokyo: Iwanami Shoten, 2007), 13–17.

72. Ernst Bloch, *Heritage of Our Times*, trans. Neville Plaice and Stephen Plaice (Berkeley: University of California Press, 1991), 104–16.

73. The classic discussion is in "Results of the Immediate Process of Production," published as the appendix to volume 1 of Marx's *Capital*, 1019–38.

74. On this point I am indebted to Harry Harootunian, *Marx after Marx: History and Time in the Expansion of Capitalism* (New York: Columbia University Press, 2015), in particular chapter 2 on Lenin and Luxemburg.

75. Harootunian, *Marx after Marx*, 38–39, 55.

76. Katai, *Inaka kyōshi*, 200, 203–4. The juxtapositions may reflect what Henshall considers Katai's growing sense during this period that the nonhuman world is indifferent to humankind. Henshall, *In Search of Nature*, 125.

77. See, for example, Katai, *Inaka kyōshi*, 11, 14, 17 (*mieta*), and 28, 38, 43 (*kikoeta*). Matthew Fraleigh discusses this aspect of the novel's prose insightfully in "Terms of Understanding: The Shōsetsu according to Tayama Katai," *Monumenta Nipponica* 58, no. 1 (2003): 70–71.

78. On this point I disagree with Fujimori Kiyoshi's argument that Katai could not maintain a distinction between the viewpoints of Seizō, the narrator, and the author. See Fujimori, *Katari no kindai* (Yūseidō, 1996), 44–46.

79. *Peinchingu*, not *desukuripushon*. Tayama Katai, "Byōsharon," in *Meiji ki III*, ed. Yoshida Seiichi and Wada Kingo, Kindai bungaku hyōron taikei 3 (Tokyo: Kadokawa Shoten, 1972), 369. The essay appeared in *Waseda bungaku* in April 1911.

80. Tayama Katai, "*Sei* ni okeru kokoromi," in *Meiji ki III*, ed. Yoshida Seiichi and Wada Kingo, Kindai bungaku hyōron taikei 3 (Tokyo: Kadokawa Shoten, 1972), 448–49. The essay was published in *Waseda bungaku* in September 1908.

81. Katai, "*Sei* ni okeru kokoromi," 448; Katai, "Byōsharon," 370. Katai's assertion weakens the connection Van Compernolle sees between *Inaka kyōshi* and Meiji-era *shaseibun*. *Shasei* is a topic in *Inaka kyōshi*, but Katai does not practice it. See Van Compernolle, *Struggling Upward*, 43–54. For a classic argument on space and interiority in *shaseibun*, see the first two chapters of Karatani Kōjin, *Origins of Modern Japanese Literature*, ed. Brett de Bary (Durham, N.C.: Duke University Press, 1993).

82. Sōma, *Nihon shizen shugi ron*, 67–69.

83. See, for example, Hiraoka, *Nichiro sengo bungaku*, vol. 1: 327, 334. Katai, a correspondent during the war, was undeniably enthusiastic about the military's achievements. On Katai's views of the war as seen in his diary, see Tomoko Aoyama, "Japanese Literary Responses to the Russo-Japanese War," in *The Russo-Japanese War in Cultural Perspective, 1904–05*, ed. David Wells and Sandra Wilson (New York: St. Martin's Press, 1999), 61–65.

84. Katai, *Inaka kyōshi*, 238. Although the diary's author died on September 22, 1904, the parade is "two or three days" after the fall of Liaoyang on September 3. The significance of the change in dates, which Katai dissembled in his memoirs, was first pointed out by Wada Kingo in "'Inaka kyōshi' no seiritsu," *Kokugo to kokubungaku* 32, no. 6 (1955): 58–59.

85. Yoshida, *Shizen shugi*, vol. 2: 194.

86. Tayama Katai, *Tōkyō no sanjūnen*, in *Tayama Katai zenshū 15* (Tokyo: Bunseidō Shoten, 1973), 648.

87. Ivan Turgenev, *Fathers and Sons*, trans. Rosemary Edmonds (Harmondsworth, Eng.: Penguin, 1975), 294–95; Katai, *Inaka kyōshi*, 241–42.

88. See Ganguly, *This Thing Called the World*; and Pheng Cheah, *What Is a World? On Postcolonial Literature as World Literature* (Durham, N.C.: Duke University Press, 2016).

89. As is well known, Benedict Anderson borrowed the phrase from José Rizal's 1887 novel *Noli me Tangere*, whose protagonist discovers he cannot see the gardens of Manila the same way after seeing the gardens of Europe. Anderson, *The Spectre of Comparisons: Nationalism, Southeast Asia and the World* (London: Verso, 1998), 2, 229.

CONCLUSION

1. In *Black Boy*, Wright recalled reading Dreiser's *Jennie Gerhardt* and *Sister Carrie*: "All my life had shaped me for the realism, the naturalism of the modern novel." Wright, *Black Boy (American Hunger): A Record of Childhood and Youth* (New York: HarperPerennial, 1993), 250. Don Dingledine shows Petry's engagement with the work of Stephen Crane in "'It Could Have Been Any Street': Ann Petry, Stephen Crane, and the Fate of Naturalism." *Studies in American Fiction* 34, no. 1 (2006): 92–95.

2. On the revival of the I-novel by the "Third Generation" writers (the *Daisan no shinjin*), see Van C. Gessel, *The Sting of Life: Four Contemporary Japanese Novelists* (New York: Columbia University Press, 1989), 60–69.

3. Rasheed El-Enany, *Naguib Mahfouz: The Pursuit of Meaning* (London: Routledge, 1993), 19.

4. Eleni Coundouriotis, *The People's Right to the Novel: War Fiction in the Postcolony* (New York: Fordham University Press, 2014), 3; Neil Lazarus, "The Retrieval of Naturalism: The Politics of Narrative in Radical African Fiction," *Critical Exchange* 22 (1987): 57–59.

5. Coundouriotis, *People's Right*, 9; Dingledine, "'It Could Have Been Any Street,'" 95; El-Enany, *Naguib Mahfouz*, 19. El-Enany speculates that Mahfouz would not acknowledge the influence of naturalism because he did not want to be associated with its deterministic ideas.

6. Reesman, *Jack London's Racial Lives*, 8, citing Paul Lauter, "London's Place in American Studies," *The Call* 14, no. 1 (2003): 11–17.

7. Antônio Cândido, "Literature and Underdevelopment," trans. Howard S. Becker, in *On Literature and Society*, ed. Howard S. Becker (Princeton, N.J.: Princeton University Press, 1995), 129.

8. Susan Stanford Friedman, "One Hand Clapping: Colonialism, Postcolonialism, and the Spatio-Temporal Boundaries of Modernism," in *Translocal Modernisms: International Perspectives*, ed. Irene Ramalho Santos and António Sousa Ribeiro (New York: Peter Lang, 2008), 22.

9. George Yúdice, "Rethinking the Theory of the Avant-Garde from the Periphery," in *Modernism and Its Margins: Reinscribing Cultural Modernity from*

Spain and Latin America, ed. Anthony L. Geist and José L. Monléon (New York: Garland, 1999), 54.

10. Yúdice reiterates Perry Anderson's classic argument identifying three aspects of the conjuncture—academicism in the arts, the incipient commodification of the art object, and the "imaginative proximity of social revolution"—to which Yúdice adds a fourth, the crisis of imperialism. Yúdice, "Rethinking the Theory," 61.

Bibliography

Åhnebrink, Lars. *The Beginnings of Naturalism in American Fiction: A Study of the Works of Hamlin Garland, Stephen Crane, and Frank Norris with Special Reference to Some European Influences, 1891–1903*. New York: Russell and Russell, 1961.

Alaoui, Setty Moretti. "Zola en Espagne: Horizon d'attente et réception." *Excavatio* 18, no. 1–2 (2003): 179–97.

Alaoui Moretti, Setty. "La Traduction espagnole de Germinal: Variation de sujet libre?" *Cahiers Naturalistes* 81 (2007): 211–27.

Allan, Michael. *In the Shadow of World Literature: Sites of Reading in Colonial Egypt*. Princeton, N.J.: Princeton University Press, 2016.

Ammons, Elizabeth. "Expanding the Canon of American Realism." In *Documents of American Realism and Naturalism*, ed. Donald Pizer, 435–52. Carbondale: Southern Illinois University Press, 1998.

Anderson, Benedict. *The Spectre of Comparisons: Nationalism, Southeast Asia and the World*. London: Verso, 1998.

Anderson, Marston. *The Limits of Realism: Chinese Fiction in the Revolutionary Period*. Berkeley: University of California Press, 1990.

Aoyama, Tomoko. "Japanese Literary Responses to the Russo-Japanese War." In *The Russo-Japanese War in Cultural Perspective, 1904–05*, ed. David Wells and Sandra Wilson, 60–85. New York: St. Martin's Press, 1999.

Appadurai, Arjun. "Disjuncture and Difference in the Global Cultural Economy." *Public Culture* 2, no. 2 (1990): 1–24.

Apter, Emily S. *Against World Literature: On the Politics of Untranslatability*. New York: Verso, 2013.

Ara, Guillermo. *La novela naturalista hispanoamericana*. Buenos Aires: Eudeba, 1965.

Arac, Jonathan. "Anglo-Globalism?" *New Left Review* 16 (2002): 35–45.

———. *Commissioned Spirits: The Shaping of Social Motion in Dickens, Carlyle, Melville, and Hawthorne*. New Brunswick, N.J.: Rutgers University Press, 1979.

Arao Yoshihide. "Shinkei." In *Kōza Nihongo no goi 10*, 236–40. Tokyo: Meiji Shoin, 1983.

Armitage, David. "What's the Big Idea? Intellectual History and the Longue Durée." *History of European Ideas* 38, no. 4 (2012): 493–507.

Arnoux-Farnoux, Lucile. "Ambiguïtés et singularités du naturalisme grec." *Cahiers Naturalistes* 77 (2003): 189–204.

Arrighi, Paul. "Zola et De Sanctis." *Revue de la Littérature Comparée* 27 (1953): 438–46.

Auerbach, Erich. "Figura." Trans. Jane O. Newman. In *Time, History, and Literature: Selected Essays of Erich Auerbach*, ed. James I. Porter, 65–113. Princeton, N.J.: Princeton University Press, 2013.

———. *Mimesis: The Representation of Reality in Western Literature*. Trans. Willard R. Trask. Princeton, N.J.: Princeton University Press, 1953.

———. "Philology and Weltliteratur." Trans. M. Said and E. W. Said. In *The Princeton Sourcebook in Comparative Literature: From the European Enlightenment to the Global Present*, ed. David Damrosch, Natalie Melas, and Mbongiseni Buthelezi, 125–38. Princeton, N.J.: Princeton University Press, 2009.

Bachleitner, Norbert. "La Traduction de Zola à Vienne: Marché littéraire, censure et goût bourgeois." *Cahiers Naturalistes* 81 (2007): 169–79.

Baguley, David. *Emile Zola: L'Assommoir*. Cambridge: Cambridge University Press, 1992.

———. "Germinal: The Gathering Storm." In *The Cambridge Companion to Emile Zola*, ed. Brian Nelson, 137–51. Cambridge: Cambridge University Press, 2007.

———. "La Fille de Nana: Palingenesis, Palimpsest?" *Romance Studies* 4, no. 1 (1986): 128–42.

———. "Les Oeuvres de Zola traduites en anglais 1877–1968." *Cahiers Naturalistes* 40 (1970): 195–209.

———. *Naturalist Fiction: The Entropic Vision*. Cambridge: Cambridge University Press, 1990.

———. "The Nature of Naturalism." In *Naturalism in the European Novel: New Critical Perspectives*, ed. Brian Nelson, 13–26. New York: Berg, 1992.

Balzac, Honoré de. *Le Père Goriot*. Paris: Gallimard, 1971.

Banfield, Ann. *Unspeakable Sentences: Narration and Representation in the Language of Fiction*. London: Routledge, 1982.

Bang, Herman. *As Trains Pass By*. Trans. W. Glyn Jones. Sawtry, Eng.: Dedalus, 2014.

Barac, Antun. *A History of Yugoslav Literature*. Ann Arbor: Michigan Slavic Publications, Dept. of Slavic Languages and Literatures, University of Michigan, 1976.

Barjonet, Aurélie. "'Le Mieux est de rester volé et content': Armin Schwarz et Gustav Grimm, pirates des oeuvres de Zola." *Cahiers Naturalistes* 81 (2007): 181–96.

Barnaby, Paul. "Nana in Milan: Cletto Arrighi and the Italian Reception of Zola." *New Comparison* 35–36 (2003): 163–78.

Barreur, Sylvain. "Zola en Hongrie." *Europe* 30, no. 83–84 (1952): 179–81.

Basilio Bénoudis, Kelly. *Le Mécanique et le vivant: La Métonymie chez Zola.* Geneva: Droz, 1993.

Becker, Colette. "De la Vénus de Gordes à la Vénus du Pont-Neuf: Jeux de réécriture." In *Lire/Dé-lire Zola*, ed. Jean-Pierre Leduc-Adine and Henri Mitterand, 79–96. Paris: Nouveau Monde, 2004.

———. "Introduction." In *Nana*, by Émile Zola. i–lxxix. Paris: Dunod, 1994.

———. "Zola, un déchiffreur de l'entre-deux." *Études Françaises* 39, no. 2 (2003): 11–21.

Beecroft, Alexander. *An Ecology of World Literature: From Antiquity to the Present Day.* New York: Verso, 2015.

Benítez-Rojo, Antonio. "The Nineteenth-Century Spanish American Novel." In *The Cambridge History of Latin American Literature*, ed. Roberto González Echevarría and Enrique Pupo-Walker, vol. 1: 417–89. Cambridge: Cambridge University Press, 1996.

Berkove, Lawrence I. "Jack London and Evolution: From Spencer to Huxley." *American Literary Realism* 36, no. 3 (2004): 243–55.

Bernheimer, Charles. *Figures of Ill Repute: Representing Prostitution in Nineteenth-Century France.* Durham, N.C.: Duke University Press, 1997.

Bertrand, Denis. *L'Espace et le sens: Germinal d'Émile Zola.* Paris: Hadès, 1985.

Bloch, Ernst. *Heritage of Our Times.* Trans. Neville Plaice and Stephen Plaice. Berkeley: University of California Press, 1991.

Borghart, Pieter. "(Greek) Naturalism in European Perspective: A Comparative Approach." *Excavatio* 19, no. 1–2 (2004): 319–33.

Borie, Jean. *Zola et les mythes; ou, De la nauseée au salut.* Paris: Livre de Poche, 2003.

Bourdaghs, Michael. *The Dawn That Never Comes: Shimazaki Tōson and Japanese Nationalism.* New York: Columbia University Press, 2003.

Bourdieu, Pierre. "The Field of Cultural Production, or The Economic World Reversed." Trans. Richard Nice. In *The Field of Cultural Production*, ed. Randal Johnson, 29–73. New York: Columbia University Press, 1993.

———. "Les Conditions sociales de la circulation internationale des idées." *Actes de la Recherche en Sciences Sociales* 145 (2002): 3–8.

Bramen, Carrie Tirado. *The Uses of Variety: Modern Americanism and the Quest for National Distinctiveness.* Cambridge, Mass.: Harvard University Press, 2000.

Brandes, Georg. "Inaugural Lecture, 1871." Trans. Evert Sprinchorn. In *The Theory of the Modern Stage*, ed. Eric Bentley, 383–97. London: Penguin, 1992.

———. "World Literature." Trans. Haun Saussy. In *Mapping World Literature: International Canonization and Transnational Literatures*, by Mads Rosendahl Thomsen, 143–47. New York: Continuum, 2008.

Brezina, Jennifer Costello. "Public Women, Private Acts: Gender and Theater in Turn-of-the-Century American Novels." In *Separate Spheres No More:*

Gender Convergence in American Literature, 1830–1930, ed. Monika M. Elbert, 225–42. Tuscaloosa: University of Alabama Press, 2000.

Brown, Donald F. "A Chilean Germinal: Zola and Baldomero Lillo." *Modern Language Notes* 65, no. 1 (1950): 47–52.

Brushwood, John Stubbs. *Genteel Barbarism: Experiments in Analysis of Nineteenth-Century Spanish-American Novels*. Lincoln: University of Nebraska Press, 1981.

Budd, Louis J. "The American Background." In *The Cambridge Companion to American Realism and Naturalism: Howells to London*, ed. Donald Pizer, 21–46. New York: Cambridge University Press, 1995.

Bueno, Eva Paulino. *Resisting Boundaries: The Subject of Naturalism in Brazil*. New York: Garland, 1995.

Cabanès, Jean-Louis. *Le Corps et la maladie dans les récits réalistes (1856–1893)*. Lille: Klincksieck, 1991.

Cady, Edwin H. *The Realist at War: The Mature Years, 1885–1920, of William Dean Howells*. Syracuse, N.Y.: Syracuse University Press, 1958.

Cândido, Antônio. *Formação da literatura brasileira: Momentos decisivos*. São Paulo: Martins, 1959.

———. "Literature and Underdevelopment." Trans. Howard S. Becker. In *On Literature and Society*, ed. Howard S. Becker, 119–41. Princeton, N.J.: Princeton University Press, 1995.

———. *O discurso e a cidade*. São Paulo: Livraria Duas Cidades, 1993.

Casanova, Pascale. *The World Republic of Letters*. Trans. M. B. DeBevoise. Cambridge, Mass.: Harvard University Press, 2004.

Ceravolo Sereza, Haroldo. "Machado de Assis and the Problem of 'Realism-Naturalism.'" In *Re-Reading Zola and Worldwide Naturalism: Miscellanies in Honour of Anna Gural-Migdal*, ed. Carolyn Snipes-Hoyt, Marie-Sophie Armstrong, and Riikka Rossi, 368–80. Newcastle upon Tyne: Cambridge Scholars, 2013.

Chakrabarty, Dipesh. *Provincializing Europe: Postcolonial Thought and Historical Difference*. Princeton, N.J.: Princeton University Press, 2000.

Charle, Christophe. *Paris fin de siècle: Culture et politique*. Paris: Seuil, 1998.

Cheah, Pheng. *What Is a World? On Postcolonial Literature as World Literature*. Durham, N.C.: Duke University Press, 2016.

Chevrel, Yves. "De Germinal aux Tisserands." *Revue d'Histoire Litteraire de la France* 85, no. 3 (1985): 447–63.

———. "Germinal en Allemagne." *Europe* 678 (1985): 89–97.

———. "Le Naturalisme à l'étranger: Croatie, Grèce, Slovénie." *Cahiers Naturalistes* 77 (2003): 183–88.

———. *Le Naturalisme: Étude d'un mouvement littéraire international*. Paris: Presses Universitaires de France, 1982.

———."Le Roman et la nouvelle naturaliste française en Allemagne, 1870–1893." Doctoral thesis, Université de Paris-Sorbonne, 1979.

———. "Peut-on proposer une périodisation du naturalisme en tant que mouvement international?" In *Le Naturalisme en question: Actes du colloque tenu à Varsovie (20–22 Septembre 1984)*, ed. Yves Chevrel, 9–20. Recherches actuelles en littérature comparée 2. Paris: Presses de l'Université de Paris-Sorbonne, 1986.

Chitnis, Bernice. *Reflecting on Nana*. London: Routledge, 1991.

Cho, Heekyoung. *Translation's Forgotten History: Russian Literature, Japanese Mediation, and the Formation of Modern Korean Literature*. Cambridge, Mass.: Harvard University Asia Center, 2016.

Coaldrake, A. Kimi. *Women's Gidayū and the Japanese Theatre Tradition*. London: Routledge, 1997.

Cohen, Margaret. *The Sentimental Education of the Novel*. Princeton, N.J.: Princeton University Press, 1999.

Coleman, Alexander. *Eça de Queirós and European Realism*. New York: New York University Press, 1980.

Corbin, Alain. *Women for Hire: Prostitution and Sexuality in France after 1850*. Trans. Alan Sheridan. Cambridge, Mass.: Harvard University Press, 1990.

Coundouriotis, Eleni. *The People's Right to the Novel: War Fiction in the Postcolony*. New York: Fordham University Press, 2014.

Cowley, Malcolm. "'Not Men': A Natural History of American Naturalism." In *Documents of American Realism and Naturalism*, ed. Donald Pizer, 225–38. Carbondale: Southern Illinois University Press, 1998.

Damrosch, David. *What Is World Literature?* Princeton, N.J.: Princeton University Press, 2003.

———. "World Literature in a Postcanonical, Hypercanonical Age." In *Comparative Literature in an Age of Globalization*, ed. Haun Saussy, 43–53. Baltimore, Md.: Johns Hopkins University Press, 2006.

Darbouze, Gilbert. *Dégénérescence et régénérescence dans l'oeuvre d'Émile Zola et celle de Manuel Zeno Gandía: Étude comparée*. New York: Peter Lang, 1997.

Davidson, Cathy N., and Arnold E. Davidson. "Carrie's Sisters: The Popular Prototypes of Dreiser's Heroine." *Modern Fiction Studies* 23, no. 3 (1977): 395–407.

Dawson, Hugh J. "McTeague as Ethnic Stereotype." *American Literary Realism* 20, no. 1 (1987): 34–44.

Debbaut, Romain. "Esthétique naturaliste et définition du naturalisme dans la littérature d'expression néerlandaise." In *Le Naturalisme en question: Actes du colloque tenu à Varsovie (20–22 Septembre 1984)*, ed. Yves Chevrel, 67–76. Recherches actuelles en littérature comparée 2. Paris: Presses de l'Université de Paris-Sorbonne, 1986.

Deleuze, Gilles. "Zola et la fêlure." In *Logique du sens*, 373–85. Paris: Éditions de Minuit, 2002.

Delvau, Alfred. *Dictionnaire de la langue verte: Argots parisiens comparés*. 2nd ed. Paris: E. Dentu, 1866.

Denning, Michael. *Culture in the Age of the Three Worlds*. New York: Verso, 2004.

Dezalay, Auguste. *L'Opéra des Rougon-Macquart: Essai de rythmologie romanesque*. Paris: Klincksieck, 1983.

Dimock, Wai-Chee. *Through Other Continents: American Literature across Deep Time*. Princeton, N.J.: Princeton University Press, 2006.

Dingledine, Don. "'It Could Have Been Any Street': Ann Petry, Stephen Crane, and the Fate of Naturalism." *Studies in American Fiction* 34, no. 1 (2006): 87–106.

Dirlik, Arif. *Global Modernity: Modernity in the Age of Global Capitalism*. Boulder, Colo.: Paradigm, 2007.

Disegni, Silvia. "La Diffusion de l'oeuvre de Zola en Italie." *Cahiers Naturalistes* 79 (2005): 109–29.

DiVanna, Isabel. "Reading Comte across the Atlantic: Intellectual Exchanges between France and Brazil and the Question of Slavery." *History of European Ideas* 38, no. 3 (2012): 452–66.

Dreiser, Theodore. *Sister Carrie*. Ed. Donald Pizer. 2nd ed. New York: Norton, 1991.

Dubois, Jacques. *L'Assommoir de Zola*. 2nd ed. Paris: Belin, 1993.

———. "Zola et les sciences humaines." *Excavatio* 19, no. 1–2 (2004): 171–84.

Duffy, Larry. *Le Grand Transit Moderne: Mobility, Modernity and French Naturalist Fiction*. Amsterdam: Rodopi, 2005.

Durkheim, Émile. *De la division du travail social: Étude sur l'organisation des sociétés supérieures*. Paris: Félix Alcan, 1893.

Eby, Clare Virginia. *Dreiser and Veblen: Saboteurs of the Status Quo*. Columbia: University of Missouri Press, 1998.

El-Enany, Rasheed. *Naguib Mahfouz: The Pursuit of Meaning*. London: Routledge, 1993.

Esty, Jed, and Colleen Lye. "Peripheral Realisms Now." *Modern Language Quarterly* 73, no. 3 (2012): 269–88.

Felski, Rita. *The Gender of Modernity*. Cambridge, Mass.: Harvard University Press, 1995.

Finocchiaro, Marzia. "De la Sicile à Milan: Itinéraire italien des réceptions du Naturalisme français." *Excavatio* 12 (1999): 177–86.

Fisher, Philip. *Hard Facts: Setting and Form in the American Novel*. New York: Oxford University Press, 1985.

Flaubert, Gustave. *Correspondance*. Paris: Charpentier, 1887.

Foster, David W. *The Argentine Generation of 1880: Ideology and Cultural Texts*. Columbia: University of Missouri Press, 1990.

Foucault, Michel. "What Is an Author?" Trans. Josué V. Harari. In *The Essential Foucault*, ed. Paul Rabinow and Nikolas Rose, 377–91. New York: New Press, 2003.

Fowler, Edward. *The Rhetoric of Confession: Shishōsetsu in Early Twentieth-Century Japanese Fiction*. Berkeley: University of California Press, 1988.

Fraleigh, Mathew. "Terms of Understanding: The Shōsetsu according to Tayama Katai." *Monumenta Nipponica* 58, no. 1 (2003): 43–78.

Franz, Thomas R. "Early Spanish Intertexts with 'L'Assommoir.'" *Horizontes: Revista de la Universidad Catolica de Puerto Rico* 32, no. 63–64 (1988): 5–20.

Friedman, Susan Stanford. "One Hand Clapping: Colonialism, Postcolonialism, and the Spatio-Temporal Boundaries of Modernism." In *Translocal*

Modernisms: International Perspectives, ed. Irene Ramalho Santos and António Sousa Ribeiro, 11–40. New York: Peter Lang, 2008.

Frierson, William C., and Herbert Edwards. "The Impact of French Naturalism on American Critical Opinion 1877–1892." *PMLA* 63, no. 3 (1948): 1007–16.

Frow, John. "Thinking the Novel." *New Left Review* 49 (2008): 137–45.

Frühstück, Sabine. *Colonizing Sex: Sexology and Social Control in Modern Japan*. Berkeley: University of California Press, 2003.

Fujimori Kiyoshi. *Katari no kindai*. Yūseidō, 1996.

Fujitani, T. *Splendid Monarchy: Power and Pageantry in Modern Japan*. Berkeley: University of California Press, 1996.

Gacoin-Marks, Florence. "Eugen Kumičić et la première réception d'Émile Zola en Croatie." In *Zola en Europe centrale*, ed. Norbert Bachleitner, Tone Smolej, and Karl Zieger, 203–26. Valenciennes: Presses Universitaires de Valenciennes, 2011.

———. "Les Débuts du naturalisme en Croatie et en Slovénie." *Cahiers Naturalistes* 77 (2003): 239–52.

Galaos, José Antonio. "Manuel Zeno Gandía y sus Crónicas de un mundo enfermo." *Cuardernos Hispanoamericanos* 59 (1964): 415–20.

Ganguly, Debjani. *This Thing Called the World: The Contemporary Novel as Global Form*. Durham, N.C.: Duke University Press, 2016.

Garon, Sheldon. *Molding Japanese Minds: The State in Everyday Life*. Princeton, N.J.: Princeton University Press, 1997.

Genette, Gérard. *Paratexts: Thresholds of Interpretation*. Trans. Jane Lewin. New York: Cambridge University Press, 1997.

Gessel, Van C. *The Sting of Life: Four Contemporary Japanese Novelists*. New York: Columbia University Press, 1989.

Gibson, Mary. *Born to Crime: Cesare Lombroso and the Origins of Biological Criminology*. Westport, Conn.: Praeger, 2002.

Gikandi, Simon. "Realism, Romance, and the Problem of African Literary History." *Modern Language Quarterly* 73, no. 3 (2012): 309–28.

Gilman, Margaret. "Two Critics and an Author: 'Madame Bovary' Judged by Sainte-Beuve and by Baudelaire." *French Review* 15, no. 2 (1941): 138–46.

Gilman, Stephen. *Galdós and the Art of the European Novel, 1867–1887*. Princeton, N.J.: Princeton University Press, 1981.

Glenn, Susan A. *Female Spectacle: The Theatrical Roots of Modern Feminism*. Cambridge, Mass.: Harvard University Press, 2000.

Goi Makoto. "Kankei toshite no 'miru' koto—Kosugi Tengai 'Hatsu sugata' no kōzō." *Rikkyō daigaku Nihon bungaku* 77 (1996): 14–23.

Goncourt, Edmond, and Jules de Goncourt. *Germinie Lacerteux*. Paris: Union Générale d'Editions, 1979.

Gonzalez-Arias, Francisca. "Parallels and Parodies: Emilia Pardo Bazán's Response to Émile Zola (La Tribuna and L'Assommoir)." *Bulletin of Hispanic Studies* 67, no. 4 (1990): 369–77.

Gosling, F. G. *Before Freud: Neurasthenia and the American Medical Community, 1870–1910*. Urbana: University of Illinois Press, 1987.

Goula-Mitacou, Polyxène. "La Traduction grecque de Nana." *Cahiers Naturalistes* 79 (2005): 141–45.

Gourg, Marianne. "Quelques aspects de la réception des thèses naturalistes en Russie." *Cahiers Naturalistes* 65 (1991): 25–36.

Grand-Carteret, John. *Zola en images*. Paris: Félix Juven, 1908.

Graves, Peter. "Afterword." In *The Red Room: Scenes from the Lives of Artists and Authors*, by August Strindberg, 307–11. London: Norvik, 2009.

Hale, Terry. "The Imaginary Quay from Waterloo Bridge to London Bridge: Translation, Adaptation, and Genre." In *On Translating French Literature and Film II*, ed. Myriam Salama-Carr, 219–38. Amsterdam: Rodopi, 2000.

Halim, Hala. "Lotus, the Afro-Asian Nexus, and Global South Comparatism." *Comparative Studies of South Asia, Africa and the Middle East* 32, no. 3 (2012): 563–83.

Hamon, Philippe. *Du descriptif*. Paris: Hachette, 1993.

Hanneken, Jaime. "Going *Mundial*: What It Really Means to Desire Paris." *Modern Language Quarterly* 71, no. 2 (2010): 129–52.

Harootunian, Harry. *Marx after Marx: History and Time in the Expansion of Capitalism*. New York: Columbia University Press, 2015.

Harrow, Susan. "Thérèse Raquin: Animal Passion and the Brutality of Reading." In *The Cambridge Companion to Emile Zola*, ed. Brian Nelson, 105–20. Cambridge: Cambridge University Press, 2007.

———. *Zola, the Body Modern: Pressures and Prospects of Representation*. London: Legenda, 2010.

Hasegawa Tenkei. "Genjitsu bakurō no hiai." In *Meiji ki III*, ed. Yoshida Seiichi and Wada Kingo, 117–26. Kindai bungaku hyōron taikei 3. Tokyo: Kadokawa Shoten, 1972.

Hayot, Eric. *On Literary Worlds*. New York: Oxford University Press, 2012.

Heckerl, David K. "'Violent Movements of Business': The Moral Nihilist as Economic Man in Jack London's The Sea-Wolf." In *Twisted from the Ordinary: Essays on American Literary Realism*, ed. Mary E. Papke, 202–16. Knoxville: University of Tennessee Press, 2003.

Helgesson, Stefan. "The World-Literary Formation of Antonio Candido." In *Re-Mapping World Literature: Writing, Book Markets, and Epistemologies between Latin America and the Global South*, ed. Gesine Müller, Jorge J. Locane, and Benjamin Loy, 225–36. Berlin: De Gruyter, 2018.

Hemmings, F. W. J. "The Origins of the Terms Naturalisme, Naturaliste." *French Studies* 8 (1954): 109–21.

Henshall, Kenneth G. *In Search of Nature: The Japanese Writer Tayama Katai (1872–1930)*. Leiden: Global Oriental, 2013.

Hijiya-Kirschnereit, Irmela. *Rituals of Self-Revelation: Shishōsetsu as Literary Genre and Socio-Cultural Phenomenon*. Cambridge, Mass.: Council on East Asian Studies, 1996.

Hill, Christopher L. "Exhausted by Their Battles with the World: Neurasthenia and Civilization Critique in Early Twentieth-Century Japan." In *Perversion and Modern Japan: Experiments in Psychoanalysis*, ed. Nina Cornyetz and Keith Vincent, 242–58. London: Routledge, 2009.

———. "Haven't We Met? On the Scales of Connection." *Verge: Studies in Global Asias* 3, no. 2 (2017): 86–89.

———. "Nana in the World: Novel, Gender, and Transnational Form." *Modern Language Quarterly* 72, no. 1 (2011): 75–105.

———. *National History and the World of Nations: Capital, State, and the Rhetoric of History in Japan, France, and the United States*. Durham, N.C.: Duke University Press, 2008.

———. "The Travels of Naturalism and the Challenges of a World Literary History." *Literature Compass* 6, no. 6 (2009): 1198–1210.

Hiraoka Toshio. *Nichiro sengo bungaku no kenkyū*. Tokyo: Yūseidō, 1985.

Howard, June. *Form and History in American Literary Naturalism*. Chapel Hill: University of North Carolina Press, 1985.

———. "Sand in Your Mouth: Naturalism and Other Genres." In *Oxford Handbook of American Literary Naturalism*, ed. Keith Newlin, 92–103. New York: Oxford University Press, 2011.

Huret, Jules. *Enquête sur l'évolution littéraire*. Paris: Charpentier, 1891.

Ingwersen, Niels. "The Modern Breakthrough." In *A History of Danish literature*, ed. Sven Hakon Rossel, 261–317. Lincoln: University of Nebraska Press, 1992.

Iwasa Sōshirō. *Seikimatsu no shizen shugi—Meiji yonjūnendai bungaku kō*. Tokyo: Yūseidō, 1986.

Jameson, Fredric. *The Political Unconscious: Narrative as a Socially Symbolic Act*. Ithaca, N.Y.: Cornell University Press, 1981.

Johnston, William. *Geisha, Harlot, Strangler, Star: A Woman, Sex, and Morality in Modern Japan*. New York: Columbia University Press, 2005.

Jurt, Joseph. "The Reception of Naturalism in Germany." In *Naturalism in the European Novel: New Critical Perspectives*, ed. Brian Nelson, 99–119. New York: Berg, 1992.

Kahanov, Alfred. "Les Traductions hébraïques des oeuvres d'Émile Zola." *Cahiers Naturalistes* 65 (1991): 113–15.

Kálai, Sándor. "La Réception de Zola en Hongrie." In *Zola en Europe centrale*, ed. Norbert Bachleitner, Tone Smolej, and Karl Zieger, 171–86. Valenciennes: Presses Universitaires de Valenciennes, 2011.

Kamakura Yoshinobu. "Shizen shugi bungaku to Makkusu Norudau—'Daraku ron' no yomare kata." *Kokubungaku gengo to bungei* 119 (2002): 60–74.

Kang U Wŏng-yong. "Nihon to Chōsen hantō ni okeru shizen shugi bungaku." *Hōsei daigaku daigakuin daigakuin kiyō* 52 (2004): 236–48.

Karatani Kōjin. *Marukusu sono kanōsei no chūshin*. Tokyo: Kōdansha, 1990.

———. *Origins of Modern Japanese Literature*. Ed. Brett de Bary. Durham, N.C.: Duke University Press, 1993.

Kawamura Kunimitsu. *Genshi suru kindai kūkan—meishin, byōki, zashiki rō, arui wa rekishi no kioku*. Tokyo: Seikyūsha, 1990.

Kawauchi Kiyoshi. *Zora to Nihon shizen shugi bungaku*. Matsudo: Azusa Shuppansha, 1990.

Kayanuma Noriko. "Geisha to jorō no shokugyō ishiki—kinsei bungaku ni miru irokoi no sekai." In *Bai-baishun to Nihon bungaku*, ed. Okano Yukie,

Hasegawa Kei, and Watanabe Sumiko, 71–80. Tokyo: Tōkyōdō Shuppan, 2002.

Keaveney, Christopher T. *The Subversive Self in Modern Chinese Literature: The Creation Society's Reinvention of the Japanese Shishōsetsu*. New York: Palgrave Macmillan, 2004.

Kim Tong-in. "The World Created by Self." *Acta Koreana* 16, no. 1 (2013): 257–60.

Kim Yoon-shik. "KAPF Literature in Modern Korean Literary History." *Positions* 14, no. 2 (2006): 405–25.

Kinmonth, Earl. *The Self-Made Man in Meiji Japanese Thought: From Samurai to Salary Man*. Berkeley: University of California Press, 1981.

Klaus, H. Gustav. "The Strike Novel in the 1890s." In *The Rise of Socialist Fiction, 1880–1914*, ed. H. Gustav Klaus, 73–98. New York: St. Martin's Press, 1987.

Kobori Yōhei. "Tayama Katai 'Inaka kyōshi' ni okeru fūkei byōsha no keisei: Utsusu koto to amu koto no aidagara." *Kokugo to kokubungaku* 92, no. 12 (2015): 56–70.

Konaka Nobutaka. "Kesareta shintai—Tayama katai 'Futon' no jidai." *Kokugakuin zasshi* 105, no. 11 (2004): 117–28.

Kōno Kensuke. "'Seishun' to iu tekusuto: Shimazaki Tōson Haru o megutte." In *Bungaku ni okeru nijūdai*, ed. Yasumasa Satō, 123–44. Tokyo: Kasama Shoin, 1990.

Kosugi Tengai. *Hatsu sugata*. Tokyo: Iwanami Shoten, 2000.

———. *Hayari uta*. Tokyo: Iwanami Shoten, 1954.

Kulczycka-Saloni, Janina. "Émile Zola en Pologne." *Cahiers Naturalistes* 32 (1966): 145–59.

Laitinen, Kai. "The Rise of Finnish-Language Literature." In *A History of Finland's Literature*, ed. George C. Schoolfield, 64–147. Lincoln: University of Nebraska Press, 1998.

Lappailainen, Païvi. "Seduced Girls and Prostitutes: The Character of the Fallen Woman in Finnish Naturalist Fiction." *Excavatio* 23, no. 1–2 (2008): 153–68.

Lazarus, Neil. "The Retrieval of Naturalism: The Politics of Narrative in Radical African Fiction." *Critical Exchange* 22 (1987): 53–62.

Lebron, Monica. "Naturalism in New Climes: Argentina and Brazil." *Excavatio* 4–5 (1994): 131–38.

Lee, Ann Sung-hi. *Yi Kwang-su and Modern Korean Literature, Mujŏng*. Ithaca, N.Y.: East Asia Program, Cornell University, 2005.

Lee, Jae-Yon. "On Kim Tong-in's 'The World Created by Self' and Yŏm Sang-Sŏp's 'Individuality and Art.'" *Acta Koreana* 16, no. 1 (2013): 253–56.

Leighton, Mary Elizabeth, and Kirsten MacLeod. "The Trials of Naturalism: Zola in the British Literary and Cultural Imagination of the Fin de Siècle." *Excavatio* 15, no. 3–4 (2001): 322–36.

Lemonnier, Camille. *Happe-Chair*. Paris: E. Monnier, De Brunhoff, 1886.

Lethbridge, Robert. "Zola and Contemporary Painting." In *The Cambridge Companion to Emile Zola*, ed. Brian Nelson, 67–85. Cambridge: Cambridge University Press, 2007.

Letourneau, Charles. *Physiologie des passions*. Paris: Germer Baillière, 1868.

Levy, Indra. *Sirens of the Western Shore: The Westernesque Femme Fatale, Translation, and Vernacular Style in Modern Japanese Literature*. New York: Columbia University Press, 2006.

Lidsky, Paul. *Les Écrivains contre la Commune*. Paris: Francois Maspero, 1970.

Link, Eric Carl. "The Five Deaths of Wolf Larsen." *Studies in American Naturalism* 5, no. 2 (2010): 151–63.

———. *The Vast and Terrible Drama: American Literary Naturalism in the Late Nineteenth Century*. Tuscaloosa: University of Alabama Press, 2004.

Liu, Lydia H. *Translingual Practice: Literature, National Culture, and Translated Modernity—China, 1900–1937*. Stanford, Calif.: Stanford University Press, 1995.

London, Jack. *The Sea-Wolf*. In *Jack London: Novels and Stories*, 479–771. New York: Library of America, 1982.

Loos, Dorothy Scott. *The Naturalistic Novel of Brazil*. New York: Hispanic Institute of the United States, 1963.

López-Beltrán, Carlos. "In the Cradle of Heredity: French Physicians and L'Hérédité Naturelle in the Early 19th Century." *Journal of the History of Biology* 37, no. 1 (2004): 39–72.

Lucas, Prosper. *Traité philosophique et physiologique de l'hérédité naturelle dans les états de santé et de maladie du système nerveux*. Paris: Baillière, 1847.

Lukács, Georg. "Narrate or Describe?" Trans. Arthur D. Kahn. In *Writer and Critic and Other Essays*, 110–48. New York: Grosset and Dunlap, 1974.

———. "The Zola Centenary." In *Studies in European Realism: A Sociological Survey of the Writings of Balzac, Stendhal, Zola, Tolstoy, Gorki and Others*, 85–96. London: Merlin, 1972.

Maeda Ai. *Text and the City: Essays on Japanese Modernity*. Durham, N.C.: Duke University Press, 2004.

Maeda Akira. "Kaisetsu." In *Inaka kyōshi*, by Tayama Katai, 243-50. Tokyo: Iwanami Shoten, 1993.

Marran, Christine L. *Poison Woman: Figuring Female Transgression in Modern Japanese Culture*. Minneapolis: University of Minnesota Press, 2007.

Marx, Jacques. "Émile Verhaeren et la poésie naturaliste en Belgique." *Excavatio* 6–7 (1995): 33–48.

Marx, Karl. *Capital: A Critique of Political Economy*. Trans. Ben Fowkes and David Fernbach. Vol. 1. New York: Penguin Books, 1976.

McDougall, Bonnie S. *The Introduction of Western Literary Theories into Modern China, 1919–1925*. Tokyo: Centre for East Asian Cultural Studies, 1971.

McFarlane, James. "Norwegian Literature 1860–1910." In *A History of Norwegian literature*, ed. Harald S. Naess, 107–99. Lincoln: University of Nebraska Press, 1993.

Mendes, Leonardo. "Sordid Literature: Naturalism and Sexuality in Brazil." *Excavatio* 21, no. 1–2 (2006): 48–62.

Mérian, Jean-Yves. *Aluísio Azevedo: Vida e obra (1857–1913)*. Trans. Claudia Poncioni. 2nd ed. Rio de Janeiro: Garamond, 2013.

———. "Les Débuts du naturalisme au Brésil." *Recherches et Études Comparatistes Ibéro-Françaises de la Sorbonne Nouvelle* 3 (1981): 27–37.

Merkle, Denise. "Germinal en Grande-Bretagne de 1884 à 1895." *Cahiers Naturalistes* 81 (2007): 197–210.

Michaels, Walter Benn. *The Gold Standard and the Logic of Naturalism: American Literature at the Turn of the Century*. Berkeley: University of California Press, 1987.

Mitchell, Lee Clark. "'And Rescue Us from Ourselves': Becoming Someone in Jack London's The Sea-Wolf." *American Literature* 70, no. 2 (1998): 317–35.

———. *Determined Fictions: American Literary Naturalism*. New York: Columbia University Press, 1990.

Mitterand, Henri. "Étude [Germinal]." In *Les Rougon-Macquart III*, by Émile Zola, 1802–80. Paris: Gallimard, 1964.

———. "Étude [L'Assommoir]." In *Les Rougon-Macquart II*, by Émile Zola, 1532–70. Paris: Gallimard, 1961.

———. "Étude [Nana]." In *Les Rougon-Macquart II*, by Émile Zola, 1650–91. Paris: Gallimard, 1961.

———. "Étude [La Fortune des Rougon]." In *Les Rougon-Macquart I*, by Émile Zola, 1532–67. Paris: Gallimard, 1960.

———. *Le Discours du roman*. Paris: Presses Universitaires de France, 1980.

———. *Le Regard et le signe: Poétique du roman réaliste et naturaliste*. Paris: Presses Universitaires de France, 1987.

———. *Zola*. Paris: Fayard, 1999.

Miyoshi Yukio. *Shimazaki Tōson ron*. Tokyo: Shibundō, 1966.

Modern Girl Around the World Research Group et al. "The Modern Girl Around the World: Cosmetics Advertising and the Politics of Race and Style." In *The Modern Girl Around the World: Consumption, Modernity, and Globalization*, ed. Alys Eve Weinbaum et al., 25–54. Durham, N.C.: Duke University Press, 2008.

———. "The Modern Girl as Heuristic Device: Collaboration, Connective Comparison, Multidirectional Citation." In *The Modern Girl Around the World: Consumption, Modernity, and Globalization*, ed. Alys Eve Weinbaum et al., 1–24. Durham, N.C.: Duke University Press, 2008.

Moretti, Franco. "Conjectures on World Literature." *New Left Review* 1 (2000): 54–68.

———. *Graphs, Maps, Trees: Abstract Models for Literary History*. London: Verso, 2005.

———. "The Novel: History and Theory." *New Left Review* 52 (2008): 111–24.

Mori Eiichi. "Kosugi Tengai to Zora." *Nihon kindai bungaku* 18 (1973): 95–104.

Mori Ōgai. "Waseda bungaku no botsu risō." In *Meiji ki I*, 193–99. Kindai bungaku hyōron taikei 1. Tokyo: Kadokawa Shoten, 1971.

Morishita Yūdō. *Shinri ōyō nōshinkeisuijaku hitsujisaku*. Tokyo: Hakubunkan, 1909.

Mosse, George L. "Introduction." In *Degeneration*, by Max Nordau, xiii–xxiii. Lincoln: University of Nebraska Press, 1993.

Mufti, Aamir. *Forget English! Orientalisms and World Literatures*. Cambridge, Mass.: Harvard University Press, 2016.

Nakayama Hiroaki. "Kettō no monogatari—'Ie' no 'yamai' ron." In *Shimazaki Tōson: Bunmei hihyō to shi to shōsetsu to*, ed. Hiraoka Toshio and Kenmochi Takehiko, 182–97. Tokyo: Sōbunsha Shuppan, 1996.

Nisetich, Rebecca. "The Nature of the Beast: Scientific Theories of Race and Sexuality in McTeague." *Studies in American Naturalism* 4, no. 1 (2009): 1–21.

Noiriel, Gérard. *The French Melting Pot: Immigration, Citizenship, and National Identity*. Trans. Geoffroy de Laforcade. Minneapolis: University of Minnesota Press, 1996.

Nolte, Sharon H., and Sally Ann Hastings. "The Meiji State's Policy toward Women, 1890–1910." In *Recreating Japanese Women, 1600–1945*, ed. Gail Lee Bernstein, 151–74. Berkeley: University of California Press, 1991.

Nordau, Max. *Degeneration*. Lincoln: University of Nebraska Press, 1993.

Norris, Frank. "A Case for Lombroso." In *The Apprenticeship Writings of Frank Norris*, ed. Joseph R. McElrath and Douglas K. Burgess, vol. 2: 127–32. Philadelphia: American Philosophical Society, 1996.

———. *McTeague: A Story of San Francisco*. 2nd ed. New York: Norton, 1997.

———. "A Plea for Romantic Fiction." In Frank Norris, *McTeague: A Story of San Francisco*, ed. Donald Pizer, 277–80. 2nd ed. New York: Norton, 1997.

———. "Zola as a Romantic Writer." In Frank Norris, *McTeague: A Story of San Francisco*, ed. Donald Pizer, 273–74. 2nd ed. New York: Norton, 1997.

Novaković, Jelena. "La Réception d'Émile Zola en Serbie." In *Zola en Europe centrale*, ed. Norbert Bachleitner, Tone Smolej, and Karl Zieger, 227–49. Valenciennes: Presses Universitaires de Valenciennes, 2011.

Nye, Robert. *Crime, Madness and Politics in Modern France: The Medical Concept of National Decline*. Princeton, N.J.: Princeton University Press, 1984.

———. "Degeneration and the Medical Model of Cultural Crisis in the French Belle Époque." In *Political Symbolism in Modern Europe: Essays in Honor of George L. Mosse*, ed. Seymour Drescher, David Sabean, and Allan Sharlin, 19–41. New Brunswick, N.J.: Transaction Books, 1982.

Nygård, Stefan, and Johan Strang. "Facing Asymmetry: Nordic Intellectuals and Center-Periphery Dynamics in European Cultural Space." *Journal of the History of Ideas* 77, no. 1 (2016): 75–97.

Odem, Mary E. *Delinquent Daughters: Protecting and Policing Adolescent Female Sexuality in the United States, 1885–1920*. Chapel Hill: University of North Carolina Press, 1995.

O'Donovan, Patrick. "The Body and the Body Politic in the Novels of the Goncourts." In *Spectacles of Realism: Body, Gender, Genre*, ed. Margaret Cohen and Christopher Prendergast, 214–30. Minneapolis: University of Minnesota Press, 1995.

Ōida Yoshiaki. "Haru ni okeru komyunikeishon no mondai." *Bai* 7 (1991): 33–47.

Oka Yasuo. "Zoraizumu no jubaku." In *Nihon bungaku no rekishi*, ed. Yoshida Seiichi and Shimomura Fujio, vol. 10: 112–41. Tokyo: Kadokawa Shoten, 1968.

Oka Yoshitake. "Generational Conflict after the Russo-Japanese War." In *Conflict in Modern Japanese History: The Neglected Tradition*, ed. Tetsuo Najita and Victor Koschmann, 197–225. Princeton, N.J.: Princeton University Press, 1982.

Pagano, Tullio. *Experimental Fictions: From Emile Zola's Naturalism to Giovanni Verga's Verism*. Madison, N.J.: Fairleigh Dickinson University Press, 1999.

Papa, James A., Jr. "Canvas and Steam: Historical Conflict in Jack London's Sea-Wolf." *Midwest Quarterly* 40, no. 3 (1999): 274–84.

Park, Sunyoung. "The Colonial Origin of Korean Realism and Its Contemporary Manifestation." *Positions* 14, no. 1 (2006): 165–92.

———. *The Proletarian Wave: Literature and Leftist Culture in Colonial Korea, 1910–1945*. Cambridge, Mass.: Harvard University Asia Center, 2015.

Pellini, Pierluigi. "Archéologie d'une 'maison de verre': Sur Zola et la folie." *Compar(a)ison* 2 (2003): 5–41.

Petrey, Sandy. *Realism and Revolution: Balzac, Stendhal, Zola, and the Performance of History*. Ithaca, N.Y.: Cornell University Press, 1988.

Pick, Daniel. *Faces of Degeneration: A European Disorder, c. 1848–c. 1918*. Cambridge: Cambridge University Press, 1989.

Pizer, Donald. "Backgrounds and Sources." In Theodore Dreiser, *Sister Carrie*, ed. Donald Pizer, 385–477. 2nd ed. New York: Norton, 1991.

———. *The Novels of Frank Norris*. Bloomington: Indiana University Press, 1966.

———. *Realism and Naturalism in Nineteenth-Century American Literature*. Carbondale: Southern Illinois University Press, 1966.

Postone, Moishe. *Time, Labor, and Social Domination*. Cambridge: Cambridge University Press, 1993.

Prendes, Manuel. "El personaje y sus libros en la novela naturalista hispanoamericana." *Excavatio* 18, no. 1–2 (2003): 392–404.

———. *La novela naturalista hispanoamericana: Evolución y direcciones de un processo narrativo*. Madrid: Cátedra, 2003.

Průšek, Jaroslav. *The Lyrical and the Epic: Studies of Modern Chinese Literature*. Bloomington: Indiana University Press, 1980.

Rachwalska von Rejchwald, Jolanta. "Apologie et aversion de Zola en Pologne." In *Zola en Europe centrale*, ed. Norbert Bachleitner, Tone Smolej, and Karl Zieger, 79–106. Valenciennes: Presses Universitaires de Valenciennes, 2011.

Ragusa, Olga. "The Study of Literary Relations: France and Italy in the Nineteenth Century." *Symposium: A Quarterly Journal in Modern Literatures* 47, no. 2 (1993): 147–55.

Ram, Harsha. "The Scale of Global Modernisms: Imperial, National, Regional, Local." *PMLA* 131, no. 5 (2016): 1372–85.

Reesman, Jeanne Campbell. *Jack London's Racial Lives: A Critical Biography*. Athens: University of Georgia Press, 2009.

Revel, Jacques. "Multiple Narratives: Scale and Discontinuity in History." In *Unsettling History: Archiving and Narrating in Historiography*, ed. Sebastian Jobs and Alf Lüdtke, 49–61. New York: Campus Verlag, 2010.

Ripoll, Roger. "Zola et les communards." *Europe* 46, no. 468 (1968): 16–26.

Roberts, Mary Louise. *Disruptive Acts: The New Woman in Fin-de-Siècle France*. Chicago: University of Chicago Press, 2002.

Rollins, Yvonne Bargues. "Une 'Danse macabre': L'Assommoir de Zola." *Nineteenth-Century French Studies* 9, no. 3–4 (1981): 233–46.

Rosenberg, Ingrid von. "French Naturalism and the English Socialist Novel: Margaret Harkness and William Edwards Tirebuck." In *The Rise of Socialist Fiction, 1880–1914*, ed. H. Gustav Klaus, 151–71. New York: St. Martin's Press, 1987.

Ross, Kristin. *Communal Luxury: The Political Imaginary of the Paris Commune*. London: Verso, 2015.

———. *The Emergence of Social Space: Rimbaud and the Paris Commune*. Minneapolis: University of Minnesota Press, 1988.

———. "Translator's Introduction." In *The Ignorant Schoolmaster*, by Jacques Rancière, vii–xxiii. Stanford, Calif.: Stanford University Press, 1991.

Rossel, Sven Hakon. *A History of Scandinavian Literature, 1870–1980*. Trans. Anne C. Ulmer. Minneapolis: University of Minnesota Press, 1982.

Rossetti, Gina M. *Imagining the Primitive in Naturalist and Modernist Literature*. Columbia: University of Missouri Press, 2006.

Rossi, Riikka. "Le Naturalisme en Finlande." *Excavatio* 17, no. 1–2 (2002): 275–87.

Saillard, S. "La Première Traduction espagnole de Germinal." *Cahiers Naturalistes* 75 (2001): 217–42.

Sakai Kosen. "Hashigaki." In *Ki no medachi*, by Émile Zola, 1–2. Tokyo: Arusu, 1921.

Salvan, Albert J. *Zola aux Etats-Unis*. New York: Kraus Reprint, 1967.

Schierenbeck, Daniel. "Is There a Doctor in the House? Norris' Naturalist Gaze of Clinical Observation in McTeague." In *Twisted from the Ordinary: Essays on American Literary Realism*, ed. Mary E. Papke, 63–85. Knoxville: University of Tennessee Press, 2003.

Schoolfield, George C. "A Sense of Minority." In *A History of Finland's Literature*, ed. George C. Schoolfield, 354–452. Lincoln: University of Nebraska Press, 1998.

Schor, Naomi. "Sainte-Anne: Capitale du délire." *Cahiers Naturalistes* 52 (1978): 97–108.

———. *Zola's Crowds*. Baltimore, Md.: Johns Hopkins University Press, 1978.

Schulz, Hans-Joachim. *German Socialist Literature, 1860–1914: Predicaments of Criticism*. Columbia, S.C.: Camden House, 1993.

Schwarz, Roberto. "Misplaced Ideas: Literature and Society in Late-Nineteenth Century Brazil." Trans. Edmund Leites and Roberto Schwarz. In *Misplaced Ideas: Essays on Brazilian Culture*, 19–32. London: Verso, 1992.

———. "National Adequation and Critical Originality." Trans. R. Kelly Washbourne and Neil Larsen. *Cultural Critique* 49 (2001): 18–42.

Seltzer, Mark. *Bodies and Machines*. New York: Routledge, 1992.

Shen, Nai-huei. "The Age of Sadness: A Study of Naturalism in Taiwanese Literature under Japanese Colonization." Doctoral dissertation, University of Washington, 2003.

Shimazaki Tōson. *Haru*. Tokyo: Iwanami Shoten, 2000.

Shin, Jiwon. "Recasting Colonial Space: Naturalist Vision and Modern Fiction in 1920s Korea." *Journal of International and Area Studies* [Seoul] 11, no. 3 (2004): 51–74.

Sibley, William F. "Naturalism in Japanese Literature." *Harvard Journal of Asiatic Studies* 28 (1968): 157–69.

Siskind, Mariano. *Cosmopolitan Desires: Global Modernity and World Literature in Latin America*. Evanston, Ill.: Northwestern University Press, 2014.

Skidmore, Thomas E. "Racial Ideas and Social Policy in Brazil, 1870–1940." In *The Idea of Race in Latin America, 1870–1940*, ed. Richard Graham, 7–36. Austin: University of Texas Press, 1990.

Skreb, Zdenko. "Le Naturalisme dans les littératures yougoslaves." In *Le Naturalisme en question: Actes du colloque tenu à Varsovie (20–22 Septembre 1984)*, ed. Yves Chevrel, 51–58. Recherches actuelles en littérature comparée 2. Paris: Presses de l'Université de Paris-Sorbonne, 1986.

Smith, Jonathan. "Naturalism and Anti-Naturalism in Italy." In *Naturalism in the European Novel: New Critical Perspectives*, ed. Brian Nelson, 151–66. New York: Berg, 1992.

Smith-Rosenberg, Carroll. *Disorderly Conduct: Visions of Gender in Victorian America*. New York: Oxford University Press, 1985.

Smolej, Tone. "Germinal en Slovénie." *Cahiers Naturalistes* 83 (2009): 289–302.

———. "La Réception d'Émile Zola chez les Slovènes à l'époque de l'Autriche-Hongrie." In *Zola en Europe centrale*, ed. Norbert Bachleitner, Tone Smolej, and Karl Zieger, 187–202. Valenciennes: Presses Universitaires de Valenciennes, 2011.

———. "L'Assommoir et l'oeuvre romanesque d'Ivan Cankar." *Cahiers Naturalistes* 77 (2003): 253–61.

Sōma Tsuneo. *Nihon shizen shugi ron*. Tokyo: Yagi Shoten, 1970.

———. *Nihon shizen shugi saikō*. Tokyo: Yagi Shoten, 1981.

Sommer, Doris. *Foundational Fictions: The National Romances of Latin America*. Berkeley: University of California Press, 1991.

Sorensen, Diana. "Alternative Geographic Mappings for the Twenty-First Century." In *Territories and Trajectories: Cultures in Circulation*, ed. Diana Sorensen, 13–19. Durham, N.C.: Duke University Press, 2018.

Sotolova, Jovanka. "Émile Zola à la tchèque." In *Zola en Europe centrale*, ed. Norbert Bachleitner, Tone Smolej, and Karl Zieger, 127–44. Valenciennes: Presses Universitaires de Valenciennes, 2011.

Spicer-Escalante, John Paul. "Civilización y barbarie: Naturalism's Paradigms of Self and Nationhood in Eugenio Cambaceres' Sin rumbo." *Excavatio* 13 (2000): 299–309.

Steene, Birgitta. "Liberalism, Realism, and the Modern Breakthrough: 1830–1890." In *A History of Swedish Literature*, ed. Lars G. Warme, 204–72. Lincoln: University of Nebraska Press, 1996.

Sutherland, Erika. "Death in the Bedroom: Eduardo López Bago and His Suspect Syphilitics." *Excavatio* 18, no. 1–2 (2003): 278–92.

Suzuki, Tomi. *Narrating the Self: Fictions of Japanese Modernity*. Stanford, Calif.: Stanford University Press, 1996.

Taine, Hippolyte. "Balzac." In *Nouveaux essais de critique et d'histoire*, 63–170. 2nd ed. Paris: Hachette, 1866.

———. *Histoire de la littérature anglaise*. Vol. 1. Paris: Hachette, 1863.

Tang, Xiaobing, and Michel Hockx. "The Creation Society (1921–1930)." In *Literary Societies of Republican China*, ed. Michel Hockx and Kirk A. Denton, 103–36. Lanham, Md.: Lexington Books, 2008.

Tarde, Gabriel. *Les Lois de l'imitation: Étude sociologique*. Paris: Félix Alcan, 1890.

Tayama Katai. "Byōsharon." In *Meiji ki III*, ed. Yoshida Seiichi and Wada Kingo, 369–84. Kindai bungaku hyōron taikei 3. Tokyo: Kadokawa Shoten, 1972.

———. *Inaka kyōshi*. Tokyo: Iwanami Shoten, 1993.

———. "Jūemon no saigo." In *Tayama Katai shū*, 53–121. Nihon kindai bungaku taikei 19. Tokyo: Kadokawa Shoten, 1972.

———. "Rokotsu naru byōsha." In *Meiji ki II*, 360–63. Kindai bungaku hyōron taikei 2. Tokyo: Kadokawa Shoten, 1972.

———. "'Sei' ni okeru kokoromi." In *Meiji ki III*, ed. Yoshida Seiichi and Wada Kingo, 448–51. Kindai bungaku hyōron taikei 3. Tokyo: Kadokawa Shoten, 1972.

———. *Tōkyō no sanjūnen*. In *Tayama Katai zenshū 15*, 445–708. Tokyo: Bunseidō Shoten, 1973.

Taylor, Charles. *Modern Social Imaginaries*. Durham, N.C.: Duke University Press, 2004.

Thornber, Karen Laura. *Empire of Texts in Motion: Chinese, Korea, and Taiwanese Transculturations of Japanese Literature*. Cambridge, Mass.: Harvard University Asia Center, 2009.

Trachtenberg, Alan. "Who Narrates? Dreiser's Presence in Sister Carrie." In *New Essays on Sister Carrie*, ed. Donald Pizer, 87–122. Cambridge: Cambridge University Press, 1991.

Trumpener, Katie. *Bardic Nationalism: The Romantic Novel and the British Empire*. Princeton, N.J.: Princeton University Press, 1997.

Tsubouchi Shōyō. "Sheekuspiya kyakuhon hyōchū." In *Meiji ki I*, 188–93. Kindai bungaku hyōron taikei 1. Tokyo: Kadokawa Shoten, 1971.

———. *Shōsetsu shinzui*. In *Tsubouchi Shōyō shū*, 39–165. Nihon kindai bungaku taikei 3. Tokyo: Kadokawa shoten, 1974.

Turgenev, Ivan. *Fathers and Sons*. Trans. Rosemay Edmonds. Harmondsworth, Eng.: Penguin, 1975.

Ueno Chizuko. "Modern Patriarchy and the Formation of the Japanese Nation State." In *Multicultural Japan: Palaeolithic to Postmodern*, ed. Donald Denoon et al., 213–23. Cambridge: Cambridge University Press, 1996.

Uryū Kiyoshi. "Tōson no shinjidai ishiki to Haru." *Fukuoka kyōiku daigaku kiyō dai-ichi bu bunka hen* 48 (1999): 1–12.

Van Compernolle, Timothy J. *Struggling Upward: Worldly Success and the Japanese Novel*. Cambridge, Mass.: Harvard University Asia Center, 2016.

Voysest, Oswaldo. "Clorinda Matto and Mercedes Cabello: Reading Émile Zola's Naturalism in a Dissonant Voice." *Excavatio* 11 (1998): 195–201.

Wada Kingo. *Byōsha no jidai—hitotsu no shizen shugi bungaku ron*. Sapporo: Hokkaidō Daigaku Tosho Kankōkai, 1975.

———. "'Inaka kyōshi' no seiritsu o meguru mondai." *Kokugo to kokubungaku* 32, no. 6 (1955): 56–62.

Wald, Priscilla. *Contagious: Cultures, Carriers, and the Outbreak Narrative*. Durham, N.C.: Duke University Press, 2007.

Wang, David Der-wei. "Mao Tun and Naturalism: A Case of Misreading in Modern Chinese Literary Criticism." *Monumenta Serica* 37 (1986): 169–95.

Wang, Dewei. *Fictional Realism in Twentieth-Century China: Mao Dun, Lao She, Shen Congwen*. New York: Columbia University Press, 1992.

Welge, Jobst. *Genealogical Fictions: Cultural Periphery and Historical Change in the Modern Novel*. Baltimore, Md.: Johns Hopkins University Press, 2015.

White, Nicholas. "Family Histories and Family Plots." In *The Cambridge Companion to Emile Zola*, ed. Brian Nelson, 19–38. Cambridge: Cambridge University Press, 2007.

Williams, Raymond. "A Lecture on Realism." *Screen* 18, no. 1 (1977): 61–74.

Wright, Richard. *Black Boy (American Hunger): A Record of Childhood and Youth*. New York: HarperPerennial, 1993.

Yasumaru Yoshio. *Bunmeika no keiken*. Tokyo: Iwanami Shoten, 2007.

Yŏm Sang-sŏp. "Individuality and Art." Trans Jae-Yon Lee. *Acta Koreana* 16, no. 1 (2013): 261–68.

———. "On the Eve of the Uprising." Trans. Sunyoung Park. In *On the Eve of the Uprising and Other Stories from Colonial Korea*, 5–112. Ithaca, N.Y.: Cornell University East Asia Series, 2010.

Yoshida Seiichi. *Shizen shugi no kenkyū*. Tokyo: Tōkyōdō Shuppanbu, 1955.

Yu, Ki-Hwan. "Le Manifeste naturaliste de Corée et Le Roman expérimental: Yeom Sang-Seob et Émile Zola." In *Re-Reading Zola and Worldwide Naturalism: Miscellanies in Honour of Anna Gural-Migdal*, ed. Carolyn Snipes-Hoyt, Marie-Sophie Armstrong, and Riikka Rossi, 312–23. Newcastle upon Tyne, Eng.: Cambridge Scholars, 2013.

Yúdice, George. "Rethinking the Theory of the Avant-Garde from the Periphery." In *Modernism and Its Margins: Reinscribing Cultural Modernity from Spain and Latin America*, ed. Anthony L. Geist and José L. Monléon, 52–80. New York: Garland, 1999.

Zakarian, Richard H. *Zola's "Germinal": A Critical Study of Its Primary Sources*. Geneva: Droz, 1972.

Zola, Émile. "Documents et plans préparatoires des Rougon Macquart." In *Les Rougon-Macquart V*, ed. Henri Mitterand, 1667–781. Paris: Gallimard, 1967.

———. *Germinal*. Paris: Gallimard, 1978.

———. "'Germinie Lacerteux' par MM. Edmond et Jules de Goncourt." In *Oeuvres critiques I*, ed. Henri Mitterand, 62–71. Oeuvres complètes 10. Paris: Cercle du Livre Précieux, 1968.

———. *La Bête humaine*. Paris: Gallimard, 2001.

———. *La Fortune des Rougon*. Paris: Gallimard, 1981.

———. *L'Assommoir*. Paris: Gallimard, 1978.

———. "Le Roman expérimental." In *Anthologie des préfaces de romans français du XIXe siècle*, ed. Herbert S. Gershman and Kernan B. Whitworth, Jr., 257–303. Paris: Julliard, 1964.

———. *Nana*. Paris: Gallimard, 2002.

———. *Thérèse Raquin*. Paris: Garnier-Flammarion, 1970.

Zwicker, Jonathan E. *Practices of the Sentimental Imagination: Melodrama, the Novel, and the Social Imaginary in Nineteenth-Century Japan*. Cambridge, Mass.: Harvard University Asia Center, 2006.

Index

FLASHPOINTS

1. *On Pain of Speech: Fantasies of the First Order and the Literary Rant,* Dina Al-Kassim
2. *Moses and Multiculturalism,* Barbara Johnson, with a foreword by Barbara Rietveld
3. *The Cosmic Time of Empire: Modern Britain and World Literature,* Adam Barrows
4. *Poetry in Pieces: César Vallejo and Lyric Modernity,* Michelle Clayton
5. *Disarming Words: Empire and the Seductions of Translation in Egypt,* Shaden M. Tageldin
6. *Wings for Our Courage: Gender, Erudition, and Republican Thought,* Stephanie H. Jed
7. *The Cultural Return,* Susan Hegeman
8. *English Heart, Hindi Heartland: The Political Life of Literature in India,* Rashmi Sadana
9. *The Cylinder: Kinematics of the Nineteenth Century,* Helmut Müller-Sievers
10. *Polymorphous Domesticities: Pets, Bodies, and Desire in Four Modern Writers,* Juliana Schiesari
11. *Flesh and Fish Blood: Postcolonialism, Translation, and the Vernacular,* S. Shankar
12. *The Fear of French Negroes: Transcolonial Collaboration in the Revolutionary Americas,* Sara E. Johnson
13. *Figurative Inquisitions: Conversion, Torture, and Truth in the Luso-Hispanic Atlantic,* Erin Graff Zivin
14. *Cosmopolitan Desires: Global Modernity and World Literature in Latin America,* Mariano Siskind
15. *Fiction Beyond Secularism,* Justin Neuman
16. *Periodizing Jameson: Dialectics, the University, and the Desire for Narrative,* Phillip E. Wegner
17. *The Practical Past,* Hayden White
18. *The Powers of the False: Reading, Writing, Thinking Beyond Truth and Fiction,* Doro Wiese
19. *The Object of the Atlantic: Concrete Aesthetics in Cuba, Brazil, and Spain, 1868–1968,* Rachel Price
20. *Epic and Exile: Novels of the German Popular Front 1933–1945,* Hunter Bivens
21. *An Innocent Abroad: Lectures in China,* J. Hillis Miller
22. *Form and Instability: East Europe, Literature, Postimperial Difference,* Anita Starosta
23. *Bombay Modern: Arun Kolatkar and Bilingual Literary Culture,* Anjali Nerlekar
24. *Intimate Relations: Social Reform and the Late Nineteenth-Century South Asian Novel,* Krupa Shandilya
25. *Media Laboratories: Late Modernist Authorship in South America,* Sarah Ann Wells
26. *Acoustic Properties: Radio, Narrative, and the New Neighborhood of the Americas,* Tom McEnaney

27. *The New Woman: Literary Modernism, Queer Theory, and the Trans Feminine Allegory*, Emma Heaney
28. *Civilizing War: Imperial Politics and the Poetics of National Rupture*, Nasser Mufti
29. *Late Colonial Sublime: Neo-Epics and the End of Romanticism*, G. S. Sahota
30. *Globalizing Race: Anti-Semitism, Empire, and the Politics of Scale in Modern French and European Culture*, Dorian Bell
31. *Domestications: American Empire, Literary Culture, and the Postcolonial Lens*, Hosam Mohamed Aboul-Ela
32. *Behold an Animal: Four Exorbitant Readings*, Thangam Ravindranathan
33. *Capital Letters: Hugo, Baudelaire, Camus, and the Death Penalty*, Ève Morisi
34. *Immaterial Archives: An African Diaspora Poetics of Loss*, Jenny Sharpe
35. *Figures of the World: The Naturalist Novel and Transnational Form*, Christopher Laing Hill